9·16·77

A
TREASURY
OF
BIRDLORE

by

Joseph Wood Krutch
& Paul S. Eriksson

PAUL S. ERIKSSON
Publisher
Middlebury, Vermont

Grateful acknowledgment is made to the following authors and publishers for permission to use and adopt copyrighted material:

AMERICAN ASSOCIATION OF RETARDED PERSONS. "Eagle Man" by Ted Shane, condensed
from *Lifetime Living*, January 1953. Copyright by Lifetime Living, Inc. Reprinted
by permission of the American Association of Retarded Persons.

AUDUBON NATURALIST SOCIETY. "The American Career of Alexander Wilson, Father
of American Ornithology," by Elsa G. Allen, from *Atlantic Naturalist*, Vol. 8, No.
2, November–December, 1952. Copyright © 1952 by Audubon Naturalist Society
of the Central Atlantic States, Inc. Reprinted by permission.

AUDUBON MAGAZINE. "Wings Across the Moon" by Robert J. Newman, from *Audubon Magazine*, July–August 1952. "Presidential Bird" by Richard L. Scheffel, from
Audubon Magazine, May–June 1961. "Snobber—Sparrow de Luxe: A Picture Story"
by Edwin Way Teale, from *Audubon Magazine*, November–December 1944. "Care
and Feeding of Wild Birds" by John K. Terres, from *Audubon Magazine*, Vol. 51,
1949. Reprinted by permission of *Audubon Magazine*.

BRIDGES, WILLIAM. "The Last of a Species" by William Bridges, from *Animal Kingdom*, the magazine of the New York Zoological Society. Reprinted by permission
of William Bridges.

BROOKFIELD, CHARLES M. "The Guy Bradley Story" by Charles M. Brookfield, from
Audubon Magazine, July–August 1955. Reprinted by permission of Charles M.
Brookfield.

COWARD-MCCANN, INC. "Remarkable History of Bird Anting" by Maurice Burton,
from *Animal Legends* by Maurice Burton. Copyright © 1957 by Maurice Burton.
Reprinted by permission of Coward-McCann, Inc.

DODD, MEAD & COMPANY. "The Story of Hawk Mountain" by Maurice Broun, from
Hawks Aloft. Copyright 1949 by Maurice Broun. "Pageant in the Sky" from *Wings
Over the Western Hemisphere* by Raymond Deck. Copyright 1941 by Dodd, Mead
& Company. "Birds Over America" from *The Big Day* by Roger Tory Peterson.
Copyright 1948 by Roger Tory Peterson. "Natural History in Times Square" from
The Lost Woods by Edwin Way Teale. Copyright 1945 by Edwin Way Teale.
"Bird Invasion" from *Days without Time* by Edwin Way Teale. Copyright 1948 by
Edwin Way Teale. Reprinted by permission of Dodd, Mead & Company.

DOUBLEDAY & COMPANY, INC. "Bald Eagles on the Hudson River," "The Hardy
Horned Owl," "Old Sicklewings," from *Footnotes on Nature* by John Kieran.
Copyright 1947 by John Kieran. Reprinted by permission.

FRONTIERS. "White House Bird Watcher" by Bates M. Stovall, from *Frontiers*, the
Magazine of the Academy of Natural Sciences, 19th and the Parkway, Philadelphia
3, Pennsylvania. Reprinted by permission.

HARPER & BROTHERS. Excerpts from *Spring in Washington* by Louis J. Halle. Copyright 1947, 1957 by Louis J. Halle, Jr. Reprinted by permission of Harper & Brothers.

HARVARD UNIVERSITY PRESS. Excerpts from *Modern Bird Study* by Ludlow Griscom.
Copyright, 1945, by The President and Fellows of Harvard College. Reprinted by
permission of the publishers.

HATCH, ROBERT MCCONNELL. "The Master of Our Woods" by Robert McConnell
Hatch, from *New Hampshire Bird News*, Vol. 7, No. 1, January 1954. Reprinted by

permission of Robert McConnell Hatch and the Audubon Society of New Hampshire.

HOLT, RINEHART & WINSTON, INC. "The Hawk and the Tern" from *The Outermost House* by Henry Beston. Copyright 1928, 1949, copyright renewed © 1956 by Henry Beston. "And I Ought to Know" from *How to Become Extinct* by Will Cuppy. Copyright 1941 by Will Cuppy. "How Long Does It Take to Paint a Bird Picture?" and "Red-tailed Hawk" from *Menaboni's Birds* by Athos and Sara Menaboni. Copyright 1950 by Athos and Sara Menaboni. Reprinted by permission of Holt, Rinehart & Winston, Inc.

HOUGHTON MIFFLIN COMPANY. Excerpt from "Birds of Massachusetts" from *Natural History of the Birds* by E. H. Forbush. Copyright 1927 by the Commonwealth of Massachusetts. Excerpt from *A Cup of Sky* by Donald Culross Peattie. Copyright 1947 by Donald C. Peattie and the Curtis Publishing Company. Reprinted by permission of and arrangement with Houghton Mifflin Company, the authorized publishers.

JAEGER, EDMUND C. "Does the Poor-Will Hibernate?" by Edmund C. Jaeger from *The Condor*, Vol. 50, No. 1, January–February 1948. Reprinted by permission of Edmund C. Jaeger. 1989526

ALFRED A. KNOPF, INC. "The Trumpeter Swan" by Sally Carrighar, from *One Day at Teton Marsh*. Copyright 1947 by Sally Carrighar and the Curtis Publishing Company. Specially adapted and abridged for this usage, with the permission of Alfred A. Knopf, Inc. "Wilderness Music" from *The Singing Wilderness* by Sigurd F. Olson. Copyright © 1956 by Sigurd F. Olson. Reprinted by permission of Alfred A. Knopf, Inc.

LAWRENCE, LOUISE DE KIRILINE. "The Voluble Singer of the Treetops" by Louise de Kiriline, from *Audubon Magazine*, May–June 1954. Reprinted by permission of *Audubon Magazine* and the author.

MACMILLAN COMPANY. Excerpt from *Flight into Sunshine* by Helen G. Cruickshank. Copyright, 1948, by The Macmillan Company. Excerpt from *Wings at My Window* by Ada Clapham Govan. Copyright, 1940, by The Macmillan Company. "On Watching an Ovenbird's Nest" by Margaret Morse Nice, from *The Watcher at the Nest*. Copyright, 1939, by The Macmillan Company. "An Adventure with a Turkey Vulture," "The Harris's Sparrow's Eggs," "Titania and Oberon" by George M. Sutton, from *Birds in the Wilderness*. Copyright, 1936, by The Macmillan Company. Reprinted by permission of the publisher.

MILLER, ROBERT CUNNINGHAM. "Bird Voices of the Autumn" by Robert Cunningham Miller, from *Pacific Discovery*, September–October 1951. "Wings of the Storm" by Robert Cunningham Miller, from *Pacific Discovery*, September–October 1951. Reprinted by permission of California Academy of Sciences. "How to Get Along with Birds" by Robert Cunningham Miller, from *National League for Women's Service Magazine*, March 1950. Reprinted by permission of the Women's City Club, San Francisco.

MURCHIE, JR., GUY. "The Perfect Flying Machine" from *Song of the Sky* by Guy Murchie, Jr. Reprinted by permission of Guy Murchie, Jr.

NATURAL HISTORY. "The Bird Doctor" by Paul H. Fluck, from *Nature*, June 1956. "Twentieth Century Audubon" by Cedric Larson, from *Natural History*, May 1956. "Refuge Pelicans of the Desert" by Lewis W. Walker, from *Natural History*, December 1949. Reprinted by permission of *Natural History*, incorporating *Nature Magazine*.

THE NEW YORKER. "Good Bag in Central Park" by Geoffrey Hellman, from *The New Yorker*, October 31, 1953, "Talk of the Town." Copyright 1953 by The New Yorker Magazine, Inc. Reprinted by permission of The New Yorker Magazine, Inc.

OXFORD UNIVERSITY PRESS, INC. "Arctic Rendezvous" from *Under the Sea-Wind Arctic* by Rachel L. Carson. Copyright 1941 by Rachel L. Carson. Excerpt from *A Guide to Bird Watching* by Joseph J. Hickey. Copyright 1943 by Joseph J. Hickey. "March: The Geese Return" from *A Sand County Almanac: and Sketches Here and There* by Aldo Leopold. Copyright 1949 by Oxford University Press, Inc. Reprinted by permission of Oxford University Press, Inc.

THE READER'S DIGEST. "Birds Live in Nature's Invisible Cage" by John and Jean

George, condensed in *Reader's Digest* from *Christian Science Monitor*. Copyright 1959 by Christian Science Monitor. Reprinted by permission of *The Reader's Digest*. WILLIAM SLOANE ASSOCIATES. "Most Dangerous Predator" from *The Forgotten Peninsula* by Joseph Wood Krutch. Reprinted by permission of William Sloane Associates. VIKING PRESS. "Reptiles Take to the Air" from *America Before Man* by Elizabeth Chesley Baity. Copyright 1953 by Elizabeth Chesley Baity. Excerpt from *Birds against Men* by Louis J. Halle. Copyright 1938 by Louis J. Halle. "Our Vanishing Condors" from *Wildlife in America* by Peter Matthiessen. Copyright © 1959 by Peter Matthiessen. Reprinted by permission of The Viking Press, Inc.

The editors wish to acknowledge the generous help of those who made suggestions of pieces for inclusion in this anthology and those who contributed towards its completion. The following is an abbreviated list of some of these people, not least of whom is Harry B. Logan:

Dean Amadon, Elizabeth Ball, G. Clifford Carl, Reginald L. Cook, Allan D. Cruickshank, Margaret Woods Eriksson, Alfred G. Etter, Edith N. Halberg, George E. Hudson, Rimsa Michel, Kenneth Morrison, Harry C. Oberholser, Dorothy C. Pallas, A. L. Rand, John Terres, John Vosburgh, Farida A. Wiley, Robert Woodward.

INTRODUCTION

Bird watching is not usually listed among the spectator sports but it is nowadays one of the most popular. Once largely a New England specialty it has spread over the entire United States. On any fine Saturday afternoon there are probably more of us out with binoculars than are congregated in all the stadia.

John James Audubon had a difficult time getting subscribers for his great work and one gentleman whom he solicited is said to have replied that he would not pay that much for all the live birds in the country, much less for pictures of them. Field guides are now among the best of bestsellers and the available current literature is amazing. Even so we have not quite caught up with the British who, so it is said, publish a book a day about their "feathered friends."

No single reason is sufficient to account for the popularity of this hobby, sport, or scientific activity, but there are half a dozen which contribute to it. Aside from the fact that there is no better excuse for being out in the open—and people seem to need an excuse whether it be golf, photography, or fishing—there is the further fact that you never draw a blank. Birds are everywhere, even in the city. Except for insects they are the most abundant and omnipresent of animal creatures and except for certain highly unpopular forms of life like mice, rats, and cockroaches they are the only ones to whom the presence of man and his activities has not always proved a disaster. Game birds and water birds may have diminished in numbers but many species of songbirds are certainly more numerous since forests have been thinned and open country become more abundant.

Another reason for the popularity of the hobby is that it may be indulged in as casually or as determinedly as you wish. Many a man and woman has begun noticing birds in the course of a walk, indulged a mild curiosity about them, and then almost before he was aware of what was happening found himself walking to see birds instead of seeing birds while he walked. Almost before he knows it, he has bought a field guide, discovered friends with the same interest, begun keeping a "life list" of those species he has identified, and perhaps even visiting the city dump—which is the least savory of the spots to which the bird watcher is attracted.

Then there is the fact that bird books and bird watchers generate one another. The books meet a demand and then create more of it. Americans were less interested in nature when they were more closely surrounded by it and the few laymen who were interested got little help until comparatively recently. Now the bookstores—and often even the drugstores—display innumerable books introducing every aspect of the natural world to everybody from the infant just beginning to read to the mature student.

Barely more than a century ago Thoreau was so handicapped by his inability to find in print anything that he wanted to know that modern readers are often astonished at his areas of ignorance. As Mr. Bradford Torrey, editor of the Thoreau *Journals,* said: "The truth appears to be that even of the commoner sorts of birds that bred in eastern Massachusetts or migrate through it Thoreau—during the greater part of his life at least—knew by sight and name only a small proportion, wonderful though his knowledge seemed to be to those who, like Emerson, knew practically nothing." To this day the curious have been unable to decide what the "night warbler" Thoreau talked a good deal about really was, and some are inclined to suspect that it was not one bird but several. Now there are thousands of mere amateurs who would be ashamed of such ignorance. In fact, the spread of expertise and the emphasis put upon it may sometimes make ornithology and ornithologists somewhat deficient in the passion and imagination which distinguished Thoreau.

The fact remains that when all the contributory reasons for the popularity of bird watching have been listed the most important of all has not been mentioned, namely, the fascination and charm of the bird itself. But what is this charm? Some species are companionable in the sense that they actually prefer nearness to human habitation—and not in every case because of the food scraps available. To some extent certain of them can also be tamed and made pets of. But in general we and they seem to occupy such discontinuous worlds that there is little intimacy of communication and for the most part they have little interest in us—desiring only to be let alone. Wrens may be an exception and they are easy to watch because they seem to be almost as curious about us as we are about them. But people watchers are few. We may call the birds "our feathered friends" but it is mostly a one-sided friendship.

Is their very remoteness, the fact that they occupy the same physical world at the same time that they seem psychically so remote, part of their fascination? They are the only animals not in the mammalian order which the vast majority of people find very attractive. Yet they are more nearly universally admired than any of the creatures more nearly related to us. There are, to be sure, societies for the protection of various animals but none is so widely supported as the National Audubon Society and a plea to "save the birds" meets a warmer public response than a similar plea to save any other creature who shares our earth with us.

Whatever the secret of their charm it has been effective since the dawn of civilization. There are birds in the Bible, birds in classical literature, and birds in folklore. The earliest known poem in the English language is addressed to a cuckoo and the last poem composed before poetry disappears from a world completely mechanized will probably also be about birds. Chaucer's description of spring inevitably included the "smale fowles"

> *maken melodye,*
> *That slepen all the night with open ye,*
> *(So priketh hem nature in hir corages)* . . .

Or, as a modern translator has it,

> *And many little birds made melody*
> *That sleep through all the night with open eye*
> *(So Nature pricks them on to ramp and rage)* . . .

The lark and the nightingale are the most worn of poetic clichés and even the most resolute of contemporary poets who have enrolled themselves in the ash-can school cannot keep them out of their verses. One is not surprised to find the song of the nightingale finding a path

> *Through the sad heart of Ruth, when, sick for home,*
> *She stood in tears amid the alien corn.*

But it is a bit surprising to find him also in *The Wasteland:*

> *Yet there the nightingale*
> *Filled all the desert with inviolable voice.*

Is the fact that the bird is the only animal except man which sings in a fashion wholly satisfying to the human ear a chief cause of the birds' popularity? Some have thought so; and though only a minority of species sing well they have certainly been the most beloved and the most celebrated. Or is the greatest charm, as others have suggested, that birds fly—as man had so long dreamed of doing and as, indeed, he still cannot do, though he may be carried aloft by a machine which can. Are birds symbols of freedom because they enjoy at least one freedom man is denied? "Had I but the wings of a dove!" seems to suggest something of the sort. So does the fact that we are promised wings when we become angels! Devils, so far as I know, have never been accorded anything more attractive than those of the bat.

It is certainly a curious fact that the most popular of animals should be those most closely related to the least popular, namely the snakes. As the fossil record shows, birds branched off from the reptilian line sometime during the Mesozoic at least one hundred and fifty million years ago, or in what is called the Age of Reptiles because the reptiles were then the most advanced of animals and reached in the dinosaurs their most imposing dimensions. Some of them, unexpectedly enterprising, took to the water, and though most of those which did so are now extinct, others took to the air and thus founded the vastly successful tribe of birds.

First, so far as is known, came those flying reptiles with light bones and membranous, featherless wings which are known as pterodactyls and of which many fossils survive in both Europe and America though they are especially abundant in Kansas. Almost contemporary is the earliest known specimen of what is undoubtedly a bird, the Archaeopteryx, whose fossil remains were discovered in Bavaria.

It was about the size of a crow, had well-developed flight feathers, and though no other land bird is known before another sixty or seventy million years had passed, there were a number of early sea birds. When we think of "bird" we usually think first of the small perching birds but the first of that kind do not appear before the Eocene (perhaps sixty million years ago) and did not become among the most numerous until the Pliocene, or some ten million years before our day when mammals were already dominating the dry land. Insects had learned to fly many millions of years before the birds but somehow or other the latter managed an astonishing step forward: unlike all the fish, amphibians, and reptiles who preceded them, they were warm-blooded and hence no longer at the mercy of the fluctuating temperatures of air or water.

And yet, for all this, even the most recent of birds are in many respects quite close to the reptiles. Their skeletons closely resemble the reptilian type; they still have reptilian scales on their legs and feet; and their feathers reveal their origin by keeping the same chemical composition as scales. Thomas Henry Huxley called them merely "glorified reptiles" and it is perhaps well for their popularity that we are not usually very much aware of this close relationship with the snakes. Perhaps that relationship is, indeed, important only to zoologists, for nothing seems further from the creeping and crawling which we associate with their ancestors than the free flight of birds. The one seems to us the most abject method of locomotion; the other the most liberated and glorious.

Inevitably the reptile which became a bird in the course of many millions of years suggests the superficially similar miracle of the caterpillar which becomes a butterfly before our very eyes in the course of a few weeks or months. If there is anything more improbable than that a lizard should become a bird it is that the essential sluggishness of a caterpillar, earthbound and to most people repulsive, should be reborn as a gay creature flitting in the sunlight and so much the very symbol of happy irresponsible freedom that we call any similar gay, irresponsible person "a butterfly." But the comparison is only fanciful. The insects who undergo metamorphosis are not recapitulating an evolutionary history. The most primitive insects are hatched as miniature adults. They know nothing of rebirth and metamorphosis. And just how the more advanced of the tribe acquired their trick of living two such different lives is one of the great mysteries of evolution.

Like all the other branches of natural history, ornithology "evolves" inevitably and organically. It is also subject to that notoriously fluctuating thing called fashion. Aims, methods, and hypotheses develop logically, but at the same time there are unpredictable fluctuations—sometimes merely whimsical. Most of the selections in this volume come from the nineteenth or twentieth centuries. But even within that brief period it will be obvious that John Burroughs, for instance, does not write about the same things, is not interested in the same things, as, say, Major Sutton. Burroughs is, first of all, a "nature lover"; Sutton first of all a scientist. And though the amateur is likely to be closer in spirit to the former he sometimes finds that what began as a passion ends as an absorbing but unemotional search for verifiable fact.

Like all the other branches of natural history ornithology has tended to become "problem oriented." The eighteenth century was the great age of classification and the discovery of new species. The nineteenth was concerned above all with establishing the fact of evolution. The "serious biologist" of the twentieth wants to answer in more or less mechanistical terms the question of what explains this or that behavior. How do birds know when the time has come to migrate? How do they find their way? Why do they sing? What makes them brood eggs when, presumably, they do not know that a baby bird will come out of them? A Thoreau disgusted that he could not find in the books available to him anything about living birds protested that he did not want to know how long the intestine of a hawk is. But that is exactly one of the kinds of things a biologist does want to find out.

Perhaps the most fundamental aspect of the difference between old and new attitudes is typified by the implied answers to the question "To what extent are birds 'fellow creatures?'" Poets have, of course, always humanized them. Shelley's *To a Skylark*, perhaps the most famous of all English poems about birds, goes the whole way in assuming human (or rather something better than human) emotions:

> *Teach us, sprite or bird,*
> *What sweet thoughts are thine:*
> *I have never heard*
> *Praise of love or wine*
> *That panted forth a flood of rapture so divine.*
>
> . . ..
>
> *Teach me half the gladness*
> *That thy brain must know,*

Such harmonious madness
From my lips would flow
The world should listen then, as I am listening now!

If a Thoreau or a Burroughs did not seriously believe in quite so perfect an identity between the human and the avian both adopted an attitude which is warmed by at least the sense that we and they are not utterly alien one to another. On the other hand, an important school of "objective ornithologists" reject even the attitude of a Thoreau or a Burroughs as involving an absurd anthropomorphism. Birds, so they insist, do not think; they only react. They do not learn; they merely become conditioned. They do not feel; they merely respond to the instincts which are triggered by hormones. If they are not quite the mere machines which Descartes believed all animals except man to be, they are something not too remote from such machines and it is only their behavior, so these scientists insist, that can be profitably studied. The poet or even the "nature lover" who attempts to establish an empathy with fellow creatures is, to them, merely the victim of a delusion.

Birds, so the argument goes, are only one step up the ladder of evolution from the notoriously unintelligent reptiles. Since they have small, primitive brains their intelligence is far more inferior to that of an ape than an ape's intelligence is to that of a man. They cannot be very acutely conscious and to read into their reactions anything even remotely analogous to what such emotion sometimes suggests to a human being is to be led into mere absurdity. The revolt against anthropomorphism leads ultimately to the conclusion that birds are essentially machinelike in their behavior.

To speak of their "love" and "devotion to their fledglings" of their "anxious concern over the intruder who disturbs their nest" is said to be mere nonsense. Battles, almost theologically fierce, have taken place over the question whether or not any one of the several species which play the "broken wing" trick to lure human beings away from their nesting place may be permissibly regarded as knowing, in any sense, what they are doing or why they are doing it. Even what seems the self-evident joy of their song then becomes a mere myth. In the first place it is not a love song but an announcement to other members of the species that a certain territory has been occupied. Here for instance is an extreme statement made by an English naturalist addressing a popular audience:

"In the human sphere the natural expression of song probably comes nearest to its fulfillment in the song of the bath, that lusty, perhaps discordant effort which threatens the panels of the bathroom door and the eardrums of unwilling listeners, and which all the world interprets as an expression of the joy of life and good will towards men though indeed it seems an odd way of expressing good will. But what has the song of the bath to do with the song of birds? Absolutely nothing! That is why I mention it, to warn you of its danger, because we are inclined, almost unconsciously, to interpret the songs of birds and other creatures from our own experience, and to look upon them as expressions of the joy of living, since sometimes they play that role with us."

On the other hand, Konrad Lorenz, the great contemporary European student of animal behavior, has coined the term "mechanomorphism" to describe the error of those who react too strongly against anthropomorphism. And not a few distinguished biologists of today have begun to protest against it. Every kind of animal lives in a psychic world of its own and the character of that world depends in part upon the balance of its senses, in even larger part upon the extent to which its behavior is fixed by instinct. Insects, for instance, live in a world of almost perfectly routined instincts so that, for instance, they are capable of the most intricate actions at a certain moment of their lives but cannot renew them if once they are interrupted. Dogs must live in a world composed largely of smells. Man is the only animal who uses words and therefore probably the only one which can have ideas. Nevertheless there is some overlapping of the worlds, not only in the case of all mammals but also in that of creatures as relatively remote as man and bird. Certainly birds can think and learn far less well than a dog or a cat. We cannot relate ourselves to them in the same way. But the capacity to think and the capacity to feel are not entirely dependent one upon another. And there is good authority behind the opinion that birds, though far from intellectual, do lead emotional lives. Sir Julian Huxley in his *Essays of a Biologist* has stated the case brilliantly and eloquently. And the truth seems to be, as Professor N. J. Berrill has stated it: "To be a bird is to be alive more intensely than any other living creature . . . Birds live in a world that is always in the present, mostly full of joy . . . with little memory of the past and no real anticipation of what is yet to come—intensely conscious of sight and sound, strongly swayed by joy and anger, and sometimes petrified by ecstasy or fear."

To what extent is all this important to the amateur? It means at least that if he began by feeling for birds something more than merely aesthetic appreciation and scientific curiosity, if he accepted them as attractive companions in the varied adventure of living, he need not reproach himself for it and need not abandon it. If he turned to nature because he was somewhat weary of machines he need not conclude that he deluded himself and that the birds which seem to be so alive are after all only exceptionally ingenious machines which can be intelligently observed only as such. If, in addition, he would prefer to remain only an amateur he may take comfort from the following statement by the late great American entomologist William Morton Wheeler who could dare be "unscientific" because he was so impeccable a scientist. At the end of a lecture called "On the Dry Rot of Academic Biology" he said: "We should all be happier if we were less completely obsessed by problems and somewhat more accessible to the aesthetic and emotional appeal of our materials, and it is doubtful whether, in the end, the growth of biological science would be appreciably retarded. It quite saddens me to think that when I cross the Styx, I may find myself among so many professional biologists, condemned to keep on trying to solve problems, and that Pluto, or whoever is in charge down there now, may condemn me to sit forever trying to identify specimens from my own specific and generic diagnoses, while the amateur entomologists, who have not been damned professors, are permitted to roam at will among the fragrant asphodels of the Elysian meadows, netting gorgeous, ghostly butterflies until the end of time."

Contents

PART THREE: BIRDS OF A FEATHER

Contents

Part

One

FLIGHT

THE RETURN

OF

THE BIRDS

John Burroughs

---

*One swallow, so we say, doesn't make a spring. But a dozen of them
—with a few robins thrown in for good measure—certainly do.
Though their return is as certain as the sun's steady climb into the sky
it touches our hearts as no merely physical happening can. Their disappearance in the autumn is as sweetly sad as the falling of the leaves;
their return is as cheering as the first flower to bloom in the woods.*

*The scientific ornithologist calls it "migration" and he studies it as
a problem. In a later section of this volume several students will explain something of the much they have learned and the much that
still remains mysterious. But the best beginning for such a book as
this is not the problem. It is the astonishing fact that the birds do return
to us—sometimes from lands many thousands of miles away which we
shall never visit. "The wild goose," wrote Thoreau, "is more of a
cosmopolite than we; he breaks his fast in Canada, takes a luncheon
in the Ohio, and plumes himself for the night in a southern bayou."*

*John Burroughs was not the first American nature writer and
neither was he the greatest but he may well be allowed to speak first,
partly because he was observant and sound, partly because he won a
wider audience than any previous writer who had invited his fellow
countrymen to consider the richness of their continent's wildlife and
the rewards to be reaped by those who saw it as something to be enjoyed rather than merely to be exploited.*

SPRING in our northern climate may fairly be said to extend from
the middle of March to the middle of June. At least, the vernal tide
continues to rise until the later date, and it is not till after the summer
solstice that the shoots and twigs begin to harden and turn to wood, or
the grass to lose any of its freshness and succulency.

It is this period that marks the return of the birds—one or two of the

From *Wake Robin*. Boston: Houghton Mifflin Company, 1895.

more hardy or half-domesticated species, like the song sparrow and the bluebird, usually arriving in March, while the rarer and more brilliant wood-birds bring up the procession in June. But each stage of the advancing season gives prominence to certain species, as to certain flowers. The dandelion tells me when to look for the swallow, the dogtooth violet when to expect the wood-thrush, and when I have found the wakerobin in bloom I know the season is fairly inaugurated. With me this flower is associated, not merely with the awakening of Robin, for he has been awake some weeks, but with the universal awakening and rehabilitation of nature.

Yet the coming and going of the birds is more or less a mystery and a surprise. We go out in the morning, and no thrush or vireo is to be heard; we go out again, and every tree and grove is musical; yet again, and all is silent. Who saw them come? Who saw them depart?

This pert little winter wren, for instance, darting in and out the fence, diving under the rubbish here and coming up yards away—how does he manage with those little circular wings to compass degrees and zones, and arrive always in the nick of time? Last August I saw him in the remotest wilds of the Adirondacks, impatient and inquisitive as usual; a few weeks later, on the Potomac, I was greeted by the same hardy little busybody. Does he travel by easy stages from bush to bush and from wood to wood? Or has that compact little body force and courage to brave the night and the upper air, and so achieve leagues at one pull?

And yonder bluebird with the earth tinge on his breast and the sky tinge on his back—did he come down out of heaven on that bright March morning when he told us so softly and plaintively that, if we pleased, spring had come? Indeed, there is nothing in the return of the birds more curious and suggestive than in the first appearance, or rumors of the appearance, of this little blue-coat. The bird at first seems a mere wandering voice in the air: one hears its call or carol on some bright March morning, but is uncertain of its source or direction; it falls like a drop of rain when no cloud is visible; one looks and listens, but to no purpose. The weather changes, perhaps a cold snap with snow comes on, and it may be a week before I hear the note again, and this time or the next perchance see the bird sitting on a stake in the fence lifting his wing as he calls cheerily to his mate. Its notes now become daily more frequent; the birds multiply, and, flitting from point to point, call and warble more confidently and gleefully. Their boldness increases till one sees them hovering with a saucy, inquiring air about barns and outbuildings, peeping into dove-cotes and stable windows, inspecting knotholes and pump-trees, intent only on a place to nest. They wage war against robins and wrens, pick quarrels with swallows, and seem to deliberate for days over the policy of taking forcible possession of one of the mud-houses of the latter. But as the season advances they drift more into the background. Schemes of conquest which they at first seemed bent upon are abandoned, and they settle down very quietly in their old quarters in remote stumpy fields.

Not long after the bluebird comes the robin, sometimes in March, but in most of the Northern States April is the month of the robin. In large numbers they scour the fields and groves. You hear their piping in the meadow, in the pasture, on the hillside. Walk in the woods, and the dry leaves rustle with the whir of their wings, the air is vocal with their cheery call. In excess of joy and vivacity, they run, leap, scream, chase each other through the air, diving and sweeping among the trees with perilous rapidity.

In that free, fascinating, half-work and half-play pursuit—sugar-making—a pursuit which still lingers in many parts of New York, as in New England—the robin is one's constant companion. When the day is sunny and the ground bare, you meet him at all points and hear him at all hours. At sunset, on the tops of the tall maples, with look heavenward, and in a spirit of utter abandonment, he carols his simple strain. And sitting thus amid the stark, silent trees, above the wet, cold earth, with the chill of winter still in the air, there is no fitter or sweeter songster in the whole round year. It is in keeping with the scene and the occasion. How round and genuine the notes are, and how eagerly our ears drink them all in! The first utterance, and the spell of winter is thoroughly broken, and the remembrance of it afar off.

Robin is one of the most native and democratic of our birds; he is one of the family, and seems much nearer to us than those rare, exotic visitants, as the orchard starling or rose-breasted grosbeak, with their distant, high-bred ways. Hardy, noisy, frolicsome, neighborly, and domestic in his habits, strong of wing and bold in spirit, he is the pioneer of the thrush family, and well worthy of the finer artists whose coming he heralds and in a measure prepares us for.

I could wish Robin less native and plebian in one respect—the building of his nest. Its coarse material and rough masonry are creditable neither to his skill as a workman nor to his taste as an artist. I am the more forcibly reminded of his deficiency in this respect from observing yonder hummingbird's nest, which is a marvel of fitness and adaptation, a proper setting for this winged gem—the body of it composed of a white, felt-like substance, probably the down of some plant or the wool of some worm, and toned down in keeping with the branch on which it sits by minute tree-lichens, woven together by threads as fine and frail as gossamer. From Robin's good looks and musical turn, we might reasonably predict a domicile of equal fitness and elegance. At least I demand of him as clean and handsome a nest as the kingbird's, whose harsh jingle, compared with Robin's evening melody, is as the clatter of pots and kettles beside the tone of a flute. I love his note and ways better even than those of the orchard starling or the Baltimore oriole; yet his nest, compared with theirs, is a half-subterranean hut contrasted with a Roman villa. There is something courtly and poetical in a pensile nest. Next to a castle in the air is a dwelling suspended to the slender branch of a tall tree, swayed and rocked forever by the wind. Why need wings be afraid of falling? Why build only where boys can climb? After all, we must set it down to the account of Robin's democratic turn: He is no aristocrat, but one of the people; and therefore we should expect stability in his workmanship, rather than elegance.

Another April bird, which makes her appearance sometimes earlier and sometimes later than Robin, and whose memory I fondly cherish, is the phoebe-bird, the pioneer of the flycatchers. In the inland farming districts, I used to notice her, on some bright morning about Easter Day, proclaiming her arrival, with much variety of motion and attitude, from the peak of the barn or hay-shed. As yet, you may have heard only the plaintive, homesick note of the bluebird, or the faint trill of the song sparrow; and Phoebe's clear, vivacious assurance of her veritable bodily presence among us again is welcomed by all ears. At agreeable intervals in her lay she describes a circle or an ellipse in the air, ostensibly prospecting for insects, but really, I suspect, as an artistic flourish, thrown in to make up in some way for the deficiency of her musical performance. If plainness of dress indicates powers of song, as it usually does, then Phoebe ought to be unrivaled in musical ability, for surely that ashen-gray suit is the superlative of plainness; and that form, likewise, would hardly pass for a "perfect figure" of a bird. The seasonableness of her coming, however, and her civil, neighborly ways, shall make up for all deficiencies in song and plumage. After a few weeks Phoebe is seldom seen, except as she darts from her moss-covered nest beneath some bridge or shelving cliff.

Another April comer, who arrives shortly after Robin redbreast, with whom he associates both at this season and in the autumn, is the gold-winged woodpecker, *alias* "high-ole," *alias* "flicker," *alias* "yarup." He is an old favorite of my boyhood, and his note to me means very much. He announces his arrival by a long, loud call, repeated from the dry branch of some tree, or a stake in the fence—a thoroughly melodious April sound. I think how Solomon finished that beautiful description of spring, "And the voice of the turtle is heard in the land," and see that a description of spring in this farming country, to be equally characteristic, should culminate in like manner—"And the call of the highhole comes up from the wood."

It is a loud, strong, sonorous call, and does not seem to imply an answer, but rather to subserve some purpose of love or music. It is "Yarup's" proclamation of peace and goodwill to all. On looking at the matter closely, I perceive that most birds, not denominated songsters, have, in the spring, some note or sound or call that hints of a song, and answers imperfectly the end of beauty and art. As a "livelier iris changes on the burnished dove," and the fancy of the young man turns lightly to thoughts of his pretty cousin, so the same renewing spirit touches the "silent singers," and they are no longer dumb; faintly they lisp the first syllables of the marvelous tale. Witness the clear, sweet whistle of the gray-crested titmouse—the soft, nasal piping of the nuthatch—the amorous, vivacious warble of the bluebird—the long, rich note of the meadowlark—the whistle of the quail—the drumming of partridge— the animation and loquacity of the swallows, and the like. Even the hen has a homely, contented carol; and I credit the owls with a desire to fill the night with music. All birds are incipient or would-be songsters in the spring. I find corroborative evidence of this even in the crowing of the cock. The flowering of the maple is not so obvious as that of the magnolia; nevertheless, there is actual inflorescence.

Few writers award any song to that familiar little sparrow, the *Socialis;* yet who that has observed him sitting by the wayside, and repeating, with devout attitude, that fine sliding chant, does not recognize neglect? Who has heard the snowbird sing? Yet he has a lisping warble very savory to the ear. I have heard him indulge in it even in February.

Even the cow bunting feels the musical tendency, and aspires to its expression, with the rest. Perched upon the topmost branch beside his mate or mates—for he is quite a polygamist, and usually has two or three demure little ladies in faded black beside him—generally in the early part of the day, he seems literally to vomit up his notes. Apparently with much labor and effort, they gurgle and blubber up out of him, falling on the ear with a peculiar subtle ring, as of turning water from a glass bottle, and not without a certain pleasing cadence.

Neither is the common woodpecker entirely insensible to the wooing of spring, and, like the partridge, testifies his appreciation of melody after quite a primitive fashion. Passing through the woods on some clear, still morning in March, while the metallic ring and tension of winter are still in the earth and air, the silence is suddenly broken by long, resonant hammering upon a dry limb or stub. It is Downy beating a reveille to spring. In the utter stillness and amid the rigid forms we listen with pleasure; and, as it comes to my ear oftener at this season than at any other, I freely exonerate the author from the imputation of any gastronomic motives, and credit him with a genuine musical performance.

It is to be expected, therefore, that "yellowhammer" will respond to the general tendency, and contribute his part to the spring chorus. His April call is his finest touch, his most musical expression.

I recall an ancient maple standing sentry to a large sugar-bush, that, year after year, afforded protection to a brood of yellowhammers in its decayed heart. A week or two before the nesting seemed actually to have begun, three or four of these birds might be seen, on almost any bright morning, gamboling and courting amid its decayed branches. Sometimes you would hear only a gentle persuasive cooing, or a quiet confidential chattering—then that long, loud call, taken up by first one, then another, as they sat about upon the naked limbs—anon, a sort of wild, rollicking laughter, intermingled with various cries, yelps, and squeals, as if some incident had excited their mirth and ridicule. Whether this social hilarity and boisterousness is in celebration of the pairing or mating ceremony, or whether it is only a sort of annual "housewarming" common among high-holes on resuming their summer quarters, is a question upon which I reserve my judgment.

Unlike most of his kinsmen, the golden-wing prefers the fields and the borders of the forest to the deeper seclusion of the woods, and hence, contrary to the habit of his tribe, obtains most of his subsistence from the ground, probing it for ants and crickets. He is not quite satisfied with being a woodpecker. He courts the society of the robin and the finches, abandons the trees for the meadow, and feeds eagerly upon berries and grain. What may be the final upshot of this course of living is a question worthy of Darwin. Will his taking to the ground and his pedestrian feats result in lengthening his legs, his feeding upon berries and grains subdue his tints and soften his voice, and his associating with Robin put a song into his heart?

Indeed, what would be more interesting than the history of our birds for the last two or three centuries? There can be no doubt that the presence of man has exerted a very marked and friendly influence upon them, since they so multiply in his society. The birds of California, it is said, were mostly silent till after its settlement, and I doubt if the Indians heard the wood-thrush as we hear him. Where did the bobolink disport himself before there were meadows in the North and ricefields in the South? Was he the same lithe, merry-hearted beau then as now? And the sparrow, the lark, and the goldfinch, birds that seem so indigenous to the open fields and so averse to the woods—we cannot conceive of their existence in a vast wilderness and without men.

But to return. The song sparrow, that universal favorite and firstling of the spring, comes before April, and its simple strain gladdens all hearts.

May is the month of the swallows and the orioles. There are many other distinguished arrivals, indeed nine tenths of the birds are here by the last week in May, yet the swallows and orioles are the most conspicuous. The bright plumage of the latter seems really like an arrival from the tropics. I see them dash through the blossoming trees, and all the forenoon hear their incessant warbling and wooing. The swallows dive and chatter about the barn, or squeak and build beneath the eaves; the partridge drums in the fresh sprouting woods; the long, tender note of the meadowlark comes up from the meadow; and at sunset, from every marsh and pond come the ten thousand voices of the hylas. May is the transition month, and exists to connect April and June, the root with the flower.

With June the cup is full, our hearts are satisfied, there is no more to be desired. The perfection of the season, among other things, has brought the perfection of the song and plumage of the birds. The master artists are all here; and the expectations excited by the robin and the song sparrow are fully justified. The thrushes have come; and I sit down upon the first rock, with hands full of the pink azalea, to listen. With me the cuckoo does not arrive till June; and often the goldfinch, the kingbird, the scarlet tanager delay their coming till then. In the meadows the bobolink is in all his glory; in the high pastures the field sparrow sings his breezy vesper-hymn; and the woods are unfolding to the music of the thrushes.

MARCH: THE

GEESE RETURN

Aldo Leopold

Aldo Leopold spent his life in forestry, game management, and conservation. His writing was for the most part scattered over various somewhat obscure technical journals and it was not until after his death that the collection of his papers called A Sand County Almanac *first revealed to any large public that he was one of the most original and charming of twentieth-century nature writers.*

ONE swallow does not make a summer, but one skein of geese, cleaving the murk of a March thaw, is the spring.

A cardinal, whistling spring to a thaw but later finding himself mistaken, can retrieve his error by resuming his winter silence. A chipmunk, emerging for a sunbath but finding a blizzard, has only to go back to bed. But a migrating goose, staking two hundred miles of black night on the chance of finding a hole in the lake, has no easy chance for retreat. His arrival carries the conviction of a prophet who has burned his bridges.

A March morning is only as drab as he who walks in it without a glance skyward, ear cocked for geese. I once knew an educated lady, banded by Phi Beta Kappa, who told me that she had never heard or seen the geese that twice a year proclaim the revolving seasons to her well-insulated roof. Is education possibly a process of trading awareness for things of lesser worth? The goose who trades his is soon a pile of feathers.

The geese that proclaim the seasons to our farm are aware of many things, including the Wisconsin statutes. The south-bound November flocks pass over us high and haughty, with scarcely a honk of recognition for their favorite sandbars and sloughs. "As a crow flies" is crooked compared with their undeviating aim at the nearest big lake twenty miles to the south, where they loaf by day on broad waters and filch corn by night from the freshly cut stubbles. November geese are aware that every marsh and pond bristles from dawn till dark with hopeful guns.

March geese are a different story. Although they have been shot at most

From *A Sand County Almanac.* New York: Oxford University Press, 1949.

of the winter, as attested by their buckshot-battered pinions, they know that the spring truce is now in effect. They wind the oxbows of the river, cutting low over the now gunless points and islands, and gabbling to each sandbar as to a long-lost friend. They weave low over the marshes and meadows, greeting each newly melted puddle and pool. Finally, after a few *pro-forma* circlings of our marsh, they set wing and glide silently to the pond, black landing-gear lowered and rumps white against the far hill. Once touching water, our newly arrived guests set up a honking and splashing that shakes the last thought of winter out of the brittle cattails. Our geese are home again!

It is at this moment of each year that I wish I were a muskrat, eye-deep in the marsh.

Once the first geese are in, they honk a clamorous invitation to each migrating flock, and in a few days the marsh is full of them. On our farm we measure the amplitude of our spring by two yardsticks: the number of pines planted, and the number of geese that stop. Our record is 642 geese counted in on 11 April 1946.

As in fall, our spring geese make daily trips to corn, but these are no surreptitious sneakings-out by night; the flocks move noisily to and from corn stubbles through the day. Each departure is preceded by loud gustatory debate, and each return by an even louder one. The returning flocks, once thoroughly at home, omit their *pro-forma* circlings of the marsh. They tumble out of the sky like maple leaves, side-slipping right and left to lose altitude, feet spraddled toward the shouts of welcome below. I suppose the ensuing gabble deals with the merits of the day's dinner. They are now eating the waste corn that the snow blanket has protected over winter from corn-seeking crows, cottontails, meadow mice, and pheasants.

It is a conspicuous fact that the corn stubbles selected by geese for feeding are usually those occupying former prairies. No man knows whether this bias for prairie corn reflects some superior nutritional value, or some ancestral tradition transmitted from generation to generation since the prairie days. Perhaps it reflects the simpler fact that prairie cornfields tend to be large. If I could understand the thunderous debates that precede and follow these daily excursions to corn, I might soon learn the reason for the priarie-bias. But I cannot, and I am well content that it should remain a mystery. What a dull world if we knew all about geese!

In thus watching the daily routine of a spring goose convention, one notices the prevalence of singles—lone geese that do much flying about and much talking. One is apt to impute a disconsolate tone to their honkings, and to jump to the conclusion that they are broken-hearted widowers, or mothers hunting lost children. The seasoned ornithologist knows, however, that such subjective interpretation of bird behavior is risky. I long tried to keep an open mind on the question.

After my students and I had counted for half a dozen years the number of geese comprising a flock, some unexpected light was cast on the meaning of lone geese. It was found by mathematical analysis that flocks of six or multiples of six were far more frequent than chance alone would dictate. In other words, goose flocks are families, or aggregations of families, and lone geese in spring are probably just what our fond imaginings had first suggested. They are bereaved survivors of the winter's shooting, searching in vain for their kin. Now I am free to grieve with and for the lone honkers.

It is not often that cold-potato mathematics thus confirms the sentimental promptings of the bird-lover.

On April nights when it has become warm enough to sit outdoors, we love to listen to the proceedings of the convention in the marsh. There are long periods of silence when one hears only the winnowing of snipe, the hoot of a distant owl, or the nasal clucking of some amorous coot. Then, of a sudden, a strident honk resounds, and in an instant pandemonium echoes. There is a beating of pinions on water, a rushing of dark prows propelled by churning paddles, and a general shouting by the onlookers of a vehement controversy. Finally some deep honker has his last word, and the noise subsides to that half-audible small-talk that seldom ceases among geese. Once again, I would I were a muskrat!

By the time the pasques are in full bloom our goose convention dwindles, and before May our marsh is once again a mere grassy wetness, enlivened only by redwings and rails.

It is an irony of history that the great powers should have discovered the unity of nations at Cairo in 1943. The geese of the world have had that notion for a longer time, and each March they stake their lives on its essential truth.

In the beginning there was only the unity of the Ice Sheet. Then followed the unity of the March thaw, and the northward hegira of the international geese. Every March since the Pleistocene, the geese have honked unity from China Sea to Siberian Steppe, from Euphrates to Volga, from Nile to Murmansk, from Lincolnshire to Spitsbergen. Every March since the Pleistocene, the geese have honked unity from Currituck to Labrador, Matamuskeet to Ungava, Horseshoe Lake to Hudson's Bay, Avery Island to Baffin Land, Panhandle to Mackenzie, Sacramento to Yukon.

By this international commerce of geese, the waste corn of Illinois is carried through the clouds to the Arctic tundras, there to combine with the waste sunlight of a nightless June to grow goslings for all the lands between. And in this annual barter of food for light, and winter warmth for summer solitude, the whole continent receives as net profit a wild poem dropped from the murky skies upon the muds of March.

THE HARDY

HORNED OWL

John Kieran

John Kieran's three reputations—as sports writer, television star, and naturalist—may overlap somewhat; but they are so far from coinciding that there are doubtless thousands who know him well in one or the other of his pursuits and little or not at all in the others. No contemporary has written with more ease, humor, and affection of the rewards of the field naturalist or has more successfully combined knowledge with the amateur spirit.

Somewhere in his writings Thoreau set it down that the human ear is not keen enough to catch the first footfalls of returning Spring. Perhaps so. Or perhaps Spring never quite goes away and is always with us to some slight degree. Who knows the first instant when the buds begin to swell on the trees or the very moment when the Skunk Cabbage first wriggles its hooked nose and starts to push up through the debris of the frozen ground?

I like to think that Spring begins on the tick of the Winter Solstice, when the sun "starts north" again. It isn't until the middle of January that there is any great difference in the height of the sun in the sky at noon or any noticeable earlier rising or later setting of the sun. But definitely—and astronomically—the Winter Solstice marks the turn for the better, if we look at it in that light despite the fact that practically all the hard weather of Winter lies ahead of us at that time. That, however, is taking a rather lofty view of things. Underfoot, conditions are more realistic. We begin to look for signs of Spring about Lincoln's Birthday or Washington's Birthday and, aside from the swelling of the buds and the Skunk Cabbage tips poking up in marshy ground, one of the early signs is the nesting of the Great Horned Owl.

One morning in late February we were walking a wooded ridge and peering at the ground around the biggest Hemlocks in the hope of finding owl pellets that might indicate a nest in the vicinity. We knew that these

From *Footnotes on Nature*. New York: Doubleday & Co., 1947.

great Hemlocks housed owls throughout the year, but it was a difficult matter to catch sight of them in any season. We had just turned to go down a slope when the Artist said: "Whoa! What's that up yonder?"

We looked overhead where he was pointing and saw a mass of leaves in a Hemlock crotch, with something like a short blunt object sticking over the edge.

"Might be an owl's tail!" said Herman the Magician, who is the leader on all our owl hunts. "Somebody skin up that big rock and take a look."

The Medical Student was along. He clambered up the rock formation to a height that put him on a level with the mass of leaves in the tree and swung his field glasses on the target. A moment later he yelled excitedly: "Holy Moses! It's a Great Horned Owl and it's looking right at me!"

We all scaled the big rock and had a look. It was February and there was snow all over the ridge. The temperature was well below freezing. Yet the Great Horned Owl already had set up housekeeping, truly a hardy bird. It might as well be recorded here that the hatching came off successfully and we saw the two young birds grow up to full size on a plentiful diet of—from the evidence we found on the ground—Rabbit and Pheasant. Shortly after they left the nest one of the young owls was found dead on the ground without a mark on it, and we never could learn the reason for its untimely end.

HUMMINGBIRDS

Donald Culross Peattie

Until the discovery of America no European had ever seen a hummingbird or anything remotely resembling it. All members of the group are found in the Western Hemisphere only, and their combination of small size, astonishing flight, and brilliant colors made them among the most sensational of the new natural wonders of the New World. In the eighteenth century the French naturalist Buffon devoted many pages to an account of them and for a time they were known in England also as what Buffon called them, "flybirds." The inhabitants of the eastern parts of our country know only one species —the ruby-throat—but there are fourteen other species in the West and more than three hundred—mostly tropical—in the world.

Like the other most beautiful birds they were once slaughtered in such numbers for their feathers that, so it is said, forty thousand skins were sold in one year by one London firm.

THE gift of wonder is a treasure safe with children and saints. To them all things from Creation's hand shine with a first lustre. This is to see them as they are. Those of us who have grown gray in the world's service have dimmer eyes. Yet even to us appear sights so sudden, of such audacious and unwearied beauty, that we too are again as children and are lifted by a quick reverence to a better state.

One such may come to you any summer day. It comes like a bomb, a bomb in feathers. You hear an insect-like thrumming, and see suspended in the air a metallic missile with propellers going at the rate of seventy-five beats a second—too fast for the human eye to perceive except as a blur. Suddenly rays of fire flash from its throat patch. As you catch your breath, the tiny visitant may dart backwards, drive off a roving bee, make a sideswipe at a kingbird, and then, in pursuit of a female of its kind, zoom away at fifty-five miles an hour, spraying the neighborhood with beauty and leaving wonder in its wake. All this in less time than it takes to say *Archilochus colubris,* the scientific name of the ruby-throated hummingbird.

This tiny comet, tipping the scales at one-tenth of an ounce, has small

From *A Cup of Sky*. Boston: Houghton Mifflin Company, 1947.

room in its fleck of body for fear. But bold and speedy though it is, it is apt to be overtaken by cold or hunger on its fall migration toward beckoning tropic warmth. How many hundreds or thousands die then, unmarked, no man knows. We can only guess at this from the numbers of those grounded little flyers which are brought to the Bronx Zoo from the streets of greater New York. In the hand a stilled hummingbird is pitiful in its frailty; by so much is the bright pride of it greater on the wing.

The wonder, indeed, is not that hummingbirds sometimes drop exhausted, but that they stay aloft. Their feats are possible because they have proportionately immense wing muscles, and are—for their size—the biggest-hearted little birds in the world. Theirs is the most perfectly controlled of bird flights; no other in the sky can, like a hummer, fly backwards. The eye cannot catch the trick in this magical dart to the rear, but slow-motion pictures reveal it. In backing away from a flower, the hummer, you might say, stands on air—tail down, wings beating horizontally. The forward wing stroke forces the air away from the bird's breast, driving it backward; then on the return stroke the wing is rotated at the shoulder joint so that the upper surface strikes the air, and this, driving the air downward, balances the pull of gravity on the tiny body.

Not only as a stunt pilot but as a lover is the hummingbird a little show-off. He will shoot back and forth before his lady, while she observes him serenely, her head flashing from side to side to follow his gyrations. The arc of his flight is like the glitter of a racing pendulum, bespeaking an ardor to match the rest of his volatile temperament. Mating follows swiftly, and egg-laying the same tempo. The nest is accomplished, like everything else in hummingbird life, at high speed; a single day has been known to suffice. Yet it is not slapped together, but is a work of consummate art. The smallest nests are no larger in diameter, on the outside, than a silver quarter; on the inside you could not drop a slim dime flat in them. Externally the nest of the ruby-throat is perfectly camouflaged with lichens, so that it is almost invisible even though usually placed in plain sight, on a branch or in such quaint and trusting spots as a loop of rope or an atom of orange on its tree. Within, the minute cradle is lined with thistledown, milkweed silk, the "wool" from the leaves of sycamores, or the stems of young cinnamon ferns. And the whole is saddled firmly on the twig with bits of spider silk woven by the needle-like bill of the female as cleverly as by any seamstress.

Here are laid two white eggs, the size of pearls or peas. When they hatch, the chicks are hardly bigger than the nail of your finger, helpless, naked, blind, all gullet and yelp. To see the mother thrust that bill in a lightning flash down the baby's throat, you would think she must surely pin the little thing to the very bough. Feeding time is about every minute or two at first; it must be a great relief to the mother when the children have to be fed only every five minutes!

Ruby-throats are the chief kind of hummingbird you will see east of the Rockies, even in tropical Florida. There is small chance of mistaking them for anything but the dusk-loving, flower-haunting sphinx moth. Out West the task of distinguishing the different species becomes confusing. In my California garden there are five species, and seldom is the bright air empty of that delicate roar, like the fury of some fairy dragon, that is made by their passionate flight. The mountains of southern Arizona have several species, some of which are found nowhere else in the United States, being Mexican species that enter our fauna from the splendid tropics. And that, of course, is the place to see hummers—in the lands of the western hemisphere lying between Capricorn and Cancer.

In those equatorial lands, hummers go to lengths of fantastic beauty as extravagant as the jungle flowers on which they feed. The tongue, unique in the bird world, consists in two tubes, but how the nectar ascends them is still unknown to scientists. (Nectar, though, is not the only fare of hummers; they like the minute insects they find in flowers, and also catch them on the wing.) In the selection of the flowers they visit, hummingbirds are skillful botanists. They delight in flowers with trumpet-shaped corollas having deeply buried nectaries. Here they fear no competition from bees; only a butterfly with her long tongue could reach into such a blossom, and the hot-tempered hummer can easily send her flying.

It used to be thought that hummingbirds prefer red flowers, but they are just as readily pleased with blue, yellow, or white, providing the shape of the flower is right and it produces abundant nectar. If you want to attract all hummers in your neighborhood, therefore, plant nectar-bearing tubular-shaped flowers. Honeysuckle, scarlet runner beans, trumpet vines and morning-glories grow for anyone, and can be trained with ease upon strings or wire to make a screen before your porch. Seated behind that screen you can watch the hummers at your ease, as they dip, sip, dart, dip again, gently buzzing, flashing off their brilliant colors, tamer than any other wild bird I know. Indeed, one may come close, and hover curiously in front of your face, wondering perhaps what sort of clumsy great creature is this? In the open garden, salvias and fuschias are favorites of the hummers and so are columbines. And, as the little creatures make the rounds of your flowers, you can know that they are at the same time pollinating them, thereby preparing seed for you. For naturally much pollen is carried from blossom to blossom on the feathers, and some flowers seem adapted especially to hummingbird pollination and, in some cases, to no other means.

But you must go to the Andean region to see in all their glory such hummingbirds as the sapphires, the rainbows, the blossomcrowns, racket-tails, fairies, sylphs, comets, trainbearers, and Incas. Altogether the family of Trochilids numbers over six hundred and fifty. Language has all but failed those whose task it has been to describe and name them. They ran through the list of gems: rubies, topazes, amethysts, beryls, emeralds, sapphires, and garnets. They scanned the heavens for suggestions, and came down with rainbow, sunbeam, sun-angel, and comet. They cast their eyes on fair woman, for comparison, and named the species the festive coquette, the frilled coquette, the adorable coquette!

Where all is dazzling beauty, how can one choose the most beautiful? Some give the prize to the white-booted racket-tail of Columbia, a glittering green elf with a forked tail almost three times as long as its body, and wings of an ethereal violet. Others yield the honors to the topaz-throated; this orchid-haunting atom of the Andean forests has a tail with two long feathers, in the male sex, crossing each other; the body is of a metallic ruby, the head a velvety black, and the throat patch icy beryl-line green in the center of which glows a topaz.

No wonder that birds of such a feather have been hunted since the days of the Aztecs, when cloaks made entirely of hummingbird skins were worn by the nobles of Montezuma's court. Even the Indians who greeted the Pilgrim Fathers of New England sometimes wore a hummingbird in one ear, like an earring. With the Victorian age of exploitation and over-adornment, the slaughter of hummers increased. The glittering skins were made into millions of artificial flowers and useless dust catchers. Thus in 1888, in Brazil, three thousand skins of the marvelous topaz-throat were mashed together into a single bale which was disposed of in London at auction, along with twelve thousand other exquisite little hummer carcasses. In that same week, four hundred thousand more hummingbird skins went under the hammer in London, soon to become mere rubbish. As many species were driven to the verge of extinction, the native collectors went deeper into the interior to levy upon new victims.

This traffic, fed by greed and vanity, was outlawed in this country by the law that forbids the importation of wild bird plumage. It was a rescue of the hummingbirds effected largely by the scientists who study them, and who thus well deserve their specimen collections. One of the finest is that of Mr. Robert Moore of Pasadena. In his treasure house I saw five hundred and eighty-eight of the six hundred-and-fifty-odd kinds of hummer, most of them collected by Mr. Moore himself. For he has led expeditions into the trans-Andean regions where even his Indian guides refused to go farther, for fear of volcano, perpetual shroud of cloud and storm, chasms, waterfalls, and smothering jungle. Thus he has discovered several species new to science and rediscovered others long lost; he has been the first scientist ever to find the nests and eggs and study the tiny life histories of a number of remote and busy creatures known before only as skins in a cabinet.

Now lovingly he laid in my palm fabulous sprites out of every country in the western hemisphere, from the tiniest bird in the world—Princess

Helena's hummer, two and a quarter inches long and weighing about one-sixteenth of an ounce—up to the giant of the family (actually only about the size of a swallow) which alone among them does not "hum" but flies with ordinary wing beats.

When I turned the light little stuffed bodies in my fingers, as one would turn a gem, they shot forth an unearthly radiance of color that made me gasp. A tiny throat, at first sight merely black, glowed suddenly emerald. Yet grind those gleaming feathers and you would have nothing but gray dust. A scarlet parrot would still be scarlet no matter how you sliced it, for the pigmentation is in the feathers. But the hummingbird's magic is all done with mirrors. The tiny barbs on each little plumule of each feather are so channeled as to break and refract the light, just as a cut diamond will do. So a hummingbird is a feathered prism, a living rainbow. Darting out of fairyland into your garden, it captures the very sunlight for you and turns it into a jewel on wings.

REPTILES

TAKE

TO THE AIR

Elizabeth Chesley Baity

The art of flying was invented by insects several hundred million years ago; reinvented by the reptiles a great many million years later; and by man within the memory of many of us still living. Insects continue to practice the art, but the reptiles surrendered it to the birds who branched off from their stock on an evolutionary line of their own and man, the only mammal (except the bat) who has ever taken successfully to the air, is too heavy in proportion to his muscular power ever to fly on his own wings. A few birds have forgotten what wings are for and it is possible that the penguins (nobody is sure) never had any wings adequate for flying. "Flight" is the first thing which "bird" suggests and despite all their fame as singers it is probably what is most responsible for their fascination.

During 1961 the discovery of a new fossil established the fact that reptiles had taken to the air, at least as gliders, thousands of years earlier than it had been hitherto supposed. But that does not change the main outlines of the story as summarized in the article which follows.

FOR at least 4000 years the Chinese have told tales about dragons, fearful creatures thought to bring thunder storms and destruction. Chinese doctors have prescribed powdered dragons' bones, which Chinese chemists have honestly and faithfully supplied. Far from being figments of a tall tale, it now appears, dragons were once a familiar part of the Chinese landscape. Today scientists scour the sands of the Gobi Desert of China for fossil dinosaurs, the "dragon" bones used by the Chinese. Practically every American schoolchild knows that flying reptiles, dragons of the air, actually did exist, though the last one was stone cold and perhaps turned to stone himself some 69 million years before the time of man.

The vertebrates ventured into the air back in the Jurassic days, millions of years after the invertebrates had taken to wings. This conquest of the

From *America Before Man*. New York: The Viking Press, 1953.

air was made by two different groups of animals, each descended from reptilian ancestors. One group was that of the real flying reptiles, the pterosaurs. This family rose in the Jurassic, flourished in the Cretaceous, and became extinct before the beginning of Cenozoic times.

The other group was that of our friends the birds, which also rose in the Jurassic. Luckily for us, they managed to survive the crisis that wiped out most of the reptiles during the difficult days that led to the Cenozoic, the era of recent life.

During the Mesozoic, reptiles became masters of the air as well as of earth and sea, and insects were no longer able to escape their enemies because they alone could fly.

The pterosaurs winged their way across America during the times that giant mosasaurs ruled the seas and enormous dinosaurs the land. Pterosaurs came in assorted sizes, ranging from the size of a sparrow to varieties larger than modern condors. They were also of assorted shapes, some with tails and crests, others with neither—a fact that caused no end of dispute among the scientists who first studied fossils. Their brains were large, for reptiles, and their sense of sight highly developed. Some fossil skeletons show teeth, indicating that there were meat-eating pterosaurs.

The leathery wings of the pterosaur had no feathers. They were membranes stretching from the extended fourth "fingers" to the back legs. These membranes show clearly in fossil imprints. The first flying reptiles to be studied were called pterodactyls, or "wing-fingers." The remaining "fingers," tipped with claws, doubtless provided anchorage to cliffs or tree limbs.

Pterosaur remains of the Jurassic are rare in North America, but those of the Cretaceous are abundant. Many fossils have been found along the shorelines of the great inland sea. During the Cretaceous the pterosaurs really spread their wings. Though some remained small, *Pteranodon* of Kansas was a real dragon in size.

The structure of this giant flying reptile shows that it must have been a glider with an enormous wing-spread. This great expanse of wings was supported by hollow bones almost paper-light. Scientists say that *Pteranodon* required only about 0.0036 horsepower to sustain his weight in flight. But what did *Pteranodon* do with those great wings when he wanted to walk? Once down, how could he have taken to the air again? Early drawings show him swooping down to seize a fish in his beak, which seems like a highly risky proceeding. Even an albatross, with only a 12-foot wing-span, has a hard time rising from the water. The chances are that *Pteranodon* glided down from cliffs or trees and was usually skillful enough to keep out of the water.

There is a possibility that the pterosaurs were warm-blooded, as are the birds. Yet, though successful for millions of years, they did not survive the crisis that led to the "recent" geologic period. The true flying reptiles became extinct, along with the dinosaurs, about 70 million years ago.

Archaeopteryx ("ancient wing"), the oldest known bird fossil, was found in Jurassic rock strata. He has been described as a "warm-blooded reptile disguised as a bird." The disguise consisted largely of feathers. *Archaeopteryx* still had file-like teeth, and claws on the ends of his wings. He had vertebrae in his tail, and his tail feathers were arranged along the sides of these vertebrae instead of spreading out fan-wise as do those of modern birds. He came very near to being a "missing link." Only three fossils of his tribe are known: two skeletons and a feather found in a quarry in Bavaria, in rocks of the Upper Jurassic. Had it not been for the imprint of the feather, scientists would have considered him a reptile.

The first bird descended from a small group of reptiles who had probably taken to trees to escape their enemies. For some reason these creatures did not remain reptiles but became feathered and warm-blooded. Feathers were the new invention to which birds hold the sole patent. Feathers provided a better flying surface than did the membrane of the pterosaur, which was no good when torn. Yet the feather, scientists tell us, is only a frayed-out reptile scale.

No one knows exactly how this fraying-out process started. Perhaps some day a fossil pre-bird will be found, older than *Archaeopteryx*, and the riddle of the feather can be solved. The first birds-in-the-making may have been small tree-climbing reptiles that jumped or sailed down from trees by spreading their limbs. A long history of accidental falls, broken by flapping forearms, seems more likely than that the birds-to-be ran along the ground, flapping their forelimbs, and then took off into the new world of the air.

Birds are rare in the fossil record. The next known fossil after *Archaeopteryx* is from strata laid down millions of years later. By this time there had been many changes in bird structure. Wings were more powerful. Yet the Mesozoic bird still had teeth and he still had a tail.

By the Eocene, some of the birds had almost fully developed their present form. Teeth were gone, and "finger" bones were hidden inside wings. The reptilian jointed tail had been replaced by a fan, or a saucy tuft of feathers.

There are good reasons why birds succeeded where pterosaurs failed. Birds have a high, constant body temperature. They show a remarkable degree of parental love, far beyond that of any reptile. The male bird has few equals as a "family man." These differences presumably enabled birds to survive the crisis that destroyed the pterosaurs.

Nevertheless, modern birds are built almost exactly like the two-legged reptiles from which they descended, and have bone structures much like those of the pterosaurs. The wings of the bird take the place of the reptile's front legs, and three reptile finger bones are concealed in them. *Archae-*

opteryx still had these fingers outside his wings; they were provided with hook-like claws which doubtless helped him scramble from one tree limb to another.

Bird legs are reptile legs in miniature, bone for bone, but are stronger than those of the pterosaurs or of primitive birds. The modern bird gets about on the ground much more easily than the pterosaur could have done. Modern birds have completely lost their teeth in favor of strong horn-like bills. A feather fan has replaced the long lizard-like tail of the early birds.

Having conquered the air, some of the early American birds decided to give up the whole idea of flying and took to the water. Such was *Hesperornis*, the great toothed diving bird of the ancient sea that washed over Kansas.

Why do birds fly? Scientists conclude that it is chiefly because they must do so in order to escape their enemies. Now and then, in certain geologic periods, conditions have been such that birds have had no dangerous enemies. In such times they grew large and remained on the ground. It may have been as a result of these periods that some kinds of birds lost the use of their wings and eventually lost the wings themselves.

Among the giant flightless birds of America's past was *Diatryma*, the flesh-eating nightmare of horses and other small mammals of his day. This bird was a great deal taller than your father, and undoubtedly much fiercer. A *Diatryma* fossil from Wyoming shows us a bird some 7 feet high.

Phororhacos of Patagonia was another flightless flesh-eating bird. Even larger than *Diatryma*, he had a ferocious beak on a head longer than that of a horse. A third Arabian Nights bird was *Brontornis*, the "thunder bird," whose leg bones were larger than those of an ox. We do not know why these giant flightless birds became extinct, but possibly the cause was some small mammal with a taste for bird eggs and fledglings.

Flightless birds are not limited in size as flying birds must be. Having lost the power of flight, however, they cannot migrate to better lands when times change, or escape new enemies by flight. Some of the extinct giant birds doubtless perished because of periods of cold weather. Others lingered in certain protected islands, out of reach of mammals, until the age of man—only to be destroyed by him. Women's fondness for the plumes of the ostrich may have saved this bird from extinction. Other living giant birds are the rhea of South America, the cassowary and the emu of Australia, and the kiwi of New Zealand. The giant "elephant bird" of Madagascar and the moa of New Zealand have become extinct fairly recently, chiefly because they were edible.

The La Brea pits of Southern California provide fossils of the largest known flying bird, *Teratornis* ("monster bird"). Feeding on the bodies of animals trapped in the La Brea tarpit, these birds were themselves trapped in the tar and unable to rise again. In body size *Teratornis* far exceeded any living flying birds. Its wings, supported by powerful muscles, had a span of 11 or 12 feet. Such a large bird could not move easily about in a forest. It is probable that the "monster bird" nested in caves or on cliffs in fairly open country. Fossils of this bird have been found in a cave in Mexico 7000 feet above sea level, as well as in low-lying Florida.

American birds may have formed the habit of wintering in South America during the cold ice-age winters that opened our modern era. When the retreating glaciers permitted, they probably returned northward, during the brief summers, to less crowded feeding grounds, by paths that led across a wide land-bridge joining the Americas—the Caribbean islands are mountain tops of this bridge. Today these former land masses have largely sunk beneath the sea, but it is likely that instincts or brain patterns formed eons ago cause birds to continue to fly this above water route, though it is now dangerous for them.

THE PERFECT
FLYING
MACHINE

Guy Murchie, Jr.

From the birds themselves man learned some of the indispensable se-
crets of successful flying but he could never have put them into
practice had he not been able to summon to his aid his own unique
invention—the art of using for his own purposes an external source of
power. Aviation first became possible when engineers had developed
the internal combustion engine to the point where the ratio of weight
to power was as low as that achieved millions of years ago by the
birds! And birds, as the author of the following article convincingly
argues, are still the most perfect of all flying machines.

1

T HE birds that we see flying successfully around us every day are
only the surviving ten per cent or so of much larger numbers that
hatch from eggs, who in turn represent far less than one per cent of all
that would be hatched if the extinct birds survived in their former numbers. In other words, our present birds are a very select bunch, being
actually only the topflight athletes, the champions who have won the flying tournament of evolution by their prodigious feats of soaring, of diving
at terrific speed, plunging deep into the sea, or fighting in the air.

Can you imagine any better example of divine creative accomplishment
than the consummate flying machine that is a bird? The skeleton, very
flexible and strong, is also largely pneumatic—especially in the bigger
birds. The beak, skull, feet, and all other bones of a 25-pound pelican
have been found to weigh but 23 ounces. Yet the flesh too is pneumatic,
and in some species there are air sacs around viscera, muscles, and, where
balance and streamlining permit, immediately under the skin. The lungs
are not just single cavities as with mammals but whole series of chambers

From *Song of the Sky*. Boston: Houghton Mifflin, 1954.

around the main breathing tubes, connected also with all the air sacs of the body, including the hollow bones. Thus the air of the sky literally permeates the bird, flesh and bone alike, and aerates it entire. And the circulation of sky through the whole bird acts as a radiator or cooling system of the flying machine, expelling excess humidity and heat as well as exchanging carbon dioxide for oxygen at a feverish rate.

This air-conditioning system is no mere luxury to a bird but vitally necessary to its souped-up vitality. Flight demands greater intensity of effort than does any other means of animal locomotion, and so a bird's heart beats many times per second, its breathing is correspondingly rapid, and its blood has more red corpuscles per ounce than any other creature. As would be expected of a high-speed engine, the bird's temperature is high: a heron's 105.8°, a duck's 109.1°, and a swift's 111.2°.

Fuel consumption is so great that most birds have a kind of carburetor called a crop for straining and preparing their food before it is injected into the combustion cylinders of the stomach and intestines, and the speed of peristaltic motion is prodigious. You may have heard of the young robin who ate fourteen feet of earthworm the first day after leaving the nest, or the house wren who was recorded feeding its young 1217 times between dawn and dusk. Young crows have been known to eat more than their own weight in food per day, and an adolescent chickadee was checked eating over 5500 cankerworm eggs daily for a week.

The main flying motors fed by this bird fuel are the pectoral muscles, the greater of which pulls down the wing against the air to drive the bird upward and onward, while the lesser hoists the wing back up again, pulling from below by means of an ingenious block and tackle tendon. This extraordinary halyard which passes through a lubricated pulley hole at the shoulder is necessary because the heaviest muscles must be kept at the bottom of the bird so that it will not fly top-heavy. Just as the motor may weigh half of a small airplane, the powerful wing muscles of a pigeon have been found to weigh half the whole bird. These pectorals, by the way, are the solid white meat attached to the breastbone or keel, a location insuring the lowest possible center of gravity—just forward of such other low-slung ballast as gizzard and liver, and well below the very light lungs and air sacs.

If you want to see the ultimate in vertebrate flexibility, you must examine a bird's neck. More pliant than a snake, it enables the beak to reach any part of the body with ease and balances the whole bird in flight. Even the stocky little sparrow has twice as many vertebrae in its neck as the tallest giraffe: fourteen for the sparrow, seven for the giraffe.

The most distinctive feature of all in a bird, of course, is its feathers, the lightest things in the world for their size and toughness. The tensile strength of cobwebs is great but feathers are stronger in proportion in many more ways, not to mention being springy and flexible.

The growth of a feather is like the unfoldment of some kinds of flowers and ferns. Tiny moist blades of cells appear on the young bird, splitting lengthwise into hairlike strands which dry apart into silky filaments which in the mass are known as down. At the roots of the down lie other sets of cells which, as the bird grows older, push the down from its sockets. These are the real feathers, and when the down rubs off they appear as little blue-gray sheaths which may be likened to rolled-up umbrellas or furled sails.

Each of these sheaths is actually an instrument of almost unimaginable potentiality and at the right moment it suddenly pops open—revealing in a few hours feathers that unfold into smaller feathers that unfold again and again. Each main shaft or quill sprouts forth some 600 dowls or barbs on either side to form the familiar vane of the feather. But each of the 1200 barbs in turn puts out about 800 smaller barbs called barbules, each of which again produces a score or two of tiny hooks known as barbicels. The complete interwoven mesh of one feather thus contains some thirty million barbicels, and a whole bird normally is encased in several hundred billion tiny clinging barbicels.

It is hard for the human mind to take in the intricacy of this microscopic weaving that is a feather. There is nothing chemical about it. It is entirely mechanical. If you pull the feather vane apart in your fingers it offers outraged resistance: you can imagine the hundreds of barbules and thousands of barbicels at that particular spot struggling to remain hooked together. And even after being torn the feather has amazing recuperative power. Just placing the split barbs together again and stroking them lengthwise a few times is sufficient to rehook enough barbicels to restore the feather to working efficiency—by nature's own zipper action.

The feather webbing is so fine that few air molecules can get through it and it is ideal material for gripping the sky. In a sense the feather is as much kith to sky as kin to bird, for by a paradox the bird does not really live until its feathers are dead. No sooner is a feather full grown than the opening at the base of the quill closes, blood ceases to flow, and it becomes sealed off from life. The bird's body does not lose track of it, however, for as often as a feather comes loose from a living bird, a new one grows in its place.

Did you ever notice how similar are a feather and a sail? The quill, though it can be bent double without breaking, is stiff enough for a mast. The forward or cutting vane is narrow as a trimmed jib, the aft or lee vane wide like a mainsail. The barbs correspond to the bamboo lugs of a Chinese junk, strengthening the sail, enabling it to withstand the full typhoon of flight. The primary feathers of some sea ducks, however, can be as jibless as catboats, having virtually no vane forward of the quill, which thus itself becomes the leading edge. The cross-section of such a feather is rather like an airplane wing and highly efficient in lift.

Besides its individual qualities a feather is a perfect part of a whole, its shaft curved to blend exactly into the pattern of the wing, its shape to fit the slipstream of the sky. Like roof tiles, feathers are arranged in overlapping rows, the forward part of the bird corresponding to the top of the roof. Which explains why birds do not feel right unless they are facing the weather, why when they turn to leeward the wind blows against their grain letting the rain soak through to the skin just as shingles reversed will funnel the wet into the house instead of shedding it away.

Different feathers naturally have different functions and shapes. The wing-tip feathers are called the primaries, usually ten in number, and serve to propel the bird. These grow out of what corresponds to the bird's hand. The forearm feathers nearer the body are the secondaries, twelve to fourteen of them—they mainly support the bird—while the upper arm tertiaries or tertial feathers fair in the secondaries with the body and stabilize the bird in the air. The tail feathers average about fourteen, overlapping from the center outwards, but they vary so much in different birds that hardly any generalization can be made about them. They are rooted in a pincushionlike muscle mound, the pope's nose, which in some species has been found to house more than a thousand individual feather muscles, each capable of moving one feather in one direction.

One might think that as a bird moults, shedding feathers from once to three times a year, the uneven loss would sometimes set the bird off balance in flight. But nature provides that at least the important primary feathers drop off exactly in pairs, one from the right wing with the corresponding feather from the left wing, waiting then for two new feathers to replace them before moulting the next pair.

2

When Leonardo da Vinci and later Otto Lilienthal and the French glider pioneers studied birds in order to learn the principles of flight, their concentration naturally was focused on the motions of wings and tail. But these movements turned out to be so fast, complex, and subtle that their analysis was extremely difficult. Even today much remains to be learned of them.

One of the first facts revealed by close observation and the high-speed camera was that wings do not simply flap up and down. Nor do they row the bird ahead like oars. The actual motion is more that of sculling a boat or screwing it ahead by propeller action, a kind of figure-eight movement.

A bird's "hand" (outer wing) is longer than the rest of its "arm" (wing) but it has almost as complete control over it as a man has. It is true that two of the original "fingers" have fused into one and the others have disappeared, but the big primary feathers have replaced them so completely that it has gained many more digits and muscles than it has lost. It can twist its "hand" to any position, spread its ten primaries, waggle or twiddle them, shrug its shoulders, even clap its "hands" together behind its head and in front of its breast. That is why wing motion is so complex, variable, and hard to comprehend.

The powerful downstroke that obviously lifts and propels the bird also is a forward stroke, so much so that the wings often touch each other in front of the breast and almost always come close at take-off and climb. Many people have trouble understanding this fact proven by the camera until they reflect that it is likewise forward motion of the airplane wing that generates lift. Just as a sculling oar or a propeller drives a boat ahead by moving at right angles to the boat's motion, so does the force of the bird's wing resolve itself into a nearly perpendicular component.

Even the wing's upstroke plays its part in driving the bird upward and onward—for the same reason. This quick flip of recovery takes half the time of the downstroke and has much less power, but is still part of the sculling motion that is almost peristaltic—like a fish in the sea or a snake in the grass—probably closest of all to the rotor screw action of a moving helicopter: forward and down, backward and up and around.

A fuller understanding of this marvel can be gained by careful study of photographs taken at very high speed, flashed in slow motion on a screen or strangely frozen in stills. The pliable feathers at the wing's tip and trailing edge are then seen to bend according to the changing pressures, revealing how the air is moving.

The downstroke plainly compresses them tightly upon each other the whole length of the outstretched wing, each feather grabbing its full hold of air, while the upstroke, lifting first the "wrist," then the half-folded wing, swivels the feathers apart like slats in a Venetian blind to let the air slip by. It is an automatic, selective process, probably nature's most graceful and intricate valve action, the different movements overlapping and blending smoothly, the "wrists" half up before the wing tips stop descending, the "forearms" pressing down while the tips are yet rising. The convexity of the wing's upper surface and the concavity of its lower aid this alternate gripping and slipping of the air—this compression of sky into a buoyant cushion below the wing while an intermittent vacuum sucks from above—this consummate reciprocal flapping that pelicans accomplish twice a second, quail twenty times, and hummingbirds two hundred times!

Birds are clearly way ahead of the airplane in aileron or roll control; and some, like ravens and roller pigeons, close their wings to make snap rolls just for fun or courting. And the same bird superiority holds in the case of flaps which brake the air to reduce speed in landing, the birds fanning out their tails for this purpose as well as their wings. Web-footed birds such as geese usually steer and brake with their feet also, and inflect their long necks like the bow paddle of a canoe to aid in steering and balancing.

The tail is of course intended primarily for steering—steering up and down as well as to right and left. Some birds with efficient tails can loop the loop, fly upside down, or do backward somersaults like the tumbler pigeon. Small-tailed birds such as ducks are handicapped by not being able to make any kind of sharp turns in the air, though their tails steer well enough in water and in slapping the waves on take-off from water. The male whidah bird has such a long tail that on a dewy morning he actually cannot get off the ground until the sun has evaporated the extra weight from his trailer. The variety of bird tails never ends, nor does the multiplicity of functions. Furled to a mere stick or fanned out 180° and skewed to any angle, tails serve for everything from a stabilizing fin to a parachute, from a flag to a crutch.

3

Man cannot hope to match the bird in sensitivity of flying control, mainly because he usually has to think air or read it off instruments, while the bird just feels air everywhere on his feathers and skin. This is not to say, however, that the bird is a faultless flyer. Birds make plenty of mistakes—even forced landings! Not a few are killed in crashes. Usually bird slip-ups happen so fast they go unnoticed. But when you get a chance to watch a flight of birds coming in to land in slow-motion movies you can see them correcting their errors by last-moment flips of tail or by dragging a foot like a boy on a sled. If a landing bird discovers he lowered his "flaps" too soon he still can ease off these air brakes by raising his wings so that his secondaries spill wind, his primary feathers remaining in position for lateral or aileron control. Buzzards do something almost similar called a "double dip" to correct a stall. But lots of times excited birds do not notice their mistakes soon enough and lose flying speed while trying to climb too steeply, or fall into a spin from tight turns or from simply misjudging the wind. Once they have ceased making headway they tumble downward just as surely as a stalled airplane.

I saw a heron one day muff a landing in a tree, stall, and fall to the ground, breaking his leg. This is particularly apt to happen to heavy birds like ducks when they are tired. Sometimes ducks lose half a pound on a long migratory flight and are so exhausted on letting down that they splash into the water and cannot take off again for hours.

The energy required of a heavy bird at take-off of course is very great. It has been estimated at five times normal cruising energy. Many birds, like the swan, need a runway in addition to the most furious beating of wings to get up enough speed to leave the ground. Others like the coot are lighter but low-powered and take off like a 1915 scout plane missing on three cylinders. All birds naturally take off against the wind for the same reason that an airplane does: to gain air speed, which is obviously more significant than ground speed at take-off. You have surely noticed that birds feeding by the lee roadside will often take off across the path of an approaching car, actually tempting death to gain the wind's help.

Heavy birds that dwell on cliffs of course have the advantage of being able to make a catapult take-off, dropping into a steep glide until they build up flying speed—but again they must beware of landing at a place where this needed gravitational asset is not available. The penalty for lack of such foresight can well be death.

I heard of a loon that made the mistake of alighting on a small pond set amid a forest of tall pines. When he wanted to take off an hour later he found himself stymied. He could not climb steeply enough to clear the trees or turn sharply enough to spiral out. He was seen thrashing along over the water, whipping the waves with his wings to get under way, even pedaling at the water desperately with his webbed feet before getting into the air. He almost made it a couple of times but also nearly got killed crashing into the big trees, then plowing back through the under-brush on his sprained wishbone. Finally he had to give up. But this particular loon was lucky. After four frustrated days in his pond jail a very strong wind came up and enabled him to take off and climb so steeply against it that he just brushed between the treetops and was free!

A very different and special capacity is required in bird formation flight or mass maneuvering. Did you ever see a puff of smoke blowing against the wind? I did—but it turned out to be a tight flock of thousands of small birds. When you get close enough to watch a large flight of starlings feeding on a field you wonder how each bird can so completely lose its individuality as to become part of that smooth, flowing mass. Sometimes the flock moves like a great wheel, individual birds alighting and rising progressively as parts of the rhythm of the rim. Now it rolls as a coach on the highroad, now with uneven grace like a tongue of sea fog folding over and over.

Sandpipers, plover, turnstones, sanderlings, and other small shore birds are all expert in this sort of flying, which seems to depend on extreme quickness of eye and a speed of selfless response not equaled elsewhere in nature—not among its counterparts in the hoofed animals of the plains, not even among the mysterious schools of the deep sea where whales and the lesser fish have been seen to dive in wonderful co-ordination miles apart. No one knows exactly how this amazing unity of action is accomplished or why. It may depend on much more than visual contact. It may be a part of one of the seams of life where the individual is granted a pretaste of absorption into a greater order of consciousness, far above and beyond his own little being.

When birds migrate they often fly in V formation and for the same reason that the Air Force does. It is the simplest way to follow a leader in the sky while keeping out of his wash and retaining good vision. Birds instinctively do it, peeling off from one heading to another and sometimes chasing after man-made gliders. They even have been seen pursuing power planes until they were unable to keep up with them. I know of a glider pilot who was followed for half an hour by a young sea gull who copied his every maneuver: figure-eights, vertical turns, spins, loops. It was only after the glider led the gull into a vertical dive for three thousand feet which blew most of the bird's feathers off that it realized it had been a little too gullible and left off the chase.

Lots of birds, far from feeling jealous of human trespassing in their ancient territory, seem to get such a kick out of airplanes that they hang around airports just like human kids watching the big ones take off and land. Many a time I've seen sea gulls at the big Travis Air Base near San Francisco flapping nonchalantly among the huge ten-engined B-36 bombers while their motors were being run up. The smoke whipping from the jets in four straight lines past the tail accompanied by that soul-shaking roar would have been enough to stampede a herd of elephants but the sea gulls often flew right into the tornado just for fun. When the full blast struck them they would simply disappear, only to turn up a few seconds later a quarter mile downwind, apparently having enjoyed the experience as much as a boy running through a hose—even coming around eager-eyed for more.

4

Of all birds the hawks have probably contributed most toward teaching man to fly—through their example of soaring over the zones of the earth where most men live. But how they accomplish their miracle has been discovered only a little at a time over long periods.

Sir George Cayley around 1810 concluded that a rook, whose weight is about a pound for each square foot of its wing area, would be able to glide horizontally as long as it could maintain a speed of at least twenty-five miles an hour. What could enable it to keep up that speed, however, he did not pretend to know.

A partial answer was revealed long afterward by a study of gulls circling close to the sea in autumn and winter, times of year when the relative warmth of the water often produces updrafts in which birds can soar indefinitely. Even in a fresh breeze when these warm columns of air are blown over to leeward until they lie almost flat upon the waves, the gulls have been observed soaring buoyantly along the invisible wind seams—gliding magically upwind upon a continuous fountain of air where two counterrotating columns adjoin.

But when they cannot thus coast "downhill" in air flowing "uphill," neither on thermal nor deflected updrafts, soaring birds somehow still manage to stay aloft on almost motionless wings—traveling at high speed as often against the wind as with it. A mission of the French scientist, Idrac, to the South Seas during the last century to solve the mystery of the albatross determined that this largest of soaring birds flies at the high average speed of forty-nine miles an hour. When soaring close to the waves and losing altitude, reported Idrac, the albatross uses his remaining speed to gain height. If he can rise only four or five times his wingspread of about eleven feet he usually gets into an air stratum fifty feet up where the wind is blowing three times as strongly as at the surface, thus giving him an extra boost just as a kite will be sent upward by a gust of wind.

The theory of this eventually expanded into one of the first real explanations of why birds soar in circles: since surface friction reduces wind speed at lower altitudes, the bird soars against the wind aiming slightly uphill to take advantage of higher wind velocity as he goes up, giving him the kite boost by *horizontal* shearing (by differences of wind speed at different horizontal levels). But as forward speed eventually falls off because of the climb, he turns away from the wind and coasts slightly downhill to leeward, again getting a boost from his increase in air speed as the tail wind decreases—then into the wind once more, and so on round and round.

The principles of "static soaring"—soaring on rising air currents—have been worked out in detail mainly during the last twenty-five years as sailplane pilots have experimented with thermal currents over sun-baked fields or up the windward slopes of hills or cold fronts. But only more recently has "dynamic soaring" come into use by man: this more difficult since it depends on the sudden variations of wind speed in gusty air to impart the kite boost by *vertical* shearing (by differences of wind speed in different vertical planes), relying of course on the pilot to be heading to windward at each increase of wind and to leeward at each decrease, a rhythm that can be irregular to the point of inscrutability.

All of these discoveries have helped explain how birds can glide on motionless wings against the wind, for it became clear that gravity is to the bird as the keel is to the sailboat or the kite string to the kite. All three hold the moving object firm against being blown to leeward, each in its own way.

The form of the wing is obviously another basic factor in flying effectiveness, and birds have adopted a great variety of special shapes just as have the airplane designers after them. There are the narrow, pointed wings of the fast and strong flyers: the falcons and swallows, the swifts and hummingbirds. There are the bent-wrist wings of the fast gliders like the nighthawk; the broad, fingered wings of the slow soarers, the red-shouldered and red-tailed hawks; the short, rounded wings of the woodland darters: grouse, quail, the small sparrows and finches.

Gulls and albatrosses also have narrow, pointed wings, theirs however adapted specially to long-range gliding and soaring over the open ocean. The albatross, in fact, so perfectly geared to the air that he cannot fold his lengthy wing restfully inside his flank feathers when on ground or sea, is thought to stretch out in sleep while actually on the wing—dozing aloft, even as some of us, but literally in his own feather bed upon the sky.

Little by little the factors of wing efficiency have resolved themselves into the separate relationships or dimensions of the wing: specifically, its aspect ratio or the proportion between its length and breadth, its degree of bluntness or pointedness, its camber or curvature fore and aft, its horizontalness or dihedral angle in relation to the other wing, its slotting or spacing of primaries (if any), its degree of sweepback, its fairing or smoothness of surface, its thickness, its flexibility, and innumerable minor points.

Aspect ratio in birds averages around 3:1. That is, their wings are generally about three times as long as they are wide. The albatross exceeds 5:1. Airplanes sometimes reach 7:1, and sailplanes as high as 18:1. Theoretically, the higher the ratio the greater the lift, but practically a limit comes when the wing gets so long and narrow that it may break in gusty air. And of course soaring birds have many considerations besides flying that affect their shape: things like catching food, preening their feathers, folding their wings, laying eggs, raising a family. Thus sailplanes, built solely for soaring, have a distinct advantage over the bird who must also be somebody's uncle or grandmother.

THE

MIGRANT

BIRDS

Gonzalo de Oviedo

Just twenty-two years after Columbus first set sail for the Indies one Gonzalo Fernandes Oviedo y Valdes was appointed Supervisor of the Gold Smeltings at San Domingo, and later, Historiographer of the Indies. In all, he paid six visits to the New World, and his Natural History of the Indies contains a mass of curious information, much of it based on original observation. He was probably the first to comment on the migration of birds in the Western Hemisphere.

E VERY yeere there passe from the end of Cuba infinite numbers of divers sorts of Birds, which come from the north of the firme Land, and crosse over the Alacrain Islands and Cuba, and flye over the Gulfe Southwards. I have seene them passe over Darien and Nombre de dios and Panama in divers yeeres, in the Firme Land; so many that they cover the skie: and this passage or march continueth a moneth or more about the moneth of March. I thinke they flie round about the World, for they never are seene to returne toward the West or North: and we see them not every yeere one after another; from morning to night the aire is covered, and some flie so high that they cannot bee seene, others lower yet higher then the mountaines tops. They come from the Northwest and North to the Southwards, and then turne South-west, occupying in length more than the eye can discerne, and a great space in breadth. The lowest are Eaglets and Eagles, and all seeme Birds of prey of many kinds and plumes: the higher cannot bee discerned in their plumes, but in manner of flying and quantitie appeare of divers sorts.

From *Summarie and Generall Historie of the Indies,* 1525, translated by Samuel Purchas.

BIRDS

OF PASSAGE

William Bartram

A vulture sailing high and effortless in the sky or a hummingbird poised before a flower are astonishing sights, but the most wonderful of all the birds' feats is one of which the incredible story has only recently become known. Even the ancient Greeks knew that some of them flew away to warmer climates when winter approached. But it is only within our own century that we have come to know about such unbelievable feats as that of the Arctic tern which migrates annually from the Arctic to the Antarctic and back again, or of the hummingbirds who fly non-stop across the Gulf of Mexico to their winter homes in Central or South America.

William Bartram, son of America's first botanist, was among the earliest of our naturalists to interest himself in the subject. The following passage is taken from the Travels *in which he describes a naturalist's journey deep into Florida. It was one of the first American books to be widely read in England and it supplied hints to both Wordsworth and Coleridge.*

THERE are but few (birds) that have fallen under my observation, but have been mentioned by the zoologists, and most of them very well figured in Catesby's, or Edwards's works.

But these authors have done very little towards elucidating the subject of the migration of birds, or accounting for the annual appearance and disappearance, and vanishing of these beautiful and entertaining beings, who visit us at certain stated seasons. Catesby has said very little on this curious subject; but Edwards more, and perhaps all, or as much as could be said in truth, by the most able and ingenious, who had not the advantage and opportunity of ocular observation; which can only be acquired by traveling, and residing a whole year at least in the various climates from north to south, to the full extent of their peregrinations; or minutely examining the tracts and observations of curious and industrious travelers who have published their memoirs on this subject. There may perhaps be some persons who consider this enquiry not to be productive of any

From *The Travels of William Bartram*, edited by Mark Van Doren. New York: Dover, 1928.

real benefit to mankind, and pronounce such attention to natural history
merely speculative, and only fit to amuse and entertain the idle virtuoso;
however the ancients thought otherwise: for, with them, the knowledge
of the passage of birds was the study of their priests and philosophers,
and was considered a matter of real and indispensable use to the state, next
to astronomy; as we find their system and practice of agriculture was in a
great degree regulated by the arrival and disappearance of birds of passage;
and perhaps a calendar under such a regulation at this time, might be useful to the husbandman and gardener.

But however attentive and observant the ancients were on this branch
of science, they seem to have been very ignorant or erroneous in their
conjectures concerning what became of birds, after their disappearance,
until their return again. In the southern and temperate climates some imagined they went to the moon: in the northern regions they supposed that
they retired to caves and hollow trees, for shelter and security, where they
remained in a dormant state during the cold seasons: and even at this
day, very celebrated men have asserted that swallows (*hirundo*) at the approach of winter, voluntarily plunge into lakes and rivers, descend to
the bottom, and there creep into the mud and slime, where they continue
overwhelmed by ice in a torpid state, until the returning summer warms
them again into life; when they rise, return to the surface of the water,
immediately take wing, and again people the air. This notion, though
the latest, seems the most difficult to reconcile to reason and common
sense, respecting a bird so swift of flight that it can with ease and pleasure
move through the air even swifter than the winds, and in a few hours time
shift twenty degrees from north to south, even from frozen regions to
climes where frost is never seen, and where the air and plains are replenished with flying insects of infinite variety, its favourite only food.

Pennsylvania and Virginia appear to me to be the climates in North
America, where the greatest variety and abundance of these winged emi-
grants choose to celebrate their nuptials, and rear their offspring, which
they annually return with, to their winter habitations, in the southern
regions of N. America; and most of these beautiful creatures, which annually people and harmonise our forests and groves, in the spring and
summer seasons, are birds of passage from the southward. The eagle
(i.e. *falco leucocephalus*), or bald eagle (*falco maximus*), or great grey
eagle (*falco major cauda ferruginea*), (*falco pullarius*), (*falco colum-
barius*), (*strix pythaulis*), (*strix acclamatus*), (*strix assio*), (*tetrao tym-
panus*), or pheasant of Pennsylvania (*tetrao urogallus*), or mountain cock
or grouse of Pennsylvania (*tetrao minor sive coturnix*), or partridge of
Pennsylvania (*picus*), or woodpeckers of several species (*corvus carnivorous*), or raven (*corvus frugivora*), or crow (*corvus glandarius s.
corvus crisatus*), or blue jay (*alauda maxima*), (*regulus atrofuscus minor*),
or marsh wren (*sitta*), or nuthatch (*meleagris*), are perhaps nearly all the

land birds which continue the year round in Pennsylvania. I might add to these the blue bird (*motacilla sialis*), mock bird (*turdus polyglottos*), and sometimes the robin red breast (*turdus migratorius*), in extraordinary warm winters; and although I do not pretend to assert as a known truth, yet it may be found on future observation that most of these above mentioned are strangers; or not really bred where they wintered; but are more northern families, or sojourners, bound southerly to more temperate habitations; thus pushing each other southerly, and possessing their vacated places, and then back again at the return of spring.

Very few tribes of birds build, or rear their young, in the south or maritime parts of Virginia and Carolina, Georgia and Florida; yet all these numerous tribes, particularly the soft-billed kinds which breed in Pennsylvania, pass in the spring season through these regions in a few weeks time, making but very short stages by the way: and again, but few of them winter there, on their return southerly; and as I have never travelled the continent south of New Orleans, or the point of Florida, where few or none of them are seen in the winter, I am entirely ignorant how far southward they continue their route, during their absence from Pennsylvania; but perhaps none of them pass the tropic.

When in my residence in Carolina and Florida, I have seen vast flights of the house swallow (*hirundo pelasgia*) and bank martin (*hirundo riparia*) passing onward north toward Pennsylvania, where they breed in the spring, about the middle of March, and likewise in the autumn in September or October, and large flights on their return southward. And it is observable that they always avail themselves of the advantage of high and favorable winds, which likewise do all birds of passage. The pewit, or black cap flycatcher, of Catesby, is the first bird of passage which appears in the spring in Pennsylvania, which is generally about the first, or middle of March; and then wherever they appear, we may plant peas and beans in the open grounds, (*vicia sativa*) French beans, (*phaseolus*) sow radishes, (*raphanus*) lettuce, (*latuca*) onions, (*cepa*) pastinaca, daucus, and almost every kind of esculent garden seeds, without fear or danger from frosts; for although we have sometimes frosts after their first appearance for a night or two, yet not so severe as to injure the young plants.

In the spring of the year the small birds of passage appear very suddenly in Pennsylvania, which is not a little surprising, and no less pleasing: at once the woods, the groves, and meads, are filled with their melody, as if they dropped down from the skies. The reason or probable cause is their setting off with high and fair winds from the southward; for a strong south and southwest wind about the beginning of April never fails bringing millions of these welcome visitors. . . .

THE

HOMING

INSTINCT

Joseph J. Hickey

Inevitably it was the mere wonder of migration that struck the mind and imagination of the early observers and the fact that some birds did migrate was known to the more enlightened for longer than is sometimes realized. As early as the first century A.D., *Pliny, the Elder knew, for instance, that storks returned year after year to the same nest. But fantastic ideas existed side by side with observation and shrewd guesses. Thus a twelfth-century bestiary having noted that storks, "those messengers of spring, those enemies of serpents, can migrate across oceans" then adds, "crows fly in front of them as pathfinders and the storks follow like a squadron." At the beginning of the eighteenth century Daniel Defoe, the author of* Robinson Crusoe, *guessed correctly that birds went South in winter in order to find the insect food which had disappeared from their summer homes, but his contemporary, the naturalist John Morton, believed that swallows spent the winter on the moon.*

Migrational Homing:

EVERYONE has heard about the marvelous homing ability of homing pigeons. Relatively few are aware, however, of the homing ability of wild birds. Between the racing pigeon and the wild species there is hardly any comparison. The pigeon is a mere novice.

Among wild birds, migrational homing behavior may be considered first, as it is known in adult birds and has been observed among young that have not yet nested. Homing has been defined as the ability of animals to return great distances over a route, part of which is entirely unknown or without landmarks. Migrating birds have this ability to a very great degree. The Greenland wheatear, which breeds in the Canadian Arctic, annually migrates to West Africa through the British Isles.

From *A Guide To Bird Watching*. New York: Oxford University Press, 1943.

Many other striking examples could be quoted. Bird banders have also proved beyond all doubt that once migratory birds have nested in a definite locality they will return there as long as they live. There appear to be only a few exceptions to this important rule. Some ducks, for instance, pair on their wintering grounds. The male may have come from central Alberta, the female from the coast of British Columbia. Obviously both cannot return home and still remain mated. It is said that the female always wins.

Do young birds have this homing ability too? It seems quite apparent that they do, although some aspects of the question are still unsettled. Many young birds migrate south before their parents. If their species is known to winter regularly only in southern California, the young birds do not, for example, winter in Florida instead. Birds never make that mistake, no matter how young.

In only a few species do the young birds accompany their parents south. Whooping cranes do this, often traveling from Canada to Texas in what are evidently family flocks. Geese are said to be another example. In some species, young and adults may winter in separate regions. During the winter the herring gulls of Boston harbor are mostly adult; those on the Texas coast are for the most part first-year birds.

Some uncertainty still surrounds the question where birds nest for the first time. Do they return to breed in the locality of their birth? Or is the selection of their first nest site fortuitous—"anywhere," as one authority has postulated, "within the natural range of the species?" The answers to these questions must rest upon the efforts of bird banders. Up to the present, however, only a few banders have provided any satisfactory information on this subject. In Holland, H. N. Kluijver once found that 44 per cent of the surviving nestling starlings that he banded returned to nest in the locality of their birth. Similarly, in Ohio, Margaret Nice concluded that 50 to 60 per cent of her fledgling song sparrows that survived returned to their birthplace. Unfortunately, many other banders never succeeded in retrapping any number of their banded fledglings.

It is now clear that one important reason for this failure is the terrific mortality suffered by young birds in their first year. Among songbirds this loss may amount to 75 per cent; in game birds it may be even higher. Another reason is said to be the failure of bird banders to search the surrounding countryside for banded birds. One of Mrs. Nice's song sparrows settled down about one mile from its birthplace, although most of her fledgling returns were between 100 and 500 yards from the original point of banding. Just how far the bander is supposed to search is hard to say.

If young birds scatter and nest almost anywhere within the breeding range of their species, the follow-up activities of bird banders would have to be Herculean. Some years ago, it occurred to me that the banding records reported only by laymen might answer this question. With this in mind, and with the kind permission of Frederick C. Lincoln, I began a search of the banding files of the United States Fish and Wildlife Service. Eventually the robin proved to be the species I wanted. Fledglings had been banded by the thousands (I never did learn how many). Sixty-one had been reported in some subsequent breeding season (mid-April to mid-July) by ordinary citizens who had no connection with the banding program. Some of the robins had been killed by cars; others had caught themselves on strings; still others had fallen victims to cats. They, one could say, were a random sample of a normal robin population. Probably in the smaller villages where a bander resided, his activities might have stimulated more people to report the band numbers on dead birds. (In large towns and suburban areas his work might be cloaked in anonymity.) This would tend somewhat to increase the percentage of returns made by the robins to the place of their birth. It would not, I think, affect reports a few miles away.

Even with this bias kept in mind, [these researches] suggests a marked tendency for robins to return to the region of their birth. Although the banders did not separate the nestlings according to first, second, and third broods, some clue to this is furnished by the banding dates. These dates do not suggest that birds in the first brood settle farther away than fledglings raised in subsequent broods. Another interesting thing about these banding records concerned the birds reported at some distance from their birthplace. All of them were somewhere *south* of their original home. Without speculating why this happened, the fact does have some significance.

Experimental Homing

Homing experiments offer special opportunities for bird watchers to explore the mysteries of migration. Some experiments deal with adults, others concern young birds. Nearly all require considerable co-operation and organization.

Granted that migratory birds are able to follow the routes of their ancestors, can they also return home over paths completely outside the range of their species? In the early part of this century, two pioneering Americans, John B. Watson and Karl S. Lashley, attempted to answer this question. Capturing five tropical noddy and sooty terns on their nests off the tip of Florida, the young men marked their birds with artists' oils and arranged for their release off the capes of Hatteras, a thousand miles north and far outside the normal range of these species.

Three birds promptly returned, two sooty terns making the journey in only five days.

Other homing experiments proved to Watson and Lashley that about 50 per cent of these birds could return from other points of the compass. Some were undoubtedly weakened by captivity, while others were suspected of following the coast. Many years later, the subject attracted the attention of German ornithologists. Using starlings, Dr. Rüppell proved that even this small species could return from any direction and with no previous knowledge of the country. Here, the absence of prominent landmarks made no difference. When sea birds were released in Italy and Switzerland, R. M. Lockley was later able to prove, they could return to their Welsh island on a straight line, and sometimes in a surprisingly short period.

Even the much maligned cowbird has been found to be an excellent homer. Once in the middle of April one of these birds was trapped by Willian I. Lyon and banded at Waukegan, Illinois. Shipping the bird westward, Mr. Lyon had it released at Denver, Colorado, on April 28. Twenty-five days later it was back in Waukegan. Sent eastward and released at Quebec on May 26, it eventually got back to Illinois and was present in Mr. Lyon's banding trap the following March. Other cowbirds, Mr. Lyon found, could return from equally remote places.

Waterfowl are no less competent. Some years ago, E. A. McIlhenny captured pintails wintering in Louisana and shipped them to distant points all over the United States. In succeeding winters, he reported, 7 returned from their point of release near Washington, D.C., 5 returned from Cape Cod, 2 from western Montana, 15 from California, and 4 from eastern Oregon.

Today the most interesting migrational homing experiments are those designed to shed light on how the homing instinct is transmitted from old to young. Mallard eggs were once shipped from England, where the species is completely sedentary, to Finland where mallards are definitely migratory. Sixty-two young birds hatched and were successfully banded. About the middle of October all but six of the Finnish birds left for southern regions; a month later these six and all the young English birds finally departed. Three of the latter were subsequently shot in Yugoslavia, one in southern France, and seven others were reported from less distant localities. None returned to England. In the following summer more than half of the English mallards returned to breed in their Finnish birthplace.

This fascinating project would at first seem to show that these young birds had no hereditary knowledge of their ancestors' home. Mallards in England must have a dormant migratory instinct of some kind, for how could the young English birds have migrated north again to their foster homeland? What would have happened if the eggs of a highly

migratory group of birds had been used instead? Some inkling is given
by the story of some sheldrake eggs that were once taken from the
island of Sylt in the North Sea and hatched in Switzerland, where the
species is practically unknown except as a very rare straggler. Out of
the 17 young that hatched, one was shot that October in the Baltic—
only 120 miles from the parental nesting site. Was this a coincidence, as
W. B. Alexander once asked, or do migratory birds have an inherited
memory of their ancestral home?

The answer will be found in careful experiments worked out on a
continental basis. Waterfowl are easily shot and yield a high percentage
of recoveries. But these records tend to become bunched in hunting
seasons when the birds are already on migration. Besides, ducks tend to
pair on their wintering grounds, which introduces a further complication.
Perhaps a more suitable species would be the herring gull, which nests on
the Pacific coast, the Great Lakes, and the Atlantic seaboard. Suppose a
mass exchange of fresh gull eggs between two of these regions was
carried out over a period of years. Would the birds hatched from Great
Lakes eggs remain, say, on the Pacific coast, or would they eventually
return to the home of their parents? What would happen if follow-up
experiments could be conducted with young birds, well grown but still
unable to fly? Would they behave the same as birds hatched from transported eggs? Would there be any difference between very young birds
and older fledglings transported just before they were ready to fly? No
one, I think, can at this time be sure of just what would happen.

The opportunities for gathering eggs (or young) obviously vary from
species to species, challenging bird clubs and students to concentrated
co-ordinated effort. Usually the transportation costs for eggs is small.
An air-mail shipment of 72 snowy egret eggs from Florida to Long Island
once cost the Linnaean Society of New York about $10. (Most of the
eggs failed to hatch in this experiment and four young nestlings died
after a week. We were inclined to believe that their white down failed
to release the normal feeding behavior patterns of the black-crowned
night herons selected as their foster parents.)

This last experiment closely paralleled others made in England, where
gray herons failed to rear young from eggs of the stork shipped from
the continent. Other possibilities along similar lines can still be successfully explored. Some years ago 260 eggs of the common gull were sent
over 300 miles to a black-headed gull colony in Rossitten, Germany. Here,
79 young were fledged by their foster parents. Although the heavy
vegetation at Rossitten was not at all adapted to their nesting needs, two
pairs of these "transplanted" birds eventually returned and successfully
raised their own young in the vicinity.

Some Homing Theories

The ability of wild birds to return over an unknown course is so far without adequate explanation. There are many theories and even the most fantastic ones are gradually being subjected to study.

Something of the history of these was reviewed not long ago by Ernst Mayr. One of the oldest and most widely accepted theories has held that homing was simply a matter of memory and random searching —when a bird is on familiar ground, it follows the known landmarks; on unfamiliar ground, it wanders about and eventually, by trial and error, picks out something familiar in the landscape. When birds were released in homing experiments, however, they almost invariably set right out in the proper direction. Proof that this theory was worthless came when it developed that birds released 500 miles from home took only 5 times longer to return than others with only 100 miles to go. If random searching were the answer, this distance would always increase geometrically instead of algebraically, as it does in nature. During the course of experiments abroad, homing birds were picked up dead—almost exactly on the theoretical straight line to their nesting localities.

Another explanation offered for homing has given the birds a marvelous ability to retrace the exact journey on which they had just been taken. The most striking proof against retracing, writes Dr. Mayr, is the triangle experiment. Suppose we have the three towns *A*, *B*, and *C* forming the corners of an equilateral triangle. We take 20 starlings from *A* and transport them to *B;* then we retain 10 at *B*, and carry the remaining 10 to *C*. We now release the 20 birds at the same moment. According to the retracing theory, it should take the *C* starlings just twice as long as the *B* birds get home to *A*, because they would have to fly via *B*. "Actual experiments, carried out in Germany, have shown that *B* and *C* starlings arrived home at the same time," Dr. Mayr reports, "thus upsetting a very fine theory."

Still another explanation of homing similarly assumes that birds have extraordinary organs that register every turn on the road of the transport. In addition, this third theory credits the bird with always knowing its geographic position in regard to its nesting locality. To check this idea, scientists shipped two cages of starlings from a German village to Berlin, over 90 miles away. Both cages were darkened, but one was mounted on the revolving disc of a phonograph and rotated during the entire journey. Of these birds, 50 to 60 percent returned home—so well, in fact, that they even bettered the record of birds that had not been subjected to this unusual treatment.

Another of the striking experiments carried out by Dr. Rüppell in Germany involved the shipment of starlings by airplane to England,

Sweden and other points in Germany, some more than 400 miles distant. Of these nesting birds, 52 out of 97 were known to return to their home localities. Moreover, the best percentage return (75.9 per cent) was obtained by birds sent the greatest distances.

It has also been suggested that birds are sensitive to terrestrial magnetism. It is argued that each part of the earth has its own magnetic field. A bird might be able to detect this through its ears and so recognize whether its home lay to the north or to the south. A few years ago Polish investigators shipped storks to various parts of Europe. Some birds had magnets attached to their heads; others, serving as "controls," carried unmagnetized weights. In spite of storms, a few birds managed to return. The head magnet had failed to impair their homing ability.

Homing today remains as much of a baffling mystery as it ever was, puzzling both biologist and bird watcher alike. The search for the mechanism of homing is, however, no more knotty than many other studies that scientists have successfully completed. Homing is now so well established in migratory birds that haphazard experiments with adults in the future can only be regarded as stunts. Nesting birds, it is now known, will return vast distances. Wintering birds are not so responsive. (They may have homing *ability*, but very little *urge* to use it outside the nesting season.) I do not think it is up to bird watchers to establish records along these lines, but they can regard the homing of young birds as their own problem. Here we are still faced with fundamental questions. Are migratory routes to a wintering ground a matter of inherited knowledge in all species? Is the recognition of a specific home locality inherited, or is it just the homing ability inherited? Do young birds memorize something about their home while they are still nestlings or just after they have left their parents?

Co-operative studies in bird migration are by no means confined to experiments in homing. An equally interesting series of projects awaits those who would like to map the weekly progress of migratory species as they traverse the length of our continent during a given season. This method of summarizing continental observations might well be taken up by bird watchers who, through some unfortunate circumstance, are no longer able to get into the field. All sorts of birds lend themselves to this type of investigation, but no more than 40 species have, I think, been so studied on our continent. Bullock's oriole would be an easy bird to map in the West, the Baltimore oriole a parallel bird in the East. Many other species that are commonly observed on village streets, in gardens, and in suburban areas might be chosen. The bird clubs . . . could be circularized in this connection. Not all of them might accurately report when the very first chimney swift arrived in their locality from South America, but they could check to observe when the swifts became common and so furnish information on this species' progress from Mexico to Canada. The postage involved in inquiries of this kind is small. It could well be carried by bird clubs anxious to have their own committees on bird migration fill in the many gaps still existing in our knowledge of this subject.

The exploration of bird migration today is obviously a many-sided one. Many observations are still needed at lighthouses and islands off the coast. Daily observations correlated with weather data at the point where migrants start their daily or nightly flight are still needed to show which species move only with favorable weather and which migrate with little regard to wind and temperature. In many regions only the vaguest correlations have been made between the exact development of local vegetation and the spring arrival of the main body of each species.

Migration watching is thus a branch of natural history in which scientific research is still fun. Narrowed down to simple rarity chasing, it is an exciting sport that in time dulls the appetite and eventually suffers from the law of diminishing returns. Within the last twenty years, I have seen many people drop bird study; they had seen "all that there was to be seen" in bird life and there was nothing more to be discovered. I think of them as belonging to those ancient orchard sitters to whom a falling apple was simply a knock on the head. In migration watching, each of us has a chance to follow in the path of Newton, to observe the wonders of creation as they are expressed in the most common phenomena, and to explore nature as assiduously as Wilson and Audubon—and with no less profit.

WINGS

ACROSS

THE MOON

Robert J. Newman

The fact that migrating birds tend to travel at night makes observation more difficult but moonlight is a help—not so much because of the dim light that it affords as because a full moon silhouettes the individuals who cross it.

BIRD!"
The voice coming out of the semi-darkness, had a lilt in it. It was as though a bird, *any* bird—not the first purple martin of spring necessarily, nor the last surviving ivory-billed woodpecker, nor a newly discovered subspecies, but just any bird at all—was a momentous matter. The voice continued:

"Eleven-thirty to five! Definition beautiful! About Two T."

A flashlight winked on. Another voice inquired, "Remarks?"

"Well, pretty fast, I'd say, but straight as an arrow."

Since 1946, this bewildering bit of dialogue, with minor variations, has been repeated more than 10,000 times. It has been heard on half-a-dozen college campuses; aboard a destroyer cruising the Gulf of Mexico; beneath the domes of astronomical observatories; at the fringe of tropical jungles; on the remote sandpits of the Dry Tortugas, and in plain backyards in the heart of great cities. But, varied as these settings have been, they have all had one thing in common. They have all been bathed in the pale light of the moon.

To understand what all this is about, we must go back to [1946] when George H. Lowery, Jr., curator of the Louisiana State University Museum of Zoology, was trying to find out whether any of the birds returning from Central America fly directly across the Gulf of Mexico or whether they all detour around it. What was needed was a means of measuring the amount of migration taking place at different times and places and in

From *Audubon Magazine*, July–August, 1952.

different directions. What is more, it had to be a method that would work at night, when most trans-Gulf flights were supposed to take place. Immediately, when you hear of this problem, you probably think of radar. So did Lowery. Radar had already on occasion detected the passage of large birds like geese. Unfortunately, so the electronics experts said, a device sensitive enough to do the same thing with small land birds would take hundreds of thousands of dollars, and a long time, to develop.

Then Lowery remembered several papers published around the turn of the century, describing the flight of migrating birds before the disc of the moon as seen through a telescope. Could these silhouettes be used somehow to obtain the information he was seeking? Lowery took the question to his friend, Professor W. A. Rense of the Department of Physics and Astronomy at Louisiana State. Rense's answer was yes, but not a simple, unqualified yes; it was an answer complicated with sines, cosines, and spherical triangles, with zeniths and azimuths, and with Greek letters like theta, eta and alpha.

Leaving these matters to the mathematicians, let us merely note what Rense eventually accomplished. The space in which one sees birds through a telescope pointed at the moon is constantly changing in size because of the movement of the moon. Rense devised equations that make adjustments for these changes. The equations permit one to use counts made with the telescope as samples to determine the probable number of birds per hour crossing over a one-mile line on the earth's surface. In order to carry out the computations, however, and to find out what the directional trend of the flight is, it is necessary to know the slant of each observed bird's pathway across the face of the moon. This information can be recorded by imagining that the moon is an upright clock with the rim marked off according to the 12 hours and with the midpoints between the hour marks considered as half-hours. Then the point on the rim where the bird appears and the point where it disappears can each be identified in terms of these hours, establishing its flight line.

This is the key to the strange snatches of conversation that are now being heard on moonlit nights all over the North American continent. "Bird!" is the call that the observer at a telescope uses to alert the recorder sitting beside him, and "eleven-thirty to five" is the description of the bird's path as it glides across the bright white background of the moon and over the silvery seas called lunar seas. Along with this "clock reading" goes other terse information regarding the speed of the bird, the curvature of its path, and the clarity of its focus.

And what about the two T? Well, that is a device to indicate the size of the bird's silhouette. Long ago the features of the moon received fanciful names, and some not so fanciful—names like the Lake of Death, the Hurricane Ocean, the Sea of Showers, the Alps and the Appenines—

and these names have stuck. One of the most prominent of these features is the crater Tycho, which stands out on the moon's surface like the navel on an immense floodlit plaster model of an orange. Moon-watchers refer to its diameter as T and use it to measure the bird's apparent length. Two T, for example, indicates a bird whose image is twice as long as the diamenter of Tycho.

Lowery eventually had the satisfaction of sitting out on the Gulf of Mexico, at the end of a wharf, a mile beyond the surf, and watching 86 birds flash across the moon in a single hour as they left the coast of Yucatan and headed out over 600 miles of open sea toward the northern Texas coast and the heel of Louisiana. The moon was high over the water so that he was looking through a mere sliver of the night sky; and the birds that he counted through his telescope were the equivalent of 11,900 birds crossing over the one mile shoreline. That was on the night of April 23, 1948. By that time it had become apparent that flight studies by means of the moon were much more than a way of finding out whether any migrants cross the Gulf. They would permit us to peer into the very heart of age-old basic mysteries of mass migration.

It is necessary to pause a moment to grasp how revolutionary this development really is. Never before have we been able definitely to measure the volume of migration, even in daylight. When we go out on a May morning bird trip to look for migrant species, we can seldom tell for sure which is the process of migration itself and which are merely effects of migration. Five thousand birds interrupting their migration to flit about for an hour in search of food *within* a square mile of fields and woodland look to the observer much the same as 5000 individuals moving *through* the same area and being replaced every 10 minutes by another 5000. Yet the one case represents no migration, while the other means migration at the rate of 30,000 birds per mile per hour! This is only one of several reasons why the impressions gotten on a bird walk may be very misleading. All of the notions we have based in the past on such impressions may be correct, but there is a good chance that some of them are quite wrong. The moon and the telescope offer an opportunity to find out.

So, before he set out for Yucatan, Lowery had suggested that some observations be made in other places at the same time. It has been said that the bird enthusiasts of America tend to shy away from the scientific aspects of their subject, being in this respect unlike Europeans. However that may be, the response to Lowery's suggestion was gratifying. Telescopes were lifted toward the moon at 30 localities scattered over the continent. Before the season ended, more than 200 people had pooled their efforts to pile up more than 1000 hours of observation.

From the resulting accumulation of data many surprising things were discovered. Some of them had to do with night migrational routes. It has been pretty generally supposed, for instance, that the peninsula of Florida is a major avenue of flight. Nevertheless, at Tampico, on the east Coast of Mexico, almost as many birds were seen in a single *hour* as were seen over the Florida station, at Winter Park, on 11 *nights* of observation. Lunar studies have also indicated that, unlike birds in the daytime, nocturnal migrants rarely fly in definite flocks; that sometimes they fly *southward* in spring, and that they tend to ride the prevailing air currents toward their destination.

But more unexpected than any of these things, perhaps, has been the discovery relating to the basic hour-to-hour pattern of their nightly activity. Ornithologists used to suppose that nocturnal migrants either traveled all night long or that they usually confined their activity to the period directly after sunset or shortly before dawn. The moon has revealed that most of them follow none of these seemingly sensible courses. After sunset the majority of the migrants seem to rest a while. Then, hour by hour, they mount in increasing numbers into the dark sky. This process typically reaches a peak between 11 P.M. and midnight. Thereafter the birds begin to drop to earth again until by the hour before dawn almost none are left a-wing.

Whatever way you look at it, it appears that many birds must get up in the middle of the night just for the sake of making three or four hours' progress toward their destinations. Why they do so we cannot guess as yet. However, it is interesting to note that the pattern of their activity corresponds closely to the pattern of migratory restlessness displayed in spring by wild European birds confined in cages with electrically wired perches that register their movements from one part of the cage to the other.

All of these results have been based on observations in spring, made mostly in the central and southern parts of the United States. We still need to know how they apply in the northern tier of states and in all the region west of the Great Plains. We still need to know whether they hold good *anywhere* in autumn. And we still need answers to a whole host of other questions. Does the moonlight itself affect the volume of migration? Do the "chip" notes of small land birds give any indication of the number passing overhead in the darkness? Do migrants funneled onto peninsulas double back? Do they advance in a wide movement, with a nearly even distribution of numbers along a broad front? Or do they travel in narrow streams? Are such streams channeled along rivers, valleys, mountain ranges and coastlines?

Finding the answers will require observations in tremendous quantity. Until recently the time needed to process that much data was a terrific obstacle to the full use of the telescopic method. For every hour that a moon observer spent behind the telescope in the spring of 1948, Lowery and his staff had to spend two man-hours working with slide rules just to get the material ready for final analysis. Now, however, graphs and tables have been prepared that make it possible to handle observations in unlimited amounts.

A plan is underway to cover the country with a network of telescopes operating simultaneously. That will require the help of interested persons everywhere. The observational procedure is a very simple one; it can be mastered in a few minutes. Anyone can participate—amateur bird watchers, professional ornithologists, or even people who know nothing of birds or bird study but would like to know. Perhaps someone else in your area is already planning to cooperate in the project. Call your local Audubon Society, bird club, observatory, or university zoology department to find out. If no one in your vicinity knows about the project, you may find out what to do by writing to the Museum of Zoology, Louisiana State University, Baton Rouge, La., for a mimeographed pamphlet, *Studying Nocturnal Bird Migration by Means of the Moon.* Almost any telescope of 19-power or more that will encompass the whole moon in its field can be used to study night migration. The spotting scopes popular among bird students are fine. If you have such an instrument but cannot find time to do any moon-watching yourself, perhaps you would like to lend it to someone else in your town who can do. If so, notify the Museum of Zoology, and an attempt will be made to coordinate telescopes and observers.

SANDERLINGS

IN THE

ARCTIC SPRINGS

Rachel L. Carson

Rachel Carson is a biologist who was little known to the lay public until The Sea around Us *became one of the most praised and widely read nature books ever written in the United States. Her* Under the Sea-Wind *from which the following chapter is taken was almost equally fine but at the time of publication attracted comparatively little attention.*

As the patches of earth spread over the snow fields, the sanderlings, plovers, and turnstones gathered in the cleared spots, finding abundant food. Only the knots resorted to the unthawed marshes and the protected hollows of the plains, where sedges and weeds lifted dry seed heads above the snow and rattled when the wind blew and dropped their seed for the birds.

Most of the sanderlings and the knots passed on to the distant islands scattered far over the Arctic sea, where they made their nests and brought forth their young. But Silverbar and Blackfoot and others of the sanderlings remained near the bay shaped like a leaping porpoise, along with turnstones, plovers, and many other shore birds. Hundreds of terns were preparing to nest on near-by islands, where they would be safe from the foxes; while most of the gulls retired inland to the shores of the small lakes which dotted the Arctic plains in summer.

In time Silverbar accepted Blackfoot as her mate and the pair withdrew to a stony plateau overlooking the sea. The rocks were clothed with mosses and soft gray lichens, first of all plants to cover the open and wind-swept places of the earth. There was a sparse growth of dwarf willow, with bursting leaf buds and ripe catkins. From scattered clumps of green the flowers of the wild betony lifted white faces to the sun,

From *Under the Sea-Wind*. New York: Oxford University Press, 1952.

and over the south slope of the hill was a pool fed by melting snow and draining to the sea by way of an old stream bed.

Now Blackfoot grew more aggressive and fought bitterly with every cock who infringed upon his chosen territory. After such a combat he paraded before Silverbar, ruffling his feathers. While she watched in silence he leaped into the air and hovered on fluttering wings, uttering neighing cries. This he did most often in the evening as the shadows lay purple on the eastern slopes of the hills.

On the edge of a clump of betony Silverbar prepared the nest, a shallow depression which she molded to her body by turning round and round. She lined the bottom with last year's dried leaves from a willow that grew prostrate along the ground, bringing the leaves one at a time and arranging them in the nest along with some bits of lichen. Soon four eggs lay on the willow leaves, and now Silverbar began the long vigil during which she must keep all wild things of the tundra from discovering the place of her nest.

During her first night alone with the four eggs Silverbar heard a sound new to the tundra that year, a harsh scream that came again and again out of the shadows. At early dawn light she saw two birds, dark of body and wing, flying low over the tundra. The newcomers were jaegers, birds of the gull tribe turned hawk to rob and kill. From that time on, the cries, like weird laughter, rang every night on the barrens. . . .

When Silverbar had begun to brood her eggs, the moon had been at the full. Since then it had dwindled to a thin white rim in the sky and now had grown again to the quarter, so that once more the tides in the bay were slacker and milder. One morning when the shore birds gathered over the flats to feed on the ebb tide, Silverbar did not join them. Throughout the night there had been sounds in the eggs under her breast feathers, now worn and frayed. They were the peckings of the sanderling chicks, after twenty-three days made ready for life. Silverbar inclined her head and listened to the sounds; sometimes she withdrew a little from the eggs and watched them intently. . . .

Now for the first time an abiding fear entered the heart of Silverbar —the fear of all wild things for the safety of their helpless young. With quickened senses she perceived the life of the tundra—with ears sharpened to hear the screams of the jaegers harrying the shore birds on the tide flats—with eyes quickened to note the white flicker of a gyrfalcon's wing.

After the fourth chick had hatched, Silverbar began to carry the shells, piece by piece, away from the nest. So countless generations of sanderlings had done before her, by their cunning outwitting the ravens and foxes. Not even the sharp-eyed falcon from his rock perch nor the jaegers watching for lemmings to come out of their holes saw the movement of the little brown-mottled bird as she worked her way, with infinite stealth, among the clumps of betony or pressed her body closely to the wiry tundra grass. Only the eyes of the lemmings who ran in and out among the sedges or sunned themselves on flat rocks near their burrows saw the mother sanderling until she reached the bottom of the ravine on the far side of the ridge. But the lemmings were gentle creatures who neither feared nor were feared by the sanderling.

All through the brief night that followed the hatching of the fourth chick Silverbar worked, and when the sun had come around to the east again she was hiding the last shell in the gravel of the ravine. A polar fox passed near her, making no sound as he trotted with sure foot over the shales. His eye gleamed as he watched the mother bird, and he sniffed the air, believing she had young nearby. Silverbar flew to the willows farther up the ravine and watched the fox uncover the shells and nose them. As he started up the slope of the ravine the sanderling fluttered toward him, tumbling to the ground as though hurt, flapping her wings, creeping over the gravel. All the while she uttered a high-pitched note like the cry of her own young. The fox rushed at her. Silverbar rose rapidly into the air and flew over the crest of the ridge, only to reappear from another quarter, tantalizing the fox into following her. So by degrees she led him over the ridge and southward into a marshy bottom fed by the overflow of upland streams. . . .

When Silverbar had led the fox far enough from her young she circled around by the bay flats, pausing to feed nervously for a few minutes at the edge of the salty tide. Then she flew swiftly to the betony clump and the four chicks on which the down was yet dark with the dampness of the egg, although soon it would dry to tones of buff and sand and chestnut.

Now the sanderling mother knew by instinct that the depression in the tundra, lined with dry leaves and lichens and molded to the shape of her breast, was no longer a safe place for her young. The gleaming eyes of the fox—the soft pad, pad of his feet on the shales—the twitch of his nostrils testing the air for scent of her chicks—became for her the symbols of a thousand dangers, formless and without name.

When the sun had rolled so low on the horizon that only the high cliff with the eyrie of the gyrfalcon caught and reflected its gleam, Silverbar led the four chicks away into the vast grayness of the tundra.

Throughout the long days the sanderling with her chicks wandered over the stony plains, gathering the young ones under her during the short chill nights or when sudden gusts of rain drove across the barrens. She led them by the shores of brimming fresh-water lakes into which loons dropped on whistling wings to feed their young. Strange new food was to be found on the shores of the lakes and in the swelling turbulence of feeder streams. The young sanderlings learned to catch insects or to find their larvae in the streams. They learned, too, to press themselves flat against the ground when they heard their mother's danger cry and to lie quite still among the stones until her signal brought them crowding about her with fine, high-pitched squeakings. So they escaped the jaegers, the owls, and the foxes.

By the seventh day after hatching, the chicks had quill feathers a third grown on their wings, although their bodies were still covered with down. After four more suns the wings and shoulders were fully clothed in feathers, and when they were two weeks old the fledgling sanderlings could fly with their mother from lake to lake . . .

Many of the cock sanderlings, who had been gathering in flocks about the fresh-water lakes almost from the time the chicks had begun to hatch, had already left for the south. Among them was Blackfoot. . . .

There came a day in August when Silverbar, who had been feeding with her grown young on the shores of the bay in company with other sanderlings, suddenly rose into the air with some twoscore of the older birds. The little flock wheeled out over the bay in a wide circle, flashing white wing bars; they returned, crying loudly as they passed over the flats where the young were still running and probing at the edge of the curling wavelets; they turned their heads to the south and were gone.

There was no need for the parent birds to remain longer in the Arctic. The nesting was done; the eggs had been faithfully brooded; the young had been taught to find food, to hide from enemies, to know the rules of the game of life and death. Later, when they were strong for the journey down the coast lines of two continents, the young birds would follow, finding the way by inherited memory. Meanwhile the older sanderlings felt the call of the warm south; they would follow the sun. . . .

MIGRATION

Charles William Beebe

There is a Power whose care
Teaches thy way across the pathless coast—
The desert and illimitable air—
Lone wandering, but not lost.

So wrote William Cullen Bryant in To a Water Fowl, once among the best known of American poems. Present-day ornithologists are little inclined to look with favor upon such notions and they are more likely to echo the words quoted in the selection which follows: "Annual migration cannot be looked upon as an act of volition, but as the automatic response to a state probably induced by a gonadial hormone" —which is after all an explanation only calling for another. It describes a mechanism which certainly exists but it does not account for the existence of that mechanism.

To write honestly and with conviction anything about the migration of birds, one should oneself have migrated.

But not every millionaire who in the autumn goes in his private car to Palm Beach and returns in the spring can claim fellow feeling with the migrant birds, although there is a firm basis of communion. A single night in a lighthouse or in the torch of the Statue of Liberty might conceivably be a better preparation. But somehow or other we must dehumanize ourselves, feel the feel of feathers on our body, and the wind in our wings, and finally know what it is to leave luxury and safety, and yield to the compelling instinct, age-old, at the moment seemingly quite devoid of reason and object. In any case the chief pleasure either in thinking or writing is pragmatic. The more I can sink my six feet to the stature of an ant, the more right I have to attempt to interpret an ant's feelings and emotions; if I am scaly instead of skinny, can know a wave and a coral reef intimately from beneath as well as above, so much the better may I hope to sense the joys and sorrows of any poor fish.

I have been lost alone in an airplane at night, I have swung so low that birds were frightened from the roosts in the tree-tops; a glow now and then through the fog ceiling made it seem as if I were contour flying

From Nonsuch. New York: Brewer, Warren & Putnam, 1932.

blindly; I have swung around and around a cluster of lights peering vainly for hint of a landing place. Finally, in deadly fear, I have climbed to temporary safety, gambled the low tide in my fuel tanks against the dawn, and won by a glimmer. Only because of this do I feel worthy of writing something about the migration of birds.

The real dramatic phase of migration is the ultimate object, enhanced by the fact that earthly creatures become helpless pawns when once this fateful hysteria claims them. With many living beings migration operates as a saver of life; to legions of others it is a forced march to certain death.

When a hawk or wild goose passes overhead, my pet monkey, Chiriqui, ducks in fear or dives into his house. A migrant bird to him merely a stimulus to inherited memory of the deadly swoop of harpy eagles. To our nth great-grand uncles—the cavemen—the coming of swallows must have meant no more than buzzing flies—possibly not so much. In historical times I seem to associate the first conscious thought of migrating birds with astrologers and the absence of sloping roofs. From the earliest times in the Far East men liked to sleep or to study the stars on the flat tops of their houses, and many an abstruse calculation of star portents of war or prophets must have been interrupted by the loud chirp of passing birds. Even this I have verified for myself, for many years ago I evaded a pair of sleepy guards and climbed by night to the apex of Cheops. There I stretched out and pretended I was an astrologer vizier of some Pharaoh of olden time. And I remember sitting up so quickly that I nearly fell down one of the giant steps, when a low *'tsip! 'tsip!* came to my ears. It was the slightest whisper of a sound but it destroyed Egypt and my vizier-ship, and replaced them with a more prosaic landscape and personality, recalling the time when, on a distant continent, as a boy, I listened each spring and autumn to the chirps of the migrating hosts.

One fortunate night I was permitted a glimpse of these vast flocks. I squatted on the swaying floor of the torch of the Statue of Liberty when the fog drifted in from the sea and closed down grey and silent. With it came birds which before had been only disembodied voices, and the fog, which obliterated the heavens and the earth, made the migrating flocks visible to my eyes. More and more they came, until a swarm of golden bees was the only simile I could think of. I dared not face them full, for now and then one struck the light with terrific impact. So I peered from behind the railing and watched the living atoms dash into view, shine for an instant, and vanish, so rapidly that when I looked through half-closed lids the driving sparks consolidated and lengthened into luminous lines. I think that I enjoyed it as a spectacle more in retrospect than at the time, for my emotion was distracted by the occasional thud at my feet of black polls and other warblers. It seemed such a cruel thing that even one of these lives which had been hatched and fed with such care in Hudson Bay or Labrador should be needlessly snuffed out because of the glare through a bit of glass.

Tens of thousands of facts have been gathered and collated concerning the migration of birds, but as to origins and causes we can only surmise and imagine.

To clarify the subject of migration I need to divorce it from the mere organism which manifests it—to emphasize the obsession, the absolute obligation to go and go, apart from the specific swallow or duck, lemming or butterfly which temporarily houses this mysterious daemon. I shall try to do this by continuing the simile of the swarm of golden bees about the lighthouse, and let the golden glow typify the migration instinct.

Even human history sheds a little light on our subject. Hannibal forged a tiny flicker of migratory flame over the Alps, the glow of which slowly died down in the plains of farther Italy. Attila and his following hordes were agleam with it when wave after wave of them broke against the Roman legions, finally to be smothered by the Eternal City itself. It is disturbing to think what our blood and mental equipment would be today had not our piratical ancestors—the winged hats—executed the most lasting migrations known to humans. A very cool, white flame burned in the Mayflower, and even today, our aforementioned Goddess of Liberty watches, perhaps a little humorously, faint sparks within the shawl-wrapped forms of the steerage, floating past, upstream, toward migration's melting-pot.

But these are all trifling migrations, whims of empire, tribe or family, variously origined and of brief duration. We must go to the lower animals to find migration in all the majesty of age-old tradition, its beginnings buried in past geological epochs, with routes fashioned by long forgotten configurations of continents, ancient before mankind had risen up on his hind legs or climbed into the trees—migrations whose times and seasons have been evolved and governed by countless centuries of revolutions of the planet earth.

From a lofty vantage point let us watch the coast lines of Labrador and Greenland and as far north as any frozen bit of earth distinguishes itself from sheer ice. It is July and the breathlessly short Arctic summer is at its height. As an icicle loses a few drops between clouds, so this northland relaxes its grip for a brief season, countable in days, and permits a few inches of thaw and of dwarfed and hasty growth of moss and flowers to slip through its icy fingers. All is grey and white—sea, old snowdrifts and birds. The birds have come, like the intermittent drops from the icicle, settling to earth from nowhere at the first hint of thaw, scratching a shallow hollow, and brooding four huddled eggs. The breast of the mother tern is a tiny oasis of warmth amid the Arctic waste; her food is inchling fish snatched at brief intervals from the edge of the ice. She stakes the hatching and the feeding of the young against the swift passing of the midnight sun, and scarcely is the brood awing before the meagre foliage blackens, the soil turns to iron, and the last ripple freezes over. She has won, but only by a margin of hours.

All along the Arctic shores from Labrador to within a few hundred miles of the pole, we from aloft now discern a faint glow—our imagined glow of the birth of the instinct of migration. It increases, and soon the restlessness of the birds is changed to impatience, and impatience to complete surrender and these bits of northernmost life beat southward across the face of the planet. There are thousands upon thousands of them. They have ceased to be every-Arctic-Tern-in-the-world, they are not *Sterna paradisaea*, they are no longer parents or young or this or that individual, but a unified cohort of organisms set apart, obsessed, glowing at fever heat with the thralldom of migration.

In the face of unknowable mystery I often imagine myself the Creator, or, as in this case, the Instigator of Instinct, and plan out what seems wisest and best. This exercise frequently shows me why the obvious is seldom probable. In regard to these migrants I should without hesitation lead them to Bermuda. Here . . . is a compact swarm of islands with an infinity of rocky crags and caves and beaches fit for safe perching and sleeping; here are multitudes of delectable fry of just the right size; here are man-made laws ensuring safety from molestation. Here also (although the least important of all natural reasons) are thousands of human eyes ready to see and admire, perhaps many human beings who would be better for having their thoughts diverted, by the sight of beauty, from the humor engendered by an ill lead at bridge or an irritating drive on the golf course.

Yet not a single migrant of this species veers eastward to these desirable isles. They hold steadfast to the south. They must sleep and eat, but, steady as the feather-end of the compass arrow, they swing on and on, covering only a little less than two hundred miles each day. If storms hold them back, they make up time, with ever warmer and warmer air whistling through their wings. Around Cape Cod, past Cape Hatteras, along Florida beaches—the hot sun of the tropics replacing the cold, blue shine of the Greenland midnight; threading the West Indies, skirting Brazilian jungles, and diving for strange fish off the shores of the Argentine. The sun swings lower, the last breath of warmth is strained from the air, as Patagonia and Magellen's Straits vanish below the horizon. After eleven thousand miles have passed behind, the birds sight the gigantic ice barrier of the Antaratic, and here the migration glow dies down and expires. Here they sleep and preen their plumage, catching fish in company with penguins instead of polar bears, their grey and white feathers illumined by the sun for all the duration of their stay.

Four months pass. The ice is just as cold, the air as bitter, there is no change in the character or abundance of food, yet again comes the restlessness, and northward goes every bird, reflying the eleven thousand miles of whirling globe, and redistributing themselves. If the gods of little birds have been kind to any single pair, the chances are they will meet and mate again, and deposit their eggs in the selfsame hollow.

These are the facts. But what about the Why? One recent answer is that "annual migration cannot be looked upon as an act of volition, but as the automatic response to a certain physiological state probably induced by a gonadial hormone." And this, in spite of itself, is very probably true, and contains a core of dramatic interest equal only to the more perspicuous phase of the subject with which we are at present concerned. It is clear that our Arctic terns must move south from their breeding grounds or be starved and frozen to death. But now that we know that they crave ice and stress of storm and small fish in frigid seas, why should they go farther south than Labrador? It would seem that this obsession of migration sometimes acquires such an impetus that only the whole long length of the planet can dissipate it.

If we find mystery in the migration of the Arctic tern we are still less able to explain the annual movements of many other birds. Of those which are not forced to move by oncoming frost, some are content to shift a few miles southward, others to cross mountain ranges and wide stretches of open ocean, to winter in unfamiliar torrid jungles. If our fancied glow of the instinct was a reality, our spring and autumn nights would show an unending blaze of avian meteors which would dim the moon and stars. After exhausting our explanations of the means of guidance, such as landmarks, sea currents, winds, stars and a magnetic sense, we must, in some instances at least, fall back on an inexplicable sense of direction. And when we have taken refuge in this pleasantly all-comprehensive phrase, we remember those species in which the young migrate before their parents—and rather willingly change the subject.

At least we have moderated our ideas as to the altitude and speed. Instead of a height of three miles above the earth, we know from airplane and other observations, that nocturnal migrants seldom average more than a half mile in height. In the daytime, however, flocks of storks, geese and plover have been seen two miles up going full speed. The record is perhaps several geese in the western Himalayas photographed at an estimated height equal to that of Mount Everest.

Until stop-watches and airplanes gave us definite data we were willing to accept with wondering credulity a speed of two hundred and forty miles an hour attributed to many birds. The cruel exactitude of definite observation has brought this down to forty miles an hour for crows and sixty for ducks. Swifts unquestionably hold the record with one hundred and very rarely one hundred and fifty miles an hour, this during their aerial feeding, not on migration.

During the two annual seasons, few vessels pass through the major lines of migration flight without affording temporary sanctuary to birds in distress. This is only a hint of the terrible dangers and toll of mortality demanded by the migration. Year after year the same number of house wrens return to our orchards, sing from our tree-tops and rear their broods in our knot-holes. If fortune is kind, a single pair of wrens may rear twenty young in a season. So in October two and twenty feathered mites take to the air some night and go to the Gulf Coast or beyond. The following spring one or both parents often return to the same nesting hollow, and as last year, a second pair is singing in the orchard. But no others are within our range. Ninety per cent—twenty out of twenty-two wrens—have perished, their little bodies devoured by hawk or owl, dashed against the glass of lighthouses, or drowned in the spray of the open ocean. Now and then a house wren spends the entire winter in the north, finding sufficient shelter and food, and yet his fellows go hundreds of miles beyond the latitude of warmth and abundance of insects, obeying some long-lost law of past initiation of this compelling instinct.

Year by year the breeding ranges of all the creatures in the world become more limited. No week passes but sees the complete wiping out of some bird or beast or insect. The way of the bird in the air is ever more perilous as the beacons and lights of humanity increase. The winter homes are being rendered barren by vast rubber plantations and other man-fashioned what-nots. Throughout a few more decades only will the old migrations still hold. For no matter how simple and easy the shortening or rerouting of a flight might be, the last surviving bird in which glows the spark of this possessing instinct will endure the new dangers, will strive to overcome the appalling handicaps thrown across its path. The method and completion of an instinct originating before man came to know he was himself can never be altered or turned aside in the few brief years of his dominance. Only the death of the last bird or animal or insect can achieve that.

A
BIRD'S-EYE
VIEW

Raymond S. Deck

Now that man has become the first mammal to take successfully to the air, he imagines a bird's-eye view of migration.

I F you and I, cruising far up in space in some Martians' super-ship, could look down with matchless vision, we would behold on any bright autumn day, four mighty rivers of birds flowing through the New World sky. The stuff of this feathered flood is Pan-American as is no other tangible resource. One of our aerial rivers, following the famed Atlantic Flyway, would be seen to drain most of the birdlife from the continent east of the Appalachian Highland. Rising actually in Greenland, fed by new streams of birds all along its course, this river would spill its tide at last over the South Atlantic States and the West Indies islands. Diminished branches would trickle on over land and ocean, to all South America.

Flowing along the Pacific coast between the Ocean and the Rocky Mountains, we would see another vast river of birds; and east of the Rockies, sweeping south over the Great Plains, the broad current of the Central Flyway, bearing its own distinctive tide. Last of the gigantic fall freshets of migrating birds, and greatest of them all, is the aerial river which roars down the Mississippi Valley. It stems like a mighty funnel from the whole area between Alaska and Baffinland.

Thence, swift-running streams of wild ducks and geese spring into life each fall, to converge at length in the region of Lake Erie. Long-legged wading-birds, diminutive songsters, are a part of such northland currents. Flowing now down the channel of the Mississippi Valley, these multitudes are joined in flight by birds which have nested along the way. The torrent multiplies prodigiously as new creeks are tributary all along its course.

From *Pageant in the Sky*. New York: Dodd, Mead, 1941.

Eventually, as it bottlenecks in the southern Valley, the Mississippi Flyway bears the vastest bird tide of any section of the world. More birds, and more species of birds may be observed in autumn in the lower Mississippi Valley than anywhere else on earth. As it finally reaches the delta of the Father of Waters, this feathered river is dammed by the Gulf of Mexico. It splatters out along the coast of Louisiana, Mississippi and Texas. Here in winter is found the world's entire supply of Blue Geese from Baffinland; of Lesser Snow Geese from the interior of Arctic America. But numerous streams of birds flow through the sky on across the Gulf to ancestral jungles in Central and South America.

Though our four rivers of birds flood the continent during the year's conventional wet seasons, they still are essentially different from everyday rivers in that their current moves south in October, north in April. Both seasons' streams, however, have their sources in proper springs, each "spring" being the nesting or wintering ground of some sort of bird. Often these flowing springs cover oddly restricted areas; sometimes they encompass strips as broad as the continent.

Part

Two

FAMILY MATTERS

BIRDS
AND POETS

John Burroughs

If the word "bird" means "flight" it means also, and almost as inevitably, "song." The usefulness of the first is obvious, but why do birds sing? Or is beauty its own excuse for being?

To the poet the answer has always been obvious. Birds sing because they are joyful, more joyful than men. Some behaviorists have, on the other hand, gone so far as to declare roundly that joy has nothing to do with it and that song in birds is not even primarily connected with the sex instinct. It is, they maintain, threatening rather than amorous, and first of all a warning to other birds of the same species: "Keep out of my territory."

Probably the truth is somewhere in between, for birds do have emotions. John Burroughs, at least, was enough poet as well as naturalist to assume that the affinity of the poet for the bird has some justification in fact.

I T might almost be said that the birds are all birds of the poets and of no one else, because it is only the poetical temperament that fully responds to them. So true is this, that all the great ornithologists—original namers and biographers of the birds—have been poets in deed if not in word . . . The very idea of a bird is a symbol and a suggestion to the poet. A bird seems to be at the top of the scale, so vehement and intense is his life—large brained, large lunged, hot, ecstatic, his frame charged with buoyancy and his heart with song. The beautiful vagabonds, endowed with every grace, masters of all climes, and knowing no bounds—how many human aspirations are realized in their free, holiday-lives—and how many suggestions to the poets in their flight and song!

Indeed, is not the bird the original type and teacher of the poet, and do we not demand of the human lark or thrush that he "shake out his carols" in the same free and spontaneous manner as his winged prototype?

From *Birds and Poets*. Boston: Houghton Mifflin, 1877.

WILDERNESS

MUSIC

Sigurd F. Olson

Sigurd F. Olson who knows the north woods as well as any man alive is like Burroughs in at least one respect. To him also the song of a bird seems to speak from one heart to another.

L AST night I followed a ski trail into the Lucky Boy Valley. It was dark and still, and the pines and spruces there almost met overhead. During the day it had snowed, and the festooned trees were vague massed drifts against the stars. Breathless after my run, I stopped to rest and listen. In that snow-cushioned place there was no sound, no wind moaning in the branches, no life or movement of any kind.

As I stood there leaning on my sticks, I thought of Jack Linklater, a Scotch-Cree of the Hudson's Bay Company. In such a place he would have heard the music, for he had a feeling for the "wee" people and for many things others did not understand. Sometimes when we were on the trail together he would ask me to stop and listen, and when I could not hear he would laugh. Once in a stand of quaking aspen in a high place when the air was full of their whispering, he dropped his pack and stood there, a strange and happy light in his eyes. Another time, during the harvesting of wild rice when the dust was redolent with the parching fires on the shores of Hula Lake, he called me to him, for he felt that somehow I must hear the music too.

"Can't you hear it now?" he said. "It's very plain tonight."

I stood there with him and listened, but heard nothing, and as I watched the amused and somewhat disappointed look on his face I wondered if he was playing a game with me. That time he insisted that he could hear the sound of women's and children's voices and the high quaver of an Indian song, though we were far from the encampment. Now that the years have passed and Jack has gone to the Happy Hunting Grounds, I believe that he actually heard something and that the reason I could not was that this was music for Indians and for those whose ears were attuned.

From *The Singing Wilderness*. New York: Alfred A. Knopf, 1956.

One night we were canoeing on the Maligne River in the Quetico on a portage trail used for centuries by Indians and voyagers. The moon was full, and the bowl below the falls was silver with mist. As we sat listening to the roar of Twin Falls, there seemed to be a sound of voices of a large party making the carry. The sound ebbed and swelled in volume with the ebb and flow of the plunging water. That night I thought I heard them, too, and Jack was pleased. Wilderness music? Imagination? I may never know, but this much I do know from traveling with Jack: he actually heard something, and those who have lived close to nature all of their lives are sensitive to many things lost to those in the cities.

We send out costly expeditions to record the feelings, expressions, and customs of primitive tribes untouched by civilization, considering such anthropological research to be worth while because it gives us an inkling of why we moderns behave as we do. We recognize that a great deal has been lost to us during the so-called civilized centuries—intuitive awarenesses that primitives still possess. Children still have them, but they soon disappear. Some individuals retain them as long as they live. All, however, have a need and hunger for them, and much of the frustration and boredom we experience is no doubt due to our inability to recapture these forgotten ways of perception.

While most of us are too far removed to hear the wilderness music that Jack Linklater heard, there are other forms—not so subtle, perhaps, but still capable of bringing to our consciousness the same feelings that have stirred human kind since the beginning of time. Who is not stirred when the wild geese go by, when the coyotes howl on a moonlit night, or when the surf crashes against the cliffs? Such sounds have deep appeal because they are associated with the background of the race. Why does the rhythmic tom-tom beat of drums affect us? Because it, too, is primitive and was part of our heritage centuries before music as we know it now was ever conceived. Wilderness music to me is any sound that brings to mind the wild places I have known.

Once during a long absence from the north I heard the call of a loon, the long, rollicking laughter that in the past I had heard echoing across the wild reaches of the Quetico lakes. It was in Tennessee that I heard it, but the instant I caught the first long wail, chills of gladness chased themselves up and down my spine. For a long time I stood there and listened, but I did not hear it again. While I waited, the north came back to me with a rush and visions of wilderness lakes and rivers crowded upon me. I saw the great birds flying into the sunsets, groups of them playing over the waters of Lac la Croix, Kawnipi, and Batchewaung. I saw the reaches of Saganaga in the early morning, a camp on some lonely island with the day's work done and nothing to do but listen and dream. And then in the recesses of my mind the real calling began as it had a thousand times in the past, the faintest hint of an echo from over the hills, answered before it died by a closer call and that in turn by another until the calling of the loons from all the lakes around blended in a continuous symphony.

There were other times that also came back to me, times when the clouds were dark and the waves rolling high, when the calling reached a pitch of madness which told of coming storm; mornings when the sun was bright and happy laughter came from the open water; nights when one lone call seemed to embody all the misery and tragedy in the world. I knew as I stood there waiting that when once a man had known that wild and eery calling and lost himself in its beauty, should he ever hear a hint of it again, no matter where he happened to be, he would have a vision of the distance and freedom of the north.

One day in the south of England I was walking through a great beech wood on an old estate near Shrivenham. There was a little brook flowing through the woods, and its gurgle as it ran through a rocky dell seemed to accentuate my sense of the age of those magnificent trees. I was far from home, as far away from the wilderness of the north as I had ever been. Those great trees were comforting to me even though I knew that just beyond them was open countryside.

Then suddenly I heard a sound that changed everything: a soft nasal twang from high in the branches, the call of a nuthatch. Instantly that beech grove was transformed into a stand of tall, stately pines; the brown beech leaves on the ground became a smooth carpet of golden needles, and beyond this cared-for forest were rugged ridges and deep, timbered valleys, roaring rivers and placid lakes, with a smell of resin and duff in the sun. The call of the nuthatch had done all that, had given me a vision of the wilderness as vivid as though for the moment I had actually been there.

How satisfying to me are the sounds of a bog at night! I like to paddle into a swampy bay in the lake country and just sit there and listen to the slow sloshing-around of moose and deer, the sharp pistol crack of a beaver tail slapping the water, the guttural, resonant pumping of a bittern. But the real music of a bog is the frog chorus. If they are in full swing when you approach, they stop by sections as though part of the orchestra was determined to carry on in spite of the faintheartedness of the rest. One must sit quietly for some time before they regain their courage. At first there are individual piping notes, a few scattered guttural croaks, then a confused medley as though the instruments were being tuned. Finally in a far corner a whole section swings into tremulous music, hesitant at the start but gradually gathering momentum and volume. Soon a closer group begins, and then they all join in until there is again a sustained and grand crescendo of sound.

This is a primeval chorus, the sort of wilderness music which reigned over the earth millions of years ago. That sound floated across the pools of the carboniferous era. You can still hear it in the Everglades: the throaty, rasping roar of the alligators and, above that, the frightened calls and screams of innumerable birds. One of the most ancient sounds on earth, it is a continuation of music from the past, and, no matter where I listen to a bog at night, strange feelings stir within me.

One night in the south of Germany I was walking along the River Main at Frankfurt. It was spring and sunset. Behind me were the stark ruins of the city, the silhouettes of broken walls and towers, the horrible destruction of the bombing. Across the river was a little village connected with the city by the broken span of a great bridge. In the river were the rusting hulls of barges and sunken boats. The river gurgled softly around them and around the twisted girders of the blown-up span. It was a scene of desolation and sadness.

Then I was conscious of a sound that was not of the war, the hurrying whisper of wings overhead. I turned, and there against the rosy sky was a flock of mallards. I had forgotten that the river was a flyway, that there were still such delightful things as the sound of wings at dusk, rice beds yellowing in the fall, and the soft sound of quacking all through the night. A lone flock of mallards gave all that to me, awoke a thousand memories as wilderness music always does.

There are many types of music, each one different from the rest: a pack of coyotes and the wild, beautiful sound of them as they tune up under the moon; the song of a white-throated sparrow, its one clear note so closely associated with trout streams that whenever I hear one, I see a sunset-tinted pool and feel the water around my boots. The groaning and cracking of forming ice on the lakes, the swish of skis or snowshoes in dry snow—wilderness music, all of it, music for Indians and for those who have ears to hear.

MORNING IN

MOUNT VERNON

Louis J. Halle, Jr.

Here Louis J. Halle, Jr., whom we shall presently meet again, pays his tribute to the contribution made by bird song to a Sunday morning's walk.

(*On Sunday, March 26, 1786, George Washington made the following entry in his diary at Mount Vernon:* "The warmth of yesterday and this day, forwarded vegetation much; the buds of some trees, particularly the Weeping Willow and Maple, had displayed their leaves and blossoms and all others were swelled and many ready to put forth.")

EASTER Sunday, April 1, was a golden day. The stars and a waning moon were out when I left for my excursion by bicycle down the river. In the darkness by the Shoreham Hotel the robins were already caroling in chorus, anticipating daybreak. The sun rose in classic splendor as I passed the airport—as it had risen among the Aegean isles three thousand years ago (the golden-throned dawn) for a lonely wanderer striving to return to his home, as it had risen a thousand years ago over the misty valley of the Loire. Robins, titmice, wrens, sparrows, thrashers, cardinals, goldfinches, purple finches were all singing. At Dyke, in the sparkling haze and freshness of the new day, a pair of wood ducks flew clamoring from the big trees beside the road, circled, landed in the trees again, took off again. Other wood ducks, in pairs, flew through the trees or out over the marshes. Pine warblers, yellow-throated warblers, blue-gray gnatcatchers, and newly arrived black-and-white warblers contributed their notes to the dawn.

A week ago I had marked the first green bloom on the woods. Now, to my eager imagination, it seemed virtually summer, the trees in flower and foliage, though one could still see through them. Later in the season the leaves would hang in heavy masses, obscuring the view. Today they were still young and tender on the trees. The borders of the woods were

From *Spring in Washington*. New York: Harper & Brothers, 1947.

everywhere illuminated by the white dogwood, the pink dogwood, and the brilliant redbud, now in full flower. Near Mount Vernon I came upon Roger Peterson and a friend, out with cameras and tripods to make color photographs of the redbud. Peterson told me the flower and foliage was between two and three weeks ahead of last year's dates, basing his calculation on the blooming of the magnolias, now over. Who could remember such an early spring as this, with everything so far ahead of schedule? At Fort Belvoir young horned larks had left their nest two weeks ago.

(On April 21, 1785, Washington at Mount Vernon wrote in his diary: "The Sassafras not yet full out, nor the Redbud—Dogwood blossom still inclosed in the button." Two days later he wrote: "The Dogwood buttons were just beginning to open as the Redwood (or bud) blossom, for though they had appeared several days the blossoms had not expanded.")

On the morning of April 3, after a night of storm, the Bonaparte's gulls were moving north along the surface of the river as far as the eye could reach, flicking their wings, sparkling in the early sunlight. They acquire their summer plumage as the trees their foliage, and through my glasses I could see that some now had black heads while the heads of others were still white or mottled. Men, it occurred to me, are among the few creatures that undergo no seasonal changes. We don't even grow shaggy coats in winter.

That morning a Louisiana water-thrush sang loud, clear and repeatedly from a ravine in Rock Creek Park as I bicycled to work. Tzee, tzee, tzee, tzippy, tzippy-tzip he sang, with emphasis, so that I should think one could have heard him half a mile off. (Birds that haunt rushing streams have loud voices to rise above the uproar.) Brown thrashers were singing in the city now—really singing, for they are among the birds that do not merely emit signals but are musicians, consciously practicing their art, as if inspired to transcend their own mortality and achieve a heaven that lies, surely, just beyond mortal reach. One that sang constantly on Woodland Drive had a whole orchestra of bells and woodwinds in his throat. His song, every phrase with its echo, bubbled like a natural spring breaking from the ground in flood season. Yet there was a method in it, a repetition and return to the same themes. Before the week was out, barn swallows, spotted sandpipers, and ruddy ducks in Washington Channel had been added to the list of new birds.

This week, however, was bountiful chiefly in its flowers. The City of Washington might have been deliberately decked for a flower festival, as when the citizens hang out their flags because it is Flag Day. The lilac clusters came out in profusion overnight, among the young leaves, freshening the air. So did the azaleas, in all their variety, transforming the woodland parks and dooryards. A man from Mars might have stopped passers-by to inquire in what god's celebration the city was so garlanded.

FREE

AS A BIRD?

John and Jean George

---

*"Behavior pattern" is a term dear to modern students of natural history
—and also to the sociologists of today. Much has been learned of the
extent to which both man and the other animals are predictable and of
the many things they "can't help doing." Perhaps it would be helpful
and encouraging if more attention were paid to the extent to which man,
at least, is also free to violate these patterns when he is intelligent enough
and strong-willed enough to do so. Perhaps also the difference between
him and the other animals is less absolute than is sometimes assumed. Is
it not largely a matter of degree? Birds, according to the authors of the
following selection, are "prisoners." But there is good evidence that they
too can on occasion be "nonconformists."*

FREE as a bird, we say; yet nearly all birds and most bird watchers
know how mistaken that saying is. The conduct of birds is so rigidly
fixed that they are prisoners to the land they fly over, slaves to the air they
fly through. Once we watched a bird go to his death because he was not
free to fly 700 feet to safety.

We were returning home along the Huron River near Ann Arbor,
Mich., where we were studying birds and mammals, and stopped to visit
a cardinal we had named Red Click because of a special clicking note he
used at the end of his song. We found him stranded on the piece of
property where he lived; the land had been scalped that day by bulldozers
so that only a few stumps and roots remained. As we watched, Red Click
flew about 400 feet, then suddenly back-winged as if he had hit an invisible wall. After flopping to earth he flew off in another direction, only
to smash into another invisible barrier.

"What's the matter with that crazy cardinal?" Jean asked. "He'll be
killed by a hawk or an owl if he doesn't fly to the woods."

"He can't fly to the woods," John said. "His 'territory' is in the middle

From *The Christian Science Monitor*, February 4, 1959.

of the cleared land. The bulldozers have taken away his trees, his bushes, his grasses, but the boundaries of his home that he and his neighbors carefully established in their bird minds are still there and he can't fly through them."

"Perhaps we could carry him to safety," Jean suggested.

"And turn him loose on some other cardinal's territory? He's a prisoner precisely because he is more terrified of intruding on another male's land than he is of remaining here without shelter."

A screech owl called from the wood lot behind us. "Hear that?" John said. "That will probably be the last chapter in the biography of Red Click."

Next morning, at the roots of a maple sapling in the wasted field, we picked up the blood-red feathers of our cardinal.

This devotion unto death to a piece of ground is probably more intense in birds than in any other vertebrate. Strongest during the breeding season, the territory fixation serves to aid in the formation of pairs, to provide shelter for the young and to ensure perpetuation of the species by spreading its population over a wide area.

By simply walking behind chickadees, pushing them around their property in the spring, we were able to map some 200 of their territories in the woods near Poughkeepsie, N.Y. The chickadees would fly to the extremities of their lands, then circle back around the edges, revealing their unseen fences. Sketched on a map, a chickadee community looks like an exurbanite settlement of people, with the size of each property varying according to the "social standing" of the occupant; the older the male, the bigger, the stronger he is, the more land he gets.

Birds which are year-round residents tend to retain the same territory for life; migrants have both summer and winter properties. The birds that stay around your home all winter may seem to be in flocks, and therefore trespassing, but they are not. They are a well-ordered bird society made up of old-timers and young, complete with a leader or "boss bird." In these winter societies the defense of the breeding territory has given way, in certain species, to the common defense of a community territory against neighboring groups of the same species. Birds will tolerate trespassers of a different species on their land, since they are not competing, but not intruders belonging to their own.

Birds' property lines are established by song. If a male bird, returning in the spring, can sing from a tree without being challenged by a neighbor, he has it as his own, to mark the limits of his real estate. If, however, another male comes winging at him and puts him back a tree or two, he knows that this land is already claimed.

By taking the best land he can and as much of it as he is able to defend, he assures himself not only a good food supply but also a mate. Female birds pick their mates by their attractive voices (each bird's voice is as distinctive as your own) and by the quality of the nesting sites in the land they have staked off. The weaker males and the late-comers, pushed into submarginal land, often go through the season as bachelors.

A bachelor song sparrow we called Mike sang so beautifully that Jean couldn't understand why the girls would not set up housekeeping with him. John said, "Your friend's territory is very small and in the woods. Song sparrows like some open fields and brush borders on their property. Getting a female to nest on Mike's territory would be like asking a debutante to live in Siberia."

Territory varies with different species from several square miles, as in the case of the horned owl, to only a square foot or so around the nest, as among the colony nesters such as terns and gulls.

Once boundary lines are settled, the feelings of the bird toward his territory mount with the progress of his nest, until he seems to do desperate things particularly near the nest site. Flying at windows and the shiny grillwork of automobiles is not bird hara-kiri. It is territory defense. His reflection in a window or grille is another male on his property, and he will fight this adversary until exhausted.

Territorial disputes, though constant in the bird world, are normally resolved by singing duels, almost always between males of the same species. Sometimes a disputed territory touches off a breast-to-breast battle in the air; the battlers seem to be rising and sliding down an invisible wall. The fight will usually be brief, and afterward each contestant will fly to a tree limb on his side of the property line and click in agitation. Usually there is a compromise and both birds will sing, in a full and exuberant song.

The female ordinarily stays within the boundaries established by her mate, but occasionally a blundering or frivolous wife can cause trouble. One season we observed a tragi-comedy in a community of vivid indigo buntings. A little female, a first-time mother, had by error built her nest on another male's property. She would fly happily to her nest, expecting her husband to usher her home, only to find that he had stopped at the edge of his territory. There he was, turning around in circles, torn between two powerful impulses: to follow his mate, and to stay off his neighbor's property. Apparently property rights proved stronger than family love. He never once crossed the barrier during the nesting period. When the young hatched, the father would catch insects for the babies, call his mate and give her the offerings. Taking them eagerly, she would return to stuff her bottomless young. We were all (including the frustrated father) greatly relieved on the day the little mother coaxed her fledglings over the border to their father's estate.

A territory boundary is not the only restraint in a bird's life. Even within their own property birds do not fly around their land on any random course, but stick to routes or "sidewalks." A bird will take the same path daily from his night roost to his feeding spot, from his nest to a certain singing post. We once saw impressive evidence that birds can map the fixed routes of other birds in the interest of safety.

A Cooper's hawk in our Michigan area staked off two square miles and soared elegantly around to attract a mate. The presence of this bird-eating intruder threw the small birds into a dither. But soon things quieted down and we wondered what adjustment they had made to the predator. In time we discovered the answer.

The big hawk, too, was a slave of habit. He nested in their woods, but always hunted in a far wood lot. Each morning he took an aerial sidewalk to the wood lot, returning home along another fixed path. The small-bird population figured out his habits, for they used fewer and fewer alarm notes to announce his coming and going. They knew he stayed on his sidewalks and never dipped down into their woods for food.

These invisible sidewalks can easily be noted in any back yard where there is a feeding station. A bird will come to the station every day about the same time from the same direction, and by way of the same sticks and twigs. There is generally a sidewalk in and another one out. We once put up a post on a bird's sidewalk, and he almost struck it, he was so confined to his route.

Each night the bird returns faithfully to his bedroom or roost, which he picks as carefully as his nesting site. In a world teeming with enemies, its loss can mean his undoing.

A woodpecker roosted in a hole in an apple tree outside our window. He went to bed at the same time every night, depending on the amount of light. As the days grew shorter, our clock showed him returning two minutes earlier each night, but our light meter registered exactly the same light value. On cloudy days he came to roost early.

One night a white-breasted nuthatch went into the woodpecker's bedroom a few minutes before he was due home. The woodpecker performed his night rituals according to his heritage. He squawked from the top of a maple. He defecated in the same spot he had used for months; he flew to the apple tree, spiraled up it and winged into his hole—where he hit the intruding nuthatch head-on.

Out they both tumbled and fought briefly. The nuthatch departed, with the woodpecker in pursuit. Sometime later we caught a glimpse of the woodpecker. It was late, but probably he could still see to get into his hole. However, he had to repeat the rituals of retirement all over again and so he went back to the maple tree. The night grew cold but the woodpecker never returned. Now it was very dark, well below his accustomed level of light. He squawked but did not fly to the apple tree. One twilight a few nights later the nuthatch cautiously investigated the empty hole and moved in. He had finally won the contest, probably because he upset the woodpecker's evening retirement habits, and the woodpecker, unable to change, was literally left out in the cold.

Almost all birds live and love and die behind the bars of nature's compulsions. They are captive in cages of their own instincts, from which, with rare exceptions, they cannot—and have no desire to—escape.

CAPACITY

AND INTELLIGENCE

OF BIRDS

Ludlow Griscom

One of the reasons why all animals sometimes seem to us almost incredibly "unintelligent" is simply this: it is we who make the definition. If intelligence were defined as the ability to perform what we want or need to do then most animals are in one respect or another more "intelligent" than we. A man lost in the woods is more helpless than a cat. And how stupid we must seem to a dog or a bird when we can't find our way home!

No one would deny the late Ludlow Griscom the right to the title "dean" of American ornithologists. In the selection given here he considers soberly the meaning of the words "capacity" and "intelligence" as applied to birds.

IT is almost impossible to avoid comparing birds with mankind, whose behavior and intelligence is not only a source of constant study and research, but often of keen anxiety. But any serious effort at comparison is positively absurd. To endow birds with "human" traits, as is popularly done, is tantamount to implying as a premise that 18,000 species of one class of vertebrates can really bear comparison with the most remarkably evolved species of a higher class. For this reason really scientific studies of bird behavior carefully avoid the use of terms and nouns used to denote human traits; they employ a special terminology which often sounds absurd in one direction, or is meaningless to the layman in another.

To develop this theme a little further, science advances by proof. If we are in doubt whether *A* is afraid or not, he can often settle the question by telling us that he is indeed "scared to death," in addition to showing the usual signs and symptoms. The emotion of fear in birds is *inferred* by their behavior, and long-continued observation raises this inference to the plane of overwhelming conviction, but it can scarcely be *proved*, like a proposition in geometry. If you wished to investigate my sense of

From *Modern Bird Study*. Cambridge: Harvard University Press, 1945.

smell, how handicapped you would be if it was understood that I could never answer any questions, would never tell whether I smelled something or not, whether the smell was strong or faint, pleasant or unpleasant.

It would appear that birds have very rudimentary senses of smell, taste, and touch, but that they are immeasurably our superiors in their powers of hearing and sight. They possess very high normal body temperatures, ranging from 103 to 112 degrees Fahrenheit. They have a normal pulse rate which is nearly double that of human beings, and they are, consequently, perfectly adapted to withstand extremes of both heat and cold.

One's outstanding impression of birds is that they are bursting with energy. Intense activity, constant alertness, extreme restlessness, are characteristic of birds, and they seem to require astonishingly little sleep and rest.

Years ago, in the spring migration in May, it was my custom to arrive at a certain field in New Jersey before dawn. I had a half-mile walk up a railroad track to some woods, which I planned to reach at daybreak. As I walked up this railroad track in the early morning, I could hear the calls and chirps of the migrating birds overhead, and as dawn arrived and daylight broke, these chirps and calls would come from a lower and lower altitude, and, finally, I would be able to make out the little forms flying north, a relatively few feet overhead. On one occasion a small warbler flew down into a little maple tree on the edge of the track, and, as a matter of interest, I stayed there and watched what it did. It kept perfectly still for twenty minutes, and for part of this time it had its head under its wing. It was obviously resting from the fatigues of its night flight, and it may have slept part of this time. During the course of this twenty minutes it became bright daylight, and I was able to identify the bird as a Nashville warbler. At the end of this twenty minutes, it seemed to revive, began to hop about the tree, and obviously found some insects to eat; then it began to sing, and in a minute or two it proceeded to fly north, presumably at least as far as the woods in the distance. The impression, of course, was that it had had sufficient rest.

The price that these small birds pay for this type of physical activity is that they are very short-lived; they burn themselves out, so to speak, in a comparatively brief span of years. Less active birds, of the less specialized orders, of greater antiquity, with lower body temperatures, live much longer.

In addition to this physical energy, birds obviously have a very vivid emotional life, but there are many curious contradictions and paradoxes.

The outstanding emotion of birds throughout the greater part of the year is fear. There is no evidence of suspense. It is true, for instance, that our small, migrating land-birds are followed north on their journey by the sharp-shinned hawk, which lives on them, but it would be most incorrect to suppose that the lives of these little creatures are clouded by the constant fear of being caught by the hawk! On the other hand, the stupidity of certain of the older groups of birds is so great as to be positively astonishing.

Returning, however, to the warblers and the sharp-shinned hawk, I remember a day in Central Park, New York City, when I was looking over a flock of warblers in the tree tops, and, to my great delight, I discovered a Cape May warbler, at that time a great rarity in the eastern states. A second later the birds all froze, the singing stopped, and a sharp-shinned hawk dashed into the tree, caught and killed one of them, and flew off with it to a near-by oak. The birds remained immobile and silent for less than a minute, and, in spite of the fact that the hawk was in plain sight and was devouring the warbler which it had just caught, the remaining warblers began to move about in the top of the tree and sing; it would appear that the incident had been completely forgotten.

Excitement and curiosity are outstanding features of the emotional life of birds, and sometimes are carried to a degree which produces fatal results. Normally shy birds can often be potshot when mating.

Excitement in birds can reach the point of extreme anger. Birds can fly into a towering rage with other birds, because of some factor which displeases them, and in addition to these blind rages there is a marked degree of jealousy between the males of any one species in adjacent areas in the breeding season. One of the curious features about birds is their antipathy to certain other species of birds, in a great many cases apparently without any rhyme or reason. Those people who run zoological gardens or who engage in the hobby of aviculture have learned that under no circumstances must certain species ever be put together in the same flight cage, no matter how large.

An outstanding illustration is the antipathy that blue jays have for all owls. Heaven knows why jays don't like owls. We haven't a single definite or authentic record, so far as I know, that any owl ever did any blue jay the slightest harm; but, it is perfectly obvious that jays detest owls on sight, and that they mob them whenever they discover them.

When it comes to death, extraordinary danger, and what human beings would call tragedy, it is astonishing how it all passes in a few minutes, all recollection seems to fade, and apparently no scar of any kind is left.

In spite of the vivid emotional life of birds, and in spite of their extreme acuity of hearing compared to that of human beings, the degree of their indifference in certain circumstances is positively incredible. In the last world war, there were many observations all going to prove conclusively that the nesting birds on the battle-fronts were much less affected and upset by the shellfire than were the human beings. At one time I was stationed in a small village back of the Second Army Front, and my dugout happened to be facing a little country churchyard with quite a variety of shrubbery. Under the somewhat dreary surroundings

I got a certain amount of enjoyment out of a robin redbreast which sang nearly all day long in the shrubbery in this churchyard. On a certain morning the Germans shelled us with 13-inch T.N.T. shells; there was a shell every five minutes for about two and a half hours; the base hospital was struck, various people were killed and wounded, and the survivors cowered in their dugouts, hoping for the best. One of these shells fell right through the roof of the church, blew it apart, and filled the garden with rubbish. Seven minutes after the last shell had fallen the robin redbreast climbed up to the top of one of the remaining bushes and began to sing, recovering from the occasion very much more rapidly than I was able to do myself.

Turning to the sex life of birds, it must be stated in no uncertain terms that the stories current in earlier years of devotion and faithfulness to the mate and young are largely "bunk" in the great majority of birds. The more usual behavior patterns can only be described as exceedingly low, provided we remember that there is no "standard," no code of ethics.

An acquaintance of mine made a very interesting, but somewhat cruel experiment some years ago with the indigo bunting. Finding a nesting pair near his house, he proceeded to shoot the male. The next day the female had secured another male, that sang in the same territory claimed by the first mate. He proceeded to shoot the second male. This kept on until he had shot *nine different* male indigo buntings, and he left the tenth male to help the female raise her family. This experiment suggests two different things. There are a larger number of un-mated birds wandering around the country in the breeding season than ordinary observation would lead one to suspect. But, as far as the sex life of the indigo bunting is concerned, what would we think of a woman who had ten husbands in one summer?

We have here ideal illustrations of the need for caution. The use of the term "faithfulness" is actually inadmissible. Marital fidelity in human beings implies prior agreement on a code of morality or ethics, and an undertaking to live up to it on the part of the married couple. Who can seriously suppose that any such premises or undertakings exist when two birds pair off in the breeding season? Certain parrots and swans, and perhaps eagles, are supposed to pair for life, but surely not because they subscribe to the principle of monogamy. Nevertheless there are some sentimental lovers of birds who are much irritated when science refuses to endow them with human moral attributes.

Coming, now, to what we might call capacity in birds, I must report that there is remarkably little outside of the standard pattern of behavior for any given species. There would appear to be little free will or choice in conduct. In spite of this extremely limited range of capacity, we have been able in certain cases to determine that there is some individual variation in capacity, as well as considerable specific variation. There are again some strange paradoxes.

The question of sex recognition in birds has received a certain amount of attention in recent years, and many ingenious and interesting experiments have been performed. To sum up the results of these experiments, there is apparently no sex recognition whatever in birds throughout the year, except at the time of the breeding season. In those birds in which the sexes are alike, or nearly alike, from our point of view, it is very clear that the only way the bird recognizes the sex of another individual of its own species is on the basis of a behavior pattern. In tame pigeons, for instance, to use a homely illustration, the male pigeon bows, struts, coos, and spreads his tail before all the pigeons near by, and he recognizes a female pigeon by the way she reacts to his performance. Apparently there is no other means of sex discrimination in these birds.

There are, however, a large variety of our smaller birds where there is marked sexual dimorphism in color. Do the birds themselves distinguish sex by these color differences? A few experiments have been performed which prove that to a certain extent they are able to do so, but at the height of the breeding season only. It is well known that the male flicker has a black facial stripe which is lacking in the female. A mated pair were trapped and banded and a blank paper strip was pasted over the black stripe of the male, whereupon its mate was no longer able to recognize it and forgot about it. The experiment was reversed, with exactly the same result.

In connection with the question of sex recognition, one of the most extraordinary things about birds is their apparent inability to discriminate between a live bird and a dead one. If you present a male of almost any bird in the northern United States with a stuffed female, the stuffed and mounted female is perfectly satisfactory to the male bird. In an experiment which Professor Allen of Cornell performed with grouse, he discovered that if he presented a male ruffed grouse in breeding condition with the skin of a male ruffed grouse which was laid on the ground, this prostrate condition of the dead grouse was "female behavior" to the male grouse, and, consequently, it was perfectly acceptable for mating purposes. On another occasion he presented the male grouse with a stuffed and mounted female grouse, and the male grouse beat this mounted female until the tail broke off, then the head broke off at the neck and hung down by a mere thread, and finally most of the feathers of the back came out; but none of this had any effect in reducing the attractiveness of the dead grouse to the male!

The ability of the house wren to discriminate between sexes is zero, when it comes to a dead mounted bird. A row of mounted wrens has been put in front of a male house wren, one of them a female house wren, the second a winter wren, which is closely like a house wren, and the third a marsh wren, which is very different from a house wren. The male house wren was not able to distinguish between the dead house wren and the winter wren, but it paid no attention to the marsh wren.

These experiments show the strange paradoxes in avian capacity and perception.

Experiments have been tried on birds as regards their ability to count. With ducks and grouse, which have very large broods of young, it is quite clear that the female is entirely unable to keep track of the total number of her original brood. It is the business of the young to keep track of the mother, and it is just too bad for one of them if it does not do so. The following experiment has been tried with small songbirds. If one egg has been laid in the nest and it is removed, all are able to perceive the loss of the egg. If, however, two eggs have been laid and one of them is taken away, the majority of birds are apparently unable to perceive that anything is missing. Those birds that are able to count up to three are exceedingly few and far between.

Birds seem to have surprisingly little power of choice in conduct and behavior in the great majority of directions. They seldom try to flirt with a type of food which is not the natural and normal one for their species. A few years ago ninety per cent of all the individuals of the brant goose in existence on the Atlantic side of the New World perished because of the strange eel-grass blight, which was so widely discussed and talked about. The brant had exceedingly specialized food habits, subsisted primarily on eel-grass, and when the eel-grass died off most of the brant perished of starvation. The survivors, however, learned to find other things to eat, and they found those other things by imitating ducks and other geese, and the species was possibly saved from extinction, in part, by that means.

There is a primitive sense of language in birds. It is clear that various notes of birds express a few of the more primary emotions. Alarm and distress notes are generally understood by a great variety of species. Noisy and alert birds like the yellow-legs and kingfisher act as a warning of the approach of danger, not only to other birds, but even to mammals and crocodiles.

The distinction between dangerous and harmless hawks is another outstanding capacity of birds, undoubtedly due to their great acuity of vision. The birds usually signal the presence of these hawks to the bird student before he has gotten around to seeing them for himself. Here is another paradox in avian powers of perception. They can discover the dangerous hawk at an extraordinary distance, but they do not seem to care or notice whether the bird is alive or a stuffed one mounted on a perch. Jays will mob a stuffed owl indefinitely.

We now come to the much-mooted subject of intelligence, and here two common terms, as the naturalist uses them, must be carefully defined.

There is a great deal of talk about the instincts of birds, and the question arises: What is an instinct? The current definition is that it is the inherited capacity or propensity to perform seemingly rational acts without conscious design or instruction. A typical example is the ability of a bird only one year old to build a most elaborate, complex, and beautiful nest, without, of course, having received any instruction. It is obviously able to do it perfectly the very first time. The proper care and feeding of the young also seems to be purely instinctive in birds, as is their knowledge of a long migration route over which they travel for the first time.

Intelligence, on the other hand, is quickness of understanding as distinct from perception, the power of reasoning, drawing an inference, or working out advantageous conduct under difficult or novel conditions.

Again, a great deal of nonsense has been written and spoken about birds in this connection. Bird lovers and popular writers have endowed birds with human-like intelligence, and they have even invented a sixth sense to account for some of the things that they do. On the other hand, a particularly cold-blooded and hard-boiled group of physiologists and animal behaviorists have denied anything to birds whatsoever, except instinct. According to this school, all their activities are purely instinctive, and birds are, consequently, to be thought of as feathered automatons. The real truth would appear to be very much nearer No. 2 than No. 1 of these two propositions. It must be admitted that some primitive birds come exceedingly close to being feathered automatons, and there is no experimental evidence whatsoever of anything remotely resembling reasoning power in birds.

Memory is remarkably good in certain very limited directions, for instance, in direction-finding. An interesting case is afforded by various small birds which are victimized by the cowbird. The cowbird egg is differently colored from most of them. It is also very much larger, but the alien egg is not recognized as such by the great majority of birds. There are a few exceptions. It is recognized by the house wren or by most house wrens, who get rid of it by stabbing it with their bills. The yellow warbler is one of the few out of seventy-five victims of the cowbird in the eastern United States that also can recognize the strange egg, and it disposes of it by building a second nest on top of the nest that contains the cowbird egg. The red-eyed vireo provides an interesting example of individual variation. Some red-eyed vireos are unable to recognize the alien egg; other red-eyed vireos are able to do so, and take one means or another of getting rid of it. We have here a question to solve, if only the necessary coöperation could be secured. It would be interesting to find out if those red-eyed vireos that can distinguish the alien cowbird egg are individuals which had been victimized by the cowbird in some preceding year!

Birds learn by experience, but very slowly indeed, and by an obvious method of trial and error, rather than by reasoning out the solution of a problem. In the great majority of difficulties, dangers, and novel situations which the white man and his civilization have brought upon birds, it has taken at least twenty-five generations for the birds to adapt themselves to any one of them. The semi-domestication of the robin is an interesting illustration in point. It has proceeded only part way. There are still a few robins which are as wild as their ancestors ever were, nesting in the deep forest in a shy and retiring manner in the north woods. Some city and town robins which have become semi-domesticated have, obviously, degenerated in many ways as the result of this domestication, and they exhibit stupidity, carelessness, and lack of competence in various directions.

In a great many birds, however, the capacity to learn something new by experience is almost zero. Boobies, for instance, are tropical sea-birds which nest on remote and lonely islets; sailors used to land from a boat and club the boobies to death for fresh meat while the remaining boobies stared solemnly at the proceedings, and waited for their turn to die. It rarely occurred to them to move or to fly away!

The plume-bearing egret was brought to the verge of extinction thirty years ago; it became so exceedingly shy that the discharge of a rifle a mile from a breeding rookery would cause all the egrets to dash wildly into the air. In the meantime, the fish crows, which always hang about egret rookeries to get a meal off the eggs or the young, were perfectly able to discriminate the fact that the rifle was in fact a mile away and, consequently, involved no danger at all, so they would remain in the rookery and would get a fine meal while the egrets wasted their time flying violently about.

Interesting evidence has been derived from certain experiments where birds are submitted to a conflict of primary emotions or instincts. Professor Allen's well-known experiment with a pair of redstarts and their young is a good illustration. At a time when the feeding instinct of the parent birds was at its height, and the young required the maximum amount of care and attention, a confederate took the young out of the nest and held them in his hand on the lawn. The question arises: "What did the parent birds do?" In this particular case the male came and fed the young, but the female would not do so. If we stop there for a moment, what interpretation do we put on these events? Was there any intelligence, and on the part of which sex? I do not see that there is any definite answer to this question. You could argue it both ways. Some people would say the "brave and noble" little male redstart conquered his fear of the dreadful human being, and stuck to his young, and that the female was cowardly and would not. On the other hand, you could argue that the female was the more intelligent of the two sexes; with her instinctive and well-earned fear of man, she played safe and did not take any chances. This experiment has been repeated with various birds many times with varying results. In one case, it is the male that feeds the young, and the female will not; again, the female feeds the young and the male will not. Sometimes both parents feed the young, and on occasion the young are at once entirely abandoned.

There is a sequel to this experiment which is by no means rare. In the case of the redstarts, for instance, the female of which would not feed the young, she discovered a near-by nest of another species, where the young were at about the same stage of development as her own, and she worked off her feeding instinct by feeding the young of the strange species. There was, consequently, no question of intelligence whatever, so far as I can see. The more powerful emotion, fear, completely erased from the mind of this female redstart all memory of her own young, and she never paid any further attention to them, even after they were put back in the nest and her own mate continued to look after them.

Observations leading to similar conclusions have been made over and over again. There is the so-called "suicide" of wounded ducks. The use of the word is, of course, most improper, because there is no departure from a normal ethical standard on the part of the duck. What actually happens is that the wounded duck has such a mortal fear of being captured by the hunter, or his retriever dog, that this is the dominant emotion of the moment, and, consequently, to escape capture it seizes hold of some vegetation or roots underneath the water and stays there until drowned. Just as the term "suicide" is entirely improper when applied to birds, so, if I may revert to the redstart for a moment, is the term "desertion" of the young. Desertion implies a moral obliquity. It is an unfavorable and a critical term which cannot fairly be applied to birds at all.

Robins and other small birds sometimes have tragic accidents, due to various unexpected causes. One day, in my garden, a great outcry arose among the robins. Various other birds clucked and called in excitement, and I stepped out of the house to see what was up. I discovered a robin hanging by one foot, which had been caught in a mass of string in a lilac bush. Taking hold of the robin and doing my best to unsnarl its foot and release it was the last straw, and it died of fright in my hand, a post-mortem dissection showing that the physiological cause had been a cerebral hemorrhage.

Another experiment yielding astonishing results was performed by Professor Allen of Cornell. In this particular case there were two male song sparrows nesting in adjacent territories. A very common thing in birds of the same species is that there is a hierarchy of dominant and weaker individuals. One male sparrow was dominant and the other was weak. The weak male would, under no circumstances, trespass on the territory of the dominant male. So he was trapped and put in a cage and the cage was deposited in the territory of the dominant male. Ludicrous and extraordinary results took place. In the first place, the dominant male fell into a rage, attacked the cage, and made every effort to get at the captive song sparrow, apparently unable to reach the conclusion that on account of the bars of the cage it could not do so, and that the situation was hopeless. All that the weak male had to do was to stay quietly in the middle of its cage, and let the other sparrow rage outside. But it was wild with fear, and dashed madly around the inside of the cage, while the other song sparrow dashed madly about on the outside. By a combination of circumstances, the wing-tip feathers of the weak male inside the cage happened to project for an instant through the bars, and the feathers were grabbed in the bill of the male outside. Whereupon the weaker male immediately died of fright and expired on the floor of the cage. Its death made no difference whatsoever to the song sparrow outside, who kept on just as madly trying to get at it, and beating against the bars of the cage as before. This absurd and unintelligent behavior merely proves that these two birds were motivated entirely by one or the other of two powerful emotions.

Parrots and members of the crow family are easily the most intelligent of birds. In spite of the wealth of amusing stories, however, I have yet to hear of a "talking" parrot where it was *absolutely certain* that it knew what it was saying, except in a few most elementary directions. Most of this "talking" is clever mimicry, aided by indispensable equipment, a fleshy and flexible tongue, for enunciation. Jays and magpies are capable of clever thieving. Ravens have been known to combine forces to capture prey too big or too fast for one bird. A pair of ravens have "ganged up" on a weasel and killed it; they have also taken turns chasing a thrush until it was exhausted and killed it. I know of no authenticated cases suggesting a higher intellectual capacity than this in birds.

AUGUST

Wilson Flagg

Whatever the meaning of a bird's song may be, the fact remains that the singing diminishes as midsummer arrives. Thoreau's contemporary Wilson Flagg (for whom he had a very qualified admiration) describes the beginning of the end of summer.

THE plains and uplands are green with a second growth of vegetation, and nature is rapidly repairing the devastation committed by the scythe of the mower. But the work of the haymaker is not completed. He is still swinging his scythe among the tall sedge-grasses in the lowlands; and the ill-fated flowers of August may be seen lying upon the greensward among the prostrate herbage. The work of the reapers is also begun, and the sheaves of wheat and rye display their wavy rows to gladden and bless the husbandman. Flocks of quails, reared since the opening of the spring flowers, are diligent among the fields, after the reapers have left their tasks. They may be seen slyly and silently creeping along the ground, and now and then lifting their timid heads as if jealous of our approach. The loud whistling of the guardian of the flock, perched at a short distance upon a wall, may also be heard, and as we saunter carelessly along the field-path, a brood of partridges, rising suddenly almost from under our feet, will often astound our ears with their loud whirring flight.

Since the fading of the roses, the birds have generally become silent, as if the presence of these flowers were necessary to inspire them with song. They have grown timid and have forsaken their usual habits, no longer warbling at the season's feast or rejoicing in the heyday of love. They fly no longer in pairs, but assemble in flocks, which may be seen rising and settling over different parts of the landscape. Some species are irregularly scattered, while others gather into multitudinous flocks, and seem to be enjoying a long holiday of festivities, while preparing to leave their native fields. Their songs, lasting only during the period of love, are discontinued since it is past, and their young are no longer awaiting their care. On every new excursion into the fields I perceive the sudden absence of some important woodland melodist. During the interval between

From *A Year with the Birds*. Published by Estes and Lauriat, 1881.

midsummer and early autumn one voice after another drops away, until the little song-sparrow is left again to warble alone in the fields and gardens, where he sang the earliest hymn of rejoicing over the departure of winter.

Since the birds have become silent, they have lost their pleasant familiarity with man, and have acquired an unwonted shyness. The warblers that were wont to sing on the boughs just over our heads, or at a short distance from our path, now keep at a timid distance, chirping with a complaining voice, and flee at our approach, before we are near enough to observe their altered plumage. The plovers have come forth from the places where they reared their young and congregate in large flocks upon the marshes; and as we stroll along the seashore, we are often agreeably startled by the sudden twittering flight of these graceful birds, aroused from their haunts by our unexpected intrusion.

It is now almost impossible for the rambler to penetrate some of his old accustomed paths in the lowlands, so thickly are they interwoven with vines and trailing herbs. Several species of cleavers with their slender prickly branches form a close network among the ferns and rushes; and the smilax and blackberry vines weave an almost impenetrable thicket in our ancient pathway. The fences are festooned with the blue flowers of the woody nightshade and the more graceful plants of the glycine are twining among the faded flowers of the elder and viburnum. The lowlands were never more delightful than at the present time, affording many a pleasant arbor beneath the shrubbery, where the waters have dried away and left the greensward as sweetly scented as a bower of honeysuckles. In these places are we tempted to linger for refreshment on summer noondays—bowers where it is delightful to repose beneath the shade of slender birches whose tremulous foliage seems to whisper to us some pleasant messages of peace. All around us the convolvulus has trailed its delicate vines, and hung out its pink and striped bell-flowers; and the clematis has formed an umbrageous trellis-work over the tops of the trees. Its white clustering blossoms spread themselves out in triumph above the clambering grapevines, forming deep shades which the sun cannot penetrate, overhanging and overarching the green paths that lead through the lowland thickets.

When the pale orchis of the meads is dead, and the red lily stands divested of its crown; when the arethusa no longer bends its head over the stream, and the later violets are weeping incense over the faded remnants of their lovely tribe, then I know that the glory of summer has departed, and I look not until the coming of the asters and the goldenrods to see the fields again robed in beauty. The meeker flowers have perished since the singing birds have discontinued their songs, and the last rose of summer may be seen in solitary and melancholy beauty—the lively emblem of the sure decline of all the beautiful objects of this life, the lovely symbol of beauty's frailty and its transientness. When the last rose is gone, I look around with sadness upon its late familiar haunts; I feel that summer's beauty now is past, and sad mementos rise where'er I tread.

It is my delight to seek these last-born of the roses, and to my sight they are more beautiful than any that preceded them, as if Nature, like a partial mother, had lavished her best gifts upon these her youngest children. The bushes that support them are overtopped by other plants, that seem to feel an envious delight in concealing them from observation, but they cannot blot them from our memory, nor be admired as we admire them. The clethra with its white odiferous flowers, and the button bush with its elegant globular heads, strive vainly to equal them in fragrance or beauty. The proud and scornful thistle rears its head close by their side, and seems to mock at the fragility of these lovely flowers; but the wild briar, though its roses have faded, still gives out its undying perfume, as if the essence of the withered flowers lingered about their former leafy habitation, like spirits about the places they loved in their lifetime.

In the latter part of the month we begin to mark the approaching footsteps of autumn. Twilight is chill, and we perceive the greater length of the nights and evening's earlier dew. The morning sun is later in the heavens, and sooner tints the fleecy clouds of evening. The bright verdure of the trees has faded to a more dusky green; and here and there in different parts of the woods may be found a sere and yellow leaf, like the white hairs that are interspersed among the dark-brown tresses of manhood, that indicate the sure advance of hoary years. The fields of ripe and yellow grain gleam through the open places in the woods, making a pleasant contrast with their greenness, displaying in the same instant the signs of a cheerful harvest and the melancholy decay of vegetation. The swallows assemble their little hosts upon the roofs and fences, preparing for their annual migration, and all things announce the speedy decline of summer.

Already do I hear at nightfall the chirping of the cicadas, whose notes are at the same time the harvest hymn of nature and a dirge over the departure of flowers. When the evenings are perceptibly lengthened and the air partakes of the exhilarating freshness of autumn, these happy insects commence their anthems of gladness; and their monotonous but agreeable melody is in sweet unison with the general serenity of nature. These voices come from myriads of cheerful hearts, but there is a plaintiveness in their modulation that calls up the memory of the past and turns our thoughts inwardly upon almost forgotten joys and sorrows. How different are our emotions from those awakened by the notes of the piping frogs that hail the opening of spring! All these sounds, though not designed particularly for our benefit, are adapted by nature to harmonize agreeably with our feelings, and there is a soothing and lulling influence in the song of the cicadas that softens into tranquility the melancholy it inspires and tempers all our sadness into pleasure.

We no longer perceive that peculiar charm of spring vegetation, that comes from the health and freshness of every growing thing; and we associate the flowers of August with the dry, withered, and dying plants that everywhere surround them. In June everything in the aspect of nature is harmonious; all is greenness and gladness, and nothing appears in company with the flowers to disfigure their charms or to affect the sight with displeasure. But August presents a motley spectacle of rank and inelegant weeds, that overshadow the flowers; and the beauty of the fields is often hidden by the withered vegetation of the last month. This appearance, however, is chiefly obvious in those places which have been disturbed by cultivation. In the wilds Nature always preserves the harmony of her seasons. Every herb and flower appears at proper time; and when one species has attained maturity it gives place to its rightful successors without any confusion, all rising and declining like the heavenly hosts of night, and clothing the face of the landscape in perpetual bloom and verdure. Seldom do we behold a parterre that equals in beauty those half wild spots where, after a partial clearing of the forest, Nature has been left to herself a sufficient time to recover from the effects of art and to rear those plants which are best fitted for the soil and the season.

Let the lover of flowers and landscapes who would learn to gather round his dwelling all those rural beauties that will meet and blend in harmony receive his lesson from Nature in her own wilds. Let him look upon her countenance before it has been disfigured by a barbarous art, to acquire his ideas of beauty and propriety, and he will never mar her features by adding gems that do not harmonize with their native expression, plucked from the bosom of a foreign clime. Then, although he may not sit under the shade of the palm or the myrtle, or roam among sweet-scented orange-groves, in the climate of northern fruits and northern flowers, he needs no foreign trees or shrubbery to decorate his grounds or to adapt them to his pleasures. In a forest of his own native pines he may find an arbor in summer and a shelter in winter as odoriferous as a grove of cinnamon and myrtle; and the fruits of his own orchards will yield him a repast more savory than the products of the Indies.

TYRANNUS TYRANNUS

Louis J. Halle, Jr.

Many birds are exemplary parents and lead ideal family lives. For that reason medieval moralists sometimes cited their example as a reproach to humankind. Modern ornithologists, on the other hand, are almost fanatically insistent upon avoiding "the anthropomorphic fallacy." Birds, they say, are creatures of instinct and perhaps of emotion, but they can't think and they are not conscious of the purpose of their seemingly purposeful actions. Here Louis J. Halle, Jr., formerly a member of our State Department and by avocation a naturalist, makes the point brilliantly in a vivid account of the family life of certain of the birds he has observed.

Does he, one asks, overstate the case—not by stressing the instinctive character of bird behavior but by seemingly making too absolute the contrast with the parallel behavior of human beings? "The kingbird," he writes, "leading the abundant life somewhere in the jungles of tropical America, was not suddenly overcome last spring by the appalling thought that if he and his mates did not act promptly his species might disappear from the earth." How many human children are conceived because their parents were struck by the fear of extinction?

I N most forms of animal life the propagation of the race seems to be a purely unintentional outcome of the sexual impulse, which is directed toward the satisfaction of the moment rather than the population of the future. A physical need exists to be satisfied, and its satisfaction involves remote consequences which were certainly not considered at the moment. Among birds, however, procreation is not the incidental consequence of an impulsive act, but the end of a chain of action that seems to have been deliberately followed with the sole purpose of bringing into being a new generation. There is no trace of capriciousness in the history of their mating. The ruling impulse seems to be the production of a family, and the physical union merely one of several incidental means to that premeditated end. They put as much passion into the choice of a nesting site, the building of the nest, the brooding of the eggs, and the feeding of the young, as into the act of union itself. The male lavishes as

From *Birds Against Men.* New York: The Viking Press, 1938.

much devotion and protecting care on his nest as on his mate, and fights as readily in its defense.

Still, I don't for a moment suppose that birds, who are creatures of impulse and incapable of contemplation, can visualize the remote future consequences of their acts. We must not allow the lower forms of life credit for spiritual faculties that even we possess imperfectly. The kingbird, leading the abundant life somewhere in the jungles of tropical America, was not suddenly overcome last spring by the appalling thought that if he and his mates did not act promptly his species might disappear from the earth. He did not think of Duty. He did not think of a nest and a clutch of fertile eggs, of embryonic life stirring, or fledglings trying out their fledgling wings over a neat green lawn some thousands of miles distant. He did not think at all. Nevertheless, he was possessed by an urge, some obscure, unrealized impulse, some restlessness which made him less content to stay where he was, even though there had been no change in his outward circumstances. The jungle still offered the same abundant food and shelter. The sun still shone, flowers bloomed, insects hummed, night and day alternated as usual. Nevertheless, the periodic urge, which scientists have guessed arises from seasonal glandular changes in the body's interior, was there. I suppose it may have been several weeks before it was strong enough to prompt action. However that may be, the time came when he found himself flying northward to alleviate the urgency which he did not understand. It was merely that he felt better about flying north than about flying east or west or south, or remaining where he was. Surely he did not picture that neatly pruned apple tree on the lawn outside our house, even though he may have nested in its immediate vicinity less than a year earlier. I doubt that at any point he saw beyond his actual physical horizon. He embarked on a journey that must have fazed him had he been capable of grasping its magnitude. A man would have to be endowed with exceptional courage to undertake it. But courage is needed only where there is imagination, and the kingbird had no need of it. . . .

The urge that had carried him across land and sea did not leave him when he arrived. But he stopped here now because it no longer satisfied that urge to go farther. Still obedient to his fate, he claimed the apple tree as his stage and waited, knowing (and not knowing) that the solitary first labor of his mission and had been accomplished, that from now on he would have a mate to share his duties. And sure enough, within a few days he was joined at his post by another kingbird, who took for granted his presence and his inclinations as he took for granted her arrival. With the apple tree as their chosen setting they played their traditional parts to a single rhythm, for both wills were bent by the same motive, prompted by the same series of momentary inspirations, subject to the same transcending intelligence that both followed blindly.

It is easy enough to conjure up the picture of a pleasant domestic scene to describe the family life of the kingbird—something on the order of the hearth-loving English vicar of the nineteenth century, surrounded by devoted wife, clay pipe, and three affectionate daughters. The early flutterings of mutual love in the respective breasts, the ripening of a maturer affection as family cares impose sobriety—protective affection in the male, devoted and worshipful in his mate. . . . The thing has been done. It was quite the fashion some years ago to draw moral sustenance from the examples of the good life set us by our feathered brethren. This was done chiefly, I believe, by ladies, closet ornithologists who rarely ventured out of sight of their pet canaries, though the literary clergy may also have had a hand in it. But the age of moral elevation has passed, and the feathered brethren, like the unfeathered, have had their manners corrupted by the literature of an irresponsible new age. Times change, birds change. . . .

I cannot conscientiously report that my kingbirds underwent any mystical or moral experience in the process of their union. As far as I could tell it was a purely practical matter. One after another, the female produced four eggs in the interior of her body, and one after another her mate fertilized them, acting exactly as though he had a perfect understanding of the mysterious processes of egg-production and embryogeny. His advances and her acceptances were spaced, as though by intelligence, to fit into the established rhythm of procreation. When, for the first time, she began to spend the night in their nest while he went off alone to roost in the woods, I knew that the spotted eggs had already been deposited in the pocket especially built to contain them.

The kingbird's days of freedom were definitely over. One may assume that his liberty had already been severely qualified ever since that urge which he had first felt in distant lands had taken possession of him. "Free as a bird" is an expression in which a bird might find ironical amusement; especially as coming from man, the only animal who has, in his individual life, succeeded in achieving some measure of independence from the discipline of nature. But now the kingbird's responsibility was embodied in four small white spheroids spotted with umber. He had a concrete treasure to guard. Those fragile shells contained the future of his race, the reason for his long migration, the cause to which he had been dedicated many weeks earlier and thousands of miles away. It was no longer enough to guard his own person from enemies. At last he had a treasure, a treasure which lay in an open nest exposed to enemies who would ravish it at the first relaxation of the vigil he shared with his mate.

Crows, especially, were dangerous. By inherited instinct, if not by experience, the kingbird knew that they would eat his eggs and young if he allowed them occasion, and, following the Napoleonic policy of his species that the best form of defense is an effective offense, he never gave the crows a chance to launch an attack. I don't suppose it was really policy. Again, he seemed prompted by a racial intelligence that was not his own. Whenever a crow appeared on the distant horizon, though he were only passing peacefully by and minding his own business, the kingbird and his mate, with piercing shrieks of anger, would project themselves at him like a pair of missiles shot out of the tree by the force of their own energy. It was unreasonable, but effective. Darting at him from above, and occasionally landing on his back in mid-flight, they would soon have him plunging like a maddened horse under a swarm of bees, and it was a pretty sure thing that he would make a long detour the next time his business carried him that way. Unreasonable, but extremely effective. The piratical crows were the first to be driven out of our neighborhood when the kingbirds set about establishing their kingdom.

In those early days, however, before the embryos had developed in the eggs, it was enough to guard them from nest-robbers. The constant brooding, to insure the proper temperature for their development, came later. The kingbirds were still free to expend their limitless vitality in exhibition flights, hawking for insects and harassing the neighborhood birds. Occasionally one or the other of them would rest for a while on the eggs, but any excuse to abandon them was good enough.

You might have thought that both birds were expert embryologists from the way they seemed to know just how much brooding was necessary, increasing the amount gradually from day to day. But they had read no book on the prenatal care of birds, attended no course of lectures, studied no diagrams. They did not know the contents of those eggs or the purpose of their brooding. They did not know why they had produced them, or why they had ever built a nest to contain them; or why they now bothered to guard them. Nor could previous experience, rule of thumb acquired through trial and error, have been a basis for their actions, since birds will follow the same established procedure whether or not they are nesting for the first time. I rather think it was the lack of any intelligent comprehension of their own actions that made those actions possible. Calculation would merely have confused the process. Completely devoid, as they were, of the capacity for reasoning, for weighing alternatives, for valuing ends, their natural instincts, shaped over millennia of evolution to the sole end of survival, had no rivalry to their leadership, authority was undivided. They acted blindly because their actions were only reflections of intuition; they acted surely, without hesitation, because only intuition prompted their actions.

The perfect co-operation between the two prospective parents was another indication of the integrity of instinct they shared in common. When the female had brooded long enough and was ready to leave the nest in search of food or exercise, she did not call her mate into consultation and ask him to take her place. She merely followed her urge and departed. The male would sometimes delay for several minutes after her departure, but you could see that the empty nest concerned him. When the·safe time had elapsed, he would fly over and settle down in her place, folding his wings carefully for a long vigil. Gradually the time between watches was reduced, as the developing embryos required more constant warmth, until in the last stages the birds would replace each other immediately.

It will be no surprise to the reader who has followed the history of the kingbirds this far to learn that their eggs did finally split open and bring forth the renewed life of the species in the form of four pink dabs of flesh, with eye-slits for eyes, with ludicrously disproportionate bills and feet, and with wing-stumps that were far from having the aerodynamic perfection of the adults' feathered pinions. And yet, how can it be otherwise than surprising? Here was an achievement out of all proportion to the kingbirds' limited powers; the culminating fourth act of a drama played over two continents, involving the most sweeping action and the most subtle dialogue, by two insignificant actors whose limited powers, placed at the disposal of the unlimited forces of nature, had produced this immortality. By themselves, these two little birds had no powers of generation. They lacked the intelligence and the knowledge to understand the necessary processes. The two kingbirds who had performed this exploit were but the instruments of an inscrutable and disembodied will, a universal purpose heard only in the echo of their own unpondered desires.

The kingbirds themselves were not surprised when they felt the eggs stirring beneath them. As passive instruments of an unfathomable fate they accepted as they had performed, without fear or question. And now the labor of the performance was increased by the necessity of filling those four bottomless gullets. Time was passing. Summer was half gone. Quantities of young robins, bluebirds, phoebes, had taken possession of the countryside and were already feeding themselves. Insects were plentiful. The kingbirds perched on the topmost twigs of the trees adjacent to their nest-tree and every minute or two sallied forth to bring in some new prey. At midday, when the sun beat down with tropical intensity, one or the other of them would stand guard on the edge of the nest, wings spread to shelter the unfeathered young from its rays. In the evening, as the heat began to wear off, the young would grow increasingly clamorous, and both parents would be hard pressed to keep them satisfied with tributes of insects until nightfall.

Up to now the kingbirds had paid little attention to me, evidently not classing my kind with such worthy opponents as crows and hawks. Along with rabbits, muskrats, groundhogs, and white-footed mice, I was considered harmless. They did not even flatter me by trying to hide their nest or dissemble their concern for it in my presence. All other birds I have been familiar with have at least had some hesitation about approaching their nests (always hidden) when I was observing them. But that was never a kingbird's way. Like the stalwart fighter he is, he has no need of trickery or deception. He builds his nest and rears his young in full view; let anyone approach at his peril. Only when I took advantage of their openness to get some photographs of them did the kingbirds change their estimate of me. That machine I carried raised me definitely to the status of a menace. From that moment I could call the crows my equals. Hovering overhead with shrill staccato shrieks, they took turns in plunging at me, their flaming crests, never displayed except in battle, standing erect on their heads, their bills snapping like the strokes of doom. So fierce was the onslaught that, despite my manifest advantages, I felt something of the terror that must accompany the insect's instant of annihilation. The first plunge brought me to my knees, my arms clasping my head for protection. But they could not drive me away. Eventually the clamor of the young for food forced them to abandon the attack, and I got the photographs I wanted. After that, however, I was a marked man. Camera or no camera, whenever I entered their territory (which was anywhere up to a hundred yards from the tree) they charged me. Other men could come and go as they pleased; I had earned their undying enmity by my invasion of their privacy. They knew now that I, different in that from others of my kind, had taken an interest in their nest and young, and they could not know that my interest was benevolent.

Of course they were right not to take any chance. They were eminently right in everything they did; as witness the fact that the four dabs of flesh grew rapidly in a few days' time to fully fledged reproductions of their elders, and were soon out of the nest. No ceremony accompanied their departure, no ostentation. In fact, it was anything but deliberate. The young birds were literally pushed out into the world by their own growth. They hatched from the nest as they had hatched from those spotted eggs, only when it could no longer contain them. Their reluctance was marked. The first day they merely tried their footing on the edge of the nest and along the adjacent twigs; and by evening all had crowded back into the cradle. One can understand their unwillingness to say farewell to the day of their infancy. But time does not wait on the pleasure of mortals. The next night the four kingbirds roosted all in a row beside an abandoned nest, and in the morning they embarked on their first experimental flights, fluttering across the great open spaces between twig and twig.

I cannot say the parent birds took any pride in the achievement. From first to last their attitude was strictly businesslike. They maintained the food-supply and kept all enemies at a distance, but I never saw them give their progeny any sign of encouragement or commendation in those first attempts to cope with the problem of flight. The young birds now had to take their share of the responsibility for their own survival. When one of them, weaker and less developed than the others, with a mere stump of tail and inadequate pinions, fell out of the tree in an abortive attempt at flight, he was left to lie where he fell, exposed to all the dangers that creep on the ground. Had it not been for my benevolent intervention, which made me the target of a series of breathtaking attacks, he would never have escaped the universal fate of weaklings. Again the kingbirds were right. According to the strictly practical ethics of nature, the Spartan code which subordinates the individual to the race, the weak must always die so that the strong may survive. But, mere man that I was, a renegade from nature and the child of a decadent humanitarian age, I followed the less practical ethics of my kind, which assume that the kingdom of nature is governed by a Bill of Rights based on the political philosophy of the eighteenth century, assuring, in the mystic name of Justice, the participation of weak and strong alike in the goods of this earth. My fault was human. But the kingbirds were right. The next day that same fledgling fell out of the tree again, and again I replaced him, in the teeth of their violent opposition. I don't suppose he survived the year, however. There are too many pitfalls in the path and only the strong and warlike can hope to hold their place on the program of nature.

I have heard a good many stories about the fierceness of a lioness in the defense of her cubs, but I would set my kingbird up against any lioness, real or legendary. Now that the young were out in the open, exposed to the attack of every passing hawk, he and his mate were transformed into a pair of Furies who anticipated the need of vengeance by harrying the countryside with a fierce, demoniac rage. The smaller birds were unmolested as long as they kept their distance. But an interdict was issued against all greater fowl, especially the hawks, who were proscribed from showing themselves anywhere within the circle of the horizon. No longer was there peace in the land. At any moment the air might be torn by the staccato shrieks of the kingbirds and I would spin about in time to see them go sizzling into the sky like a pair of rockets after a distant speck of a hawk passing through on the way to his feeding grounds. They always attacked from above, and the harassed hawk never made any attempt to meet the challenge except by escape.

I must not give the impression that the kingbirds were prompted to assault an enemy so much more powerful than themselves by mere recklessness. As children of nature they were far too practical for that. Napoleon may have been a romanticist in his aims, but he was an utter realist in policy; until the end he never attacked except with a realistic confidence in his own superiority. The kingbirds, similarly, knew his own powers and the strength of the enemy, and he reckoned accordingly. Note that he always attacked from above, the one position in which he was safe from retaliation. For no large bird, however much advantage it may have in speed or sustained flight, can climb as rapidly as a small bird. The small birds have not the weight necessary for high speed or for gliding flight, but for the same reason they are more buoyant, more easily raised by the strokes of their wings. Often too easily. Most of the small birds must fold their wings and drop down at regular intervals to maintain a level course. The typical rising falling flight of the perching birds is directly due to this excess buoyancy. The kingbird's manner is different. He is exceptional in the control he can exercise over his speed and pitch by varying the depth of his wing-strokes rather than their frequency. But the same buoyancy is his. I have seen my kingbird ascend almost vertically for twenty or thirty feet to capture some insect passing overhead. A hawk cannot make so steep a grade. His method is to rise slowly in sweeping circles till he has reached his pitch, and from there to prey on what lies below him. The kingbird knew that he was safe in his attack as long as he remained above. Even so, he never quite closed in, as he did with crows, being careful always to keep a few inches' leeway between himself and the hawk he was storming. His tactics were always shrewd, rather than reckless.

I mention the kingbird's realism in this respect with no derogation to his valor. He had no more use for romanticism in making war than in making love. With confidence in his own powers, he used them fully, but he reflected the will of nature too exactly to be other than strictly practical in his policy. As with all great rulers, his sovereignty was a masterly achievement of *Realpolitik*. There was no nonsense in his make-up.

I am not much given to hero-worship, but before the summer was over I was persuaded that the kingbird could do no wrong. To a human being, endowed with the intelligence and imagination that distract men from their purpose, confuse their policy, and lead them into a morass of doubts and hesitations, the kingbird's ever-unhesitating choice of the right course could only command admiration. He never wavered between alternatives. He never questioned. He was never uncertain. And he was always amazingly right. The triumph of his sovereignty was inevitable from the first because it was inevitable that he should always use his powers to their best advantage. In the strength of his single-mindedness that little mite, not so big as my first, became a symbol of invincible purpose in nature.

The kingdom which he had come up from the south to establish in our apple tree was now justified by four brand-new princes clothed in the traditional black-and-white of their kind, their breasts immaculate, their tails tipped with white, the feathers of wing and back still fresh and unworn. It had taken them only a few days to learn proper kingbird flight, and now they knew all the tricks: how merely to vibrate their wing-tips for hovering and how to dig deep in the sprints, how to spread their tails for sudden turns, how to change their pace without interval, and how to glide in to their landings on motionless pinions. They accompanied their parents about the countryside in a screaming procession and flew after them to snatch prey from their bills in mid-air. Only the fact that their plumage was now shabby, that their breasts had darkened and the white edges of their wing-feathers worn off, distinguished the parents from their offspring. But the moulting season was at hand, and when the six kingbirds took their separate departures for the tropics there would no longer be any way of telling them apart.

Simultaneously with the development of the young birds' capacity to care for themselves, the inscrutable urge which had driven the kingbird over thousands of miles of land and sea, had prompted him to build a nest and take a mate, and had aroused in him a concern for the fledglings that resulted from the union, lost its strength. When the young birds no longer depended on him they became strangers and possible rivals who might, when the next nesting season came round, be attacked with as much vigor as they had been cherished during their upbringing. His mate became merely another bird whose existence did not concern him. Once more he was free of ties and responsibility.

Almost free, but not quite. As long as mortal beings are subject to the passage of time, the constant revolution of the four seasons, the steady march of days and hours—each minute leaving its faint, ineffaceable mark so that there can be no turning back from the universal end—as long as the earth and all its inhabitants continue to grow older, they can never be quite free. The kingbird's mission had been successfully accomplished, another generation had been produced. But there was some loss: a whole season of life had passed away. In a few more weeks the insects on which he depended for his livelihood would be gone, the leaves would be stripped from the trees, the first wintry frosts would wither the verdure of summer. Again he must move.

With millions of other birds, the majority pursuing their first migration, (he no longer recognized his offspring among them), he began to drift southward. He had no vision of the approach of winter, for he could never have experienced it. But now a new urge had taken possession of him, growing stronger with the weeks. His life was once more shaped to a deliberate will which commanded it. That southern course was not new to him, but time had passed since he had last flown it, another year had been taken from the term of his life.

I like to picture my kingbird arriving once more in tropical lands on a warm November evening, after his long flight across the high seas, and resting for the night among the grass-covered ruins of some city of the jungle over which a monarch, centuries dead, had once held sway. It would be only poetic justice for him to enjoy the posthumous hospitality of a vanished empire, while in a bare apple tree to the north a bundle of grasses, tilted more than ever, now, and capped with a little mound of snow, remained as the last monument of his own temporal sovereignty.

COURTSHIP

OF THE

DUCK HAWK

A. C. Bent

Man likes to give himself credit for being the only animal who manages to transmute the sex impulse into love—with a capital L. Perhaps. Nevertheless some present-day ornithologists are so impressed by the emotional intensity of some mating birds that, as Sir Julian Huxley said of himself, it made him wishful for a moment to be one. At least this is certain: birds had evolved an elaborate ritual of courtship long before the time when (if you can believe the comic papers) our cave-man ancestors had thought of nothing more subtle than a blow over the head with a stone axe. Perhaps no American bird can rival certain tropical species in the complexity and splendor of their courtships but, as the following selection demonstrates, even the duck hawk feels the elevating influence of Venus.

I N Massachusetts adult duck hawks reoccupy the breeding stations before the end of February, and since the first eggs are not laid before March 25 or April 1, there is a long and interesting courtship. So wonderful are the aerial evolutions of the peregrines during this season that I am inclined to think that no observer can fully appreciate their powers of flight who has not seen them at the nesting site on a windy March day; every movement, no matter how extended, is centered about the home cliff, so that its whole course may be traced, which is not usually the case at other seasons and places.

There is some evidence that it is the male bird that is strongly attached to the cliff—that he returns there first and endeavors to attract a female, but if unsuccessful, remains there throughout the summer, while unmated females apparently roam about from place to place. Whether the duck hawk mates for life, and the female of the previous season returns directly to the cliff, if still alive (as has been generally assumed), I am not

From *Life Histories of North American Birds of Prey*. U. S. Government Printing Office, Washington, D.C., 1938.

yet prepared to say, but I do recall very vividly a little drama that throws considerable light on the initial stages of courtship. This took place at Mount Sugarloaf on March 16 and involved a male peregrine that at that date, some three weeks after his return to the mountain, appeared to be still unmated. I had been watching him for more than an hour as he sat quietly on a dead pine above the cliff and during this whole period had heard no call or seen no such animation as is associated with the courting period. Suddenly, at about 9 o'clock, he launched out from his perch and began to sail back and forth along the face of the cliff, repeatedly giving the *wichew* or rusty-hinge note. A moment later I spotted a large female peregrine coming up the valley from the south, some 200 feet above the mountain. Arriving abreast of the cliff, she began to describe wide circles over the crest, flying very leisurely and seeming to watch the proceedings below her; the tercel redoubled his cries and flew from one shelf to another, alighting for a moment on each one and then swinging along to the next, with every appearance of the greatest excitement. The falcon, having presently completed three or four circles, now straightened her course toward the north, and picking up speed with every stroke of her wings soon disappeared in the haze along North Sugarloaf; the male continued his vain activity, wailing and *wichew*-ing for nearly a minute after she had passed from sight. He then made a short silent sally out over the valley and finally returned to sit hunched up and quiet on his dead tree for many minutes, before leaving on a hunting expedition behind the mountain. This episode introduces several of the elements of the courtship—the flight display, the shelf display, the coaxing *wichew* note—and it remains only to elaborate on their use and to mention the food-bringing routine.

The male assumes an aggressive role throughout the first part of the period, seeming to arouse and lead on the female from step to step of the reproductive cycle. With both birds at a cliff, early in March, the first business of each morning is feeding. Shortly after daylight the falcons will be discovered perched on their favorite dead trees on the upper part of the cliff, watching closely for the passing of some smaller bird suitable for prey. If none appears near at hand the male will sally out at intervals and go far across the valley, returning perhaps at the end of 20 or 30 minutes with a blue jay hanging limp in his talons. He wails while still at a distance, and the female, wailing in return, flies to meet him and receives the bird in the usual way. Or perhaps his search has been in vain, and he suddenly plunges down from a great height, empty-footed, to resume the watch from his perching tree. Perchance a flicker now appears flying up the valley at a considerable height above the trees, but still below the level of the hawks; they both start out from their trees and, stroking steadily, converge on the unfortunate bird with a speed and deadly earnestness chilling to the onlooker. The female takes the lead. The flicker sees its peril too late, and in a trice the falcon snatches it dead in the air and, turning sharply about, heads back for the cliff while her mate convoys her from behind. She lights on her tree, holding the bird against the branch with one foot, and in another moment flicker feathers are drifting down-wind as she eagerly plucks her booty. Meanwhile the tercel sallies forth again over the valley and this time returns with his bird. There are many variations of this morning scene—the birds may go away hunting together, the male may make his kill near the cliff, or the female may miss her stoop, in which case the tercel often stoops at the same bird—but certain parts of the pattern are quite invariable. In general, the female stays closer to home; if they both chase the same bird, the female makes the first stoop; and she eats the first bird whether she kills it herself or the male brings it to her.

Having fed, the hawks are likely to sit quietly for some little time, occasionally wailing to each other, preening their feathers, perhaps lazily stretching first one wing and then the other. At length the tercel starts off his perch and begins to soar and swoop about the cliff, describing a series of figure-eights in the air, sometimes in a horizontal, sometimes a vertical, plane. At times he lights on little shelves and *wichews*; again he returns to his tree and wails, or perhaps he soars higher and higher in the air, farther and farther out across the valley, until at last he shuts his wings to his sides and plunges down in a mile-long swoop that brings him back to the cliff. Sometimes the falcon accompanies him on these flights, but for the most part she is distinctly passive. The culmination of these flight displays depends much on the weather, but eventually the patient watcher will see an exhibition of flying that is literally breathtaking. I have seen it at many nest sites, but never to better advantage than one beautiful spring morning at Black Rock when a rising southerly gale was whipping along the flanks of Mount Everett. We were hidden in the woods below the south end of the cliff, and the peregrines were quite unconscious of our presence at the time; again and again the tercel started well to leeward and came along the cliff against the wind, diving, plunging, saw-toothing, rolling over and over, darting hither and yon like an autumn leaf until finally he would swoop up into the full current of air and be borne off on the gale to do it all over again. At length he tired of this, and, soaring in narrow circles without any movement of his wings other than a constant small adjustment of their planes, he rose to a position 500 or 600 feet above the mountain and north of the cliff. Nosing over suddenly, he flicked his wings rapidly 15 or 20 times and fell like a thunderbolt. Wings half closed now, he shot down past the north end of the cliff, described three successive vertical loop-the-loops across its face, turning completely upside down at the top of each loop, and roared out over our heads with the wind rushing through his wings like ripping canvas. Against the background of the cliff his terrific speed was much more apparent than it would have been in the open sky. The sheer excitement of watching such a performance was tremendous; we felt a strong impulse to stand and cheer.

As March advances, the male peregrine tries more and more to entice the female to certain shelves he has picked out. Between hunting trips and exercising flights above the valley he spends long intervals on these shelves, scratching around in the debris, *wichew*-ing in his most persuasive tones, standing at their front edges breast out to the sun, wailing mournfully now and then, and even flying to the female's roost tree to *wichew* at her in soft conversational tones. At first she pays no attention, nor leaves her tree, but gradually her passivity gives way to mild interest; she flies to the shelf where he is working and lights there; they both walk back out of sight and for a moment there is an outburst of argumentative *wichew*-ing and creaking as she seems to disagree emphatically with all his plans. Either bird may come off first, leaving the other to scratch and dig around, but as a rule they do not both stay. At any time now the female may be seen to return to her tree alone; the male *wichews* excitedly at one or more shelves and then comes off the cliff, flies directly to her with no other preliminaries, and copulation takes place to the accompaniment of a low, conversational, chuckling noise, which is entirely distinct from the usual notes. Coition is more likely to occur near the middle of the day and is usually repeated within an hour or so; it is also repeated on succeeding days until at least two eggs are in the nest.

The interest of the male in nesting shelves now begins to wane in inverse proportion to the female's increasing, though somewhat furtive, activity. While he is away hunting she may be seen going all over the cliff, squeezing into the most inadequate cracks and niches, scratching and scraping with bill and feet, turning round and round to get the feel of tentative nest hollows. At length she chooses the site, apparently with no reference to the male's previous selection, and in the course of a few days makes a smooth well-rounded scrape an inch or two deep. If disturbed at this time she is very likely to pick a new site at once and hurriedly prepare it, and I have several times had the experience of watching a falcon carefully form a nest hollow only to return after a short interval and discover the first eggs in quite a different spot on the cliff. The eggs are laid at intervals of every other day, with often two full days between the third and fourth.

THE

COURTSHIP

OF THE

CANADA GOOSE

John James Audubon

---

*Part of the greatness of Audubon lies in the fact that he was both
rigidly scientific within the limitations of his time and yet capable both
of emotion himself and of recognizing it in birds.*

I T is extremely amusing to witness the courtship of the Canada Goose
in all its stages; and let me assure you, reader, that although a Gander
does not strut before his beloved with the pomposity of a Turkey, or
the grace of a Dove, his ways are quite as agreeable to the female of his
choice. I can imagine before me one who has just accomplished the defeat
of another male after a struggle of half an hour or more. He advances
gallantly towards the object of contention, his head scarcely raised an
inch from the ground, his bill open to its full stretch, his fleshy tongue
elevated, his eyes darting fiery glances, and as he moves he hisses loudly,
while the emotion which he experiences causes his quills to shake, and
his feathers to rustle. Now he is close to her who in his eyes is all
loveliness; his neck bending gracefully in all directions, passes all round
her, and occasionally touches her body; and as she congratulates him on
his victory, and acknowledges his affection, they move their necks in a
hundred curious ways. At this moment fierce jealousy urges the defeated
gander to renew his efforts to obtain his love; he advances apace, his
eyes glowing with the fire of rage; he shakes his broad wings, ruffles up
his whole plumage, and as he rushes on the foe, hisses with the intensity
of anger. The whole flock seems to stand amazed, and opening up a
space, the birds gather round to view the combat. The bold bird who has
been caressing his mate, scarcely deigns to take notice of his foe, but

From *The Birds of America*. New York: George R. Lockwood & Son, 1870.

seems to send a scornful glance towards him. He of the mortified feelings, however, raises his body, half opens his sinewy wings, and with a powerful blow, sends forth his defiance. The affront cannot be borne in the presence of so large a company, nor indeed is there much disposition to bear it in any circumstances; the blow is returned with vigour, the aggressor reels for a moment, but he soon recovers, and now the combat rages. Were the weapons more deadly, feats of chivalry would now be performed; as it is, thrust and blow succeed each other like the strokes of hammers driven by sturdy forgers. But now, the mated gander has caught hold of his antagonist's head with his bill; no bull-dog could cling faster to his victim; he squeezes him with all the energy of rage, lashes him with his powerful wings, and at length drives him away, spreads out his pinions, runs with joy to his mate, and fills the air with cries of exultation.

OUR

VANISHING CONDORS

Peter Matthiessen

The California condor holds several records. It is the largest bird in the United States and it is also—along with the similar Andean condor—the largest bird capable of flight now living anywhere in the world. Gigantism seems to have run in the family since an extinct relative, Teratornis incredibilis, was, so far as the fossil record shows, the largest flying bird which ever lived anywhere on earth. The two living giant condors have each a wingspread of nearly ten feet and weigh up to twenty-five pounds. During the Pleistocene incredibilis soared over Nevada on wings estimated to have spread nearly seventeen feet.

The California condor is also one of our rarest birds and it has probably been going slowly the way of the mastodon and the sabertoothed tiger for many thousands of years. Since the Pleistocene, so the fossil finds indicate, its range has been gradually narrowing until now it is found only in a very restricted area centering in the California Coast Range. The total number of living specimens could probably be counted by scores and the chances are that before long there will be none. Some of the many reasons for its approaching death as a species are given in the article which follows. Man and the changes which he brings about when he invades an area have no doubt hastened its disappearance but it was probably doomed long before he became a factor. Animal species do die a sort of natural death and those which attained immoderate size seem in several instances to have found it difficult to compete with smaller competitors.

Fossil remains of the California condor have been found as far east as Florida, and it circled the desert mountains from Nevada to Texas no more than two thousand years ago. It is now confined, however, to the coastal mountains of the Pacific. Lewis and Clark reported it from Oregon, where one was observed perched on a stranded whale, and in this period it may still have strayed north to the Canadian border and east as far as Utah. The appearance of the white man doubtless hastened

From *Wildlife in America*. New York: The Viking Press, 1959.

its withdrawal, for it was last seen in the state of Washington about 1830, and in Oregon in 1913. Recently it has retired northward from Baja California, and is now present only in the Los Padres National Forest, in south-central California.

At the time of its disappearance from Washington, Richardson termed it common in California, and Coues, nearly half a centruy later, attested also to its abundance. In the first part of the nineteenth century, the condor's decline had probably been slow, although Indian tribes are said to have killed it as a burial fetish, a messenger from the living to the dead, and the Forty-niners apparently used its gigantic quills as containers for their gold-dust. But the next half-century witnessed the general settlement of California, and by 1900 the condor was fading fast.

Like most members of its family, this huge vulture is not particular about its food, provided that the food is carrion. When the great game animals roamed freely in the West, it must have fed abundantly, and the sheep ranches operated by the Spanish also provided ample nourishment. As the sheep were replaced by the less numerous cattle, however, the domestic source of food decreased, and the game animals had already declined. The condor's plight was compounded further by the reduction of livestock mortality effected by modern treatment of diseases, and by the sanitary practice of burning or burying dead animals. The carcasses of marine animals became less frequent along the coast, and the coast itself, more and more populated, was gradually forsaken by the shy birds. In the present century the condors have come to depend for food on small mammal remains and other meager fare; a few ranchers have cooperated with conservationists by leaving dead stock unburied, and trappers have been asked to skin fur animals in the fields, but the condors have dwindled to an estimated sixty in number, at which level they are presently maintaining themselves.

Food, however, is but one of the serious problems. The other great birds of the continent—the trumpeter swan and the whooping crane, the white pelican and the eagles—have all been seriously reduced, and, though the causes vary, one common to them all is conspicuousness, which draws man's malevolent attention. The truly enormous condor, with its wingspread of ten feet, is a tempting target for the idle rifle.

Furthermore, its optimum reproductive rate of one young every second year, per pair, is the lowest of all North American birds, barely offsetting the annual mortality. Conceivably, the condors could be helped by artificial rearing, since experiments with the very similar Andean condor of South America, in which the removal of the first egg for artificial incubation inspired the parents to produce another, and the removal of the second fledgling encouraged a nesting the following year, have shown that four young might be produced in the time required in the wild for one. In practice, eleven Andean condors were raised from a single pair over a period of six years. But efforts to assist the California condor in this manner have to date been resisted by the National Audubon Society and other groups, which apparently feel that the removal of eggs or a pair of adult condors from the remnant population might prove disastrous. The last nests are located almost entirely in the Sespe Wildlife Preserve of the Los Padres, to which even naturalists are forbidden access without special permit.

At least one authority believes that over two hundred condors still exist, many of them in the mountains outside the Preserve which stretch away northward toward San Francisco. The figure of sixty, presented originally in the Audubon Society's exhaustive monograph on the species, is more generally accepted. These forlorn survivors, scattered across the ridges of the coast range, seem barely suited to a world which has gone on without them. The birds have declined through long epochs of animal abundance dating back to the days of the giant bears and bisons, mammoths and mastodons, ground sloths, dire wolves, and saber-toothed tigers, and one may suppose that their last days began with the passing of this prehistoric fauna. The condor's ancient relative, *Teratornis*, with its wingspread of twelve feet, is long since gone, though it flew once in company of the condor; the condor, in turn, shares its mountains today with the much smaller turkey vulture, a bird better adapted to the lean pickings of civilized landscapes. Silent, swaying patiently on intent wings, the turkey vulture remorselessly usurps the condor's range.

The ivory-bill, whooping crane, and condor may all be senile species, better suited to other ages, other climates, and too old to change. The last two, at least, were eking out the million and more years of their existence long before the first red nomads spread south from Bering Strait, and their history with the white man has occupied no more than one fleeting autumn of a great old age. In consequence, their passing, when it comes, will bear a quite different import from that of the passenger pigeon, a species cut down in the prime of its existence. But it is also true that, had mankind not altered the shape and nature of the land, their withdrawal from the earth would have been a slow one, lived out gracefully over centuries to come. And so we must assume responsibility, even for these.

The ancient condor, bare-headed and ragged, is not a pretty bird at rest, but in flight, soaring stiff-winged on the air currents of the Los Padres, it achieves all the dignity of its years. To see it—and one should —one must usually climb into the mountains which surround its last preserve. The most simple route, perhaps, is via Piru Canyon, which lies not far north of the city of Los Angeles. In the canyon one follows a road which traces the contours of the western face, reaching its highest point high above and beyond the lake at San Felicitas Dam. Forsaking the car, one climbs a fire break up the spine of the mountain, gaining a brushy summit in an hour's journey. Though the summit commands a view of many miles in all directions, no sign of man is any longer visible. Great rolling brown ridges mount, one upon another, to the westward horizon, and to the north the shadowed canyon narrows, disappears. Jutting cliffs form the eastern face of Piru Canyon, falling steeply from the distant high plateaus, and to the south the mountains open out into the bright open lands of the Santa Clara Valley. The world is as it was long, long ago, its life breathing quietly beneath the sun.

A light wind stirs the chaparral, muting an insistent rock wren, and raptors of several sorts—buteos, eagles, small falcons, turkey vultures—are almost constantly in sight, casting neat shadows as they slide across a canyon face, curl upward, and sweep slowly back, yet seeming to drift always in a fixed direction. A raven flaps aimlessly across the scene, and white-throated swifts swoop past in violent arcs. As the sun rises, so, often, do the birds, forsaking the early morning hunt with the drying of the dew and circling upward into oblivions of blue too bright to contemplate. But the great condor, sulking on some remote ledge in the fastnesses of its preserve, fails to appear. One by one its small relatives vanish, black specks which trick the eye, then are no more. Midday comes, and the songbirds sit stone still in the brush. There is sun, heavy silence, a pervasive scent of parched vegetation, a lizard materialized on a rock.

The condor, appearing, does not break the silence. There are two. They crest the horizon to the westward, several miles away, but even at that distance, seen through binoculars, they can be only condors or eagles, for their posture is too bold, their flight too firm, for hawks or vultures.

They sail down across the dry ravines, across this high country where few men have stalked and none have stayed, coming on swiftly, unswerving. A mile away, they no longer can be eagles, and the heart stops. Sweeping forward, a scant hundred feet above the brush, they descend the grade of ridges, one bird four wing spreads behind the other, and the definitive broad band of white of the wing's shoulder glints powerfully now in the hard light. They pass the ridge summit at eye level, implacably, and in that moment the naked orange of the head is bright. Then, as swiftly as they had come, they glide away, broad-backed as they sink across the canyon, alone in a world of gray-green brush, brown mountain, ocher cliffs, blue sky. The birds do not circle at the canyon but forge straight on, dark silhouettes against the pale plateaus in the far distance, as if, striking eastward on some ancient errand, they meant to return across the continent.

THE

COURTSHIP

OF THE

ENGLISH SPARROW

A. C. Bent

A. C. Bent's Life Histories of North American Birds *is perhaps the most monumental modern work dealing with ornithology. Its fifteen volumes, published one by one between 1919 and 1953, are the lifework of a dedicated man. In part a compilation, they draw upon both printed works and upon private communications from hundreds of observers. No other account of the subject is fuller or more authoritative.*

T HE courtship of the English sparrow is more spectacular and stren- uous than elegant. It used to be a common experience to see a group of these dirty, soot-begrimed street gamins struggling and fighting al- most under our feet in our streets and gutters, oblivious to their sur- roundings. Charles W. Townsend (1909) thus describes the actions of the ardent male:

"With flattened back, head held up and tail down (up?), wings out from the body, the tips of the primaries touching or nearly touching the ground, he hops back and forth before the coy female as if on springs. Not one but several dance thus before a lady who barely deigns to look at them, and then only to peck in feigned disgust at the love- lorn suitors. These pecks are often far from love pats. At times she stands in the middle of a ring of males at whom she pecks viciously in turn as they fly by, all chirping excitedly at the top of their lungs. The casual observer might think the lady was being tormented by a crowd of un- gallant males, but the opposite is in reality the case for the lady is well pleased and is showing her pretended feminine contempt for the male sex, who on their part are trying their best to attract and charm her.

From *Life Histories of North American Blackbirds, Orioles, Tanagers, and Allies.* Smithsonian Institution, Washington, D.C., 1958.

At other times she plants her bill firmly on the head of the suitor, and pecks at him violently from time to time without letting go her hold. I have seen several such one-sided fights, for the oppressed rarely fights back, where the male seemed to be on the verge of exhaustion, lying panting on the ground, but on being disturbed both birds flew off apparently none the worse. About a year ago I watched two males in fierce encounter on a small grass plot in front of my house. One had the other by the bill and held him back downwards on the grass. They were both using their claws vigorously and bracing with their wings. Occasionally they would roll over, or go head over heels. Breaking apart they would fly up at each other like enraged barn-yard cocks. Although I stood within two feet of them, so intent were they that they did not notice me until I made an incautious movement and they fled to fight elsewhere.

A disgraceful fight between two female English Sparrows occurred in front of my house one April day. Catching each other by the bills they pulled and tugged and rolled over on the grass. When they broke away the fight was renewed a few inches above the ground in fighting cock style. Three males appeared, and watched the fight. One, evidently scandalized, endeavored to separate the Amazons by pecking at them, but they paid no attention to him and only after some time flew away, one chasing the other."

Claude T. Barnes has sent me the following interesting account of the mating of this strenuous species: "The incredible English sparrow is the best illustration of *furor amatorius*. The male suffers from satyriasis, the female from nymphomania. In the several years that we have observed them breeding, in two instances copulation took place fourteen times in succession, with a stopwatch record of five seconds for the act and five seconds for the interval. In each instance it was the soft *tee tee tee tee tee tee* of the female, sitting with outstretched wings that attracted our attention, and our count one was perhaps in reality two or three. Since other males within 20 feet took no interest, we believe that despite its reputation for promiscuity the domestic sparrow, after earlier imbroglios are settled, actually does mate with at least a short period of fidelity. Once mated, however, the female seems willing to continue the venery beyond the capacity of the male, for in every instance we have observed she continued her fluttering chant until he ceased to respond."

THE

HOUSE WREN'S

NOTION OF

ARCHITECTURE

Elliott Coues

The wrens are among the relatively few birds who seem to take a genuine and sympathetic interest in men. The bird watcher is likely to find them stalking him for a change, and of course one species (the house wren) gets its name from its preference for the neighborhood of human habitation. No bird is "cuter," but his morals are not of the best and it is said that certain respectable old ladies took down their wren boxes when it was discovered some years ago that house wrens are likely to change mates in the middle of the season. The fanciful may imagine that this giddiness of character explains why they build the messy nests complained of below. Bohemians are notoriously not neat housekeepers.

THE birds seem to be afflicted with an *insanabile construendi cacoëthes* (to borrow a simile from Juvenal), which impels them to keep on building after they have built enough for any practicable purpose. Their notion seems to be, that whatever place they select, be it large or small, must be completely filled with a lot of rubbish before they can feel comfortable about it. When they nest in a knot-hole, or any cavity of inconsiderable dimensions, the structure is a mass of sticks and other trash of reasonable bulk; but the case is otherwise when they get behind a loose weather-board, for instance, where there is room enough for a dozen nests; then they never know when to stop. I witnessed a curious illustration of their "insane" propensities in one case where a pair found their way through a knot-hole into one of those small sheds which stands in the back-yard, with a well-worn path leading to the house, showing

From *Birds of the Colorado Valley*. Washington: U. S. Government Printing Office, 1878.

its daily use. (It should be premised that a wren likes to get into its retreat through the smallest possible orifice; if the entrance be small enough, there cannot be too much room inside; and, when the hole is unnecessarily large, it is often closed up to the right size.) Having entered through a nice little hole, into a dark place, the birds evidently supposed it was all right inside, and began to build in a corner under the roof, where the joists came together. Though annoyed by frequent interruption, the indefatigable little creatures, with almost painful diligence, lugged in their sticks till they had made a pile that would fill a bushel, and I cannot say they would not have filled the whole shed had they not been compelled to desist; for they were voted a nuisance, and the hole was stopped up. The size of the sticks they carried in was enormous in comparison with their own stature; it seemed as if they could not lift them, much less drag the crooked pieces through such a narrow orifice. These coarse materials, it will be remembered, are only the foundation of a nest, as it were; their use in places where there is no real occasion for such a mass of trash is evidently the remaining trace of primitive habits. Inside this pile of material, there is a compact cup-like nest proper, of various fine soft vegetable and animal substances. The birds are extremely prolific, ordinarily laying six or eight eggs; and they will continue to deposit more if the nest be robbed—sometimes to the number of three or four full clutches. The eggs themselves are too well known to require description. As to the sites of the nest, it is almost impossible to speak in specific terms. The old hat Audubon drew has become historic; the sleeve or pocket of a coat hung up in an outhouse— a box in a chaise from which the birds were often ejected, and to which they as often returned—boxes, jars, or gourds set up for Martins—skull of an ox or horse—nest of another bird—are among the odd places the birds have been known to fancy. In the West, favorite locations for Parkman's Wren are a rift in an old stump or log, or the crevice between a strip of partially detached bark and the trunk of a tree—places which give full scope for its inveterate liking to fill up a cavity to an unlimited extent and then barricade the entrance.

ON WATCHING

AN

OVENBIRD'S NEST

Margaret Morse Nice

The loud, almost earsplitting song of the ovenbird is familiar to every inhabitant or commuter in rural New England but he is a skulker in the underbrush and few except bird watchers even connect the song with the inconspicuous singer. He gets his name, of course, from the oven-shaped nest which he constructs on the ground.

ONE Monday in July as I wandered through the woods, I was suddenly stopped by loud protestations. Looking about I saw an Ovenbird on a branch with his bill full of grubs while below on the ground beside the Dutch oven of a nest stood the mother bird, staring up at me absolutely motionless. As I walked towards her, she flew up, adding her objections to those of her mate. Inside the nest were two tiny infants, blind and naked. I retired behind a bush twenty feet away, effacing myself as much as possible, but the commotion kept on unabated. All the neighbors came to sympathize or look on—another pair of Ovenbirds, a Black and White Warbler, a Chestnut-sided Warbler, a Black-throated Green Warbler, a Phoebe, and a Chewink.

After awhile father with a moth in his bill descended to the ground, flew up again, scolded and scolded, raising his orange crown and jerking his tail; then he flew down again and ran towards the nest still objecting. His mate became frantic with alarm, on seeing such rash conduct; he reconsidered, flew up above the nest, ate his insect, and devoted himself to reproaches.

Seeing that the situation was hopeless, I moved forty feet away across the brook, seating myself beside a rock and behind a small hop hornbeam tree; with my glasses I could see the happenings at the nest. At once there was peace, and in two minutes mother went to the young to brood them. Soon Father came with a big spider and caterpillar; his mate slipped

From *The Watcher at the Nest*. New York: The Macmillan Company, 1939.

out and waited while he fed the babies, returning to them when he left. Mother brooded and brooded, then slipped quietly off and walked away. For a long time she stayed away, finally reappearing as stealthily as she had left, bringing with her a large meal. The most striking thing about the routine of an Ovenbird's household is its deliberateness—broodings three-quarters of an hour long, meals sometimes an hour and a half apart—all in marked contrast to the ways of most warblers, whose broodings are short, and who bring food every five to ten minutes.

It seemed as if life stood still for me while I devoted myself to this nest, as if I had endless leisure to look, to enjoy, to think, alone in this pleasant place in the woods. The stately clusters of evergreen wood fern, the sun-dappled water beeches and hemlocks, the tiny waterfall—to these I could give but fleeting glances, for always I had to concentrate on the rocks and brown leaves about the center of activities of mother Ovenbird. A baby tree bowed; I seized my glasses, for any movement in that region was fraught with possible meaning. But the alarm was false. It is curious how one small branch will bend with a breeze that nothing else feels. In these vigils I learned much of the ways of the wind.

Often there was no sound but the tumbling brook. Sometimes there were discordant notes. A soft pattering across the leaves, and suddenly a red squirrel vented his wrath at my presence by the strangest squeaks and squeals, more like those we expect from a toy than those from a real animal. A gray squirrel flirted his handsome tail in quirks and curlicues and then exploded into a snarling, jarring string of vituperations, extraordinary noises to proceed from such a soft and furry little beast.

The birds were pure delight. The Scarlet Tanager threw a wild, proud challenge to the woods in keeping with his gorgeous plumage. The solemn, continuous strain of the Red-eyed Vireo embodied the very spirit of serenity and content. Most beautiful of all was the song of the Hermit Thrush; when heard near by it has a note of courage, of triumph over the difficulties of life; at a distance it expresses ineffable sweetness and peace.

Mother Ovenbird had her notions; she did not mind me looking at her when she was by the nest, but if ever I caught sight of her on her way there, she froze at once, and would not be reassured until I had put down the offending glasses. It was curious that on Tuesday morning, of the five intervals between the meals she brought, four lasted exactly forty-eight minutes each.

That afternoon I noted:

"How pretty mother looks inside her rustic bower! She steps out and views the weather, which is threatening; then withdraws again to shelter."

Father was an almost negligible factor in the home life during the first half of the week, for he seldom came with food, sometimes absenting himself for an afternoon at a time, and he did not even proclaim his territory with the loud, insistent *teacher teacher teacher teacher*, as is the custom of his kind earlier in the season. On Wednesday I was shocked to see a Hermit Thrush chase him three times, when he had had one of his rare impulses to bring food to the young.

Although most of the authorities state that male and female Ovenbirds are identical in appearance, I was glad to find that I could distinguish my birds, not only by the brighter orange crown of the male, but particularly by the color of their backs, father's being more golden brown, and mother's having more of an olive cast.

Mr. Mousley "never once approached the nest" of the Ovenbirds he was studying; but by choosing my time I could steal across the brook each day and admire the progress of the babies without the parents being any the wiser. Although little Ovenbirds are fed so seldom in comparison with most other baby birds, their meals make up in size what they lack in number. I was repeatedly astonished at the enormous mouthfuls of spiders, caterpillars and moths that were brought to the young.

Thursday afternoon there came a change in the schedule. Mother gave up brooding and guarded instead, mounting a near-by bush and sitting quietly for fifteen minutes or so, her handsome black-streaked breast puffed out—a picture of motherly satisfaction. Father suddenly woke up to his responsibilities, and for the rest of the week outdid his mate in bringing food. Instead of meals appearing once every forty-two minutes, they now came at the rate of once in twenty minutes, the difference being largely due to father's zeal, since mother kept on the even tenor of her way, hardly hastening her return at all.

On Saturday morning the young had been fed at 10:35 and I was beginning to feel that it was full time they received further attention: "11:35. A bird flies down two yards from the nest. She feeds; then the male comes walking over the leaves. She steps aside for him while he feeds. Strangely enough a gaping, reproachful mouth waves at them as they leave, like a comic picture of a ferocious snake. Did both large portions go into one maw?"

On Sunday morning as I neared the familiar spot, I heard mother scolding very hard and fast. It was plain that something had happened; I went directly to the nest and found it empty. I had never dreamt that the precocious little creatures would leave so soon. How could they have deserted their warm, dry, cozy home for the wild wet woods?

Sadly I returned to my accustomed post; soon it was evident that one baby was near the nest in mother's charge, while the other was in a bed of ferns tended by the father. So I watched the family for some time, not realizing how far a little Ovenbird may travel at such a tender age; when I went to investigate, mother's babe was far away and well hidden. The fern bed was a baffling place to search, but all at once I heard a shrill *peep peep peep;* following the sound I discovered baby looking like a little light brown leaf, the fuzz of down outside his feathers giving him a very odd appearance. His tail had barely sprouted, and his flight feathers were not unsheathed; he could not possibly have flown, but his legs were strong and well developed.

I gently picked him up and he was not a bit afraid; in a few minutes he went to sleep in my hand. Father appeared with a caterpillar, but instead of going through the extravagant demonstration of alarm I expected, merely gave a loud *tchip* and vanished. Baby begin to preen himself, then said *peep* and again *peep.* A mosquito started to bite my hand, and I brought it in front of the little bird as a small tidbit; but he did not peck at it till it flew. Another alighted on his wing and sucked itself full, while I perceived a new bond of sympathy between birds and people.

Presently baby grew hungry and called more and more frequently, so I returned him to his twig and went back to my hornbeam. Louder and more persistent came his far-reaching cries, until I could not help thinking how easily an enemy might find him. It was time for me to go home; as I passed the fern bed I stepped on a dead twig that snapped—instantly there was silence. I do not suppose the little fellow had ever heard this sound before, but something in his inherited make-up told him it spelled danger. I was not able to visit this family again, but I hope they escaped the perils of youth, and journeyed South in safety.

By good fortune the next summer I again discovered an Ovenbird's nest in the Grey Rocks woods in mid-July. The mother flew quietly away from her three eggs, but the following day she behaved differently. While her mate scolded at my approach, she hurried off, then turned back, and ran about in a peculiar attitude with her back hunched, wings dragging, tail spread fanwise and body feathers puffed out. There was no simulation of injury, but she certainly did look strange and conspicuous and well suited to draw the attention of an unsophisticated enemy to herself.

The next morning (which happened to be Monday) two babies had hatched. I settled myself twenty feet away behind a little hemlock, thankful that neither parent had seen me look at their progeny. Before long there was a rustle in the great hemlock to the south and I became motionless while mosquitoes settled over my face. I felt like St. Macarius who, inadvertently crushing a gnat and thereby missing an opportunity of enduring mortification patiently, stationed himself for six months in the marshes of Scete. Fortunately for me, little mother took only three minutes to decide that I was not too alarming a neighbor. She flew to the ground and walked to the nest where she fed the babies and stepped in to brood. Then I began once more on my occupation of reducing the pests of the world.

Mother hovered her children for fifty-four minutes, then walked away, but to my surprise returned in ten minutes with another large meal—the other mother had never spent less than seventeen minutes away. This time she waited in the hemlock two minutes and the next time only one, and after that bothered no more about me. How my heart warmed to her for her good sense and devotion!

Her mate, unfortunately, felt differently about me. He came once that morning to bestow a morsel on his offspring, but upon spying me, he started to scold and for one half-hour he protested; then he departed, not to be seen again that day nor the next. In an attempt to calm his nerves, I moved farther away; but even that concession did not reassure him. Sometimes I hear his loud announcement of ownership and very occasionally the ecstatic flight song; but he refused to risk his precious skin by coming near me.

For three days the routine varied very little; long broodings; sometimes long, sometimes short, absences from the nest; ten large meals brought during eight hours the first day, eleven the next, and fourteen the next—and every bit of the work done by mother. Oddly enough there were two intervals of forty-eight minutes on this Tuesday, one of forty-six, and one of forty-four.

Wednesday father appeared with a contribution; but instead of feeding his babies all he did was to reprove me, raise his crest, flutter his wings, and give a curious, soft, three-syllable note to his mate. She, as if in a spirit of bravado to show him the unreasonableness of his fears, did a thing without precedent, for she dropped directly down to the nest from a branch above it. (Every other time she walked from quite a distance to the nest.) Still he remained stubbornly distrustful.

One day I had a philosophic thought; namely, that pleasure was given to three sets of beings by the occasional visits from the biting flies: First, it must seem like a banquet to the flies to discover me still and tasty in the woods. Next, there was a distinct feeling of achievement within me when I dispatched the creatures. And finally the carcass was a boon to the ant that carried it off for a dinner with her sisters. My philosphizings vanished, however, the next day when I was attacked by an army of deer flies. I used to think the etymology of Beelzebub—"king of the flies"—was a prophetic reference to the noxious germs given us by our satellite the housefly, but now I knew better; it was these little demons that were meant.

This year as last, Thursday afternoon showed a change in the home life; but this time the male had no part in it. First, mother gave up brooding; then, instead of walking directly away when leaving the nest as heretofore, she browsed around for a few minutes in front of the nest, finding small insects for herself; twice she flew away instead of leaving on foot; and finally she fed her three children twice as often as before.

The first three and one-half days she had brought meals once in forty minutes on an average; this afternoon she presented them once every nineteen minutes. I looked forward eagerly to what the next day would bring forth, in further variations in her behavior and a possible reform on the part of her mate.

As I watched little mother, I longed to know more of her life. I wished I could have seen the courtship, could have viewed the construction of the quaint little home, and then could have followed the fortunes of the young family after their first venture into the world, and somehow could have known how they found their way on the incredible journeys of South America and back to these Massachusetts woods. A great admiration for this quiet little bird arose in me, for her self-sufficiency, the simplicity of her life unencumbered by the possessions that overwhelm us human beings. Here she was her own architect, her own provider, bringing up her babies independently of doctors, nurses, books, and even her husband, facing unaided the elements and prowling enemies.

Each morning I left a blessing with the brave little bird, and each morning was happy to find all well. But Friday as I walked through the woods, I noticed that big mushrooms that had been standing for several days were now lying low, gnawed by some animal. A sense of foreboding caused me to go straight to the nest as soon as I reached my hemlock; the home was empty and beside it lay five feathers from little mother's wing. I trust the gallant bird had escaped with her life.

THE

HARRIS'S SPARROW'S

EGGS

George Miksch Sutton

To the layman, a sparrow is simply a sparrow. Actually there are more than fifty kinds in the eastern half of the United States and many others found only in the West. Since many species look much alike they are the despair of the tyro and the pride of the expert.

I F you are not an ornithologist you probably never have heard of a Harris's Sparrow. And if you have never heard of a Harris's Sparrow you cannot be expected to know that it took us learned scientists almost a hundred years to find its eggs; that the long search ended in two weeks of warfare between the Americans and the Canadians; and that the final, decisive battle of this conflict was won by the Americans.

The Harris's Sparrow is a handsome member of the finch tribe. It is considerably larger than an English Sparrow. It has a pink bill; black crown, face, and throat; streaked back and sides; and white underparts. It inhabits the middle part of North America, nesting in the stunted spruce woods at the edge of the Barren Grounds, migrating across south central Canada and our midwestern States, and wintering in Kansas, Oklahoma, and Texas. It was discovered, in 1837, by a young naturalist named Thomas Nuttall, who described it three years later, naming it *Fringilla querula*, the Mourning Finch. A few years later the famous ornithologist-artist, John James Audubon, rediscovered the bird, bestowing upon it, in honor of his excellent and constant friend Edward Harris, Esq., the common name it now bears. Ornithologists since the time of Nuttall, Audubon, and Maximilian, Prince of Wied, have been observing it, tracing its routes of migration northward, hoping to find its summer home. Its breeding grounds were discovered in 1900, or thereabouts; but even so recently as [1931] its eggs were yet unfound and undescribed.

From *Birds in the Wilderness*. New York: Macmillan Company, 1936.

On June 16, in [that year], a few minutes before nine o'clock in the morning, the Harris's Sparrow's eggs were discovered. They were in no way extraordinary in appearance. In size, shape, and color they were much like the eggs of several closely related Fringilline species. They were very light greenish-blue, heavily blotched with brown. A complete description of them appeared in our leading ornithological journals. . . . But the story of finding these eggs—of the battle waged at the edge of the tundra between the Americans and the Canadians—this story has never been published. I purpose to tell this story here, although I have no desire to disturb the peace that has so long existed along our northern boundary line.

The story begins a good many years ago. As a boy of fifteen I dreamed fond dreams of discovering the Harris's Sparrow's eggs. As I read in my bird books such statements as "the eggs of this sparrow are unknown," I squirmed, felt strange stirrings inside me, and pondered. Where would the nest of such a sparrow be—on the ground, under a thick bush, in a tree? Would it be hidden away in some shadowy place, or would it be at the tip of some high, cone-bearing bough? And how many eggs would be in it?

In the early fall of 1930, while returning from my year with the Eskimos of Southampton Island, I had occasion to wait some days at Churchill, Manitoba, for the train that would carry me south. There at Churchill, on the west coast of Hudson Bay, I for the first time encountered the Harris's Sparrow on its breeding ground. I did not see much of it, to be sure, for I had little opportunity to walk through the country which it preferred to frequent. But I could see that it had nested thereabouts, and the idea of finding the unfound eggs took fresh hold upon me.

I talked the matter over with my good friend JB.[1] Characteristically enthusiastic over the prospect of such a quest he decided to organize an expedition to Churchill the following Spring. "We must be there early," I advised. "The nest has been found, remember, and the young birds have been described; so we must be there early enough to get the eggs!"

We got there early enough, all right. Alighting from our comfortable Pullman on that evening of May 24, 1931, we found ourselves standing in snow two feet deep. A strong wind from the Bay struck us full in the face. The drifts along the ridge just to the north of us were, we learned, over twenty feet deep. Springtime indeed! The Churchill River was frozen shut miles back from the mouth. The Bay was a vast field of ice chunks that rose and sank with the tides. Husky dogs were pulling sledges to an encampment on the opposite side of the River. Our thin, short

[1] John Bonner Semple

topcoats and shining oxfords were ridiculous in this Arctic land. But we were there!

There were four of us: our good friend J.B., he of the eagle's eye and unquenchable enthusiasm; Sewall Pettingill, at that time my fellow graduate student at Cornell, and an expert photographer; Bert Lloyd, an ornithologist who had collected birds extensively and who knew the Churchill region from personal experience; and myself.

We were eager as fox terriers. Each of us dreamed of discovering those eggs. We didn't give voice to our inner feelings in the matter, but there was an ardent glitter in every eye. True, the River was covered with ice four feet thick. True, the Harris's Sparrow had not yet returned from the south. But Spring would come. The tamaracks would turn green with the sinking away of the snow, the ptarmigan would doff their winter garb, and the tundra lakes would thaw. And somewhere out in those silent, all but colorless, half-buried spruce woods there would be a Harris's Sparrow's nest. And in that nest there would be eggs. And one of us, one of us four men, would find them!

We piled our luggage on a tractor-truck, picked our way across the winter-bound construction camp to some lighted windows, and interviewed the Department of Railways and Canals. We were, we explained, strangers in a strange land. We had come to study birds. We had the necessary permits from the government. We hoped to be able to establish camp somewhere near the mouth of the River. We would not be in anybody's way, we promised, nor cause any disturbance.

The Department of Railways and Canals contemplated us a full moment, cleared his throat with a bark, and informed us that he would find us beds for the night; that he would get a tent for us on the morrow, that we could take our meals with the sixteen hundred workmen if we wanted to, but that we'd have to be at the mess hall on time and clear out when we were through. Thanking the Department for his courtesies and creeping off like thieves caught in the act we went to bed. I am not sure that my three confreres felt as I did. As for me, I felt myself wholly unwanted at Churchill—decidedly a *persona non grata*. But what about those Harris's Sparrow's eggs? Could they be found without me?

And next morning we felt better. We were at breakfast at the appointed hour—six o'clock. The food was good and there was plenty of it. We were hungry. A long day was ahead of us. We tried a little conversation between the first mouthfuls, but gave that up. Our "pleases" and "thank yous" drew frowns. We were not there to talk. We were there to stoke our furnaces. And stoke we did. The flapjacks were grand, and easy to manage. We got them down almost without chewing or swallowing. Prunes took more time because the pits had to be discarded somehow. And bacon rinds slowed us up. But in the first three minutes we learned from our hosts how to spread butter on a slice of bread and pour canned milk with the other. In the next three minutes we learned to stuff cookies and oranges into our pockets while gulping coffee. And at the end of the next three minutes we were rising, wiping our mouths with our sleeves, and "clearing out." Breakfast that morning must surely have taken us all of nine minutes. Our hosts finished long before we did. Though I am breaking the strict continuity of my story in telling you this, we learned in time to eat more rapidly.

Churchill was an incredible place. It was not a town, for there were only one or two dwellings and one or two women. It was an enterprise. Huge dredges were gouging away the river bottom. A vast cement grain elevator was rising. Under the snow about us lay a network of narrow-gauge tracks over which "dinkey engines" were soon to pull cars filled with gravel, workmen, and water. On the higher ground between the River and the Bay stood row upon row of barracks, a little hospital, some mission buildings, one or two banks, a motion picture palace of sorts, the headquarters of the Royal Canadian Mounted Police, and a wireless station. Churchill, an ocean port in the making!

We got our big tent and J.B.'s little silk tent up that day, built ourselves a worktable, unpacked our equipment, and unrolled our sleeping bags. And Bert Lloyd and I, eager to make certain that the sparrows were not ahead of us, walked six miles upriver to the spruce woods, wallowed for hours through slushy drifts, dark-brown muskeg streams, and waist-deep, ice-filmed pools. The sparrows had not come. We saw some Snow Buntings and Lapland Longspurs, a few Pipits and Horned Larks, and three Pintail Ducks. We got back just in time for dinner—dead tired. At dinner we stoked again.

On May 27, the Harris's Sparrow arrived from the south. We had beaten him by three days. We thought he looked a bit disconsolate, but the notes of his whistled song reassured us that Spring was on its way.

We continued to eat at the mess hall, but we usually missed the noon meal. Walking six miles in order to begin our day's work took time and energy. We were glad when the gravel trains began running. We became acquainted with the engineers and firemen and sometimes had a chance to bum a ride. By the time we got back from our day afield we were half-starved. Our evening meal, large as it invariably was, invariably made us sleepy. Existence was simple. We rose, dressed, stoked, walked or rode six miles to the spruce woods, tramped the tundra, woodlands and muskeg for hours, walked or rode six miles back from the spruce woods, stoked, undressed, and went to bed. Here and there during this busy program of nest-hunting we found time to prepare birdskins, write notes, make drawings, and take photographs.

Whenever we four men conversed we usually conversed about the Harris's Sparrow, though there were other interesting birds in the region. Bert Lloyd, as we learned, had once found what he thought was a Harris's

Sparrow's nest. This nest had been under a little bush. Yes, it had been the right size for a Harris's Sparrow. No, it hadn't been completely hidden by leaves and moss. Yes, it had been made of grass. But Bert had had no chance to identify the parent birds. So, in the last analysis, we knew next to nothing about a Harris's Sparrow's nest. We were prepared for anything. The fact that the one or two nests on record had been described thus and so didn't help us much. At night I was wont to say to my companions: "We must look everywhere—on the ground, under bushes, in trees, in holes in the ground—everywhere. And we must watch the birds constantly. The easiest way to find some nests is to watch a bird that has a wisp of grass, or a feather, or a twig in its bill."

We came to an agreement concerning our procedure in the event a nest was found. If a full set of eggs were discovered, these were to be collected immediately, lest in our absence from the nest they be destroyed by some Whiskey Jack, weasel, or other predatory creature. We wanted photographs of the first nest if possible, to be sure, but the important thing was to collect and preserve those eggs so that an adequate description of them might be published. By the end of our first week we were somewhat fagged by our exertions, puzzled by our failure to find what we felt to be mated pairs, annoyed at our inability to distinguish male and female birds in the field (their coloration was almost precisely the same), and more fervently, desperately, even frantically eager than ever. Personal pride was at stake by this time. There were reputations to uphold. J.B., the oldest of our party, was also the sharpest eyed—an exceedingly keen observer with an enviable record as a rifle, shotgun and revolver shot. Sewall Pettingill was a youngster, a grand chap too, who felt that his name would flash in electric lights across the land if only he could find that nest. Bert Lloyd had been in the Churchill region before. He had become familiar with the summertime ways of the Harris's Sparrow, and what was more, thought he had already seen a nest. As for me, I was half mad, half downright crazy. I'd dream, quite literally dream at night, about sparrows as big as cows, with huge black eyes and long white lashes. That sort of thing. The less we say about it the better.

And then came the Canadians! One week after our arrival, almost to the minute, on the very train that had brought us, came four stalwart Canadians from the Province of Alberta—four men quite as capable and quite as eager as ourselves, each one of them just as determined as each one of us to be the first to find the Harris's Sparrow's eggs.

We were in bed when the Canadians came. In fact, we were asleep, dreaming about sparrows with long eyelashes. All at once we heard a booming voice outside our tent. The Canadians were making a call. We did out best at wakening, half sat up, rubbed our eyes, and tried to talk. No, we hadn't found a Harris's Sparrow's nest. Oh yes, there were lots of Harris's Sparrows about, dozens of them, but we weren't even sure

these birds were mated yet. I fail to remember whether we rose to light
a candle or not. I think we didn't. We weren't very hospitable, I fear.
And J.B., our indomitable leader, was nettled. "These Canadians!" he
was saying as soon as they left. "What do they mean by trying to spoil
our game? We came up here to do this thing ourselves and they haven't
a right to bust in this way!" There was quite a bit of muttering from the
little tent in which J.B. slept. We all felt a good deal the same way, I
guess, but Sewall, Bert and I didn't mutter. We lay in our sleeping bags
with eyes wide open, wondering how we could beat these unexpected,
unwelcome newcomers. If only they'd play fair and go to bed and not
begin their search until the morrow!

Next morning there was a new light in our eyes. We four men were
no longer pitted against each other. We were pitted against a new, a
formidable, a mighty foe—the Canadians.

We three younger men, generous creatures that we were, had decided
amongst ourselves that if we possibly *could* do so we'd let J.B. find the
first nest. There is nothing written down in black and white to prove this,
but I am telling the truth. J.B. had been a good scout. Finding the nest
would be a sort of peak in his ornithological career. We younger men
could do something else some time that would win us renown. In our
inner hearts we hoped that Fate would somehow force us to find that first
nest, but our tongues spoke phrases that were as unselfish and altruistic
as any ever spoken.

The coming of the Canadians changed all this. The contest was a free-
for-all now. And come what may, America must win. We had been the
first on the ground. We had made the greater sacrifice in getting there.
Feeling ran high.

The egg-hunting tactics of the Canadians were different from ours.
Armed with what must have been dishpans, sections of stove-pipe, tin
trays and canes they marched through the spruces making the wildest sort
of noise. Their purpose was to frighten the mother sparrows from the
nests. We laughed as we listened, but scowled as we laughed. This was
a silly, childish procedure—a ridiculous method of bird study—but what
if it worked! After all, *we* had not found a nest. Our irreproachable
methods had thus far failed. We went on with our quiet, determined,
methodical searching, but the sound of the enemy's drums made us nervous. Perhaps at this very moment they are finding the nest, we would
think. Perhaps a bird is flitting out from under their feet—and in her
flitting is giving away the century-old secret! Each and every evening we
talked about our experiences of the day, and wondered if the enemy had
won. We did not go to see them. They did not come to see us. We had no
friendly symposiums of the habits of Harris's Sparrows. We were on
speaking terms, yes; but we were uncomfortable whenever we met each
other. Occasionally, out on the tundra, we ran into them face to face.

At such times we conversed about the weather (and there is weather to talk about at Churchill); about the interesting birds we had been seeing; and about the methods of bird-skinning. Sooner or later, of course, the matter of *the nest* was sure to come up, and at this juncture we blushed and fidgeted and looked afar off and did our doomed-to-failure best to appear uninterested and casual. The enemy continued to tell us that they had not found the nest. We wondered if they were telling us the truth. They may have had similar doubts concerning us.

The enemy was encamped in a freight car that stood on a siding at the edge of the construction camp. Here they slept and ate and prepared their specimens. We passed the place at least twice a day, sometimes more frequently. But we never called. And we rarely saw them.

The precious days passed. By June 10, I began to be genuinely and deeply worried. Unless we found the nest before the summer waned there would be young birds, not eggs. We had heard the male birds singing day after day. We felt that by this time they must surely have chosen their nesting-territories. But we had found no sign of a nest.

On the evening of June 15, Sewall (by this time we were calling the lad "Sewall the Beautiful" and "Sewall the Cruel") drew me aside to tell me that he had seen a Harris's Sparrow with grass in its bill; that he had watched the bird for hours; and that he had found a nest! Sewall was excited, to say the least. He was fairly shaking. And when I looked upon him and listened to his words a pang shot me through. What right had Sewall, unlettered, callow, inordinately smug youth that he was, to find the nest! "Do you think we'd better say anything about it to the others?" he was asking in a wobbly whisper. "The nest is down under the moss, at the end of a sort of burrow. I watched the bird for a long time, and followed it on hands and knees—but I saw it with grass in its bill only once."

That nest (poor, beautiful, downcast Sewall!) proved to be the nest of a mouse.

And then came the morning of June 16. That morning a strange, in fact very strange, thing happened—something in the nature of an omen. I had walked to a favorite part of the section of woodland I had been studying most closely. I was watching a pair of Harris's Sparrows, wondering as usual which was the male and which the female, when all at once one of the birds flew across a clearing to an old box that had been tossed aside by the men who had built the railroad through the woods. As the bird sat on the box it began to sing. I watched it with my binocular and chanced to note that there were large black letters on the box. Looking at the letters one by one I found to my complete amazement that the word HARRIS was printed there. It was a box in which bacon or ham had been shipped from the Harris Abbatoir, a Canadian meatpacking firm.

S. AND H. KIMBALL

Canada Geese in flight

[2] Great Horned Owl (immature)

[3] Great Horned Owl

[4a] Male Rubythroated Hummingbird

] Rubythroat hovering

[4c] In backward flight

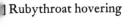

sapsucker holes in birch tree

[5] Sanderlings in flight showing characteristic back and wing markings

[6] Sanderlings

Bald Eagle, by Mark Catesby, c. 1679–1749
(*see also* Audubon, Wilson, and Fuertes versions)

Morinellus marinus   Frutex 3.?

[8] Turnstone, or Sea Dottrel, by Mark Catesby
(See Catesby, "The Bald Eagle"; "The Hooping Crane"; "The Turnstone or Sea Dottrel")

White-billed woodpecker, by Mark Catesby (See Catesby, "Carpenteros")

[10] Turkey Buzzard, by Mark Catesby
(See George Miksch Sutton, "An Adventure with a Turkey Vulture")

:regrine or Duck Hawk

[12] Red-tailed Hawk

lifornia Condor

[14] House Wren

[15] Ovenbird

[16] Towhee (Chewink)

Wild Turkey

Canada Geese

[19] Whooping Cranes

Whiteheaded or Bald Eagle, by John James Audubon, c. 1785–1851
Catesby, Wilson, and Fuertes versions)

[21] Wild Turkey, by John James Audubon (cf. Thomas Morton, "Turkies")

Snowy Heron, or White Egret, by John James Audubon
(Helen G. Cruickshank "Snowy Egrets at East River Rookery")

[23] Passenger Pigeons, by John James Audubon (cf. Audubon, "The Passenger Pigeon")

I fairly gasped when I realized that a fine male Harris's Sparrow was perching there in front of me on a box that was labeled HARRIS. I rose with the determination of a Perseus or a Columbus and marched through the woods. I cannot very scientifically explain my feelings, but I knew that a sign had been given.

At a little before nine o'clock, while marching across an all but impassable bog, I frightened from a sphagnum island underfoot a slim, dark-backed bird. It made no outcry, but from the explosive flutter of its wings I knew it had left a nest. I searched a moment, parting with my hand the tough, slender twigs of flowering Labrador tea. And there was the nest—with four eggs that in the cool shadow had a dark appearance. The mother bird, by this time was chirping in alarm. I looked at her briefly with my glass. A Harris's Sparrow! I raised the gun, took careful aim, and fired. Marking the nest, I ran to pick her up. Upon my return, the male appeared. I shot him also, for I knew the record would not be complete unless I shot both parent birds. To say that I was happy is to describe my feelings all too tamely. I was beside myself. Shooting those important specimens had taken control. I had been so excited I had hardly been able to hold the gun properly. As I knelt to examine the nest a thrill the like of which I had before never felt passed through me. And I talked aloud! "Here!" I said. "Here in this beautiful place!" At my fingertips lay treasures that were beyond price. Mine was man's first glimpse of the eggs of the Harris's Sparrow, in the lovely bird's wilderness home.

Then I began to wonder how many other nests had been found that morning. The enemy! My comrades! Had they, too, been favored by Heaven with a sign? I had a wild desire to gather everybody about me— friend and foe alike—so that we might work together, compare notes, make plans, take photographs. I looked at my watch. Perhaps some Canadian had found a nest at eight o'clock! Perhaps several nests had been found before nine o'clock that morning! I fired my shotgun loudly as I could (have you ever tried this?) three times, and was a little surprised, as the echoes died, that no familiar form of friend nor unfamiliar form of foe materialized. I fired again. There was no answer.

So, happy in a way that was quite new to me, but dubious as to the priority of my achievement, I hippity-hopped across the bogs. I wasn't much of an ornithologist those next few hours. I was too gay for Ornithology. At a little before noon I chanced to see Bert Lloyd ahead of me. I started to call him—then decided not to. A wild fear seized me. Perhaps all this happiness of the last three hours was unwarranted. Perhaps all this had been some weird hallucination. I knelt on the moss, opened my collecting creel, got out those two specimens I had shot at the nest, and looked at them closely. Yes, they were Harris's Sparrows, there could not be the slightest doubt of that. They were not White-crowned Sparrows, nor Fox Sparrows, nor Tree Sparrows. No, there was nothing wrong with me this time.

"Bert!" I shouted, trying to keep my voice normal. And Bert turned and came. "What luck?" I asked. And Bert gave me the usual report—plenty of birds, mated pairs too, but no nest. Queer that he couldn't see how boiling over I was with excitement.

So I told him. And Bert's response was the response of a good friend, a good sport, a good ornithologist. His words were cordial and the exultant delight that shone from his face was genuine. I showed him the specimens. And from that time until the reunion of our party that evening, two of us wondered how many other nests had been found that day.

To be perfectly honest, I was hoping that nobody else had found a nest. In a vague sort of way I wanted my good friend J.B. to have the thrill of it all—but he had been successful in so many ways that I felt this purely ornithological triumph might quite justly be mine. And Sewall —well, if Sewall had found a nest before nine o'clock that morning he was just too lucky for tolerance. But the Canadians!

Bert and I got back about six o'clock. We were a little late at the mess hall. The workmen frowned as we came in, for they knew the cook would be angry, and we were wet and dirty. But we didn't care. Let them frown. Let them despise us. We were above being despised. J.B. and Sewall were busy stoking—almost too busy to notice us. We sat down. When there was a clatter of departing workmen I leaned toward J.B. and said, "Did you find the nest today?" J.B. said he hadn't. "I found one— with four eggs in it," I rejoined. And the stoking stopped.

I have never, neither before nor since, seen J.B. look as he looked at precisely that moment. He may have been wishing that he had found the nest. He may have been as jealous as a successful, vigorous, fair-minded, generous sportsman can at times be. He may quite possibly have hated me for my insolence. But I think he was happy. For I know he felt, as I did, that beating dishpans in the woods was no way to study birds; that our Harris's Sparrow was a bird of rare discernment; that in this hectic battle of the past sixteen days it was only right that the Americans should win. For they had.

Part

Three

BIRDS

OF A

FEATHER

THE SOCIAL

BIRDS

William Bartram

All men are alike, said Montaigne, or we would not know that they were men; all men are different, or we could not tell them one from another. The thing which makes them different is what we call "personality" and no other species has so much of it as man has. Individual men have, in other words, more individuality; individual members of every other species are more like one another. Nonconformity (of which we now hear so much) is a conspicuous trait of the human being.

Though ornithologists have recently come to realize that even birds sometimes exhibit more individual personality than used to be supposed and that there are nonconformists sometimes found among them, the fact remains that when we speak of the "character" of this bird or that, we usually mean the character of the species to which it belongs. And how different those characters are! The rigidly scientific object to our saying that eagles have dignity, that wrens are impudent, or that peacocks are vain, but we will go on saying it nevertheless. And the scientist himself will stress the fact that species are sometimes so different from one another that it is only by anatomical and other analyses that we are able to say of, for instance, the penguin and the chimney swift that both are birds.

There are approximately 8500 different kinds now living and about 900 known only as fossils. The most obvious of the extremes to which two species may go, and yet be unquestionably members of the same great order, is size. The smallest, extinct or living, is the Cuban bee-hummer which is actually not much larger than a bumblebee. It measures only two and a quarter inches from the tip of its beak to the tip of its tail and weighs less than two grams. The largest, which became extinct probably only a few hundred years ago, was the New Zealand Moa, a flightless, ostrichlike creature of which the largest stood some twelve feet high.

The present section of this volume deals with a few outstanding

From *The Travels of William Bartram*. Philadelphia: James & Johnson, 1791.

personalities among American birds. It can appropriately begin with some remarks by William Bartram, the late eighteenth-century American naturalist whom we have met before.

Birds are in general social and benevolent creatures; intelligent, ingenious, volatile, active beings; and this order of animal creation consists of various nations, bands, or tribes, as may be observed from their different structure, manners, and languages, or voice; each nation, though subdivided into many different tribes, retaining its general form or structure, a similarity of customs, and a sort of dialect or language, particular to that nation or genus from which those tribes seem to have descended or separated. What I mean by a language in birds, is the common notes or speech, that they use when employed in feeding themselves and their young, calling on one another, as well as their menaces against their enemy; for their songs seem to be musical compositions, performed only by the males, about the time of incubation, in part to divert and amuse the female, entertaining her with melody, etc. This harmony, with the tender solicitude of the male, alleviates the toils, cares and distresses of the female, consoles her in solitary retirement whilst sitting, and animates her with affection and attachment to himself in preference to any other. The volatility of their species, and operation of their passions and affections, are particularly conspicuous in the different tribes of the thrush, famous for song. On a sweet May morning we see the red thrushes (*turdus rufus*) perched on an elevated sprig of the snowy Hawthorn, sweet flowering Crab, or other hedge shrub, exerting their accomplishments in song, striving by varying and elevating their voices to excel each other; we observe a very agreeable variation, not only in tone but in modulation; the voice of one is shrill, of another lively and elevated, of others sonorous and quivering. The mock-bird (*turdus polyglottos*) who excels, distinguishes himself in a variety of action as well as air; from a turret he bounds aloft with the celerity of an arrow, as it were to recover or recall his very soul, expired in the last elevated strain. The high forests are filled with the symphony of the song of the wood thrush (*turdus minor*).

Both sexes of some tribes of birds sing equally finely; and it is remarkable, that these reciprocally assist in their domestic cares, as building their nests and sitting on their eggs, feeding and defending their young brood, etc. The oriolus (*icterus, Cat.*) is an instance of this case; and the female of the *icterus minor* is a bird of more splendid and gay dress than the male bird. Some tribes of birds will relieve and rear up the young and helpless, of their own and other tribes, when abandoned. Animal substance seems to be the first food of all birds, even the granivorous tribes.

SIGHT

AND SOUND

IN BIRDS

Montague Chamberlain

Here from one of the older standard manuals is a description of some of the general characteristics of birds.

COMPARING animals with each other, we soon perceive that *smell*, in general, is much more acute among the quadrupeds than the birds. Even the pretended scent of the Vulture is imaginary, as he does not perceive the tainted carrion, on which he feeds, through a wicker basket, though its odor is as potent as in the open air. This choice also of decaying flesh is probably regulated by his necessities and the deficiency of his muscular powers to attack a living, or even tear in pieces a recent, prey. The structure of the olfactory organ in birds is obviously inferior to that of quadrupeds; the external nostrils are wanting, and those odors which might excite sensation have access only to the duct leading from the palate; and even in those, where the organ is disclosed, the nerves, which take their origin from it, are far from being so numerous, so large, or so expanded as in the quadrupeds. We may therefore regard *touch* in man, *smell* in the quadruped, and *sight* in birds, as respectively the three most perfect senses which exercise a general influence on the character.

After sight, the most perfect of the senses in birds appears to be *hearing*, which is even superior to that of the quadrupeds, and scarcely exceeded in the human species. We perceive with what facility they retain and repeat tones, successions of notes, and even words; we delight to listen to their unwearied songs, to the incessant warbling of their tuneful affection. Their ear and throat are more ductile and powerful than in other animals, and their voice more capacious and generally agreeable. A Crow, which is scarcely more than the thousandth part the size of an ox, may be heard as far, or farther; the Nightingale can fill a wider space

From *A Popular Handbook of the Ornithology of the U.S. and Canada, based on Nuttall's Manual*. Little, Brown and Co., 1891.

with its music than the human voice. This prodigious extent and power of sound depend entirely on the structure of their organs; but the support and continuance of their song result solely from their internal emotions.

The windpipe is wider and stronger in birds than in any other class of animals, and usually terminates below in a large cavity that augments the sound. The lungs too have greater extent, and communicate with internal cavities which are capable of being expanded with air, and, besides lightening the body, give additional strength to the voice. Indeed, the formation of the thorax, the lungs, and all the organs connected with these, seems expressly calculated to give force and duration to their utterance.

Another circumstance, showing the great power of voice in birds, is the distance at which they are audible in the higher regions of the atmosphere. An Eagle may rise at least to the height of seventeen thousand feet, for it is there just visible. Flocks of Storks and Geese may mount still higher, since, notwithstanding the space they occupy, they soar almost out of sight; their cry will therefore be heard from an altitude of more than three miles, and is at least four times as powerful as the voice of men and quadrupeds.

THE GOBBLER

IN

HISTORY

Glover M. Allen

What is our national bird? Officially, of course, it is the bald eagle. But do we not think more often of the turkey—as the founding fathers certainly did? It is odd that a name which suggests the Near East should be applied to a fowl which is native only to the Americas and so exclusively New World in its associations. Though the name has nothing to do with the Ottoman Empire, it has had, nevertheless, a curious history. First applied to a kind of African guinea fowl it was transferred to the American game bird soon after the discovery of the western continent. The etymology is somewhat dubious but the common name may have referred to the turquoiselike iridescence of the neck feathers.

Though once very abundant, the species was disappearing from its native woods until they were restocked with cage-grown specimens, many of which have now gone wild and are fairly well established again.

T HE Turkey is the only bird of the New World (except the Muscovy Duck) that has been successfully added to the category of domesticated animals. It first appears in print in the account of the West Indies and Mexico published in 1527 by Oviedo, a Spaniard, who spent several years in these newly discovered countries. The Mexican Turkey had already been domesticated by the natives of that part of America, and it was from them that the Spaniards obtained it and brought it to Europe, where it was established as early at least as 1530. It seems not to have been known in England much before 1541. The name was also applied mistakenly sometimes to the Guinea Fowl. The earliest published figures of the Turkey were those by Belonius and by Gesner, both, through a coincidence, in the same year, 1555. From Europe the bird was reintroduced into America by our Pilgrim forefathers, who likewise

From *Birds and Their Attributes*. London: George G. Harrap.

found a related race wild here in New England in the earlier days. Morton, in his "New English Canaan," written in 1637, tells of Turkeys "which divers times in great flocks have sallied by our doores; and then a gunne being commonly in a redinesse, salutes them with such a courtesie, as makes them take a turne in the cooke roome." There is some reason to suppose that the New England Turkeys were sometimes kept tame here, but they were not truly domesticated. The Mexican bird differs from ours in having whitish-tipped feathers, and this distinguishing character the domestic race persistently retains. The Wild Turkey in New England was not wholly exterminated until about the middle of the last century when a few still remained on Mt. Tom in western Massachusetts and ranged the wild country of that region. Gradually the flocks became broken up and the birds ceased to breed. A few old gobblers remained here and there and were either finally hunted down and killed or, if by reason of their great wariness they escaped being shot, they eventually disappeared from other causes. The late William Brewster relates how a single old and wary Turkey cock lived in the Concord region about 125 years ago, the last of its race in these parts. Though many hunters sought its life, it was never shot, but finally succumbed to other enemies or died of old age. In England Turkeys were early dedicated to the Christmas feast. It was natural therefore that our forefathers having the wild Turkey here at their doors, regarded it as a proper bird for their Thanksgiving feasts. To this day the Vermont- or Rhode Island-bred Turkey is famed for its excellent flesh. It will not occur to many, however, that the English Sparrow has any connection with the present scarcity and high cost of our Thanksgiving dinner. This is nevertheless the case, and is a point of great interest in its bearing on the interrelations of diverse species. For it seems that young Turkeys are highly susceptible to a disease of the intestine called "blackhead," which is due to the activity of a microscopic amoeba-like creature belonging to the same group of one-celled beings as many other disease-organisms—the Protozoa—and to that group of Protozoa provided with a whip-like appendage, by the lashing of which it is able to move about. This minute organism passes one of its stages in damp ground, and is carried and spread by the sparrow, which, however, is immune from its attack. The sparrows in visiting the barnyards for grain infect the Turkeys' surroundings, so that in some localities the raising of these birds for the table has had to be almost completely abandoned. In this boomerang fashion do we reap our reward for upsetting Nature's balance by bringing in new and untried elements among creatures whose systems have not become accustomed to cope with them.

TURKIES

Thomas Morton

Most of the early American colonists were little interested in birds beyond their edibility. Thomas Morton was no exception in this respect, but he was an exception in many others. He was so far from being a puritan that he called the settlement of which he became the head Merrymount, set up a maypole there, and thus scandalized his neighbors in Plymouth Colony. Hawthorne immortalized him in Twice Told Tales but he seems, unfortunately, to have been in fact a rather scurrilous character whose reputation was dubious even before he left England. In the New World he violated the law by supplying firearms to the Indians and he was at one time sentenced to banishment. His book, New English Canaan, published in 1637, was denounced by a rival author as "full of lies and slanders, and full fraught with profane calumnies." However, he seems to have been sound enough on the turkey.

T URKIES there are, which divers times in great flocks have sallied by our doores; and then a gunne (being commonly in a redinesse), salutes them with such a courtesie, as makes them take a turne in the Cooke roome. They daunce by the doore so well.

Of these there hath bin killed, that have weighed forty eight pound a peece.

They are mainy degrees sweeter than the tame Turkies of England, feede them how you can.

I had a Salvage who hath taken out his boy in a morning, and they have brought home their loades about noone.

I have asked them what number they found in the woods, who have answered Neent Metawna, which is a thosand that day; the plenty of them is such in those parts. They are easily killed at rooste, because the one being killed, the other sit fast neverthe lesse, and this is no bad commodity.

From *New English Canaan*, or *New Canaan*. Printed at Amsterdam by Jacob Frederick Stamm, 1637.

THE

BALD EAGLE

Mark Catesby

*One of the important pioneer explorers of the natural history of what
is now the United States was Mark Catesby who came here first in
1710 and returned to England a few years later with what was called
the best botanical collections that had ever been made on our continent. He later came back to America, lived for a while in the Carolinas, and finally settled in California where he died in 1749 after
publishing in two volumes an excellent* Natural History of Carolina,
Florida, and the Bahama Islands.
Here are three of his bird portraits.

THIS Bird weighs nine pounds: the Iris of the eye white; over which
is a prominence, cover'd with a yellow skin; the Bill yellow, with the
Sear of the same colour: the Legs and Feet are yellow; the Tallons black,
the Head and part of the Neck is white, as is the Tail; all the rest of the
Body, and Wings, are brown.

Tho' it is an Eagle of a small size, yet has great strength and spirit,
preying on Pigs, Lambs, and Fawns.

They always make their Nests near the sea, or great rivers, and usually
on old, dead Pine or Cypress-trees, continuing to build annually on the
same tree, till it falls. Though he is so formidable to all birds, yet he
suffers them to breed near his royal nest without molestation; particularly
the fishing and other Hawks, Herons, etc. which all make their nests on
high trees; and in some places are so near one another, that they appear
like a Rookery. This Bird is called the BALD EAGLE, both in Virginia
and Carolina, though his head is as much feather'd as the other parts of
his body.

Both Cock and Hen have white Heads, and their other parts differ very
little from one another.

From *The Natural History of Carolina, Florida, and the Bahama Islands.* London:
Printed for C. Marsh, in Round Court in the Strand; and T. Wilcox, over-against
the New Church, in the Strand, 1754.

THE "HOOPING" CRANE

Mark Catesby

THE Hooping Crane is about the size of the common Crane. The bill is brown, and six inches long; the edges of both mandibles, towards the end, about an inch and half, are serrated. A deep and broad channel runs from the head more than half way along its upper mandible. Its nostrils are very large. A broad white list runs from the eyes obliquely to the neck; except which, the head is brown. The crown of the head is callous, and very hard, thinly beset with stiff black hairs, which lie flat, and are so thin that the skin appears bare, of a reddish flesh colour. Behind the head is a peek of black feathers. The larger wing feathers are black. All the rest of the body is white. This description I took from the entire skin of the Bird, presented to me by an Indian, who made use of it for his tobacco pouch. He told me, that early in the Spring, great multitudes of them frequent the lower parts of the Rivers near the Sea, and return to the Mountains in the Summer. This relation was afterwards confirmed to me by a white Man; who added, that they make a remarkable hooping noise; and that he hath seen them at the mouths of the Savanna, Aratamaha, and other Rivers nearer St. Augustine, but never saw any so far North as the Settlements of Carolina.

From *The Natural History of Carolina, Florida, and the Bahama Islands*. London: Printed for C. Marsh, in Round Court in the Strand; and T. Wilcox, over-against the New Church, in the Strand, 1754.

THE TURN-STONE,

OR

SEA-DOTTREL

Mark Catesby

THIS Bird has, in proportion to its body, a small head, with a strait taper black bill, an inch long. All the upper part of the body is brown, with a mixture of white and black. The quill feathers of the wings are dark brown; the neck and breast are black; the legs and feet light red. In a voyage to America, in the year 1722, in 31 deg N. Lat. and 40 leagues from the coast of Florida, the Bird, from which this was figur'd, flew on board us, and was taken. It was very active in turning up stones, which we put into its cage; but not finding under them the usual food, it died. In this action it moved only the upper mandible; yet would with great dexterity and quickness turn over stones of above three pounds weight. This property Nature seems to have given it for the finding of its food, which is probably Worms and Insects on the Sea-shore. By comparing this with the description of that in Will. Ornitholog. which I had then on board, I found this to be the same kind with that he describes.

From *The Natural History of Carolina, Flordia, and the Bahama Islands*. London: Printed for C. Marsh, in Round Court in the Strand; and T. Wilcox, over-against the New Church, in the Strand, 1754.

THE KING

OF SONG

Edward Howe Forbush

Thoreau once commented indignantly upon the fact the state of Massachusetts, like most of its citizens, was indifferent to nature except in so far as it affected the pocketbook and that its only entomological publication was called Injurious Insects—*as though they alone could concern anyone. Perhaps he would have been mollified if he could have foreseen the official publication from which the following is selected.*

I HAVE written elsewhere as follows regarding the Mockingbird as a songster: "The Mockingbird stands unrivaled. He is the king of song. This is a trite saying, but how much it really means can be known only to those who have heard this most gifted singer uncaged and at his best in the lowlands of the Southern States. He equals and even excels the whole feathered choir. He improves upon most of the notes that he reproduces, adding also to his varied repertoire the crowing of chanticleer, the cackling of the hen, the barking of the house dog, the squeaking of the unoiled wheelbarrow, the postman's whistle, the plaints of young chickens and turkeys and those of young wild birds, not neglecting to mimic his own offspring. He even imitates man's musical inventions. Elizabeth and Joseph Grinnell assert that a Mockingbird was attracted to a graphophone on the lawn where, apparently, he listened and took mental notes of the performance, giving the next day, a week later, or at midnight an entertainment of his own and then repeating it with the exact graphophone ring. Even the notes of the piano have been reproduced in some cases and the bird's vocalization simulates the lightning changes of the kaleidoscope.

"The Mocker is more or less a buffoon, but those who look upon him only as an imitator or clown have much to learn of his wonderful originality. His own song is heard at its best at the height of the love season, when the singer flutters into the air from some tall tree-top and impro-

From *Birds of Massachusetts and Other New England States*. Published by the Commonwealth of Massachusetts, 1929.

vises his music, pouring out all the power and energy of his being in such an ecstasy of song that, exhausting his strength in the supreme effort, he slowly floats on quivering, beating pinions down through the bloom-covered branches until, his fervor spent, he sinks to the ground below. His expanded wings and tail flashing with white in the sunlight and the buoyancy of his action appeal to the eye as his music captivates the ear. On moonlit nights at this season the inspired singer launches himself far into the air, filling the silvery spaces of the night with the exquisite swells and trills, liquid and sweet, of his unparalleled melody. The song rises and falls, as the powers of the singer wax and wane, and so he serenades his mate throughout the live-long night. One such singer wins others to emulation and, as the chorus grows, little birds of the field and orchard wake just enough to join briefly in the swelling tide of avian melody."

THE

VOLUBLE SINGER

OF THE

TREETOPS

Louise de Kiriline Lawrence

The vireo is the only bird who has a verb for a name—"vireo" literally is Latin for "I am green." So he is; but not brilliantly so and that is one of the reasons why the layman who is not even a bird watcher hardly notices him despite the fact that some members of the genus are among the most abundant of our birds. Nearly everyone who has ever been in the country has heard a vireo sing but not one in ten has seen or at least noticed him.

ONE of my favorites among birds is the red-eyed vireo. I know him well and he appeals to me particularly because in looks and comportment he is such a smooth and elegant bird. Slow motion is his specialty, but sometimes he is brimming with nervous energy and moves faster than the arrow in a streamlined fashion all his own. I do not think that the epithet "sluggish," so often used about him, fits him particularly well. It seems to me that we shall need to find another and a better word, one that contains the elements of sobriety and fluidity.

About his singing, terms have been used that are not altogether complimentary—monotonous, repetitious, preacher-like—and I was always inclined to question the aptness of these descriptions. Was he as tireless as his reputation would have him? When in the day did he start singing, when did he stop? Was there any relation between his manner of singing and his character which, if known, would dispel the impression of what might seem monotonous and repetitious? Were his moods, needs, and temperament reflected in the nuances of tone, in the speed and the manner of the delivery of his songs? What I hitherto knew of the red-eyed vireo's singing gave only part of the answer to these questions.

From *Audubon Magazine*, May–June, 1954.

When the call came from the British ornithologist, Noble Rollin to make an all-day study of some special bird activity, I thought this was a fine opportunity to devote to the red-eye. Everything fitted in very well, too, because the day I was able to do the survey was May 27, 1952, a few days after Male A had taken up territory in my study area at Pimisi Bay which, as the crow flies, is about 180 miles north of Toronto, Canada. But at this time my bird was still without a mate and there would, presumably, be few claims upon his attention other than singing and feeding.

Pre-dawn, the most enchanting and mysterious moment in the 24 hours, reigned when I came out at 3 A.M. A soft, misty light prevailed, not enough to see but enough to surmise the outlines of the trees and the opening in the woods through which the trail led, the delicate luminosity of the night. A whip-poor-will called at close quarters, a loud song and passionate of tempo, for he was in the midst of his love-making. I counted 37 whip-poor-wills; then silence. Then he began again.

I walked into the vireo territory, armed with notebook and flashlight and wearing a warm sweater. It was chilly, the temperature was 43 degrees, and the wind light from the west. A faint streak of dawn appeared at the eastern horizon, stealing the light from the stars.

Across my path, two veeries began calling, soft interrogative notes that never waited an answer. Then, muted like a heavenly whisper, the thrushes begin to sing. Penetrating the dusk and hanging deliciously upon the air, these whisperings seemed unearthly, but they represented the most potent reality of these birds' lives. For this was the time when competition between their males was strong, when pairing took place and nesting locations were chosen, when the blood within them ran fast and their sensations were acute.

A purple finch flew over, *tuck*-ed, and gave a burst of song sweeter than honey. His season was a little ahead of the veeries', beyond the culmination of passions, and his song, therefore, was like an afterthought, a reminiscence of what had stirred in him before the nest-building and the laying of the first eggs.

As the light increased, the singing of the veeries became louder and intermingled with the weirdest discordant notes and exclamations, suggesting an excitement which intensified with the approach of day. Startling and strange was this conversation between the thrushes, as it emanated explosively from the depths of the underbrush close to the path where I stood, now here, now over there. Then, all of a sudden, the swish of rapid flight low through the bushes from one place to another. Since their beginning, these rituals and displays, these unanswered and unanswerable queries from one tawny thrush to the other, evolved into the charming game I just now witnessed.

But no vireo was yet awake.

Beyond the valley of the spring, the rose-breasted grosbeak began to sing, songs so deliciously lyrical that the bird himself seemed loath to end such a fine performance and took to his wings the better to enact an accomplished finale. In the top of a green birch, the robin caught the theme of the grosbeak's impassioned utterance, but geared it down to a song modulated to please a mate sitting quietly on well incubated eggs. For at this moment, the robin's song was not of territorial announcement or self-assertion, but one symbolizing the bond between two closely attached creatures.

Light came and at 4 o'clock I could see to write without the flashlight. During the next 22 minutes, the number of birds that had testified to their awakening rose to 20. A pair of yellow-bellied sapsuckers breakfasted on the sap of a white birch before resuming work on their nest-hole. A crow flew over, welcomed by no one, but busy on its own nest and eggs. A porcupine, climbing an aspen for a feed of green bark, sounded to me like a black bear, and a great blue heron flew over my head and croaked so loudly that, weak-kneed, I nearly sat down on the spot.

By this time, had I not known that my vireo was somewhere on this piece of land whereupon I stood, I would have despaired of his intention ever to sing again. But then, surprisingly, because I had waited so long, exactly nine minutes before sunrise, the red-eyed vireo serenely began dropping phrase upon phrase of song into the confusion of all the other bird-voices. With such casual dreaminess did this long-awaited awakening happen that it required some seconds to penetrate into my consciousness, and forced me to start counting his inaugural sets of two and three notes at five.

I found him high in the crown of a trembling aspen. There he wandered about, hopping from twig to twig, looking around, up and down, from side to side. His bill opened and closed, his throat bubbled, and his crest rose lightly and fell with the rhythm of his utterances. He sang, phrase following upon phrase, with just enough interval to mark a disconnection between them. He sang with an aloof intensity and confluence that seemed totally to divorce his performance from any special objectives and reasons. This bird sang simply because self-expression in song was as much a part of his being as his red eye.

In the next 100 minutes, when the birds filled the woods with the greatest volume of music, our vireo achieved all his vocal records of the day. Thus, from 5:00 to 6:00 A.M., he sang the greatest number of songs in any hour—2155 phrases. From 4:22 A.M., just as he began singing, to 5:00 A.M., he attained his highest speed of delivery, an average of nearly 44 songs per minute; from 6:05 to 6:10 A.M., he sang the most songs in any five-minute period of the day, an average of 70 songs per minute.

Yet, breathless would not properly describe the performance of this bird. He continued to sing for the next three hours with a perfectly calm and casual continuance that at the end amassed him a total of 6063 songs, delivered at a speed of 40 songs per minute. During this time, he allowed himself six pauses from one to six minutes each which he divided equally among the three hours. While he sang, he wandered leisurely from one part of his two-acre territory to the other, selecting his way through the foliated crowns of the tallest aspens and birches. Had not his trail been so clearly marked in song, it would have been a problem for me to follow this bird which moved at such heights and blended so well with his surroundings.

Although my vireo often fed while he sang, and sang with his mouth full, more concentrated feeding called for silence, and the important business of preening claimed all of his attention. Once a trespassing vireo, a stranger, interrupted him. Abruptly he stopped singing and, like an arrow released from a taut bow, he shot down from his tall perch directly in pursuit of the intruder. And with that, the incident closed. With his only red-eye neighbor settled on an adjacent territory to the north, our vireo had no altercations. On one occasion during the afternoon, the two happened to come close to their common border at the same time; but from this nothing more serious resulted than that the birds for about a quarter of an hour indulged in competitive singing.

A little before 9 o'clock in the morning, my vireo stopped singing. Up to this time he had spent almost four out of four-and-a-half hours singing continuously. This was a remarkable record as, apart from the need of advertising himself and his territory, nothing occurred to call forth extraordinary vocal efforts on his part. Red-eyed vireos do not always sing as persistently as this bird did, especially during the first days after arrival from the South when leisurely feeding is often the keynote of existence to many of them. Nor do all individuals possess the same capacity for vocal expression. I have known at least one other red-eyed vireo whose total number of songs in a day, even at the most exciting period, probably never reached four figures. As to the pursuit of the strange vireo, I surmised that this was a passing female, because my male *stopped singing* and dashed off chasing it, instead of challenging it by voice and gesture. That nothing came of it only suggests, that for the female, the moment was not auspicious.

The next half-hour my bird spent feeding and preening. He descended from the heights of the tree crowns to the middle strata of the woods where, one may presume, he found more privacy in the secluded leafy niches. Then, once more, he resumed singing. While he still attained a speed of 38 songs when he sang, his average from 9:00 to 10:00 A.M. was only about six songs a minute for the whole hour. This proved to be an interesting fact, because, regardless of his hourly averages, his speed of singing consistently and gradually declined throughout the day. In other words, he sang more and more slowly as the day advanced.

After his hour of rest, the vireo achieved a forenoon peak of singing that lacked only 13 songs in reaching as high a total as that obtained from 5:00 to 6:00 A.M. He worked up to this peak in the hour before noon, but would, I think, have reached it earlier had he not wandered into a grove of trees heavily infested with the forest tent caterpillar. Here he distracted himself with a great deal of flycatching on the wing. If his objective were the eating of the tachanid flies, which prey upon the tent caterpillars, this activity, from a human viewpoint, may not have been useful. But, of course, I could not be sure that these were the insects he caught. As to the caterpillars, my vireo tramped lightly over the masses of them, apparently without recognizing them as good. When, through my binoculars I saw these worms as wriggling shadows on a translucent leaf, then the bird knew instantly what to do with them—he snapped them down, dashed them to pulp on the twig at his feet, and ate them.

From dawn till noon, the vireo reached a grand total of 14,027 songs, but after this time his singing diminished notably. The interruptions between groups of songs became longer and more frequent, even as he sang more and more slowly. From noon until going to roost, he gave only a little more than half as many songs as during the early part of the day. But even this was a remarkable number and his voice continued to be heard when most of the other birds sang but little or were altogether silent. Moreover, compared with the all-day record of 6140 songs of an unmated European blackbird made by Noble Rollin on April 5, 1948, my vireo's afternoon performance alone exceeded this by 2030 songs.

The lesser peak of singing, which occurred during the afternoon, was perhaps partly due to the encounter at the territorial border with the neighboring red-eye to the north. For quite a while, certainly, this stimulated both birds to greater vocal effort. But the time of afternoon rest came in the next following two hours, when my vireo wandered about within a small area, or feeding or sitting on a twig, trimming and polishing every feather in his plumage, and when he sang only a little.

The last hour of his day the vireo spent in the top of a quaking aspen. Here he moved about from perch to perch. I saw the easy opening and closing of his bill and heard his notes drop, one by one, upon the calm air.

All day I had heard him singing thousands of songs, of two to four, seldom five, notes. Monotonous, repetitious, preacher-like? His singing was all this, if an utterance that was so intrinsic a phase of a creature's character, so innate an expression of self, could be any of these attributes. What I had heard all day, set to music, was this vireo's instinctive emotions and preoccupations, the wherefores and the end of his very existence.

Lovely and clear, simple and eloquent, his song and intonations continued to reach me from the top of the aspen. Hitherto his voice had been unaffected by his day-long singing. But now, as if he had reached the end, yet only with reluctance gave in, his songs shortened and were often just softly whispered. Then the sun hid behind alto-cumulus clouds and it grew dusky in the vireo territory, while out yonder, at the edge of the forest, the sun still threw its gold upon the trees and hillsides.

Between 6:00 and 6:13 P.M. my vireo sang 44 songs. Two minutes later, with wings closed, he dropped from the crown of the aspen into a thick stand of young evergreens. From here, like an echo of his day's performance, he gave six more songs. Then he fell silent and was heard no more. Officially, the sun set one hour and 39 minutes later.

Fourteen hours, less six minutes, my red-eye vireo had been awake, and of this time he spent nearly 10 hours singing a total of 22,197 songs. This was his record. But the most important is not the record, but my introduction to an individual bird and the glimpse he gave me of his true character.

OLD

SICKLE WINGS

John Kieran

The many-talented John Kieran (whom we have met before) used to go regularly on "nature walks" with a very select company. It is no secret that the drama critic who figures in this passage is Brooks Atkinson—one of the few Broadwayites who maintain a passionate interest in doings remote from Times Square.

OUR afternoon record was spotty—just a hawk here and there—but one was a Duck Hawk, a bird that I never see without a thrill. This is the American cousin of the Peregrine Falcon of medieval history and romance. It is the avian ace of the air, the fastest thing on wings in our part of the country, a marauder, a fierce and fearless predator for its weight and size. We have seen Duck Hawks swooping at Bald Eagles, apparently just for the fun of it, and Dick Herbert, who keeps a census of all the Duck Hawks that breed along the Palisades, told us that he had seen a Duck Hawk knock down a Great Horned Owl that happened to pass too close to the Duck Hawk's nest.

There is no mistaking the Duck Hawk when it stoops to conquer. It comes down with a lightning plunge on half-shut wings. How fast it drops is a matter of estimate, and some estimates I have seen I believe are much too enthusiastic. The Falconer, when he was a fighter pilot in France in World War I, found himself flying parallel to a Peregrine Falcon as he was returning from a foray over enemy territory in the Champagne sector. He turned to test the speed of the bird and followed it down when it dived to get away from the plane. He knew the speed of which his plane—a Spad—was capable and of this experience he wrote:

"I would say that the Duck Hawk has a cruising speed of about 75 miles per hour and a diving speed of about 150 miles per hour. At least, this one did."

The Dramatic Critic told me that once on a Winter day he was watching a line of ducks winging swiftly northward just a few feet above the

From *Footnotes on Nature*. New York: Doubleday & Co. Inc., 1947.

water of the Hudson River. For some reason the ducks seemed to be in a tearing hurry as he watched them through his field glasses. Suddenly a Duck Hawk, coming from the rear, shot past the line of ducks so fast that, as the Dramatic Critic solemnly stated, it made the ducks look as though they were walking on the water. Once the Medical Student and I went across the Hudson River and along the foot of the Palisades in the hope of seeing a Duck Hawk. It was in early Spring and the ground was muddy, so that walking was a heavy process. We plodded along for hours and saw nothing except a few stray ducks and hundreds of Herring Gulls on the river. By late afternoon we were worn and weary and a cold wind had come up to add to our discomfort. Just as we were going down the slope to take the ferry home in the dusk, the Medical Student grabbed my arm and said: "Look!" I looked and all I saw was a darkish speck shooting downward across the sunset sky with almost incredible speed. There was just one bird in our region that could fly in such fashion—the Duck Hawk! We were dog-tired and our shoes were a mass of clotted mud, but there was a glow of satisfaction in our hearts as we went aboard the ferry. We had seen "Old Sickle Wings," which is our nickname for any Duck Hawk because of its shape in hunting flight, and we were well content.

MASTER

OF

THE WOODS

Robert McConnell Hatch

Clerical bird watchers are common in England. In fact natural history in general owes much to rural clergyman who had the leisure and the inclination to take up sometimes improbable hobbies. One such, Gilbert White, might be called the first English "nature writer"—though of course not the first English naturalist. As the following selection by Bishop Hatch will show, the United States has produced at least one churchman birdwatcher—and a highly placed one at that.

SOMETIMES a bird can cast its spell over a whole countryside. Other birds may live there, but they become mere bit players in the drama. Dominating the scene is a single massive personality.

Such is the case on a wooded hillside in Lancaster, New Hampshire. Far up the hill and tucked deep in the forest is a one-room board camp built by a neighbor of mine when he was cutting logs. His name was Orrin Wentworth, and his wife's name was Lottie. They called the little building Camp Owl, using the first letter in each of their names, O and L, and adding the W for Wentworth. It was a fitting family designation for the camp, but I soon learned that it applied for quite another reason.

On my first overnight visit to the camp I was walking up the trail alone in the dark of the moon. I had reached a murky part of the trail, under some tall fir trees, when the night air was split by a series of eight spine-tingling hoots. The last hoot slurred downward, indentifying its source as a barred owl. I had heard barred owls before, but always at a respectable distance. The proximity of the sudden hoots unnerved me, and I continued up the trail at top speed.

Again and again that summer I heard the barred owl. The woods echoed with hoohoo, hoohoo, hoohoo, hoohooaw. Sometimes the hooting was close to the camp. Sometimes it was so far up the hillside that I could

From *New Hampshire Bird News, January* 1954.

barely hear it. Once in the dead of night the owl awoke me, not hooting this time, but clucking, cackling and snarling from a point directly over the camp. In fact, I still wonder if the owl was not perched on the ridgepole of the building during this performance.

Other birds inhabit the hillside—black-throated blue warblers, redstarts, black and white warblers, oven birds, hermit thrushes, brown creepers, whitethroats and juncoes, nuthatches and chickadees, hairy and downy woodpeckers, to name only a few. I have eaten supper listening to the music of olive-backed thrushes, and I have breakfasted to the song of black-throated green warblers. I have watched red-tailed hawks circling over the camp, and one day I saw a goshawk as I sat on the porch. But none of these birds, not even the goshawk, could match the owl. Every night the hoots rang through the forest, now from this direction, now from that, until the owl seemed the master of these woods and all the other birds mere satellites.

Finally I resolved to see the owl. I strained my eyes for him at dusk. I tried to catch him in the beam of my flashlight. I craned my neck throughout the day as I searched dense evergreens and looked for cavities in trees. I felt sure that he saw me repeatedly, and I had an uneasy suspicion that I was affording him a summer's entertainment. But, to save my life, I could not find him. I could only hear his hooting in the night.

My vacation came to an end. My last day in New Hampshire was a rainy one. I felt depressed and decided to walk up to the camp, more to relive old memories than anything else. For once I gave no thought to the owl.

I reached the camp late in the afternoon. It was raining hard, and the woods were growing dark. I sat on the porch and dwelt once more on some of the great memories of that summer—the nesting pair of broadwinged hawks I had found, the kestrels in our pasture, the Lincoln's sparrow on the edge of a bog, the white-winged crossbills singing like canaries on the shores of a wilderness pond. They were stirring memories, but they were abruptly shattered! A large bird flew moth-like to the branch of a tree in front of the camp. He relaxed on his perch and gazed at me calmly for what seemed an age. I gazed back, not so calmly. It was the barred owl. I felt as though our long acquaintance had changed into friendship. When at last he flew away I murmured, "So long, old friend! I'll see you again next summer."

And so I did, because barred owls have been known to inhabit a locality for many years. I am at home with him now and because of this I am also at home with the tract of woods that belongs so exclusively to him.

THE

MALIGNED CATBIRD

Elliott Coues

The catbird is a mimic second only to the mocker. Like the mocker also he is unusually tolerant of the intruder, man. Why then are his virtues not recognized—as the author of the following portrait says that they are not. Is it because his name prejudices those who look with suspicion on the cat? Or is it, perhaps, because he is given to interrupting his most elaborate flights of song with a derisive "meouw" which seems to say: "Fooled you that time. You thought I was some other bird."

IT is not easy to account for the vulgar prejudice against this bird. The contempt he inspires cannot be entirely due to familiarity; for other members of the household, like the Robin, Bluebird, and Swallow, do not come under the ban. If his harsh, abrupt, and discordant note were the cause, the croaking Crow and chattering Blackbird would share the same disgrace. Yet the fact remains that the Catbird is almost always regarded unfavorably, not so much for what he does, perhaps, as for what he is, or is not. To eyes polite, he seems to be "off color" in the best society, he is looked upon as *un peu compromis*. There must be a reason for this—the world is too busy to invent reasons for things—for there never was a popular verdict without roots in some fact or principle. It is instinctive; the school-boy despises a Catbird just as naturally as he stones a frog; and when he thinks a thing is mean, no argument will convince him to the contrary.

For myself, I think the boys are right. Like many of the lower animals, they are quick to detect certain qualities, and apt to like or dislike unwittingly, yet with good reason. The matter with the Catbird is that he is thoroughly common-place. There is a dead level of bird-life, as there is of humanity; and mediocrity is simply despicable—hopeless and helpless, and never more so than when it indulges aspirations. Yet it wears well, and is a useful thing; there must be a standard of measure, and a foil is often extremely convenient. The Catbird has certainly a good deal

From *Birds of the Colorado Valley*. Washington: U. S. Government Printing Office, 1878.

to contend with. His name has a flippant sound, without agreeable suggestiveness. His voice is vehement without strength, unpleasant in its explosive quality. His dress is positively ridiculous—who could hope to rise in life wearing a pepper-and-salt jacket, a black velvet skull-cap, and a large red patch on the seat of his pantaloons? Add to all this the possession of some very plebian tastes, like those which in another case render beer-gardens, circuses, and street-shows things possible, and you will readily perceive that a hero cannot be made out of a Catbird.

But to be common-place is merely to strike the balance of a great number of positive qualities, no single one of which is to be overlooked. It is accomplished by a sort of algebraic process, in which all the terms of an equation are brought together on one side, which then equals zero. There is said to be a great deal of human nature in mankind, and I am sure there is as much bird-nature in the feathered tribe. There is as much life in the kitchen as in the parlor: it is only a matter of a flight of stairs between them. We who happen to be above know none too much of what goes on below—much less, I suspect, than the *basse-cour* often learns of the *salon* and the *boudoir*. I sometimes fancy that the Catbird knows us better than we do him. He is at least a civilized bird, if he does hang by the eyelids on good society; if he is denied the front door, the area is open to him; he may peep in at the basement window, and see the way up the back stairs. His eyes and ears are open; his wits are sharp; what he knows, he knows, and will tell if he chooses. His domesticity is large; he likes us well enough to stay with us, yet he keeps his eye on us. His is the prose of daily life, with all its petty concerns, as read by the lower classes; the poetry we are left to discover.

Explain him as we may, the Catbird is inseparable from home and homely things; he reflects, as he is reflected in, domestic life. The associations, it is true, are of an humble sort; but they are just as strong as those which link us with the trusty Robin, the social Swallow, the delicious Bluebird, or the elegant Oriole. Let it be the humble country-home of toil, or the luxurious mansion where wealth is lavished on the garden—in either case, the Catbird claims the rights of squatter sovereignty. He flirts saucily across the well-worn path that leads to the well, and sips the water that collects in the shallow depression upon the flag-stone. Down in the tangle of the moist dell, where stands the spring-house, with its cool, crisp atmosphere, redolent of buttery savor, where the trickling water is perpetual, he loiters at ease, and from the heart of the greenbrier makes bold advances to the milkmaid who brings the brimming bowls. In the pasture beyond, he waits for the boy who comes whistling after the cows, and follows him home by the blackberry road that lies along the zigzag fence, challenging the carelessly thrown stone he has learned to dodge with ease. He joins the berrying parties fresh from school, soliciting a game of hide-and-seek, and laughs at the mishaps that never fail when children try the brier patch. Along the hedge row, he glides with short easy flights to gain the evergreen coppice that shades a corner of the lawn, where he pauses to watch the old gardener trimming the boxwood, or rolling the gravel walk, or making the flower bed, wondering why some people will take so much trouble when everything is nice enough already. Ever restless and inquisitive, he makes for 'the well-known arbor, to see what may be going on there. What he discovers is certainly none of his business: the rustic seat is occupied; the old, old play is in rehearsal; and at sight of the blushing cheeks that respond to passionate words, the very roses on the trellis hang their envious heads. This spectacle tickles his fancy; always ripe for mischief, he startles the loving pair with his quick, shrill cry, like a burlesque of the kiss just heard, and enjoys their little consternation. "It is only a Catbird," they say reassuringly—but there are times when the slightest jar is a shock, and pledges that hang in a trembling balance may never be redeemed.

"Only a Catbird" meanwhile remembers business of his own, and is off. The practical question of dining recurs. He means to dine sumptuously, and so, like the French philosopher, place himself beyond the reach of fate. But nature, in the month of May, is full of combustible material, and the very atmosphere is quick to carry the torch that was kindled in the arbor where the lovers sat. His fate meets him in the only shape that could so far restrain masculine instincts as to postpone a dinner. The rest is soon told—rather it would be, could the secrets of the impenetrable dark-green mass of *Smilax* whither the pair betake themselves be revealed. The next we see of the bird, he is perched on the topmost spray of yonder pear tree, with quivering wings, brimful of song. He is inspired; for a time at least he is lifted above the common-place; his kinship with the prince of song, with the Mockingbird himself, is vindicated. He has discovered the source of the poetry of every-day life.

THE
GREAT SHRIKE

John Burroughs

---

*The most dangerous and relentless of all predators is man himself.
Yet he is very quick to call "savage" and "cruel" the animal who kills
for food and to forget that, with very few exceptions, he alone either
takes more prey than he needs, kills for the sake of killing, or calls
wanton slaughter of other creatures "sport." As Bernard Shaw once
said: "When a man wants to murder a tiger he calls it sport; when the
tiger wants to murder him he calls it ferocity."*

*John Burroughs was too good a naturalist not to know all this and
not to know, besides, that without the predator the balance of nature
could not maintain itself. Yet the soundest of naturalists is not wholly
free from the human prejudice and Burroughs (only half seriously,
no doubt) yields to it in this vivid account of the demure-looking
little bird with the habits and soul of a great hawk.*

BUT let me . . . contemplate for a few moments this feathered bandit
—this bird with the mark of Cain upon him, *Lanius borealis*—the
great shrike or butcher-bird. Usually the character of a bird of prey is
well defined; there is no mistaking him. His claws, his beak, his head, his
wings, in fact his whole build, point to the fact that he subsists upon live
creatures; he is armed to catch them and to slay them. Every bird knows
a hawk and knows him from the start, and is on the lookout for him. The
hawk takes life, but he does it to maintain his own, and it is a public and
universally known fact. Nature has sent him abroad in that character, and
has advised all creatures of it. Not so with the shrike; here she has concealed the character of a murderer under a form as innocent as that of
the robin. Feet, wings, tail, color, head, and general form and size are all
those of a song-bird—very much like that master songster, the mocking
bird—yet this bird is a regular Bluebeard among its kind. Its only characteristic feature is its beak, the upper mandible having two sharp processes and a sharp hooked point. It cannot fly away to any distance with
the bird it kills, nor hold it in its claws to feed upon it. It usually impales

From *Locust and Wild Honey*. Boston: Houghton Mifflin Company, 1879, 1895.

its victim upon a thorn, or thrusts it in the fork of a limb. For the most part, however, its food seems to consist of insects—spiders, grasshoppers, beetles, etc. It is the assassin of the small birds, whom it often destroys in pure wantonness, or merely to sup on their brains, as the Gaucho slaughters a wild cow or bull for its tongue. It is a wolf in sheep's clothing. Apparently its victims are unacquainted with its true character and allow it to approach them, when the fatal blow is given. I saw an illustration of this the other day. A large number of goldfinches in their full plumage, together with snowbirds and sparrows, were feeding and chattering in some low bushes back of the barn. I had paused by the fence and was peeping through at them, hoping to get a glimpse of that rare sparrow, the white-crowned. Presently I heard a rustling among the dry leaves as if some larger bird was also among them. Then I heard one of the goldfinches cry out as if in distress, when the whole flock of them started up in alarm, and, circling around, settled in the tops of the larger trees. I continued my scrutiny of the bushes, when I saw a large bird, with some object in its beak, hopping along on a low branch near the ground. It disappeared from my sight for a few moments, then came up through the undergrowth into the top of a young maple where some of the finches had alighted, and I beheld the shrike. The little birds avoided him and flew about the tree, their pursuer following them with the motions of his head and body as if he would fain arrest them by his murderous gaze. The birds did not utter the cry or make the demonstration of alarm they usually do on the appearance of a hawk, but chirruped and called and flew about in a half-wondering, half-bewildered manner. As they flew farther along the line of trees the shrike followed them as if bent on further captures. I then made my way around to see what the shrike had caught, and what he had done with his prey. As I approached the bushes I saw the shrike hastening back. I read his intentions at once. Seeing my movements, he had returned for his game. But I was too quick for him, and he got up out of the brush and flew away from the locality. On some twigs in the thickest part of the bushes I found his victim—a goldfinch. It was not impaled upon a thorn, but was carefully disposed upon some horizontal twigs—laid upon the shelf, so to speak. It was as warm as in life, and its plumage was unruffled. On examining it I found a large bruise or break in the skin on the back of the neck, at the base of the skull. Here the bandit had no doubt gripped the bird with his strong beak. The shrike's bloodthirstiness was seen in the fact that it did not stop to devour its prey, but went in quest of more, as if opening a market of goldfinches. The thicket was his shambles, and if not interrupted he might have had a fine display of tidbits in a short time.

The shrike is called a butcher from his habit of sticking his meat upon hooks and points; further than that, he is a butcher because he devours but a trifle of what he slays.

A few days before, I had witnessed another little scene in which the shrike was the chief actor. A chipmunk had his den in the side of the terrace above the garden, and spent the mornings laying in a store of corn which he stole from a field ten or twelve rods away. In traversing about half this distance, the little poacher was exposed; the first cover going from his den was a large maple, where he always brought up and took a survey of the scene. I would see him spinning along toward the maple, then from it by an easy stage to the fence adjoining the corn; then back again with his booty. One morning I paused to watch him more at my leisure. He came up out of his retreat and cocked himself up to see what my motions meant. His forepaws were clasped to his breast precisely as if they had been hands, and the tips of his fingers thrust into his vest pockets. Having satisfied himself with reference to me, he sped on toward the tree. He had nearly reached it, when he turned tail and rushed for his hole with the greatest precipitation. As he neared it, I saw some bluish object in the air closing in upon him with the speed of an arrow, and, as he vanished within, a shrike brought up in front of the spot, and with spread wings and tail stood hovering a moment, and, looking in, then turned and went away. Apparently it was a narrow escape for the chipmunk, and, I venture to say, he stole no more corn that morning. The shrike is said to catch mice, but it is not known to attack squirrels. He certainly could not have strangled the chipmunk, and I am curious to know what would have been the result had he over-taken him. Probably it was only a kind of brag on the part of the bird— a bold dash where no risk was run. He simulated the hawk, the squirrel's real enemy, and no doubt enjoyed the joke.

On another occasion, as I was riding along a mountain road early in April, a bird started from the fence where I was passing, and flew heavily to the branch of a near apple-tree. It proved to be a shrike with a small bird in his beak. He thrust his victim into a fork of a branch, then wiped his bloody beak upon the bark. A youth who was with me, to whom I pointed out the fact, had never heard of such a thing, and was much incensed at the shrike. "Let me fire a stone at him," he said, and jumping out of the wagon he pulled off his mittens, and fumbled about for a stone. Having found one to his liking, with great earnestness and de-liberation he let drive. The bird was in more danger than I had imagined, for he escaped only by a hair's breadth; a guiltless bird like the robin or sparrow would surely have been slain; the missile grazed the spot where the shrike sat, and cut the ends of his wings as he darted behind the branch. We could see that the murdered bird had been brained, as its head hung down toward us.

The shrike is not a summer bird with us in the Northern States, but mainly a fall and winter one; in summer he goes farther north. I see him most frequently in November and December. I recall a morning during the former month that was singularly clear and motionless; the air was like a great drum. Apparently every sound within the compass of the horizon was distinctly heard. The explosions back in the cement quarries ten miles away smote the hollow and reverberating air like giant fists. Just as the sun first showed his fiery brow above the horizon, a gun was discharged across the river. On the instant a shrike, perched on the topmost spray of a maple above the house, set up a loud, harsh call or whistle, suggestive of certain notes of the blue jay. The note presently became a crude, broken warble. Even this scalper of the innocents had music in his soul on such a morning. He saluted the sun as a robin might have done. After he had finished he flew away toward the east.

The shrike is a citizen of the world, being found in both hemispheres. It does not appear that the European species differs essentially from our own. In Germany he is called the nine-killer, from the belief that he kills and sticks upon thorns nine grasshoppers a day

To make my portrait of the shrike more complete, I will add another trait of him described by an acute observer who writes me from western New York. He saw the bird on a bright mid-winter morning when the thermometer stood at zero, and by cautious approaches succeeded in getting under the apple-tree upon which he was perched. The shrike was uttering a loud, clear note like *clu-eet, clu-eet, clu-eet*, and, on finding he had a listener who was attentive and curious, varied his performance and kept it up continuously for fifteen minutes. He seemed to enjoy having a spectator, and never took his eye off him. The observer approached within twenty feet of him. "As I came near," he says, "the shrike began to scold at me, a sharp, buzzing, squeaking sound not easy to describe. After a little he came out on the end of the limb nearest me, then he posed himself, and, opening his wings a little, began to trill and warble under his breath, as it were, with an occasional squeak, and vibrating his half-open wings in time with his song." Some of his notes resembled those of the bluebird, and the whole performance is described as pleasing and melodious.

This account agrees with Thoreau's observation, where he speaks of the shrike "with heedless and unfrozen melody bringing back summer again." Sings Thoreau: —

> "His steady sails he never furls
> At any time o' year,
> And perching now on winter's curls,
> He whistles in his ear."

But his voice is that of a savage—strident and disagreeable.

I have often wondered how this bird was kept in check; in the struggle for existence it would appear to have greatly the advantage of other birds. It cannot, for instance, be beset with one tenth of the dangers that threaten the robin, and yet apparently there are a thousand robins to every shrike. It builds a warm, compact nest in the mountains and dense woods, and lays six eggs, which would indicate a rapid increase. The pigeon lays but two eggs, and is preyed upon by both man and beast, millions of them meeting a murderous death every year; yet always some part of the country is swarming with untold numbers of them. But the shrike is one of our rarest birds. I myself seldom see more than two each year, and before I became an observer of birds I never saw any.

In size the shrike is a little inferior to the blue jay, with much the same form. If you see an unknown bird about your orchard or fields in November or December of a bluish grayish complexion, with dusky wings and tail that show markings of white, flying rather heavily from point to point, or alighting down in the stubble occasionally, it is pretty sure to be the shrike.

THE

WATER-OUZEL

John Muir

Perhaps the most famous single passage describing an American bird is John Muir's rapturous account of his own favorite, the water-ouzel. Though it has often been reprinted, the editors of the present volume cannot bring themselves to omit it. Muir was a first-rate naturalist, a daring, lonely explorer, and a brilliant writer. Unlike many contemporary naturalists he saw no reason why he should strive for "objectivity" or to either conquer or conceal his "love of nature." He gloried in his passion for everything which was wild and grand in the natural world and it is the intensity of his emotions which is in part responsible for the greatness of his books. No other native writer of the past or present is more eloquent.

THE waterfalls of the Sierra are frequented by only one bird—the Ouzel or Water Thrush (*Cinclus Mexicanus, Sw.*) He is a singularly joyous and lovable little fellow, about the size of a robin, clad in a plain waterproof suit of bluish gray, with a tinge of chocolate on the head and shoulders. In form he is about as smoothly plump and compact as a pebble that has been whirled in a pot-hole, the flowing contour of his body being interrupted only by his strong feet and bill, the crisp wing-tips, and the up-slanted wren-like tail.

Among all the countless waterfalls I have met in the course of ten years' exploration in the Sierra, whether among the icy peaks, or warm foothills, or in the profound yosemitic cañons of the middle region, not one was found without its Ouzel. No cañon is too cold for this little bird, none too lonely, provided it be rich in falling water. Find a fall, or cascade, or rushing rapid, anywhere upon a clear stream, and there you will surely find its complementary Ouzel, flitting about in the spray, diving in foaming eddies, whirling like a leaf among beaten foam-bells; ever vigorous and enthusiastic, yet self-contained, and neither seeking nor shunning your company.

If disturbed while dipping about in the margin shallows, he either sets

From *The Mountains of California*. New York: The Century Company, 1894.

off with a rapid whir to some other feeding-ground up or down the stream, or alights on some half-submerged rock or snag out in the current, and immediately begins to nod and courtesy like a wren, turning his head from side to side with many other odd dainty movements that never fail to fix the attention of the observer.

He is the mountain streams' own darling, the humming-bird of blooming waters, loving rocky ripple-slopes and sheets of foam as a bee loves flowers, as a lark loves sunshine and meadows. Among all the mountain birds, none has cheered me so much in my lonely wanderings—none so unfailingly. For both in winter and summer he sings, sweetly, cheerily, independent alike of sunshine and of love, requiring no other inspiration than the stream on which he dwells. While water sings, so must he, in heat or cold, calm or storm, ever attuning his voice in sure accord; low in the drought of summer and the drought of winter, but never silent.

During the golden days of Indian summer, after most of the snow has been melted, and the mountain streams have become feeble—a succession of silent pools, linked together by shallow, transparent currents and strips of silvery lacework—then the song of the Ouzel is at its lowest ebb. But as soon as the winter clouds have bloomed, and the mountain treasuries are once more replenished with snow, the voices of the streams and ouzels increase in strength and richness until the flood season of early summer. Then the torrents chant their noblest anthems, and then is the flood-time of our songster's melody. As for weather, dark days and sun days are the same to him. The voices of most song-birds, however joyous, suffer a long winter eclipse; but the Ouzel sings on through all the seasons and every kind of storm. Indeed no storm can be more violent than those of the waterfalls in the midst of which he delights to dwell. However dark and boisterous the weather, snowing, blowing, or cloudy, all the same he sings, and with never a note of sadness. No need of spring sunshine to thaw *his* song, for it never freezes. Never shall you hear anything wintry from *his* warm breast; no pinched cheeping, no wavering notes between sorrow and joy; his mellow, fluty voice is ever tuned to downright gladness, as free from dejection as cock-crowing.

It is pitiful to see wee frost-pinched sparrows on cold mornings in the mountain groves shaking the snow from their feathers, and hopping about as if anxious to be cheery, then hastening back to their hidings out of the wind, puffing out their breast-feathers over their toes, and subsiding among the leaves, cold and breakfastless, while the snow continues to fall, and there is no sign of clearing. But the Ouzel never calls forth a single touch of pity; not because he is strong to endure, but rather because he seems to live a charmed life beyond the reach of every influence that makes endurance necessary.

One wild winter morning, when Yosemite Valley was swept its length from west to east by a cordial snow-storm, I sallied forth to see what I might learn and enjoy. A sort of gray, gloaming-like darkness filled the valley, the huge walls were out of sight, all ordinary sounds were smothered, and even the loudest booming of the falls was at times buried beneath the roar of the heavy-laden blast. The loose snow was already over five feet deep on the meadows, making extended walks impossible without the aid of snowshoes. I found no great difficulty, however, in making my way to a certain ripple on the river where one of my ouzels lived. He was at home, busily gleaning his breakfast among the pebbles of a shallow portion of the margin, apparently unaware of anything extraordinary in the weather. Presently he flew out to a stone against which the icy current was beating, and turning his back to the wind, sang as delightfully as a lark in springtime.

After spending an hour or two with my favorite, I made my way across the valley, boring and wallowing through the drifts, to learn as definitely as possible how the other birds were spending their time. The Yosemite birds are easily found during the winter because all of them excepting the Ouzel are restricted to the sunny north side of the valley, the south side being constantly eclipsed by the great frosty shadow of the wall. And because the Indian Cañon groves, from their peculiar exposure, are the warmest, the birds congregate there, more especially in severe weather.

I found most of the robins cowering on the lee side of the larger branches where the snow could not fall upon them, while two or three of the more enterprising were making desperate efforts to reach the mistletoe berries by clinging nervously to the under side of the snow-crowned masses, back downward, like woodpeckers. Every now and then they would dislodge some of the loose fringes of the snow-crown, which would come sifting down on them and send them screaming back to camp, where they would subside among their companions with a shiver, muttering in low, querulous chatter like hungry children.

Some of the sparrows were busy at the feet of the larger trees gleaning seeds and benumbed insects, joined now and then by a robin weary of his unsuccessful attempts upon the snow-covered berries. The brave woodpeckers were clinging to the snowless sides of the larger boles and overarching branches of the camp trees, making short flights from side to side of the grove, pecking now and then at the acorns they had stored in the bark, and chattering aimlessly as if unable to keep still, yet evidently putting in the time in a very dull way, like storm-bound travelers at a country tavern. The hardy nut-hatches were threading the open furrows of the trunks in their usual industrious manner, and uttering their quaint notes, evidently less distressed than their neighbors. The Steller jays were of course making more noisy stir than all the other birds combined; ever coming and going with loud bluster, screaming as if each had a lump of melting sludge in his throat, and taking good care to improve the favorable opportunity afforded by the storm to steal from the acorn stores of the woodpeckers. I also noticed one solitary gray eagle braving the storm on the top of a tall pine-stump just outside the main grove. He was standing bolt upright with his back to the wind, a tuft of snow piled on his square shoulders, a monument of passive endurance. Thus every snow-bound bird seemed more or less uncomfortable if not in positive distress. The storm was reflected in every gesture, and not one cheerful note, not to say song, came from a single bill; their cowering, joyless endurance offering a striking contrast to the spontaneous, irrepressible gladness of the Ouzel, who could no more help exhaling sweet song then a rose sweet fragrance. He *must* sing though the heavens fall. I remember noticing the distress of a pair of robins during the violent earthquake of the year 1872, when the pines of the Valley, with strange movements, flapped and waved their branches, and beetling rock-brows came thundering down to the meadows in tremendous avalanches. It did not occur to me in the midst of the excitement of other observations to look for the ouzels, but I doubt not they were singing straight on through it all, regarding the terrible rock-thunder as fearlessly as they do the booming of the waterfalls.

What may be regarded as the separate songs of the Ouzel are exceedingly difficult of description, because they are so variable and at the same time so confluent. Though I have been acquainted with my favorite ten years, and during most of this time have heard him sing nearly every day, I still detect notes and strains that seem new to me. Nearly all of his music is sweet and tender, lapsing from his round breast like water over the smooth lip of a pool, then breaking farther on into a sparkling foam of melodious notes, which glow with subdued enthusiasm, yet without expressing much of the strong, gushing ecstasy of the bobolink or skylark.

The more striking strains are perfect arabesques of melody, composed of a few full, round, mellow notes, embroidered with delicate trills which fade and melt in long slender cadences. In a general way his music is that of the streams refined and spiritualized. The deep booming notes of the falls are in it, the trills of rapids, the gurgling of margin eddies, the low whispering of level reaches, and the sweet tinkle of separate drops oozing from the ends of mosses and falling into tranquil pools.

The Ouzel never sings in chorus with other birds, nor with his kind, but only with the streams. And like flowers that bloom beneath the surface of the ground, some of our favorite's best song-blossoms never rise above the surface of the heavier music of the water. I have often observed him singing in the midst of beaten spray, his music completely buried beneath the water's roar; yet I knew he was surely singing by his gestures and the movements of his bill.

His food, as far as I have noticed, consists of all kinds of water insects, which in summer are chiefly procured along shallow margins. Here he wades about ducking his head under water and deftly turning over pebbles and fallen leaves with his bill, seldom choosing to go into deep water where he has to use his wings in diving.

He seems to be especially fond of the larvae of mosquitos, found in abundance attached to the bottom of smooth rock channels where the current is shallow. When feeding in such places he wades up-stream, and often while his head is under water the swift current is deflected upward along the glossy curves of his neck and shoulders, in the form of a clear, crystalline shell, which fairly incloses him like a bell-glass, the shell being broken and re-formed as he lifts and dips his head; while ever and anon he sidles out to where the too powerful current carries him off his feet; then he dexterously rises on the wing and goes gleaning again in shallower places.

But during the winter, when the stream-banks are embossed in snow, and the streams themselves are chilled nearly to the freezing-point, so that the snow falling into them in stormy weather is not wholly dissolved, but forms a thin, blue sludge, thus rendering the current opaque —then he seeks the deeper portions of the main rivers, where he may dive to clear water beneath the sludge. Or he repairs to some open lake or millpond, at the bottom of which he feeds in safety.

When thus compelled to betake himself to a lake, he does not plunge into it at once like a duck, but always alights in the first place upon some rock or fallen pine along the shore. Then flying out thirty or forty yards, more or less, according to the character of the bottom, he alights with a dainty glint on the surface, swims about, looks down, finally makes up his mind, and disappears with a sharp stroke of his wings. After feeding for two or three minutes he suddenly reappears, showers the water from his wings with one vigorous shake, and rises abruptly into the air as if pushed up from beneath, comes back to his perch, sings a few minutes, and goes out to dive again; thus coming and going, singing and diving at the same place for hours.

The Ouzel is usually found singly; rarely in pairs, excepting during the breeding season, and *very* rarely in threes or fours. I once observed three thus spending a winter morning in company, upon a small glacier lake, on the Upper Merced, about 7500 feet above the level of the sea. A storm had occurred during the night, but the morning sun shone unclouded, and the shadowy lake, gleaming darkly in its setting of fresh snow, lay smooth and motionless as a mirror. My camp chanced to be within a few feet of the water's edge, opposite a fallen pine, some of the branches of which leaned out over the lake. Here my three dearly welcome visitors took up their station, and at once began to embroider the frosty air with their delicious melody, doubly delightful to me that particular morning, as I had been somewhat apprehensive of danger in breaking my way down through the snow-choked cañons to the lowlands.

The portion of the lake bottom selected for a feeding-ground lies at a depth of fifteen or twenty feet below the surface, and is covered with a short growth of algae and other aquatic plants—facts I have previously determined while sailing over it on a raft. After alighting on the glassy surface, they occasionally indulged in a little play, chasing one another round about in small circles; then all three would suddenly dive together, and then come ashore and sing.

The Ouzel seldom swims more than a few yards on the surface, for, not being web-footed, he makes rather slow progress, but by means of his strong, crisp wings he swims, or rather flies, with celerity under the surface, often to considerable distances. But it is in withstanding the force of heavy rapids that his strength of wing in this respect is most strikingly manifested. The following may be regarded as a fair illustration of his power of sub-aquatic flight. One stormy morning in winter when the Merced River was blue and green with unmelted snow, I observed one of my ouzels perched on a snag out in the midst of a swift-rushing rapid, singing cheerily, as if everything was just to his mind; and while I stood on the bank admiring him, he suddenly plunged into the sludgy current, leaving his song abruptly broken off. After feeding a minute or two at the bottom, and when one would suppose that he must inevitably be swept far down-stream, he emerged just where he went down, alighted on the same snag, showered the water-beads from his feathers, and continued his unfinished song, seemingly in tranquil ease as if it had suffered no interruption.

The Ouzel alone of all birds dares to enter a white torrent. And though strictly terrestrial in structure, no other is so inseparably related to water, not even the duck, or the bold ocean albatross, or the stormy-petrel. For ducks go ashore as soon as they finish feeding in undisturbed places, and very often make long flights overland from lake to lake or field to field. The same is true of most other aquatic birds. But the Ouzel, born on the brink of a stream, or on a snag or boulder in the midst of it, seldom leaves it for a single moment. For, notwithstanding he is often on the wing, he never flies overland, but whirs with rapid, quail-like beat above the stream, tracing all its windings. Even when the stream is quite small, say from five to ten feet wide, he seldom shortens his flight by crossing a bend, however abrupt it may be; and even when disturbed by meeting some one on the bank, he prefers to fly over one's head, to dodging out over the ground. When, therefore, his flight along a crooked stream is viewed endwise, it appears most strikingly wavered—a description on the air of every curve with lightning-like rapidity.

The vertical curves and angles of the most precipitous torrents he traces with the same rigid fidelity, swooping down the inclines of cascades, dropping sheer over dizzy falls amid the spray, and ascending with the same fearlessness and ease, seldom seeking to lessen the steepness of the acclivity by beginning to ascend before reaching the base of the fall. No matter though it may be several hundred feet in height he holds straight on, as if about to dash headlong into the throng of booming rockets, then darts abruptly upward, and, after alighting at the top of the precipice to rest a moment, proceeds to feed and sing. His flight is solid and impetuous, without any intermission of wing-beats—one homogeneous buzz like that of a laden bee on its way home. And while thus buzzing freely from fall to fall, he is frequently heard giving utterance to a long outdrawn train of unmodulated notes, in no way connected with his song, but corresponding closely with his flight in sustained vigor.

Were the flights of all the ouzels in the Sierra traced on a chart, they would indicate the direction of the flow of the entire system of ancient glaciers, from about the period of the breaking up of the ice-sheet until near the close of the glacial winter; because the streams which the ouzels so rigidly follow are, with the unimportant exceptions of a few side tributaries, all flowing in channels eroded for them out of the solid flank of the range by the vanished glaciers—the streams tracing the ancient glaciers, the ouzels tracing the streams. Nor do we find so complete compliance to glacial conditions in the life of any other mountain bird, or animal of any kind. Bears frequently accept the pathways laid down by galciers as the easiest to travel; but they often leave them and cross over from cañon to cañon. So also, most of the birds trace the moraines to some extent, because the forests are growing on them. But they wander far, crossing the cañons from grove to grove, and draw exceedingly angular and complicated courses.

The Ouzel's nest is one of the most extraordinary pieces of bird architecture I ever saw, odd and novel in design, perfectly fresh and beautiful, and in every way worthy of the genius of the little builder. It is about a foot in diameter, round and bossy in outline, with a neatly arched opening near the bottom, somewhat like an old-fashioned brick oven, or Hottentot's hut. It is built almost exclusively of green and yellow mosses, chiefly the beautiful fronded hypnum that covers the rocks and old drift-logs in the vicinity of waterfalls. These are deftly interwoven, and felted together into a charming little hut; and so situated that many of the outer mosses continue to flourish as if they had not been plucked. A few fine, silky-stemmed grasses are occasionally found interwoven with the mosses, but, with the exception of a thin layer lining the floor, their presence seems accidental, as they are of a species found growing with the mosses and are probably plucked with them. The site chosen for this curious mansion is usually some little rock-shelf within reach of the lighter particles of the spray of a waterfall, so that its walls are kept green and growing, at least during the time of high water.

No harsh lines are presented by any portion of the nest as seen in place, but when removed from its shelf, the back and bottom, and sometimes a portion of the top, is found quite sharply angular, because it is made to conform to the surface of the rock upon which and against which it is built, the little architect always taking advantage of slight crevices and protuberances that may chance to offer, to render his structure stable by means of a kind of gripping and dovetailing.

In choosing a building-spot, concealment does not seem to be taken into consideration; yet notwithstanding the nest is large and guilelessly exposed to view, it is far from being easily detected, chiefly because it swells forward like any other bulging moss-cushion growing naturally in such situations. This is more especially the case where the nest is kept fresh by being well sprinkled. Sometimes these romantic little huts have their beauty enhanced by rock-ferns and grasses that spring up around the mossy walls, or in front of the door-sill, dripping with crystal beads.

Furthermore, at certain hours of the day, when the sunshine is poured down at the required angle, the whole mass of the spray enveloping the fairy establishment is brilliantly irised; and it is through so glorious a rainbow atmosphere as this that some of our blessed ouzels obtain their first peep at the world.

Ouzels seem so completely part and parcel of the streams they inhabit, they scarce suggest any other origin than the streams themselves; and one might almost be pardoned in fancying they come direct from the living waters, like flowers from the ground. At least, from whatever cause, it never occurred to me to look for their nests until more than a year after I had made the acquaintance of the birds themselves, although I found one the very day on which I began the search. In making my way from Yosemite to the glaciers at the heads of the Merced and Tuolumne rivers, I camped in a particularly wild and romantic portion of the Nevada cañon where in previous excursions I had never failed to enjoy the company of my favorites, who were attracted here, no doubt, by the safe nesting-places in the shelving rocks, and by the abundance of food and falling water. The river, for miles above and below, consists of a succession of small falls from ten to sixty feet in height, connected by flat, plume-like cascades that go flashing from fall to fall, free and almost channelless, over waving folds of glacier-polished granite.

On the south side of one of the falls, that portion of the precipice which is bathed by the spray presents a series of little shelves and tablets caused by the development of planes of cleavage in the granite, and by the consequent fall of masses through the action of the water. "Now here," said I, "of all places, is the most charming spot for an Ouzel's nest." Then carefully scanning the fretted face of the precipice through the spray, I at length noticed a yellowish moss-cushion, growing on the edge of a level tablet within five or six feet of the outer folds of the fall. But apart from the fact of its being situated where one acquainted with the lives of ouzels would fancy an Ouzel's nest ought to be, there was nothing in its appearance visible at first sight, to distinguish it from other bosses of rock-moss similarly situated with reference to perennial spray; and it was not until I had scrutinized it again and again, and had removed my shoes and stockings and crept along the face of the rock within eight or ten feet of it, that I could decide certainly whether it was a nest or a natural growth.

In these moss huts three or four eggs are laid, white like foam-bubbles; and well may the little birds hatched from them sing water songs, for they hear them all their lives, and even before they are born.

I have often observed the young just out of the nest making their odd gestures, and seeming in every way as much at home as their experienced parents, like young bees on their first excursions to the flower fields. No amount of familiarity with people and their ways seems to change them in the least. To all appearance their behavior is just the same on seeing a man for the first time, as when they have seen him frequently.

On the lower reaches of the rivers where mills are built, they sing on through the din of the machinery, and all the noisy confusion of dogs, cattle, and workmen. On one occasion, while a woodchopper was at work on the river-bank, I observed one cheerily singing within reach of the flying chips. Nor does any kind of unwonted disturbance put him in bad humor, or frighten him out of calm self-possession. In passing through a narrow gorge, I once drove one ahead of me from rapid to rapid, disturbing him four times in quick succession where he could not very well fly past me on account of the narrowness of the channel. Most birds under similar circumstances fancy themselves pursued, and become suspiciously uneasy; but, instead of growing nervous about it, he made his usual dippings, and sang one of his most tranquil strains. When observed within a few yards their eyes are seen to express remarkable gentleness and intelligence; but they seldom allow so near a view unless one wears clothing of about the same color as the rocks and trees, and knows how to sit still. On one occasion, while rambling along the shore of a mountain lake, where the birds, at least those born that season, had never seen a man, I sat down to rest on a large stone close to the water's edge, upon which it seemed the ouzels and sandpipers were in the habit of alighting when they came to feed on that part of the shore, and some of the other birds also, when they came down to wash or drink. In a few minutes, along came a whirring Ouzel and alighted on the stone beside me, within reach of my hand. Then suddenly observing me, he stooped nervously as if about to fly on the instant, but as I remained as motionless as the stone, he gained confidence, and looked me steadily in the face for about a minute, then flew quietly to the outlet and began to sing. Next came a sandpiper and gazed at me with much the same guileless expression of eye as the Ouzel. Lastly, down with a swoop came a Steller's jay out of a fir-tree, probably with the intention of moistening his noisy throat. But instead of sitting confidingly as my other visitors had done, he rushed off at once, nearly tumbling heels over head into the lake in his suspicious confusion, and with loud screams roused the neighborhood.

Love for song-birds, with their sweet human voices, appears to be more common and unfailing than love for flowers. Every one loves flowers to some extent, at least in life's fresh morning, attracted by them as instinctively as humming-birds and bees. Even the young Digger Indians have sufficient love for the brightest of those found growing on the mountains to gather them and braid them as decorations for the hair. And I was glad to discover, through the few Indians that could be induced to talk on the subject, that they have names for the wild rose and the lily, and other conspicuous flowers, whether available as food or otherwise. Most men, however, whether savage or civilized, become apathetic toward all plants that have no other apparent use than the use of beauty. But fortunately one's first instinctive love of song-birds is never wholly obliterated, no matter what the influences upon our lives may be. I have often been delighted to see a pure, spiritual glow come into the countenances of hard business-men and old miners, when a song-bird chanced to alight near them. Nevertheless, the little mouthful of meat that swells out the breasts of some song-birds is too often the cause of their death. Larks and robins in particular are brought to market in hundreds. But fortunately the Ouzel has no enemy so eager to eat his little body as to follow him into the mountain solitudes. I never knew him to be chased even by hawks.

An acquaintance of mine, a sort of foot-hill mountaineer, had a pet cat, a great, dozy, overgrown creature, about as broad-shouldered as a lynx. During the winter, while the snow lay deep, the mountaineer sat in his lonely cabin among the pines smoking his pipe and wearing the dull time away. Tom was his sole companion, sharing his bed, and sitting beside him on a stool with much the same drowsy expression of eye as his master. The good-natured bachelor was content with his hard fare of soda-bread and bacon, but Tom, the only creature in the world acknowledging dependence on him, must needs be provided with fresh meat. Accordingly he bestirred himself to contrive squirrel-traps, and waded the snowy woods with his gun, making sad havoc among the few winter birds, sparing neither robin, sparrow, nor tiny nuthatch, and the pleasure of seeing Tom eat and grow fat was his great reward.

One cold afternoon, while hunting along the river-bank, he noticed a plain-feathered little bird skipping about in the shallows, and immediately raised his gun. But just then the confiding songster began to sing, and after listening to his summery melody the charmed hunter turned away, saying, "Bless your little heart, I can't shoot you, not even for Tom."

Even so far north as icy Alaska, I have found my glad singer. When I was exploring the glaciers between Mount Fairweather and the Stikeen River, one cold day in November, after trying in vain to force a way through the innumerable icebergs of Sum Dum Bay to the great glaciers at the head of it, I was weary and baffled and sat resting in my canoe convinced at last that I would have to leave this part of my work for another year. Then I began to plan my escape to open water before the young ice which was beginning to form should shut me in. While I thus lingered drifting with the bergs, in the midst of these gloomy forebodings and all the terrible glacial desolation and grandeur, I suddenly heard the well-known whir of an Ouzel's wings, and, looking up, saw my little comforter coming straight across the ice from the shore. In a second or two he was with me, flying three times round my head with a happy salute, as if saying, "Cheer up, old friend; you see I'm here, and all's well." Then he flew back to the shore, alighted on the topmost jag of a stranded iceberg, and began to nod and bow as though he were on one of his favorite boulders in the midst of a sunny Sierra cascade.

The species is distributed all along the mountain ranges of the Pacific Coast from Alaska to Mexico, and east to the Rocky Mountains. Nevertheless, it is as yet comparatively little known. Audubon and Wilson did not meet it. Swainson was, I believe, the first naturalist to describe a specimen from Mexico. Specimens were shortly afterward procured by Drummond near the sources of the Athabasca River, between the fifty-fourth and fifty-sixth parallels; and it has been collected by nearly all of the numerous exploring expeditions undertaken of late through our Western States and Territories; for it never fails to engage the attention of naturalists in a very particular manner.

Such, then, is our little cinclus, beloved of every one who is so fortunate as to know him. Tracing on strong wing every curve of the most precipitous torrents from one extremity of the Sierra to the other; not fearing to follow them through their darkest gorges and coldest snow-tunnels; acquainted with every waterfall, echoing their divine music; and throughout the whole of their beautiful lives interpreting all that we in our unbelief call terrible in the utterances of torrents and storms, as only varied expressions of God's eternal love.

THE

SCAVENGERS

Mary Austin

Mary Austin was not an ornithologist. She was a mystic, a visionary, and, in the opinion of many, a prophetess and seer besides. Born in Illinois she grew up in Bakersfield, California, fell under the spell of the desert, and there evolved her curious theory of the influence of landscape upon culture. Americans, she argued, were eternally different from the people of the Old World because the land they inhabited was different. They would find their true selves when they learned, as the Indians had learned before them, the lessons this land could teach them.

Of her many books the best was probably The Land of Little Rain *(1903) from which the following selection is taken The vultures she describes are actual birds that an ornithologist will recognize. But they are also symbols and riddles to be read. They know and they can teach one aspect of the mystique of the desert.*

FIFTY-SEVEN buzzards, one on each of fifty-seven fence posts at the rancho El Tejon, on a mirage-breeding Sptember morning, sat solemnly while the white tilted travelers' vans lumbered down the Canada de los Uvas. After three hours they had only clapped their wings, or exchanged posts. The season's end in the vast dim valley of the San Joaquin is palpitatingly hot, and the air breathes like cotton wool. Through it all the buzzards sit on the fences and low hummocks, with wings spread fanwise for air. There is no end to them, and they smell to heaven. Their heads droop, and all their communication is a rare, horrid croak.

The increase of wild creatures is in proportion to the things they feed upon: the more carrion the more buzzards. The end of the third successive dry year bred them beyond belief. The first year quail mated sparingly; the second year the wild oats matured no seed; the third, cattle died in their tracks with their heads towards the stopped watercourses. And that year the scavengers were as black as the plague all across the mesa and up the treeless, tumbled hills. On clear days they betook themselves to the upper air, where they hung motionless for hours. That year there were vultures among them, distinguished by the white patches

From *The Land of Little Rain*. Boston: Houghton Mifflin, 1903.

under the wings. All their offensiveness notwithstanding, they have a stately flight. They must also have what pass for good qualities among themselves, for they are social, not to say clannish.

It is a very squalid tragedy—that of the dying brutes and the scavenger birds. Death by starvation is slow. The heavy-headed, rack-boned cattle totter in the fruitless trails; they stand for long, patient intervals; they lie down and do not rise. There is fear in their eyes when they are first stricken, but afterward only intolerable weariness. I suppose the dumb creatures know nearly as much of death as do their betters, who have only the more imagination. Their even-breathing submission after the first agony is their tribute to its inevitableness. It needs a nice discrimination to say which of the basket-ribbed cattle is likeliest to afford the next meal, but the scavengers make few mistakes. One stoops to the quarry and the flock follows.

Cattle once down may be days in dying. They stretch out their necks along the ground, and roll up their slow eyes at longer intervals. The buzzards have all the time, and no beak is dropped or talon struck until the breath is wholly passed. It is doubtless the economy of nature to have the scavengers by to clean up the carrion, but a wolf at the throat would be a shorter agony than the long stalking and sometime perchings of these loathsome watchers. Suppose now it were a man in this long-drawn, hungrily spied upon distress! When Timmie O'Shea was lost on Armogossa Flats for three days without water, Long Tom Basset found him, not by any trail, but by making straight away for the points where he saw buzzards stooping. He could hear the beat of their wings, Tom said, and trod on their shadows, but O'Shea was past recalling what he thought about things after the second day. My friend Ewan told me, among other things, when he came back from San Juan Hill, that not all the carnage of battle turned his bowels as the sight of slant black wings rising flockwise before the burial squad.

There are three kinds of noises buzzards make—it is impossible to call them notes—raucous and elemental. There is a short croak of alarm, and the same syllable in a modified tone to serve all the purposes of ordinary conversation. The old birds make a kind of throaty chuckling to their young, but if they have any love song I have not heard it. The young yawp in the nest a little, with more breath than noise. It is seldom one finds a buzzard's nest, seldom that grown-ups find a nest of any sort; it is only children to whom these things happen by right. But by making a business of it one may come upon them in wide, quiet cañons, or on the lookouts of lonely, table-topped mountains, three or four together, in the tops of stubby trees or on rotten cliffs well open to the sky.

It is probable that the buzzard is gregarious, but it seems unlikely from the small number of young noted at any time that every female incubates each year. The young birds are easily distinguished by their size when feeding, and high up in air by the worn primaries of the older birds. It is when the young go out of the nest on their first foraging that the parents, full of a crass and simple pride, make their indescribable chucklings of gobbling, gluttonous delight. The little ones would be amusing as they tug and tussle, if one could forget what it is they feed upon.

One never comes any nearer to the vulture's nest or nestlings than hearsay. They keep to the southerly Sierras, and are bold enough, it seems, to do killing on their own account when no carrion is at hand. They dog the shepherd from camp to camp, the hunter home from the hill, and will even carry away offal from under his hand.

The vulture merits respect for his bigness and for his bandit airs, but he is a sombre bird, with none of the buzzard's frank satisfaction in his offensiveness.

The least objectionable of the inland scavengers is the raven, frequenter of the desert ranges, the same called locally "carrion crow." He is handsomer and has such an air. He is nice in his habits and is said to have likable traits. A tame one in a Shoshone camp was the butt of much sport and enjoyed it. He could all but talk and was another with the children, but an arrant thief. The raven will eat most things that come his way—eggs and young of ground-nesting birds, seeds even, lizards and grasshoppers, which he catches cleverly; and whatever he is about, let a coyote trot never so softly by, the raven flaps up and after; for whatever the coyote can pull down or nose out is meat also for the carrion crow.

And never a coyote comes out of his lair for killing, in the country of the carrion crows, but looks up first to see where they may be gathering. It is a sufficient occupation for a windy morning, on the lineless, level mesa, to watch the pair of them eying each other furtively, with a tolerable assumption of unconcern, but no doubt with a certain amount of good understanding about it. Once at Red Rock, in a year of green pasture, which is a bad time for the scavengers, we saw two buzzards, five ravens, and a coyote feeding on the same carrion, and only the coyote seemed ashamed of the company.

Probably we never fully credit the interdependence of wild creatures, and their cognizance of the affairs of their own kind. When the five coyotes that range the Tejon from Pasteria to Tunawai planned a relay race to bring down an antelope strayed from the band, beside myself to watch, an eagle swung down from Mt. Pinos, buzzards materialized out of invisible ether, and hawks came trooping like small boys to a street fight. Rabbits sat up in the chaparral and cocked their ears, feeling themselves quite safe for the once as the hunt swung near them. Nothing happens in the deep wood that the blue jays are not all agog to tell. The hawk follows the badger, the coyote the carrion crow, and from their aerial stations the buzzards watch each other. What would be worth knowing is how much of their neighbor's affairs the new generations learn for themselves, and how much they are taught of their elders.

So wide is the range of the scavengers that it is never safe to say, eyewitness to the contrary, that there are few or many in such a place. Where the carrion is, there will the buzzards be gathered together, and in three days' journey you will not sight another one. The way up from Mojave to Red Butte is all desertness, affording no pasture and scarcely a rill of water. In a year of little rain in the south, flocks and herds were driven to the number of thousands along this road to the perennial pastures of the high ranges. It is a long, slow trail, ankle deep in bitter dust that gets up in the slow wind and moves along the backs of the crawling cattle. In the worst of times one in three will pine and fall out by the way. In the defiles of Red Rock, the sheep piled up a stinking lane; it was the sun smiting by day. To these shambles came buzzards, vultures, and coyotes from all the country round, so that on the Tejon, the Ceriso, and the Little Antelope there were not scavengers enough to keep the country clean. All that summer the dead mummified in the open or dropped slowly back to earth in the quagmires of the bitter springs. Meanwhile from Red Rock to Coyote Holes, and from Coyote Holes to Haiwai the scavengers gorged and gorged.

The coyote is not a scavenger by choice, preferring his own kill, but being on the whole a lazy dog, is apt to fall into carrion eating because it is easier. The red fox and bobcat, a little pressed by hunger, will eat of any other animal's kill, but will not ordinarily touch what dies of itself, and are exceedingly shy of food that has been manhandled.

Very clean and handsome, quite belying his relationship in appearance, is Clark's crow, that scavenger and plunderer of mountain camps. It is permissible to call him by his common name, "Camp Robber": he has earned it. Not content with refuse, he pecks open meal sacks, filches whole potatoes, is a gormand for bacon, drills holes in packing cases, and is daunted by nothing short of tin. All the while he does not neglect to vituperate the chipmunks and sparrows that whisk off crumbs of comfort from under the camper's feet. The Camp Robber's gray coat, black and white barred wings, and slender bill, with certain tricks of perching, accuse him of attempts to pass himself off among woodpeckers; but his behavior is all crow. He frequents the higher pine belts, and has a noisy strident call like a jay's, and how clean he and the frisk-tailed chipmunks keep the camp! No crumb or paring or bit of eggshell goes amiss.

High as the camp may be, so it is not above timber-line, it is not too high for the coyote, the bobcat, or the wolf. It is the complaint of the ordinary camper that the woods are too still, depleted of wild life. But what dead body of wild thing, or neglected game untouched by its kind, do you find? And put out offal away from camp over night, and look next day at the foot tracks where it lay.

Man is a great blunderer going about in the woods, and there is no other except the bear makes so much noise. Being so well warned beforehand, it is a very stupid animal, or a very bold one, that cannot keep safely hid. The cunningest hunter is hunted in turn, and what he leaves of his kill is meat for some other. That is the economy of nature, but with it all there is not sufficient account taken of the works of man. There is no scavenger that eats tin cans, and no wild thing leaves a like disfigurement on the forest floor.

RED-TAILED

HAWK

Athos and Sara Menaboni

Since the days of Audubon, ornithologists have often devoted much of their time to bird portraiture. Photography opened a new field and its possibilities have been greatly extended within the last few years by the invention of the stroboscopic flash which can stop even the incredibly fast motion of a hummingbird's wing. But photography is inevitably to some extent impersonal and the personal vision of a painter or draftsman still has its special value. Athos and Sara Menaboni are passionate bird lovers whose tenderness (not always a characteristic of ornithologists) contributes something to the great charm of their work.

THIS morning I am reminded of a story that goes something like this: The Poverello of Assisi, after hearing the villagers' tale of woe about a wolf destroying their sheep and, worse than that, eating their children, persuaded the men not to go kill the wolf, and said he would go outside the village walls to talk the matter over with the beast. In fear and trembling the townsmen watched St. Francis calmly approach the ferocious animal saying, "Brother wolf, why are you a killer?"

The wolf answered that he could find food in no other way, but that if he were regularly fed by the people of the village he would do them no more harm. St. Francis promised the wolf that food would be set out every day for him. The promise was kept, and never again was there trouble.

Formerly I thought this story farfetched, but now I do not think it so improbable.

Let me go back to the day when Athos and I chanced upon a wounded female red-tailed hawk. Obviously someone had shot her, yet she had escaped with only a broken wing. Helpless on the ground, she would have died of starvation had we not come along. Her eyes were fierce, and she had just cause to hate human beings. At the sight of us she lay on her back, terrified, brandishing her feet with the long talons in the

From *Menaboni's Birds*. New York: Rinehart & Co., 1950.

air. She knew that her only method of defense would be to tear our flesh.

Athos threw his leather jacket over her and in a moment had wrapped her securely in it. He held her legs firmly, and before we reached Valle Ombrosa she had ceased struggling. She behaved nicely while her wounds were swabbed with antiseptic, a splint was applied to hold the broken bones in place, and both wings were tied to her body to keep her from flapping them.

While she was "taking the cure," it was imperative that she be put in a warm, enclosed spot with not to much light, and that she see us often enough so that she would recognize us as her friends. In our tiny house there was not much choice as to where she could be put—of course the shower-bath enclosure! Once there, terror and hate left her eyes and were supplanted by curiosity and wonder. We gave her a piece of meat and left her alone, to get her bearings in peace.

Within three days she was eating out of our hands. She found that we meant no harm when we scratched the back of her head and neck and smoothed her breast feathers, and she closed her eyes, apparently in ecstasy when we petted her. She learned to ride on our gloved hands to the kitchen when we wanted the shower bath to ourselves, and after a few more days she learned to perch on our ungloved hands without sinking her long talons in our flesh. She looked forward to our visits to break the monotony of her existence and came to enjoy her excursions to the living room to be shown off to visitors. She let anyone stroke her head and hold her with bare hands. I wondered if she understood and appreciated it when Athos said, "I am crazy about hawks. They are so intelligent."

After three weeks Athos took off her bonds to allow her to use her wings to flap about the bathroom. After a couple of days he set a post into the ground on the front terrace, put jesses on her legs, and attached her with a chain to the post. Quickly she learned that she could fly just so far—to the brick wall—and no farther. She liked her exercise that first day, and when dusk came she kept trying to fly to the house. Athos took her upon his hand and she rode docilely into her bathroom for the night, where she knew she was safe from harm.

After a few days of the hawk being outdoors during the day and brought into the house at night, Athos tried an experiment: after he untied her from the post he dropped the chain to the ground beside her. She walked directly to the front door, waited for him to open it, and entered the house. Would she know what to do next? She turned left to go into the bunkroom alone; there she turned right to go into the bathroom, and in the bathroom she hopped over the floor sill into the shower enclosure. She knew as well as we did where her bed was! Patiently she waited for Athos to come take off the chain for the night, and after that was done she promptly went to sleep. Every night thereafter she repeated the performance.

How nice that she liked our home! "Our home?" Why, it was hers just as much as it was ours, for she helped pay for it by posing for the pictures Athos painted of her. She owned us just as much as we owned her.

Daily we watched her exercising or in repose, and were sorry to observe that the broken wing, though the bones had knitted, drooped somewhat. We hoped that in flying exercises this would be corrected, and the next step was to place her in the large aviary, where she could use her wings fully.

She could fly well enough to enjoy herself in the aviary, but in the months that followed we saw that she could not fly sufficiently well to be set free in the wild to look after herself. She was destined to live out her life span with the Menabonis; destined to give us a constant reminder of the gunman who had shot her; destined to make me ask people to please, please not shoot red-tailed hawks.

A year—two years—in confinement. She did not appear unhappy, yet I wondered what her thoughts were when high in the sky she could see other hawks of her kind in their element, free to go where they chose, to mate, and to live normally. I hoped that it was some compensation to know that her food would come every morning, from Athos's hands. Then, too, she was not alone, for in the next partition in the aviary was the Sergeant, not too different from her kind.

There she was, a perfectly healthy bird with a drooping wing. One morning Athos said to me, "I'm going to release her, to see if she can fly. After all, we could be mistaken; if we are, she ought to have her freedom." It was a gamble, but Athos wanted to risk it for her sake.

After being taken from the aviary, she slowly flapped her wings to gain a perch on a pine close by. For half a day she stayed there, looking about her familiar territory from a different vantage point. Then she opened each wing its full spread of sixteen inches, and flew off. She *could* fly well!

We wondered if we should ever see her again. Days passed, and once high in the sky we saw what appeared to be a red-tailed hawk soaring above Valle Ombrosa, but at that distance we could not determine if it was our pet or not. But a strange sound came from our aviary. After years of silence the Sergeant had let out a peculiar call, not a bit like the sound we had imagined a golden eagle to make, but like a small dog barking. Could it be that he recognized his former aviary mate? Was he calling to her?

A week went by, and one morning we heard a great commotion of chickens clattering alarm, ducks quacking, and pigeons flying. We rushed outside to see what was the cause, and there on a pine branch directly over the aviary sat our red-tailed hawk! The Sergeant was barking at her!

Athos looked at her and said, "Her crop is flat, she must be hungry. Perhaps she cannot fly well enough to catch her own food, and has come home for a handout." He rushed to get meat from the refrigerator.

Under the pine he stood with the meat on his outstretched hand. He called up to her, "Come on down. Here is your breakfast."

She opened her wings, dived downward, and glided to his feet. She walked a couple of steps to him and took the proffered piece of meat from his hands. After she had eaten it, she cried in a soft pitiful voice for more. Athos handed her another piece and another, until her crop bulged. When satisfied, she sprang into the air, and flew to a near-by tree, where she sat for hours. Then we saw a most peculiar thing happen. She flew onto the wire top of the eagle cage and stayed there. The Sergeant, in his cramped space, jumped off his perch, flipped himself upside down, and through the wire locked claws with the hawk! For five minutes the Sarge hung upside down in that clasp with her. She must have liked it, for after he turned her loose, and righted himself to go back to his perch, she waited on the wire for him to return to go through the same antic ten minutes later. Were they in love with each other? Was the Sergeant only playing?

With a loud, eerie, and weird scream she flew off. It was the kind of scream we should have expected to come from the eagle, but he only barked like a puppy as she left.

All right, she had come home, but a problem presented itself: would the hawk catch our other free birds? We soon found out that our fears were groundless, for the next morning she came back for breakfast. Every morning thereafter she returned, without once molesting the pigeons, ducks, or chickens. Why should she, when Athos is such a good provider?

And we always know by the barking of the Sergeant when she has arrived. Time after time we have seen them lock claws.

At the moment I see Athos on the hill by the hawk's favorite pine, and she is looking down at the rabbit in his hand, which he secured for her yesterday. I hear him saying, "Come on down. I can't stay here all day waiting for you to make up your mind! Come now."

And now she flies to his feet. The hawk of Valle Ombrosa is having her breakfast. She is so tame that, as she eats, I see Athos scratching the back of her head.

CHEWINKS

IN

THE SUN

Ada Clapham Govan

Despite the passion with which they have been spied upon, birds can still surprise not only the amateur but sometimes even the professional—as the anecdotes published in natural-history magazines prove again and again. Here is an especially charming little example.

SPEAKING of chewinks reminds me of a shock they gave me one hot summer day. Looking out my window I was startled and alarmed to find the yard strewn with bird bodies, as if a machine gun had sprayed it. Ten chewinks already lay sprawled out, apparently having breathed their last. Then an eleventh, who until that moment had looked in the pink of condition, suddenly slumped in a heap, tilted his right side uppermost, lifted his right wing, and unfolded like an accordion. It was positively uncanny to see so much bird evolve from so little substance. Every feather on his body now pointed in the wrong direction, as if an electric shock had stood it on end. His lower jaw swung loose. Finally, twisting his neck at an angle that must have put a crick into several vertebrae, he leveled one glassy eye at the sun and proceeded to out-stare Old Sol.

Suddenly I realized that our back yard was being used as a sort of bird nudist camp. Apparently these tiny sun-worshippers were out to make a record-breaking catch of all the healthful beauty rays on hand!

Presently the prostrate bodies began to return to life. With their upper sides frizzled to a turn, the distended feathers miraculously laid themselves down as if someone had just turned off the electric juice. Each wing and tail folded back into its alloted space. Looking almost normal again, the devotees were scrambling to their feet. But not a chewink in the bunch believed in being only half-baked.

One by one, again, they dropped in their tracks, but with the under-

From *Wings at My Window*. New York: The Macmillan Company, 1940.

done side now on top. Why each and every bird opened his mouth I don't know, unless as a vent to let off steam. I almost expected to find small pools of gravy dotting the ground when the youngsters finally picked themselves up—this time for keeps. Each gave himself a vigorous shake to reassemble his disassociated parts into the proper chewink model. Then, thoroughly permeated by vitalizing sunbeams, they dashed into their never-ending business of foraging for good substantial "eats."

CALL TO

A TRUMPETER

Sally Carrighar

Sally Carrighar is a gifted and indefatigable observer in remote northern lands who has developed a personal and original approach to the problem of describing the intimate life of birds and other animals. Like Ernest Thompson Seton, her aim is to make us realize that they do actually "lead lives" rather than merely "exhibit behavior patterns" and to establish in this way an empathy between them and us. But she is also aware how sternly official biologists usually disapprove of anything which suggests "anthropomorphism." Walking carefully between the Scylla of mere behaviorism and the Charybdis of the anthropomorphic she is astonishingly successful in making the subjects of her accounts humanly understandable without attributing to them any exclusively human traits.

T HE late, yellowing sun shot its rays through the willow brush. The willows grew out of the water in clusters like giant fistfuls. They met at the top in a wide glinting blur. Below was the lucent brown gloss, now frosted lightly with autumn dust. In flowing water the dust had wrinkled against the stems. On sheltered bays swimming animals had left shining paths.

The Trumpeter Swan was gliding beneath the wilderness of the brush. Where the overhead boughs spread apart, his breast broke a pale blue sheen. Under the leaves that joined, he was scattering green-gold flakes. He was crossing reflections of the stems, red with a violet bloom on the bark. But all the willows were not bursts of color. Among them were dead thickets, bare and silvered by the sun so that they looked ice-coated, tangles with the crystal magic of winter. Any day the sheaths of ice would become real, and the tremulous water no longer would yield to a white feathered bow.

Here the willows became so dense that the Swan must keep swinging to wind among them. He paddled faster, with his throat tensely upright. He could not relax when he felt so enclosed, although he was more

From *One Day at Teton Marsh*. New York: Alfred A. Knopf, 1947, 1954.

concerned for his family, following him, than for himself. A moose and her calf were browsing near on the leaves. They were out of sight, but the plunge of their hoofs was disquieting. And he could hear their talk, rough murmurs that may have seemed a violence to the Swan, whose own voice was a ringing clear channel for his emotions.

The thickets beyond were spaced thinly, and he came out on a small lagoon. His throat fell into a flow of curves, a tranquil sway forward and back over his wings, a lift to capture a mayfly, a downward folding to layer a feather, a revolving to scan the shoreline. The fly and feather and shore may have been only excuses for the elegant pleasure of motions so slowly graceful. He seemed more quiet than if he had not moved at all.

Now, late in the afternoon, little wind touched the responsive water. It was a stillness quick to stir, like the Swan's awareness. But a flock of mergansers splashed into the bay. They were learning how to drive fish to the shallows. The one they pursued dodged away to the willow canals, and several of the ducks dived. The Swan returned to the willows himself. Mergansers, with their habit of swimming underwater, made him nervous. For no one could tell where they would come up again. The Swan had a poise so sensitive, controlling such immense power, that lively animals often were subdued by it. Much of the time he lived in a peace he partly created; but no duck respected it. Nor did the winds. And the snows would not, and even more disastrously human beings had entered it.

He was leading his family to the beaver pond, a width from which they could rise in flight. Since the day drew to its end, his mate might follow him into the sky, if she ever would. Rounding a thicket, he missed the silent movement behind, of the others. He strengthened the stroke of one foot to pivot, and paddled back. His three cygnets had stopped to dabble for insects in floating leaves. Their mother was not with them.

The Swan was patient. He held his place with a weaving pressure of one web and the other and watched the fledglings. Their winter plumage was nearly complete. At first they had been all violet-gray, but their heads now were pinkish rust. Their bills were violet, mottled with rose. And did their colors please their father, whose eyes could distinguish them but were used to adult swans' vivid white?

The cygnets were two-thirds grown, larger than ducks but doubtless small to him. Their necks were shorter-proportioned than they would be later, and their heads were fluffier. One was beating his wings, a stretching that half-lifted him into the air, with his olive-brown feet patting the water. The other two also began to flap—little mimics still. In many ways they were not mature, needing yet to be watched. See how heedlessly they are switching their bills through the leaves, concerned only with food. They have not learned a swan's exquisite caution. At their age most birds were meeting the world by themselves, but in those species the new generation numbered thousands, even millions. The Swan was protecting his cygnets as if he had known that less than a hundred new broods of trumpeters had hatched this year, throughout the world.

Their mother should not expose them to danger by lingering so. Surely she was not far behind, concealed by the brush, but why not here? Her manner lately had made the Swan uneasy. She had seemed separate, most of the time near the family but not careful to guard the cygnets on one side while he guarded them on the other, not balancing her moves with his, with a matching grace as harmonious as a single swan's; not coming into the air with the others, not once since the young had begun to fly.

The mother had not been in the air since the flightless weeks of her summer molt. But the Swan's own wing feathers were grown out now; hers should be too. This was the season when swans should be making expeditions around the valley, around the peaks cupping the sky, up the Snake to its highest rill. Always on other years he and his mate had taken their young on autumn flights.

A swan's nature widened as the fall of leaves widened horizons. And these short family tours were the only ones they would make. No trumpeters anywhere migrated southward now. Once they did; even the grandparents of these two had been in the spindrift of wings scudding down the continent to the marshes that do not freeze. But human beings had come to those marshes to shoot swans for their down. And some of the ponds had been drained. Wildness was gone from the south—knowledge that older swans seemed to have given the recent ones. This Jackson Hole pair never had seen the devastation of the wintering grounds; yet their impulse to go was checked.

Actually human beings had stopped killing trumpeters everywhere. They had found that their spirits were lifted by the resonant voices and the great translucent wings. And so they had made a law that no one might destroy these birds. But how could that news be conveyed to the wild discouraged instincts?

The birds' down kept them warm in the northern winters, but too often their food was lost. They would stay on the narrowing ponds until the underwater plants were glazed over completely; then would starve. So quickly a species can die: of the immense flocks of trumpeters less than a thousand birds, anywhere, now remained alive.

These two had been fortunate. They had been reared on the Red Rock Lakes, where there was permanent open water. Then on one of their fall flights they had found this Teton Marsh, even warmer, and had stayed. Men had come here to kill ducks however, and some of their shot had fallen into the shallows. The mother swan had found several and had swallowed them, believing them snails perhaps. By this time the shot had eroded away, but she was sick of lead poisoning—sick of civilization really, as much as the swans who starved.

The father and the cygnets rounded the island and walked up into the sedges. The mother stayed in the water. She no longer spent the nights on their hillock; that was one of her strange new ways. The young ones let themselves down on the spongy roots. Sleepiness soon dazed their eyes. The Swan too folded his feet beneath him. He plucked a few sedge seeds and turned his neck backward so that his head lay at the upper edge of one wing. Most of his bill was under the feathers, but his eyes were out.

His mate appeared tense. He raised his head, for she was pushing against the island. With fumbling, broken motions she was trying to come ashore. But her legs were not strong enough to support her, and she sank back in the water.

She slept. For a long time the Swan stayed awake, watchful and now with a deep uneasiness. The sky was a merging of faded daylight and coming moonlight, a bright dust that anywhere might be stars. The yellow and green of the shoreline grasses still faintly showed. Their reflection was touched by the shine on the pond, which gave them the delicacy of grasses in spring, when they were tremulous, with their stirrings yet uncertain. Below the vertical blurs the water was mauve and blue-silver, the shades in the sky. A dragonfly passed, drained of his color. The grasses grayed. Overhead then was only a dark immensity, pricked by stars.

As soon as the sun was up, the cygnets began to stir. Piping a soft impatience, they slipped down in the water and filed away toward the willow thickets. Their father overtook them; more slowly their mother followed. The family passed other sedge hillocks and a corner of the meadow. The sun, coming in levelly, filled the grasses with light, and glanced off the water, striking the swans' plumage twice.

Even the father's own feeding was an aid to his young. The willow channels were ice-bordered this morning, but he paddled along the open center, watching the liquid brown depths. Some plants grew too deep, but finally he found a bed of clasping-leaf pondweed that he could reach. He swung down his head and first raked in the muck. The sensitive skin on his bill touched a dragonfly nymph. He nibbled it up and probed for more. Meanwhile, in brushing between the rippled leaves, he had broken off some of them. They floated up, nourishment for the cygnets. And when he pulled up a whole spray, waterboatmen and scuds were dislodged, and the young swans caught them. Several ducks—mallards and the consistent little thieves, baldpates—sped up to share the food. The Swan did not object. He cleared the channel of the weeds, satisfying his own hunger, the cygnets', and that of various smaller birds.

When the meal was finished, the cygnets paddled off to the meadow.

They were sleepy, climbed out into the grass, and cuddled down. Their mother had stayed in the willows, but their father joined them. He laid his head between his wings and closed his eyes. He also wished to sleep, for his day's vigilance had begun too early. Late in the night the beaver had been moving with sounds that were harmless, but toward morning a slap of his tail had sent a warning over the marsh. Peering up from the sedges, the Swan had discovered an otter.

The enemy swam about, underwater or sculling through the surface. Moonlight silvered his wakes, and the ripples swished into the sedge blades of the swans' roost. Finally he went away, but he might return. The Swan had felt too alarmed to relax again.

Even now, in the reassuring light of day, he could not sleep. For the weather was making all the creatures restless. It made the swans, too, nervous, but they did not hop, flutter, or call continually, or fight. They showed their discomfort by letting the others' movements unsettle them. The cygnets were aroused by a varying hare, thumping her own tension.

At once they wished to be somewhere else. The Swan was disturbed at the prospect of taking them out alone. He called to his mate, but she did not come. Perhaps he could lead the young ones to the backwash, usually a quiet place. No; they would go past the dam. Two parents might have distracted them. They ignored their father's urging. He paddled faster and swung in advance.

Beyond the dam was the wooded bank with the beaver's canal cut into it and his house built against it. The adult swans never had brought the young here; an enemy could steal toward them too secretly through the grove. Now the cygnets swung up the shore, piping their pleasure in the new place. They stopped near the canal and jabbed for water-skaters in the debris drifted against the bank.

The current, draining toward the dam, was a swifter movement against the Swan's feet than the flow in the sedge beds or thickets. But his webs could detect another, uneven surge, no doubt stirred by the otter. An otter might swim up under a cygnet and pull it down. He was likely to do it only if he could find no fish, and this pond fairly swayed with fish; yet an otter's caprice was not to be trusted.

The Swan's eyes strained across the pond. The otter was submerged and not visible through the surface, dazzled with sunlit ripples. The smallest cygnet, a female, sensed her father's alarm. She showed the first stilling of her impulsiveness, the first touch of a swan's caution. While her brothers hunted more insects, she moved farther along the shore, where she could take flight more easily.

The heavy irregular surge became stronger. No more waiting; the father must take his young ones into the air. He called and had made the first leaping strokes with his feet when a marsh hawk swung over the grove.

The Swan could outdistance the hawk in flight, but the cygnets could not. Here then they must stay. The harrier had seen them. He would torment them—a prospect that put a more sensuous grace in his wing-beat. This was one of his great days. The swift wind had given him op-position, and that he loved. Here could be more of it.

With a shrill cry he turned down and straightened out, hanging above the young female. His yellow claws dropped. His hovering face would be terrible to a cygnet; ruffed and flat, it combined the look of a hawk and an owl.

The father was down-wind of the harrier. He could rise only by turn-ing his back on the cygnets. He paddled instead to the little one's side, whipping a violent spray with his wings. The hawk cried another taunt, and the Swan replied with a louder warning. His neck was drawn back and his beak was open, ready for a murderous lunge if the hawk should drop lower.

At a sag in the wind the harrier swayed, lost his position, and circled above the pond to advance again over the cygnet. With that brief break the father sped into the wind, was soon off the water and pursuing the hawk. The harrier swept away, across the meadow and river and on over the sagebrush plain. The Swan was close behind, calling threats. The har-rier went into a steep dive, a winding ascent, and another dive—sinuous turns that the larger Swan could not closely follow. But in fleeing, the hawk had admitted that he was vanquished. The father hastened back toward the pond and the greater threat of the otter.

The young ones had been subdued by their fright. Now they would be obedient. The marsh no longer beat with the otter's swimming, but the family filed to the sedge beds and their roost. There, secluded behind the tall, upright blades, they would wait out this tumultuous morning.

Soon after noon the wind blew down a dead tree that anchored the beavers' dam. It crashed on the pond with the high, metallic clatter of shattered water. Ducks exploded from the surface. The pelican sailed away. The great blue heron flopped up with a *quonck* in a loud collapsing voice. And out from the willows, like mosquitoes from beaten grass, rose smaller birds, incredible numbers seen together, of magpies, and mourn-ing doves, belted kingfishers, yellow warblers, mountain and black-capped chickadees, pink-sided juncos, and tree swallows. Only the swans did not fly. Over their hillock the white and gray wings briefly waved; then were folded.

Soon the fears, too, were folded. The boldest birds came down, each leading a flock of excited followers.

The storm was close to Jackson Hole. Now the winds whirling around its center had passed on east. The water lay heavy and still, repeating with darkened colors every shoreline twig and root, every russet, cream, or brown-striped breast of a floating duck.

The Swan's mate spread the clearest outline on the surface. Below her perfectly was reflected the white sway of her side. It ended in the black knob of her knee, high because her legs were pulled up in discomfort. The Swan came off the roost to float beside her, and the cygnets followed. The family drew together, seeming to sense a crisis. A strange new sound was roughening the air.

The first hint of its meaning came to the Swan when he found that his toes touched the muck. They never had done that here. Now his webs were flat on the bottom, and he stood. Then the cygnets' feet touched, as their mother may have seen, for she lowered her own webs. At once she started toward the pond. Not being able to walk, she must stay on water deep enough so that she could paddle. She stopped at the outer border of the sedge beds, and the others with her. But she soon had to move again.

The dam had not been visible from the sedge roost. When the swans came out into the pond they discovered a break in the beaver's masonry. Around the roots of the upset tree the water was pouring down to the creek below. This was the reason for the roar they were hearing. The shores of the pond were drawing inward; its size was shrinking. Behind the swans were channels and slopes of bare mud.

Several times the family let the shallow water drive them on. Then they went to the center of the pond and huddled there near the end of the fallen tree. The father was facing the backwash, but into his sidewise vision a shadow flowed. It was the otter, topping the dam with his lilting step.

The mother too saw him. They swung together, enclosing the cygnets. The otter dived in the pond. But he emerged and began to tour the borders. No switch of his tail-tip and no toss of his arrogant head was missed by the eyes of the Swan.

The otter tumbled and swam in the draining pond. He rode the cascade through the break and caught a fish and climbed up on the prostrate trunk of the tree to eat it. The swans went out on the open surface.

A second otter came. The lively creatures were splashing together. The swans turned toward the shore, then back on the pond again, for the otters went out on the silt. The father Swan shifted about, tense and frantic.

Over the earth swept a sudden darkening, and a quick wind stirred the leaves. The air was oppressive. It lay in the Swan's lungs so heavily that each breath must be pushed out. Limpness lowered the arch in the mother's throat.

Down from the sky fell a soft tumult of snow. The flakes dissolved on the water; on the shores, the dam, and the brush they spread a cover. The downy mist thickened. An enemy could pounce from it. The swans heard the otters' cries but they could not see them. They could not see, in fact, to the other side of the pond. They heard also the brutal hoarseness of ravens, brawling over something, somewhere out there in the close white shower.

But loudest for the father may have been the calls of competing instincts. Surely he should be loyal first to his sick mate. He should stay here and protect her, helpless, needing him so desperately. His devotion to her was a lifelong emotion; his concern for the cygnets would pass before another brood could hatch.

Yet his full care of the young ones, recently, had strengthened his sense of responsibility for them. To save them, he should leave this vanishing marsh. He should take them to a new home, probably on the Red Rock Lakes, where he had spent his own years as a cygnet. Safety and food depended on water, and soon apparently none would be here.

To protect his mate or his fledglings—both calls rose from the deepest instincts in his nature. And the conflict may have been no less an anguish because conscious reasoning did not weigh it. Decided either way, one almost-irresistible urge must be denied.

He knew which call he would answer when he felt his wings lift. Into the dense enveloping snow he sped. He trumpeted to the cygnets and then slowed his flight, listening for the skitter of their feet, the air thrashed by their wings. When all three were aloft, a different note came into his voice. It spoke to his mate, though not with a summons. He was aware now that she could not rise. But he sent down his cry, for her to understand if she could. Twice he led the cygnets in low circles above the marsh, trumpeting to the white bird, so quiet upon the black pond. Finally her throat straightened, her bill lifted upward, and she trumpeted one answering call.

He turned his course west toward the Teton slope. Along the base of the mountains was a row of lakes, familiar enough so that he could find them in blind flying. He held his speed to the cygnets' and constantly urged them on, so that none would be lost. He was taking them to the smallest lake, on Mount Moran, near the northern tip of the range. It could not be a home, for these lakes froze from shore to shore. But on its breadth were the tops of several muskrat lodges. One would be a roost where the family could await the end of the storm.

He still was awake when the storm broke up. The mountain and the long range south took shape. The overhead thickness began to lift and shred. For a while clouds, luminous with moonlight, continued to cross the frosted blue of the dark night sky. Their shining passage seemed the only happening, now that the earth was covered by the wide monotony of the snow. As smoothly as swans the clouds appeared from over the Teton crest, to stream above the valley and beyond the eastern range. With a lingering hold one pulled away from another . . . lost the touch . . . moved on alone. Two united . . . blended . . . started to separate

. . . clung . . . tore apart. Always they were changing, but their world did not change. It was a world of inviolate wildness.

A new wind swept the clouds away, and in the sky was only the moon, a hanging ball of light that dimmed the stars.

The bugling of an elk awakened the cygnets in the morning. He stood on a granite cliff above the lake and sent his challenge over the valley with a rising flow of notes almost as clear and vibrant as the Swan's.

The early light was coloring the snowy peaks with the nacreous pink of sea shells. Coming down the slope, the sunshine gilded the ivory crown upon the elk's head. It passed the pines and spruces at the shore and stretched back over the misty surface of the lake to the lodge.

The Swan allowed the cygnets to feed for a brief time. Soon he called them and rose from the pond to start their flight to the Red Rock Lakes. The sky felt crisp and electric, for with the storm's departure ozone from above the stratosphere was raining earthward. The pressure of the air was heightened, heightening in turn each animal's vitality. Never had the cygnets flown so swiftly.

Everything seemed changed, and for the better. That may have been the reason why the Swan reversed his course. Or possibly the danger to his mate was, after all, the stronger call. He circled back at the head of the valley, turning south instead of north. Setting an almost-adult speed for the young swans, he was following the Gros Ventre crest.

The indigo river shone between the white flats of the valley floor. One of its curves, there, held the marsh. The pond was smaller than before the tree fell, but it was not empty. The Swan was spiraling down.

His glide along the water stopped him near the dam. During the night the beaver partly had repaired it, and the inflow of the brook had filled the marsh up to the level of the dam's unfinished top. The willow channels still were drained, but the surface spread back past the sedge beds, past the Swan's roost. Floating near the hillock was his mate.

He hastened toward the roost, so eagerly that now the ripples did not melt out from his sides but splashed away. The cygnets stopped at a bed of milfoil, which the lowering of the pond had brought within their reach.

The mother watched her family's return. Her eyes were more intense this morning, with a more accessible look. And there were other proofs that she was slightly stronger. Her wings lay higher on her back, and her throat was swinging slowly. Her head was turning in the sunlight. If she had swallowed more of the shot, she might not have recovered. She might not if the weather had remained depressing. But its most invigorating benefits had come together at her crisis. She would live, though never again to mother cygnets, for the poison had made her barren.

As the Swan approached, he thrust his head beneath the surface, tossed it back with a shower of crystal drops upon his wings. He beat the wings and half-rose from the water. Slowing the stroke, he let himself down but again reared, framed in his wings' great pulsing gleam of white.

The motion may have been stirred by instinct's memory of the autumn when they plighted their devotion. The ritual had been a kind of dance, in which the two, advancing toward each other, lifted from the water, breast to breast. This later day his mate could only once and briefly raise her wings—the merest opening along her sides, yet a wish expressed.

He tilted his bill as if to trumpet, but swung it down and glided closer to her. Both birds turned their attention to the sunny day, the cygnets, and the life that they would share once more, beginning with this new and silent clasping of their spirits.

TITANIA

AND OBERON

George Miksch Sutton

Roger Tory Peterson says that the question he is most often asked by visiting naturalists is, "Where can I see the big cuckoo that runs on the ground?" The answer is, "In the arid Southwest," and the bird in question is the famous road-runner, the cockiest and most impudent as well as the strangest bird of our American deserts. He does not look like a member of the cuckoo tribe—he is actually almost chicken size and he waves his long tail up and down to express his emotions. Neither does he have the reprehensible habits of the European cuckoo since he is actually a good family man. His favorite foods are snakes (even rattlesnakes) and lizards, which he chases madly and captures expertly. No bird is more at home in the desert and it is easily tamed. Here one of the most distinguished American ornithologists describes his meeting with this rather unbirdlike bird who, incidentally, can fly into a tree if necessary but much prefers his legs to his wings.

THE stories that Texans tell to Yankee newcomers in their midst are blood-chilling stories of rattlesnakes, coiled ready to strike; of water moccasins that line the shaded banks of streams; of death-dealing coral snakes, ringed with scarlet, gold and black; of scorpions, lightning-quick of tail, that dart from the roadside; of tarantulas, emerald-eyed and steel-fanged, that leap from every clump of cactus; of foot-long centipedes, with formidable pincers, that lie in wait for passers-by in caves. "Should one of these crawl over you," I was told, "your flesh will rot and fall from your bones!"

These impressive lectures, delivered in an awed and ominous voice, served to make my every walk an adventure. Armed with a stout club, I was ready to meet death at any turn.

Of all the descriptions of prairie creatures, that of a certain bird charmed me most. This was the Road-Runner, a blood-thirsty killer whose eyes were "flaming red," and whose speed was the speed of a race

From *Birds in the Wilderness*. New York: The Macmillan Company, 1936.

horse. He was known by such colloquial names as Chapparal Cock, Ground Cuckoo, and Snake Killer. He was the ancient foe of the rattlesnake, round whom he built walls of cactus and whom he fought to the death. What prowess, what strength, what craftiness must be the Road-Runner's, I thought, as I longed to see this terror of the sandy wilderness. I was not anxious, however, that our first meeting should be intimate.

This meeting was inevitable. Walking across the prairie, I entered a ravine whose nearer bank was covered with bushes and vines. Instantly, hearing a sharp rattle, I halted. Was I in a snake's den? Turning cautiously I saw a bird, about two feet long, with coarsely streaked plumage. For a second he looked at me, then raised his high, steel-black crest, disclosing a red-orange, featherless patch back of his eye. Again I heard the arresting rattle as his mandibles clapped together. He bounded with unbelievable ease over some low bushes, then, spreading his short wings which were obviously unfit for sustained flight, soared down the gully, dropped into the maze of gray-green, and was gone. I had met the Road-Runner! I had been close enough to ascertain that not his eyes, but the bare patches *back of his eyes* were red, and that his tail was very long. His perfectly calculated leaping haunted my memory for days.

During the following care-free years I was to learn much about this famous bird. I saw him often. I found his nest. Finally, I took it upon myself to raise two young from early infancy.

One day in late April, 1914, while pushing my way through a dense, cobweb-hung thicket, I spied not far in front of me a crude mass of twigs. Instantly on the alert, I wiped the caterpillar silk from my eyelashes and looked at the unshapely structure more closely. A hopelessly lopsided, poorly anchored nest it was, but above it, parallel with a supporting branch, was the long, iridescent tail of a bird. In moving, I disturbed a small vine. At once there peered over the rim an angular face with lifted crest and blazing eyes. There was a flash of scarlet then, with scarcely a rustle of leaf or tremor of tendril, the muscular creature slid away. There was a soft thud as strong feet touched the ground. A thin form faded into the weeds. Wings unspread, the mother Road-Runner had bounded clear of the dense tangle.

There was a weird nestful. Crouching beside a soiled egg were five ugly youngsters whose dark-skinned bodies were sparsely covered with long, white hairs, and whose beaks were tipped with the hard egg-tooth of babyhood. Their flabby feet, two toes pointing forward, two backward, were dull blue. Their eyes were gray-brown, with steel-blue pupils and a reptilian stare. Pinfeathers had just begun to appear on the edge of the wings. Were these four-inch, greasy-looking, uncouth things really baby birds? Though I had no experience in caring for such charges I decided to take two of them home.

As I stood there I wondered what I was to feed these infant dragons.

Accidentally I touched an upturned beak and four great mouths, wabbling uncertainly on scrawny necks, rose in unison. I jerked back my hand—the pink-blotched lining of those mouths had an almost poisonous appearance. From the depths of the small frames came a hoarse, many-toned buzzing which gave the impression that a colony of winged insects had been stirred to anger.

Puzzled by the motionlessness of one of the young I examined him more closely and was startled at finding an inch of the tail of a large lizard protruding from his mouth. He had been fed enough to keep his digestive apparatus busy for some time; for, as the gastric fluids would make assimilable that part of the lizard which had entered the stomach, he had only to swallow a little more to prolong his meal. For a four-inch Road-Runner a lizard nine inches long should furnish an enduring repast.

I had learned at least that my pets were carnivorous. At home my long-suffering family gathered round the unattractive pair, exhibiting all the enthusiasm at their command, and wondering, no doubt, when this gathering of crawling, creeping, buzzing and squeaking creatures was to end. We found an old bucket, lined it with dry grass, and placed the birds in their new nest. It took them but an instant to adjust themselves. Once they had assumed their normal attitude they began buzzing for food. For the following two weeks this clamor was almost incessant. It greeted us early in the morning; the merest human whisper or footfall near the bucket roused it instantly. I was to learn much, sometimes to my annoyance, about the rapidity with which young Road-Runners digest their food.

At first my charges could not stand; they merely lay on their bellies, bills upraised, ready to beg for food. Soon, however, they began toddling about in the bucket, jostling each other, and raising their bodies unsteadily when in most importunate mood. Pinfeathers began to burst, each glossy vane tipped with the fragile white hair of babyhood. The young Road-Runners were becoming pretty.

No complete record was kept of the thousands of grasshoppers and other insects, lizards, mice, and small snakes which were endlessly thrust into those insatiable gullets. My friends at school learned that I needed help and it was not unusual to see a small troop of boys approaching our house with mice in pasteboard boxes, or snakes and lizards dangling from their hands. Most of these creatures the birds swallowed entire, head first. An eighteen-inch snake could not be consumed at one gulp, to be sure, but it disappeared soon enough, once it was well started. Although bones, fur, feathers, and scales were swallowed indiscriminately, no pellets of indigestible material were tossed up; the powerful juices of the stomach dissolved all arrivals.

When they were strong enough to stand on their toes, the stub-tailed birds were allowed to wabble about the yard. The bare patch back of the eye was now brightening to orange, and about the round pupil appeared a narrow pale ring, giving to the fully lashed eye a fierceness which checked most admirers at a respectful distance.

The young adventurers found the world exciting. Vultures soaring in the distant sky roused at once their interest and suspicion. Floating milk-weed-down they eyed with gravity. Strange voices sent them scuttling to a familiar retreat. The warm light penetrated their loose plumage; yielding, they spread their wings, fluffed out the feathers of their backs and shoulders, and took long sun-baths. They bathed in dust also, but never in water. They recognized me as their protector and provider, and followed me, when they could, wherever I went. If I lay on the grass they ran about over my body, toying with my clothing and seeking the highest perch they could reach, not failing of course to beg for food.

Since they were now so personable and were attracting so much attention—they even had visited the Fort Worth Public Library, where they were shown to a hundred wide-eyed children—my family decided they should receive names. Our final choice was Titania and Oberon, though the harsh-plumaged, athletic creatures did not even remotely suggest fairy royalty, nor had I the faintest knowledge of their sex. But we thought these names were pretty and that they reflected good literary taste.

The pets were called by their euphonyms only when visitors were to be properly impressed; consequently, they paid no attention to the meaningless titles. To a snap of the fingers, a whistle, the shutting of a door, or the calling of a homely, but honest "Birdie, Birdie!" however, they came with an overwhelming rush.

After three weeks they became sturdy enough to catch part of their own food. With patient coaxing they were taught to pick up grasshoppers tossed to them, and finally to run after and capture crippled insects. Content at first, perforce, with sluggish, wingless nymphs which were abundant, they stole about through the weeds, wings pressed neatly against their slender bodies, snapping up the insects as fast as they could find them. Grasshoppers, often still alive and kicking, they swallowed with a toss of the head and a hollow gulp. Large green or gray cave-crickets which lived in piles of boards, or in damp, shadowy places, were especially prized. When a yellow- or coral-winged grasshopper rose noisily from the path, the birds crouched in momentary fear, but soon began to mark the return to earth of the clackety aeronaut and to steal up behind tufts of grass, intent upon a killing.

Finally they learned to capture the biggest, noisiest, and wariest grasshoppers on the prairie. They would watch a coral-wing in his courtship flight and, running stealthily, wait until the performer dropped to the ground. With a bound over low weeds, a dart across the open, and a final rush with outspread wings and tail they would frighten their prey into the air, leap nimbly after him, nab him unerringly with their bills, and descend gracefully on outspread wings to beat him to insensibility with a whack or two on a stone.

Once they had learned to capture grasshoppers, their food problem was largely solved and, since they showed no inclination to run away, they were at liberty most of the time. They ran about the yard, playing with each other, or catching insects. In the heat of mid-day they sought shelter of broad, cool leaves, and sprawled in the sand. Daily, often many times daily, I took them for a walk across the prairie. Following me closely or running at my side, they watched the big world with eyes far keener than my own. Grasshoppers which I frightened from the grass they captured in side expeditions. If I paused near a flat stone, they urged me on with grunts, bit gently at my hands, and raced back and forth in an ecstasy of anticipation.

I entertained misgivings concerning these flat stones. What savage creatures might not they conceal! Could young Road-Runners manage swift-tailed scorpions, sharp-toothed mice, or poisonous spiders? Under the first stone there were scorpions. The Road-Runners hesitated an instant, as if permitting an untried instinct to take possession of their brains, then rushed forward, thrust out their heads, and attacked the scorpions precisely at their tails. Perhaps these venomous tails received more than the usual benumbing blows, but the scorpions were swallowed with gusto.

I had not supposed that a Road-Runner would capture and devour a tarantula. One day, however, we paused at the tunnel of one of these big, furred spiders. Somewhat in the spirit of experimentation, and following the method known to all Texas boys, I teased the black Arachnid from her lair by twirling a wisp of grass in her face. She popped out viciously and jumped a good ten inches to one side. With a dash one bird was upon the monster before she had opportunity to leap a second time. A toss of the bird's head and one of the eight legs was gone. Free again, the spider leaped upon her captor. The other bird now entered the combat, snatched up the spider, and sliced off another leg. One by one the legs went down, and finally the two birds pulled apart and gulped the sable torso.

Tarantulas were now our prey. Whenever we came upon a burrow the birds ran about wildly, looked longingly at the hole, begged noisily for food, then rushed back and forth flashing their tails. Imagine my delight, my wonder too, one day, at seeing one of the birds pick up a tiny pebble and, after creeping up slyly, drop it into the neat orifice.

The pretty race-runner lizards which lived along the roads tantalized the birds almost to a frenzy. These reptiles were at first too wary and too speedy to be caught. Day after day the birds gave chase only to return with hang-dog expression, shaking their heads sadly, grunting half-heartedly, and begging penitently for food. One day we surprised a lizard and had the advantage of being close to him at the start. Running as rapidly as I could, I headed him off, and in the twinkle of an eye one of the Road-Runners had him by the tail. We were all surprised, upon examining our quarry, to find a tail, twitching and wriggling in the road—but no lizard! *Sans* tail, which had broken off at the proper instant, the lizard was now safe in his den. The birds seemed in doubt as to whether they should consume so mysterious a morsel. Within a week or two these exceedingly nimble lizards were captured every day; and now and then we saw a tail-less one making off in mad haste.

To the comparatively sluggish though well-armored horned lizards, which were to be found in grassless areas, the birds paid no attention unless they were very hungry. A horned lizard, confronted by his foe, would flatten out, rise high on his legs, and sway back and forth as if about to leap or inflict a dangerous bite. But Road-Runners are not to be bluffed. Grasping their tough victim by the head or back they beat him against a convenient stone. Thirty or forty blows were sometimes needed to render him sufficiently quiescent for ingestion. I felt a tightening at the throat as I watched these reptiles being swallowed. But the birds evinced no pain or discomfort. Occasionally, indeed, horned lizards were swallowed while yet quite alive, and had to be coughed up for further battering.

The conquest of certain individual animals became an obsession with the redoubtable pets. There was, for instance, an old scaly swift lizard whose fortress and sunning place was a lumber pile not far from the house. Attempt after attempt was made to surprise, head off, or corner this sage veteran, but he was always too quick. There were too many convenient crevices into which he could dive, and his favorite sunning spots were so prominent that he could survey his surroundings with ease. He was so handsome and he matched his wits so successfully with those of his feathered tormentors that I grew rather fond of him. One day I saw one of the birds stealing upon him from behind a huge burdock plant. That day might have been his last had I not thrown a stone which popped sharply on a board sending him pellmell into one of his retreats.

There was also a round-bodied cotton rat which had a nest in a rough stone wall that extended along one side of our property. Two or three times a day he scurried across a gap in the wall, and the birds came to look upon him as a possible meal. At first his speed and considerable size kept the enemy at a safe distance, but their interest sharpened daily, and eventually they formed the habit of loitering near the runway. One day I heard a squeal of terror and ran up in time to see the bewildered animal running this way and that, trying to escape the two lightning-quick demons who never really held him, but pinched him, tossed him, dealt him blows, buffeted him, made him weary with fighting for life. Over his limp form the Road-Runners had an argument. He was heavy. No sooner would one bird start to swallow than the other would be tugging at the hind foot or tail, and down he would drop. I finally cut the rat in two. From the first of our foraging expeditions the birds had killed with ease the small snakes which we found under rocks. Now having attained full size, they were ready for combat with their traditional foe, the rattle-snake; but I never saw them actually killing a large snake of any kind.

Large dead snakes were frequently given to the birds, however, and their attempts to swallow a four-foot meal were vastly amusing. Having beaten the dead reptile's head on the ground to make assurance doubly sure, they engaged in a spirited wrangle to settle ownership. Sometimes one Road-Runner actually got the head-end of the snake swallowed and stood awkwardly gasping for breath while the other bird tugged at the tail-end. What futility! The scales of a snake's skin are so constructed that it would be almost as easy for a snake to move backwards through the grass as for a bird to swallow it tail first.

After they had worn themselves down to a state of philosophical ac-ceptance of their physical limitations, I usually cut the snake into three or four pieces and let them while away the hours in swallowing. At such times they wandered unhappily about, mouths agape, the fore part of their meal safely down and being digested, but the latter part annoyingly in the way, awaiting its hour of engulfment. The unswallowed portion usu-ally hung from one side of the mouth for half an hour until the bird, tir-ing of this attitude, would step over and about the dangling meal, shifting it to the other side of his mouth, and exhibiting in every movement a mighty determination to keep it from slipping out.

My six-year-old sister, Evangel, was frankly afraid of these pet Road-Runners. While wearing a certain pair of brown sandals she once kicked in self-defense at a bird which ran at her, begging for food. This bird, recognizing that he had the upper hand, rushed at the little girl whenever she wore those sandals. She came screaming into the house one day, a Road-Runner flopping about her neck, his hard bill grasping firmly the lobe of her ear.

A neighbor's small dog seemed to derive immense pleasure from chas-ing the birds. They never really had to run to out-distance this noisy pest, but he was persistent. Tired of being chased, they would slip under the porch through an opening in the foundation which the dog could not enter. Here, at last, was an animal too large to swallow!

On an interurban car track not far from our house, lizards were wont to sun themselves on the hot ties, and grasshoppers to perform their courtship flights. The birds frequently visited this rich preserve. When a car approached they did not flee in terror but stood their ground, then, bounding from tie to tie, raced just ahead of the roaring, swaying mon-ster. Often they ran thus for a hundred yards or more, when, panting with the unusual exertion, they shot off to one side to rest in the shade of the weeds.

Life on the prairie was pleasant and eventful. Each dawn promised new conquests; each expedition along the roads had its excitement and rewards. But these happy days were numbered. In July, when the birds were almost three months old, we moved to northern West Virginia. I was exceedingly fond of my pets, and feared that leaving them behind would mean their early death. We made a wire cage, covered it with cloth, and took them with us on the train.

The trip was hot and unpleasant. The birds were so frightened that they jumped about, injuring their bills and breaking their feathers so badly that their tails had to be cut off. I was constantly afraid the poor captives would raise such a commotion that they would be sentenced to the baggage car. They ate raw beefsteak; but their appetite was far from normal.

Arrived at our destination, a hamlet sequestered among cool hills, I thought first of all of the Road-Runners. Chilled by fog, sick from lack of exercise and improper food, and, worst of all minus their handsome tails, they were forlorn indeed as they walked about sedately on the cement walks and neat lawn of the college campus. Titania and Oberon! For the first time the names seemed significant and fitting! Smitten with remorse at having brought these sun-dwellers to a hostile land, I was determined to get food for them—grasshoppers, snakes, birds—anything but beefsteak.

By noon the birds and I felt better. The beneficent sun had drawn off the fog, and a few grasshoppers were to be found on the baseball diamond. Furthermore, the creek which threaded the hills was teeming with watersnakes. These fields were not the windy prairies to be sure; but life was endurable so long as there was food for the Roadrunners.

The odd, bobtailed birds soon became popular, especially with children, who wanted to chase them or to watch them eating. Every day snakes or mice were brought to them, and their usual sprightliness returned.

The birds evidently foresaw that they would have to conquer new kinds of prey, for they began to take unusual interest in the English Sparrows which fed about the college buildings. Within a few days they captured the birds with little difficulty. Walking about with a non-committal air that was comically suggestive of the chickens which fed near by, they gradually drew nearer to a sparrow, then, with a dash to one side, and a tremendous leap, snatched the fleeing victim from the air! It was odd that the usually sagacious sparrows did not, as a community, learn to fear these new enemies; instinct, however, seemed to warn them only against prowling cats, or hawks which always attacked from above.

In September the campus hummed with the return of students. Frosty mornings with their lavender-colored asters and scarlet maple leaves heralded a winter which would be difficult indeed for the aliens. I was so busy that I could not properly care for my pets, which now ran hither and yon through the countryside. For a week or two I saw little of the Road-Runners, though daily I heard reports of strange birds seen here and there along the roads sometimes some distance from town.

Winter in West Virginia is rarely severe; but it is damp, and there is little in the way of food for Road-Runners. I made plans for sending them back to their Texas prairie. I considered feeding and keeping them indoors for winter. But when I tried to locate them, they were not to be found. I spent many hours, day after day, in searching. Through likely meadows, now rank with iron-weed and strewn with silken milkweed balloons, I wandered in the morning, or after school hours, eager to glimpse a familiar slender form, or to hear the sharp rattle of mandibles. But I failed to find the birds.

One afternoon, when I returned from college, my mother told me of a dead bird, wrapped in newspaper, brought by a man who had heard I was interested in collecting specimens. Two odd creatures had rushed up to him from the roadside, he had said, fluttering their wings as if they were baby birds, begging for food; and he had killed one of them with a stick.

I did not need to unwrap the slender package, for I saw a familiar foot sticking out at the end. I should not have known, anyway, whether it was Titania or Oberon who had been returned to me.

THE

GREAT

HORNED OWL

Edward Howe Forbush

It is no wonder that owls were among the first birds to strike strongly the imagination of Western man. Their eerie cries, their great, glowing eyes, the silence of their flight, and the very fact that they, unlike us, are creatures of darkness rather than of light has surrounded them with an air of mystery. It is still difficult not to think of them as fascinatingly sinister and possibly even wise in some esoteric way. Actually, of course, they are first of all neither philosophers nor evil spirits but ratcatchers and hence among the most economically useful of birds. The great horned owl, common over most of the United States, is the largest of our species. Here is a strictly light-of-common-day account of this nighttime predator.

EVERY living thing above ground in the woods on winter nights pays tribute to the Great Horned Owl except the larger mammals and man. Ordinarily when there is good hunting this owl has a plentiful supply of food, and when there is game enough it slaughters an abundance and eats only the brains; but in winter when house rats and mice keep mostly within the buildings, when woodchucks and shunks have "holed up" and when field mice are protected by deep snow—then if rabbits are scarce and starvation is imminent, the owl will attack even the domestic cat, and usually with success. A farmer brought me a Great Horned Owl one winter day that had killed his pet tom cat on the evening of the previous day. The cat was out walking in the moonlight on one of his usual expeditions in search of unattended females, when the farmer heard a wail of mortal agony and opening the door saw Mr. Cat in the grasp of the owl. Before he could get his gun and shoot the bird the cat was no more. Its vitals had been torn out. Usually the noiseless flight of the owl enables it to take the cat by surprise and seize it by the back of the neck and the

From *Birds of Massachusetts and Other New Engand States*. Published by the Commonwealth of Massachusetts, 1927.

small of the back, when all is soon over; but if the cat is not taken by surprise and is quick enough to turn on the owl, the episode is likely to have a different ending. Sometimes the owl "wakes up the wrong customer" as the following incident related to me by Mr. J. A. Farley clearly shows:

"Mr. Zenas Langford, for many years superintendent of streets in the southern part of Plymouth, tells me that a few years ago in the Pine Hills, he came upon a Horned Owl in trouble with a black snake. As he went along the cart road, the two suddenly 'fell into it.' Plainly the owl had caught the snake, but the reptile had twisted itself around the bird so that it was unable to fly, and fell to the ground with its prey. Mr. Langford says that the owl had grasped the snake about six inches below its head, but the part of the snake below the owl's talons had twisted itself around the bird tightly. There was at least one light turn around the owl's neck. Mr. Langford could not see that the snake had bitten the owl, which however, was nearly exhausted. The owl nevertheless had not relaxed its hold on the snake. Neither of the creatures had given up. Mr. Langford killed the snake, which measured 4 feet. The owl was so weakened and helpless that it could not fly; it seemed to have been choked. Mr. Langford wrapped it in a blanket, took it home, kept it for a week and then let it go." The porcupine, also, does not yield up his life, without doing all the harm possible. Witness the Horned Owl, liberally besprinkled with porcupine quills, which was shot in the Province of Quebec in December 1907, and reported by Rev. G. Eifrig.

Horned Owls kill and eat many skunks, and seem to care little for the disagreeable consequences of attacking these pungent animals. Many of the owls that I have handled give olfactory evidence of the habit. They kill both wild and domesticated ducks, picking them up skillfully out of the water at night, and no goose is too large for them to tackle. Occasionally, however, the owl comes to grief in its attack on some water-fowl. At Lanesboro, Massachusetts, in February, 1918, one was found floating dead in a pool with a duck that it had killed. No one knew the details of this midnight tragedy. It may be that the owl was weakened by hunger and was unable to rise from the water. Where hens, chickens and turkeys are allowed to roost at night in the trees, many fall victims to this owl, which is said to alight on the branch beside its chosen prey, crowd it off the limb and then strike it in the air. Some guinea hens roosting in trees on my farm disappeared in some such manner. Usually the owl does not stop to eat his victim on the spot but bears it away.

Mr. A. A. Cross of Huntington informed me that in December, 1918, one of his neighbors left a live guinea hen in a sack and it disappeared. The next day he found the remains of the fowl in the orchard. The sack had been torn open and about half of the bird had been eaten. Two traps were set near it and the next night a splendid specimen of the Great Horned Owl was taken.

In eating its prey this owl usually begins at the head and eats backward. The birds are plucked, but small mammals such as mice and rats are swallowed whole, head first. Mr. E. O. Grant says that he saw an owl strike a Ruffed Grouse in a bush and bear it away without even checking his flight. "The owl flew up a stream with a stream of feathers trailing in his wake. I think," says Mr. Grant, "that he must have had that bird pretty well plucked before he had gone 60 rods." The Horned Owl is no respecter of persons. It kills weaker owls from the Barred Owl down, most of the hawks and such nocturnal animals as weasels and minks. It is the most deadly enemy of the Crow, taking old and young from their nests at night and killing many at their winter roosts. Game birds of all kinds, poultry, a few small birds, rabbits (especially bush rabbits), hares, squirrels, gophers, mice, rats, woodchucks, opossums, fish, crawfish and insects are all eaten by this rapacious bird. It is particularly destructive to rats. Mr. E. O. Niles tells of a nest of this owl on his farm containing two young owls and several dead rats. On the ground below the nest were the bodies of 113 rats, recently killed, with their skulls opened and the brains removed. When we find young in the nest of one of these owls, they are well supplied with game. Mr. H. O. Green writes that he found remains of a skunk, a Crow and a Pheasant at one nest and Mr. Joseph Peters says that the parent birds that supplied another nest brought black ducks, rabbits, rats, snakes, a Red Phalarope, a Virginia Rail, two Woodcocks, a Bob-white, a Northern Flicker, a Pheasant and some small birds. In eating their food the fierce young birds grasped the game firmly in the talons and tore at it with their beaks. They began their feast on the larger birds and mammals by consuming the head and then working backward through the carcass. Of 127 stomachs of Great Horned Owls examined by Dr. A. K. Fisher, 31 contained poultry or game birds; 8, other birds; 13, mice; 65, other mammals; 1, a scorpion; 1, fish; 10, insects; and 17 were empty.

In the wilderness the Great Horned Owl exerts a restraining influence on both the game and the enemies of game, for it destroys both and thus does not disturb the balance of nature. But on the farm or the game preserve, it cannot be tolerated.

SNAKE BIRDS

William Bartram

---

*One of the prize exhibits of the National Audubon Society's Ever-
glades Sanctuary in southern Florida is the anhinga or, as it is sometimes appropriately called, the snakebird, from its long, writhing
neck; and sometimes most inappropriately the water turkey—for no
good reason. This creature always strikes the most casual visitor as
somehow queer, and its queerness is no doubt due to the fact that
it is a very ancient bird and in many ways archaic. Though perhaps
distantly related to the cormorants, anhingas are not sea birds and
the few species are usually put in a group by themselves. Fossils suggest that they are descended from an extinct group of which bones
have been recovered from the Eocine sediments something like eighty
million years old.*

*William Bartram observed them during his late-eighteenth-century
exploration of Florida, called them snakebirds, and noted their remote
similarity to the cormorants. The more dignified appellation, anhinga,
comes from a native Amazonian word.*

H ERE is in the river and in the waters all over Florida, a very curious
and handsome bird, the people call them Snake Birds, I think I
have seen paintings of them on the Chinese screens and other India
pictures: they seem to be a species of cormorant or loon (*Colymbus
cauda elongata*) but far more beautiful and delicately formed than any
other species that I have ever seen. The head and neck of this bird are
extremely small and slender, the latter very long indeed, almost out of
all proportion, the bill long, straight and slender, tapering from its ball to
a sharp point, all the upper side, the abdomen and thighs, are as black
and glossy as a raven's, covered with feathers so firm and elastic, that
they in some degree resemble fish-scales, the breast and upper part of
the belly are covered with feathers of a cream colour, the tail is very
long, of a deep black, and tipped with a silvery white, and when spread,
represent an unfurled fan. They delight to sit in little peaceable communities, on the dry limbs of trees, hanging over the still waters, with
their wings and tails expanded, I suppose to cool and air themselves, when

From *Travels through North and South Carolina, Georgia, East and West
Florida*. Printed by James & Johnson, Philadelphia, 1791.

at the same time they behold their images in the watery mirror: at such times, when we approach them, they drop off the limbs into the water as if dead, and for a minute or two are not to be seen; when on a sudden at a vast distance, their long slender head and neck only appear, and have very much the appearance of a snake, and no other part of them are to be seen when swimming in the water, except sometimes the tip end of their tail. In the heat of the day they are seen in great numbers, sailing very high in the air, over lakes and rivers.

I doubt not but if this bird had been an inhabitant of the Tiber in Ovid's days, it would have furnished him with a subject, for some beautiful and entertaining metamorphoses. I believe they feed entirely on fish, for their flesh smells and tastes intolerably strong of it, it is scarcely to be eaten unless constrained by insufferable hunger.

WINGS

OF THE

STORM

Robert Cunningham Miller

The Greeks thought that the Halcyon, or kingfisher, nested on the sea during a season of unusual calm. It doesn't, and neither does any other bird, though we still use the phrase "Halcyon days" to describe a time of unusual tranquillity.

As happens in the case of so many exploded myths, there are even more wonderful truths to take its place. Many sea birds do incredible things, such as wandering over millions of square miles of ocean, spending almost their entire lives above or on the water, and coming to land only to nest. Food is abundant; but why do they not, like the Ancient Mariner, cry in despair, "Water, water everywhere, nor any drop to drink?" Physiologists have long pooh-poohed the notion that they could drink sea water. No kidney is capable of removing so high a concentration of salt. Perhaps the question is not quite settled yet to everyone's satisfaction but some recent investigation seems to indicate the presence in some sea birds of a special gland which separates the dissolved salts from the water.

O F all the habitats available to birds, the wide and lonely reaches of the open sea might appear to be one of the most inhospitable. Yet there are birds that are just as much at home over vast and turbulent waters as is the red-winged blackbird in a marsh, or a robin on a lawn. So completely are they adapted to the marine environment that they may go weeks or months without sighting land, and indeed have no need of the land whatever except for nesting, which is carried out on remote oceanic islands. If all the land on earth were to be submerged beneath the sea, years after the human race had become extinct there would still be birds winging their way about this global ocean, able to live out their normal life span completely at home in a world of water.

Nine persons out of ten, asked to name a bird of the ocean, would

From *Pacific Discovery*. September–October, 1955.

promptly reply "sea gull," or name one of the numerous species of gull. Even as good a sea-faring man as John Masefield might not win a prize on this quiz program, for in "Sea-fever" he refers in one breath to "the gull's way and the whale's way," although the paths of gulls and whales only occasionally and accidentally cross. Gulls by and large are not birds of the ocean, but birds of the shore and even of inland lakes.

To a person spending a summer at the seashore, the gulls, with their attractive plumage, wheeling flight and plaintive cries, are likely to be a memorable part of his seaside experience. But as a matter of fact, and with no disrespect to either, they are a good deal like himself. They like the sea shore and the sea wind, and enjoy beach-combing, but they don't care for too much salt water. An exception is the kittiwake, one of the smallest and most maritime of the gulls. In our book this little gull is really a sea-faring bird.

But when we speak of birds of the open ocean, we mean primarily storm petrels, shearwaters, fulmars, and albatrosses. All belong to a single order, the Tubinares, or tube-nosed swimmers, characterized by nostrils which open well forward along the sides of the beak. This article, in case you haven't guessed, is about albatrosses, and more specifically a common albatross of the North Pacific. The fulmars and shearwaters are essentially just smaller versions of the albatross, and though they are remarkable birds in their own right, to whom we would like to return in future, they will be mentioned here only in passing. But the storm petrels are so different and so remarkable that we cannot pass them up without comment.

The name petrel is derived from that of St. Peter who, according to the Gospel of Matthew (xiv:29), walked on the water. Moreover, the scientific name of the family to which the petrels belong (*Hydrobatidae*) means the same thing; it is derived from two Greek words meaning "one who treads on water." Petrels are little sea birds, smaller than a robin, who wing their way across some of the stormiest waters of the world. They fly close to the surface of the sea, and look like tiny, storm-tossed paper kites at the mercy of wind and wave. But each time a wave sweeps up and threatens to engulf them, they let down their slender legs with broad webbed feet and skip lightly along the surface of the water. Thus by an amazing combination of flying and skipping that keeps the onlooker breathless with excited admiration they negotiate the roughest seas.

Albatrosses apparently never use their feet in this manner, but they do make a great deal of use of their feet in taking off and landing. When alighting on the water they drop their legs like the landing gear of an airplane, spread out their webbed feet and thrust them forward to act as a brake when they strike the water. When taking off, they face into the wind, spread their long wings, and kick the water vigorously with both feet, once, twice, thrice or more, until they are airborne, leaving a wake of splashes a yard or two apart, visible for a few moments until they are blotted out in the endless movement of the ocean.

The lighter the wind, the more difficulty the albatrosses have in taking off, and the harder and longer they have to kick their feet. Robert Cushman Murphy, in *Oceanic Birds of South America,* recounts an instance in which, in a calm and fog, he encountered numerous albatrosses sitting on the water. As his boat approached them, they would swim away, or splash away kicking with their feet for as much as a hundred yards before taking to the air. This situation was complicated by the fog, so that it is not entirely clear whether it was the calm or the fog that discouraged the birds from taking off. But some observers believe that albatrosses require wind for flight, and are unable to fly in a dead calm.

My own observations do not entirely bear this out, as I have seen albatrosses take off from a calm sea in nearly still air and flap along heavily like oversize gulls. But they do not go far in this manner, and many observers have noted that in calm weather albatrosses give up flying and spend their time sitting on the water. It is an interesting thought that these masters of flight are so much creatures of the wind that they find themselves at a disadvantage without it. In fact, it is not an unreasonable theory that the tropic belt of calms is an important barrier in preventing albatrosses from moving freely back and forth across the equator. The species found in the northern and southern hemispheres are altogether distinct, and only rarely does a stray turn up in the wrong hemisphere.

In 1860 a black-browed albatross, native to the southern hemisphere, appeared in the Faeroe Islands, midway between Scotland and Iceland, and was seen regularly in this vicinity for 34 years, until it was shot in 1894.

Most species of albatross are found south of the equator, where the great southern ocean that encircles the globe between Antarctica and Australia, South Africa and South America provides the conditions of almost perpetual wind and swell in which these great birds are most at home. There is no albatross in the North Atlantic, its place there being taken in large part by the fulmar. But the North Pacific has its complement of albatrosses, whose flight is just as impressive as that of the wanderers of southern seas. So much has been written of the flight of the wandering albatross, the largest in its wing expanse of any existing bird, that we are inclined to underrate the other albatrosses, especially those we can find nearer home.

Once there were three species of albatross in the North Pacific—the short-tailed albatross, the Laysan albatross, and the black-footed albatross.

The first of these is apparently extinct, through the raiding of its nesting sites many years ago for the feather trade. Not a single individual of the short-tailed albatross has been definitely identified in recent years. The Laysan albatross is still moderately common in mid-Pacific, and occasionally strays to the Pacific coast of North America. It is the only white-bodied albatross to be seen off our coast. The black-footed albatross is happily still abundant, and may be seen in off-shore waters all the way from North America to Japan.

This dark brown albatross, with the whitish forehead and rump patch, and occasionally some other light feathers in its plumage, is known to sailors as the "gooney." Its nondescript appearance is unlikely to arouse any excitement in a seasick voyager. But it is really a magnificent bird, its seven-foot spread of wing not being exceeded by any North American birds except the eagles and the California condor. In powers of flight it is second to none.

Its long knife-like wings, with an aspect ratio (ratio of length to width) of around eleven to one, are especially adapted to horizontal gliding, and to maneuvering in the "bumpy" air that occurs over the surface of the ocean when a sea is running. Each wave or swell has an invisible counterpart in the air immediately above it; the albatross rides these waves of air, adjusting instantly to every draft, and taking maximum advantage of the upward component.

Maneuvering (from the Latin via the French, meaning "to work with the hands") is in fact a particularly apt word in describing the flight of the albatross. The bend of the wrist comes a little more than one-third of the distance in from the tip of the wing. The portions of the wing corresponding to the upper arm and forearm provide a gliding surface; but it is the outer section of the wing, corresponding to the human hand, that "feels" the wind and adjusts to every changing gust. There is even a certain amount of finger movement; the alula or bastard wing, corresponding to the human thumb, carries several stiff feathers which can be moved independently to raise or lower a section of the leading edge of the wing.

If you would like to imagine yourself a black-footed albatross, stretch out your arms as far as possible and think of them as being further extended to a total span of seven feet, and transformed into narrow wings, about eleven times as long as they are wide. Next think of your body size being reduced till your total weight is somewhere around seven pounds. Now, except in small matters of detail (no puns, please), you are a working model of an albatross, and ready to take off in a high wind.

While the albatross is the best of all known gliders, we must remember that it is not only a glider, but a combination of glider and light airplane, able to switch on the engine in an instant to pull itself out of any difficulty. I have seen albatrosses glide for long periods of time with scarcely any visible motion of the wings; but under conditions a little less favorable I have seen them swinging in mile-wide arcs astern of a steamer, flapping the wings once or twice at the end of each long glide. If one attributed human psychology to albatrosses, he might think they were trying to live up to their advance billing by slipping in a few surreptitious flaps now and then when too far away from the ship to be readily observed. Actually they are doing whatever comes naturally to them. As the wind dies down they flap more and more, and at last, as stated above, they give up flying and settle down on the water.

Black-footed albatrosses are seldom seen closer to shore than fifteen or twenty miles. Occasionally they will venture a short distance into wide inlets, like Monterey Bay, the Strait of Juan de Fuca, or Dixon Entrance. There are no records for San Francisco Bay. They can be seen any day from the deck of a trans-Pacific steamer; but the only way to really get to know them is to go well off shore in a fishing boat or other small craft. . . .

When a vessel is hove to for hauling nets or handling oceanographic gear, albatrosses would settle down on the water near by and wait hopefully for hand-outs from the galley. They have an inordinate appetite for pancakes, either with or without syrup. They feed at the surface of the water, or occasionally turn bottoms-up like the non-diving ducks and reach as far down into the water as they can stretch their necks. They never dive. Although they are wild birds and maintain a good deal of wariness, by judicious baiting they can be lured within camera range.

These hours of fraternizing with albatrosses in a calm sea, over pancakes or crusts of bread, are all too brief and infrequent. When the wind freshens and the sea comes up, and it becomes too rough for oceanographer or fisherman to work, then the albatrosses take to the air and give a truly magnificient demonstration of their powers of flight. In many months at sea over a period of twenty-five years, I have never seen weather so rough that the albatrosses seemed to be in the least difficulty. The cold, wet seafarer aboard a small vessel laboring through heavy seas in a full gale, gazes with admiration and envy at these majestic birds, and inevitably thinks of them in terms of the title of this article.

CARPENTEROS

Mark Catesby

Next to the passenger pigeon the most famous of vanished or vanishing birds is the spectacular ivory-billed woodpecker of the southern forests. A pair or two may just possibly still live in some remote fastness but it has been some years since one was last seen. In this case extinction is not due to deliberate persecution by man but simply to the fact that even good management of forests for human use involves the removal of the many dead trees upon which the ivory-bill depends for its food supply.

Mark Catesby, the eighteenth-century naturalist whom we have met before, took note of this remarkable bird.

T HE Largest White-bill Woodpecker weighs twenty ounces; and is about the size, or somewhat larger than a Crow. The bill is white as ivory, three inches long, and channelled from the basis to the point: the iris of the eye yellow: the hind part of the head adorned with a large peaked crest of scarlet feathers: a crooked white stripe runs from the eye on each side of the neck, towards the wing: the lower part of the back and wings (except the large quill feathers) are white: all the rest of the Bird is black.

The bills of these Birds are much valued by the Canada Indians, who make coronets of them for their Princes and great warriors, by fixing them round a wreath, with their points outward. The Northern Indians, having none of these Birds in their cold country, purchase them of the Southern people at the price of two, and sometimes three buck-skins a bill.

These Birds subsist chiefly on Ants, Wood-worms, and other Insects, which they hew out of rotten trees; nature having so formed their bills, that in an hour or two they will raise a bushel of chips; for which the Spaniards call them *Carpenteros*.

From *The Natural History of Carolina, Florida, and the Bahama Islands*. London: Printed for C. Marsh, in Round Court in the Strand; and T. Wilcox, over-against the New Church, in the Strand, 1754.

THE "MIRACLE"

OF THE

GULLS

Hubert Howe Bancroft

The age of skepticism began soon after what is now the United States was colonized. We have not, therefore, so many legends about birds as the Europeans have. Perhaps the most famous of ours is the "miracle" of the sea gulls which appeared from nowhere to save the crops in the new Mormon settlement in Utah. These gulls must have decided to stay around since there are now many at the Great Salt Lake near by.

T HE spring saw everybody busy, and soon there were many flourishing gardens, containing a good variety of vegetables. In the early part of March ploughing commenced. The spring was mild and rain plentiful, and all expected an abundant harvest. But in the latter part of May, when the fields had put on their brightest green, there appeared a visitation in the form of vast swarms of crickets, black and baleful as the locust of the Dead Sea. In their track they left behind them not a blade or leaf, the appearance of the country which they traversed in countless and desolating myriads being that of a land scorched by fire. They came in a solid phalanx, from the direction of Arsenal Hill, darkening the earth in their passage. Men, women, and children turned out en masse to combat this pest, driving them into ditches or on to piles of reeds, which they would set on fire, striving in every way, until strength was exhausted, to beat back the devouring host. But in vain they toiled, in vain they prayed; the work of destruction ceased not, and the havoc threatened to be as complete as that which overtook the land of Egypt in the last days of Israel's bondage. "Think of their condition," says Mr. Cannon—"the food they brought with them almost exhausted, their grain and other seeds all planted, they themselves 1200 miles from a settlement or place where they could get food on the east, and 800 miles

From *History of Utah* (1540–1887). San Francisco: The History Company, 1891.

from California, and the crickets eating up every green thing, and every day destroying their sole means of subsistence for the months and winter ahead."

I said in vain they prayed. Not so. For when everything was most disheartening and all effort spent, behold, from over the lake appeared myriads of snow-white gulls, their origin and their purpose alike unknown to the new-comers! Was this another scourge God was sending them for their sins? Wait and see. Settling upon all the fields and every part of them, they pounced upon the crickets, seizing and swallowing them. They gorged themselves. Even after their stomachs were filled they still devoured them. On Sunday the people, full of thankfulness, left the fields to the birds, and on the morrow found on the edges of the ditches great piles of dead crickets that had been swallowed and thrown up by the greedy gulls. Verily, the Lord had not forgotten to be gracious!

To escape the birds, the crickets would rush into the lake or river, and thus millions were destroyed. Toward evening the gulls took flight and disappeared beyond the lake, but each day returned at sunrise, until the scourge was past.

DOES THE

POOR-WILL "HIBERNATE?"

Edmund C. Jaeger

The correction of one error often leads to another. Thus the belief, current from classical times and well into the eighteenth century, that swallows hibernate under the water of ponds was hardly disposed of before most ornithologists would have been willing to say, "No bird hibernates." That some of them do is one of the most startling of recent discoveries. Here the tale is told by the man who first observed the strange phenomenon.

WHILE going up through a very narrow, high-walled, almost slot-like cañon in the Chuckawalla Mountains of the Colorado Desert two of my students and I saw on December 29, 1946, a most unusual sight. On the side-wall about two and a half feet above the sand of the cañon bottom was a Poor-will (*Phalaenoptilus nuttallii*) resting head-upward in a vertical rock-hollow, its gray and black, mottled plumage blending so perfectly with the coarse gray granite that we had to look twice to convince ourselves it was really a Poor-will. The shallow crypt, with deepest part above, was just a little more than large enough to hold the bird, hence its back was almost flush with the rock surface. When we had observed the bird quietly for more than ten minutes without noticing any motion, I reached forward and touched the bird without evoking any response. I even stroked the back feathers without noticing the slightest movement. Was our bird dead, sick or just deep in winter sleep? We left the place for awhile, then about two hours later returned. The Poor-will was still in the same position. I now reached forward and picked it up, freely turning it about in my hands. It seemed to be of unusually light weight and the feet and eye-lids when touched felt cold. We made no further attempt to be quiet; we even shouted to see if we could arouse our avian "sleeper." I finally returned it to its place in the crypt; but while I was doing this I noticed that it lazily opened and shut an eye, the only sign I had that it was a living bird. Unfortunately

From *The Condor*. January–February, 1948.

we soon had to leave the place and return home without making further observation.

Ten days later at about ten o'clock in the morning I returned with Mr. Lloyd Mason Smith. To our great surprise and satisfaction the Poorwill was still there in its rock niche, with every indication that it had not moved "even so much as a feather" in the intervening time. I reached forward and as before carefully picked it up. But this time instead of remaining perfectly quiet, it gave several "puffy" sounds as if expelling air from the lungs, opened an eye, and began to make a variety of queer high-pitched whining or squeaky mouse-like sounds. After some moments it opened its mouth widely as if yawning and then resumed its quiet. As Mr. Smith further handled it, it again made the whining notes; then suddenly it raised both wings and held them in rigid, fully outstretched upright position. The eyes remained closed. After the bird had held the wings stiffly upward for several minutes we worked together to put them back in normal position; several times we attempted this but the wings came quickly back high above the head until the tips almost touched. Some five minutes later while one of us still held the bird, we tried again, this time more successfully, for we got the wings at least partially in position. We now put the Poor-will back in its crypt as best we could and left. The morning was cool (42° F.), the sky overcast.

That afternoon while the sky was still gray with clouds we returned for further observations. We had put the bird into its crypt not quite in normal position and with feathers somewhat ruffled and wings askew, and so it was now when we found it after an absence of three hours. Mr. Smith picked up the Poor-will hoping to photograph it while I held it in my hand. But to our great surprise it whipped open its wings and flew out of hand in perfectly normal flight as if it had only been playing 'possum all the time but now had suddenly become alert to danger. It flew about forty feet up-cañon into an iron wood tree (*Olneya tesota*). We walked toward it and again it flew, alighting this time among some rocks high above us and where we were unable to reach it.

On this day there were fresh coyote tracks directly below the Poor-will's roosting site. The position of the foot prints indicated that the coyote had stopped and turned toward the bird. There were fresh feces and claw marks in the sand, all indications that he had remained there a number of minutes. Perhaps he even saw or smelled the bird, for it probably was perching there on the side of the rock at about the level of his eye.

On November 26, 1947, a Poor-will, probably the same bird, was in the same crypt, and again it was lethargic. On December 6 it was banded.

I am not venturing to state any conclusions, but this experience leads me strongly to suspect that one reason that so little is known and written about the winter habits of Poor-wills is because the birds then for the most part hide away and perhaps spend a short period in a kind of somnolence at least somewhat akin to true hibernation. Culbertson (Condor, 48,1946:158–159) found a Poor-will hidden in a rotten log and in sort of a torpid state of low metabolism. I take this as a partial corroboration of my belief that a period of winter inactivity among Poor-wills may be more common than we have supposed.

Part

Four

BIRDS AND MEN

WHITE HOUSE BIRD WATCHER

Bates M. Stovall

Theodore Roosevelt, ardent naturalist and great conservationist, was also a mighty hunter whose exploits were satirized by some and aroused the anger of others who objected to killing for fun. Mark Twain, for example, made him the subject of one of his famous "eruptions." The fact remains that Roosevelt was, more than any other one man, responsible for our national parks and that he never ceased to work for the preservation of wild life. To Frank M. Chapman he once wrote: "When I hear of the destruction of a species I feel as if all the works of some great writer had perished."

Close by Theodore Roosevelt's grave at Oyster Bay is a bird fountain. And near it stands a rock on which one reads that the fountain was erected by the National Association of Audubon Societies as a memorial to "Theodore Roosevelt, Friend of the Wild Birds."

This is no mere flattering phrase, for the late President was a born nature lover who made birds a part of his life. And with the information obtained about them through his prolific reading and from his close friendship with ornithologists of repute, he combined a rare knowledge of the subject gleaned from observations in the field. His powers of observing natural objects were remarkable. Nothing escaped his notice, whether elephant or hummingbird.

His interest in birds was evidenced at the age of nine, when he noted in his diary that several hundred swallows had descended upon a house in which he was staying near Tarrytown, N.Y. They swarmed about the place. Many got inside. One even attached itself to his pants. He caught some of them and put them out the windows.

By the time he was fourteen, he had a fair knowledge of American birds and had taken lessons in taxidermy. Also, with two of his cousins, he had begun what the three described as the Roosevelt Museum of Natural History. When his parents took him and their other children to Egypt, he was careful to take along a supply of printed pink slips labeled "Roosevelt Museum." They were to be used in marking specimens.

The Egyptian trip marks the beginning of his serious attention to

From *Frontiers Magazine*. February 1955.

collecting as a student of natural history. He took along a taxidermy out-
fit and his father gave him a shotgun. At Cairo he obtained a book with
descriptions of Egypt's birds. He had plenty of opportunity, for the
elder Roosevelt hired a boat in which the family spent two months on
the Nile. The boy scoured the river's vicinity, collecting ibis, plover
and other birds. His father trailed along behind through bog and over
solid ground, being hard put to keep up.

Many specimens obtained in Egypt and Palestine eventually reached
the Smithsonian Institution in Washington. Others found their way to
the American Museum of Natural History, New York.

When living as a ranchman in the West, Roosevelt didn't let cattle
interfere with his interest in bird life. Although he found many of the
western birds, especially in the river bottoms, representative of those in
the East, similarities were hardly ever absolute. In some cases the difference was in the songs; in others in the markings.

Sagamore Hill, his Long Island home, was a fertile center of bird
life, though the winged population was not as large as that around Washington. During one period of twenty-four hours, the owner of Sagamore
Hill counted forty-two different kinds of birds in its vicinity.

While President, he was frequently found early in the mornings
rambling about the White House grounds with his wife. Sometimes he
carried field glasses with him, the better to examine the skies and the
tops of tall trees.

"The people who saw me gazing up into a tall tree like one demented,"
Roosevelt afterward said, "no doubt thought me insane."

To which his wife added: "Yes, and as I was always with him, they
no doubt thought I was the nurse who had him in charge."

Among the visitors to the White House grounds were warblers. The
various kinds, with their differences in color and song, perplexed even
experienced ornithologists. But Roosevelt knew most of them.

John Burroughs was one of his closest friends. Burroughs said that
although he had given his whole life to ornithology, Roosevelt knew
almost as much about it as he did.

While the two were in Yellowstone National Park they heard a distant
call like someone blowing in an empty bottle. It came from the spruce
woods above their camp. They concluded the noise was made by a bird,
but were unable to decide what kind. Roosevelt, who was President at
the time, exclaimed: "Let's go run that bird down!"

So they crossed a stream and hot-footed it over a snow-streaked plain.
When they got into the woods they discovered their quarry high up in
a tree. Burroughs imitated the creature's call and caused it to turn toward
him. But they still couldn't make out its species.

"You stay here and keep that bird treed, and I'll fetch the glasses,"
said the President.

So he rushed off to camp, got the field glasses and returned. And with their help, it was found that the feathered object was a pygmy owl. "I think the President was as pleased," said Burroughs afterward, "as if he had bagged some big game, for he had never seen the bird before."

Though Roosevelt loved to hear birds sing, he pointed out it is hard to be an impartial observer of their music. The listener's mood, his keenness of sense and the surroundings, all have a part in the attractiveness of the song.

On one occasion near Nashville, he spent the night in a room with windows overlooking a large magnolia tree. It was spring-time; the magnolia was bathed in the light of a full moon. A mockingbird serenaded Theodore the live-long night. He was enthralled, afterward declaring the bird poured forth such a rapture of ringing melody "as I have never listened to before or since."

A man's mood on occasions might be such, Roosevelt believed, that even the loveliest of bird songs would make little impression on him. Yet at such times, wilderness cries like those made by prairie fowl, wild geese, eagles and sandhill cranes might have strong appeal.

In 1909, he went on his expedition to collect specimens of African birds, mammals, reptiles and plants. And he took with him special instructions from John Burroughs to observe the habits of the honey-bird.

From his observations, Roosevelt found how the bird performed. It chattered loudly to draw attention to itself, and then flew from tree to tree, making sure, however, that it was being followed. In this way it eventually led men to a honey tree. Here the bird would flit from branch to branch, and call loudly as if saying: "Come and get it." When sure the honey had been found, the winged guide would sit solemnly by and watch. Then, as soon as the men had taken the honey, the bird swept in and ate the grubs. The natives believe that misfortune descends upon honey gatherers who fail to leave the bird its share of the booty.

The black whydah finch was another unique bird Roosevelt saw in Africa. A cock of this species, dressed in his dark, glossy suit and long tail feathers, alights in a two-foot ring having a tuft of foot-high grass remaining in the center. He jumps a couple of feet into the air, wings spread, tail drooping, head thrown back. Landing again in the ring, he might make a few hops forward, then jump into the air as before. He repeats these activities over and over again. Along the Kamiti river were numerous rings, and Roosevelt found it startling to see so many birds doing their unique dance at the same time.

Camouflage engineers might learn a thing or two from the flight of the African nightjar. When Roosevelt first saw one of these in flight it seemed to him that two large moths or butterflies were flying along together. Then he took another look and saw the bird ahead, discovering that the supposed insects were really feather patches at the end of long quills. Each of the bird's wings trailed a quill which was twice as long as the creature's body and tail.

In point of tameness, Roosevelt put the wagtails of Africa on a par with the whisky jacks and Hudsonian chickadees of the northern woods. He also marvelled at the fearlessness shown by a small cormorant in Africa which plumped into the water beside the naturalist Loring while he was swimming. And in South America he was greatly taken with Moses, a little owl, which Miller, a naturalist, had gotten in the Chaco. Moses was kept in a basket. When Miller was around the owl would make queer little noises to show it wanted to be taken up and petted. Sometimes its owner would let it perch on his hand or on a bar near him. When stroked or tickled, it chuckled delightedly.

To hear the bird songs of England about which he had read, Roosevelt took a long walk through the Valley of the Itchen and through the New Forest. He had Sir Edward Grey, a bird enthusiast, for a guide.

At one point in a flooded lowland, the two had to walk through breast-deep water. While they were drying themselves in the sunshine shortly afterward, the musical notes of a bird sounded. Teddy beamed. "Of all the songs we have heard today," he exclaimed, "that is the only one which resembles in any degree an American song bird."

"That," said Sir Edward, "is the goldencrested wren."

Afterward, Teddy became curious as to the accuracy of his companion's statement, so he asked a bird expert in the British Museum about it. In reply, he was told the song was the only one they could have heard on such a walk which was like that of an American bird.

During their walk, conversation often went somewhat like this:

Grey: "Did you hear that?"

"Yes: what bird is it?"

"A blackcap."

"So that is the song of the blackcap."

Roosevelt didn't have to ask further about the bird. He knew the rest.

Though he thought the blackcap warbler to be the most musical songster heard during the walk, it was the blackbird which impressed him most of the birds he came across in England. Its habits and appearance, he found, were greatly like that of an American robin.

It was during his administration as President that national bird reservations became realities, and when he retired there were more than fifty scattered through our country and its possessions.

PRESIDENTIAL

BIRD

WATCHER

Richard L. Scheffel

Theodore Roosevelt may have been the only American President whose earliest ambition was to be a professional naturalist but Thomas Jefferson had considerable interest in the subject. He "took all knowledge for his province" and like more than one country gentleman in England he recorded in a diary many observations, not only of his crops, but of every natural phenomenon which came under his wide-ranging scrutiny.

I T had been an average spring. The days had warmed and the hills were green until now it was the 8th of June, 1790. At Philadelphia it already seemed like summer; on that day the season's first peas and strawberries appeared in the markets.

He may have been writing, or calling on friends at the time—we do not know. But we do know that on the evening of that same June 8, Thomas Jefferson heard the insistent call of the whip-poor-will for the first time that year. These simultaneous entries on the stage of spring struck Secretary of State Jefferson as curious and he immediately wrote to his daughter, Mary, asking when these signs of the season had appeared in Virginia.

"Take notice hereafter whether the whip-poor-wills always come with the strawberries and peas," he advised her.

Mary Jefferson replied that the peas at home had been ripe since May 10, and those few strawberries that had survived the late frost had been ready for picking on May 17.

But Mary had to admit to "Dear Papa" that ". . . as for the whip-poor-wills, I was so taken up with my chickens that I never attended to them, and therefore can not tell you when they came, though I was so unfortunate as to lose half of the chickens."

Our third President was, it seems, a dedicated, if amateur, naturalist. He

From *Audubon Magazine*. May–June, 1961.

meant it when he said there is "not a sprig of grass that shoots uninterest-
ing to me, nor anything that moves." He was constantly alert to life
around him and kept prodigious records of his observations. If he saw his
first robins on February 28 in Philadelphia, it prompted him to wonder
when they had returned to Monticello. His letters to his daughters are, as
a result, filled with his observations and requests for information in order
that "we shall be able to compare the climates of Philadelphia and Monticello."

He eventually concluded that the purple martin could be expected at
Monticello sometime between March 18 and April 9, just about the time
the first asparagus should be ready in his kitchen garden each spring.
And he came to expect the whip-poor-will's arrival in Albemarle County
during the first three weeks of April while redbud and dogwood still
glowed from the hills—more than a month before the bird showed up
in Philadelphia.

Nor were Jefferson's thoughts devoted exclusively to affairs of state
while he crossed the Atlantic in 1784 to take up his new duties as
Minister to France. His personal log of the voyage tells us he spent
a good deal of time scanning sea and sky. He kept a record of the
shearwaters and petrels, sharks and whales he sighted, as well as of passing
sails.

While in Europe, Jefferson left his post long enough to tour southern
France and the Italian Riviera where he wrote enthusiastically of the
superb climate and the great numbers of nightingales, beccaficcas, ortolans,
quail and other birds. Of these, he said, he would have liked especially
to bring back to America the pheasants and partridges of France, though
he never was able to.

He probably imagined them in the extravagant park he had pictured,
as a young man, surrounding his hilltop mansion. For young Tom
Jefferson had written of a plan for a park which should harbor peacocks,
guniea hens, pheasants and partridges. It would also include feeding stations to attract squirrels and rabbits, deer and "every other wild animal
(except those of prey)." And, besides a buffalo, he wanted to "procure a
buck elk, to be, as it were, monarch of the woods; but keep him shy,
that his appearance may not lose its effect by too much familiarity."

The buffalo and elk, unfortunately, eluded Jefferson, but Isaac, one of
his former slaves, has assured us that partridges were especially abundant
at Monticello. And a French visitor has left us an idyllic picture of
Jefferson strolling over his grounds of an evening with his score or so of
tame deer coming up to take Indian corn from his hands.

Like many other Americans visiting Europe, Jefferson was smitten by
the nightingale. What a bird it would be in America!

"We must colonize him thither," he wrote.

To his daughter, Martha, he described his thrill at sailing on the canal of Languedoc with "cloudless skies above, limpid waters below," while a row of nightingales sang from each bank. He told her of the fountain of Vaucluse, where water gushed from a secluded mountain valley, and Petrarch's chateau perched on the cliff above.

"To add to the enchantment of the scene," he recalled, "every tree and bush was filled with nightingales in full song."

Not that America couldn't do as well, of course. Notice the nightingale's song, Jefferson advised Martha, and remember it for comparison with the mockingbird's song back in America. The mockingbird "has the advantage of singing through a great part of the year, whereas the nightingale," he added, "sings but about five or six weeks in the spring, and a still shorter term, and with a more feeble voice, in the fall."

The mockingbird seems to have been Jefferson's special favorite. While congratulating Martha one spring on the songster's return to Monticello, he added that he hoped all the new trees and shrubs becoming established around the house would attract more mockingbirds ". . . for they like to be in the neighborhood of our habitations if they furnish cover." He even suggested that Martha teach her children to venerate the mockingbird "as a superior being in the form of a bird, or as a being which will haunt them if any harm is done to itself or its eggs."

One mockingbird actually became Jefferson's personal pet. Margaret Bayard Smith, whose husband was editor of Washington's first newspaper, described Jefferson's pet mockingbird as a "constant companion" who followed him about in the White House. It often perched on his couch to serenade him as he napped and would even land on his shoulder and take food from his lips.

Birds, however, were more than just playthings to Jefferson. He considered a man's education incomplete if it did not include study of Alexander Wilson's "American Ornithology."

He also was well acquainted with Mark Catesby's mammoth two-volume work, "The Natural History of Carolina, Florida and the Bahama Islands." In fact, he commented that Catesby's "drawings are better as to form and attitude than color."

He was, after all, the president who organized the Lewis and Clark Expedition. Even before negotiations for the purchase of the vast Louisiana Territory had been completed, Jefferson had secured an appropriation from Congress to finance the expedition by Meriwether Lewis and William Clark.

In three years of explorations up the Missouri, across the Rockies and down the Columbia to the Pacific, Lewis and Clark sent hundreds of herbarium specimens, skins, skeletons and seeds to Jefferson. They even sent him a live prairie chicken and four magpies.

Many species were entirely new to science, and it was Jefferson who filled the vital role of assembling records and distributing specimens among qualified scientists for study, for the expedition discovered hundreds of unknown plants and varieties of wildlife.

Jefferson's other contribution to our knowledge of birds appeared in a work called "Notes on the State Virginia," the only book he ever published. It was inspired by a series of questions submitted to him by the Marquis de Marbois, Secretary of the French Legation at Philadelphia, who was gathering information on the American states for dissemination in Europe.

Jefferson took advantage of this opportunity to organize his vast file of notes and memoranda, "which I did in the order of Mr. Marbois' queries, so as to answer his wish, and to arrange them for my own use." The result was a book that has been called the most important scientific work, except for Benjamin Franklin's on electricity, published in America up to that time. It included information on the geography, climate, commerce, laws and the plants and animals of Virginia. Several pages of the "Notes" are given over to a listing, by both scientific and common names, of over 100 of the birds of Virginia, qualified by the comment that there were "doubtless many others which have not yet been described and classed."

It is an impressive list but not enough, of course, to establish Jefferson as an expert ornithologist. Some people have exaggerated his accomplishments in this field. Elsa Allen, historian of American ornithology, has analyzed his list critically, pointing out its many weaknesses and errors along with its strong points, in order to dispel the legend.

We have to agree with Mrs. Allen that Jefferson was not an ornithologist, although even this strict critic concedes "he had a tolerable familiarity with some 60 or 70 birds."

But whether he knew 70 or 100 species is not of monumental importance. What is intriguing is the fact that this busy and learned statesman considered bird study one of his major secondary interests.

Only a man of intense devotion to wildlife would take the time, for instance, to observe and write of the "chattering plover or killdee" as it flew down the lane ahead of him at Monticello.

This Founding Father enjoyed an intimate kinship with nature which he liked to describe as an "interest or affection in every bud that opens, in every breath that blows."

FATHER

OF AMERICAN

ORNITHOLOGY

Elsa G. Allen

---

*The first great American ornithologist was not Audubon but his
slightly younger contemporary, the Scotsman Alexander Wilson
whose reputation has always been blighted by the shadow of his
famous contemporary. Born in 1766 and growing up in poverty,
Wilson was one of those obscure Europeans who came alone and
unsponsored to the New World, not to seek their fortunes, but to
see for themselves its natural wonders and beauties. For ten years he
supported himself in the United States by schoolteaching until a
meeting with William Bartram marked the turning point of his career. The first volume of his* American Ornithology *was published
in 1808 and the eighth was in the press when he died in 1813. Of his
work Elliot Coues, one of the greatest ornithological authorities,
wrote: "Probably no other work of ornithology of equal extent is
equally free from errors; and its truthfulness is illumed by a spark
of the divine fire."*

Back in 1794 in Old Philadelphia, adjacent to Peale's Museum, a zoological garden was founded. The principal attraction was an eagle
with this sign on his cage—"Feed me well and I'll live a hundred years."
I think of this fine old bird as a cynosure of American ornithology, a
science which was indeed reared and fledged in Philadelphia, and which
later, when it came of age, spread throughout the land.

Seventeen ninety-four was also the year that brought to our shores
the immigrant Scot, Alexander Wilson, who became Aamerica's first
ornithologist. He had space on the deck of the American ship, Swift,
sailing from Belfast for Philadelphia on May 23, and he took his young
nephew, William Duncan, with him.

Times had been hard for Wilson in Paisley, his native town. At thirteen,
soon after his mother died, he was taken out of school and bound appren-
tice and servant to a weaver. For three long years he rebelled against

From the *Atlantic Naturalist*. November–December, 1952.

this unnatural confinement and finally, when the indenture expired and he was free, he wrote these feeling lines:

"Be't kent to a' the world in rhime
That wi right meikle wark and toil
For three lang years I've ser't my time,
Whiles feasted wi' the hazel oil."

Yet, so limited was young Wilson's education that he had to continue at weaving, and he stooped over the webs another four years. He was then twenty years of age, and loath to face another year of weaving, he took to the road with a pack on his back, and a few of his poems in his pocket. He had decided to study nature and write verse.

Two slender little volumes of his poetry came out with indifferent success, and another, a humorous ballad called, *Watty and Meg*, with a homely and witty philosophy on marriage, was published anonymously. It was popular at once, and thousands of copies were sold. The beloved poet of the people, Robert Burns, was thought to be the author, but instead it was the humble and dissatisfied weaver, Alexander Wilson.

Wilson's early twenties were divided between the weavers' craft and the journeyman's uncertain lot. When he was weaving, his employers complained of his indifference to his work and his constant scribbling, while his customers along the road cared little for his wares or his poetry.

Though Wilson could write feelingly of the beautiful Scottish landscape, he could not refrain from using his bitter and sarcastic wit against the political and industrial ills of the times, and finally, in a personal attack on a certain manufacturer in his poem, *The Shark*, he was found guilty of libel. It was the repercussion of this unfortunate incident, with his imprisonment, his trial, his fine and at last his sentence requiring him to burn his offensive lampoon on the steps of the Tolbooth, that determined him in his plan to go to America.

Accordingly, he took leave of his few good friends the last of April, 1794, and after fifty-three days at sea, he and his young companion arrived at New Castle, Delaware. Here they disembarked with their guns and luggage, and walked thirty-five miles to Philadelphia, although the ship was bound for that port.

The first bird that Wilson saw was a red-headed woodpecker. He shot it and made a skin of it, and he thought it the most beautiful bird he had ever seen.

Wilson's Early Years in America

A new world spread out before him; strange birds, new trees and flowers stirred his love of nature; and life at once was full of promise. He scanned the landscape and settlements for possible employment, ruefully aware that weaving was the only trade he knew. Duncan got a job at the looms of James Robertson, of Philadelphia; Wilson took one in a copper-plate print shop, abandoned it, and returned to weaving, in the service of Mr. Joshua Sullivan, of Pennsypack Creek, ten miles from the city.

But the birds were on his mind; he had arrived at the height of the nesting season and he could not forget the abundant whistling cardinals so striking in their red plumage nor the wood thrushes with their lovely morning and evening singing, and many lesser songsters of the roadside. In a few weeks he was a peddler again, carrying a pack of silk and cotton fabrics. He reasoned that in this way he could at least study birds and he set out for Virginia, settled for a few months at Sheppardstown, then up to Bustletown, Pennsylvania, where he served as a country schoolmaster. Finally he went to Milestown, Pennsylvania, where he lived for several years.

Here Wilson began his self-education and worked at mathematics, surveying, German, drawing, and music. He became much interested, too, in American politics and on the day of Jefferson's inauguration March 4, 1801, he delivered at Milestown an *Oration on Liberty*, in which he displayed an amazing command of English.

"Pedagoging" was his scornful way of referring to school teaching, and he liked it little better than weaving. He had to study hard at night to keep ahead of his pupils, and during his week-ends, he worked at surveying to help out the wretched pittance he was paid as schoolmaster. He hated the community and branded the village as a settlement of canting, preaching, praying, ignorant Presbyterians. His general unhappiness was augmeted by an unfortunate love affair in the summer of 1801, that caused him great anxiety. He wrote to his intimate friend, Charles Orr, a writing master of Philadelphia: "Do come," he said; "your friendship and counsel may be of the utmost service to me. I have no friend but yourself and *one*, whose friendship has involved us both in ruin, or threatens to do so. You will find me at the schoolhouse." In another letter Wilson says:

> "Of all the events of my life nothing gives
> me such inexpressible misery as this.
> O, my dear friend, if you can hear
> anything of her real situation, and
> whatever it is, disguise nothing to me."

He concludes his letter to Orr thus:

> "I have no company and live unknowing and
> unknown. I have lost all relish for this
> country and if Heaven spares me, I shall
> soon see the shores of Old Caledonia."

Who the woman of Milestown was we cannot learn from any of Wilson's letters, but she apparently was married and the situation for him was hopeless, except that this love enriched his life and matured his writing. He turned more and more to poetry, studied the Scottish pastoral poets, Pope, Thomson, Shenstone, Ramsay, and Fergusson, and yearned to make his own name live among the Scottish bards. To Orr again he unburdened his heart:

"The idea (of poetry) is transporting and such a
recompense is worth all the misfortunes
penury and deprivations here that
the most wretched sons of science have ever suffered."

He was torn between two desires: to write poetry and to study nature. Could he combine these two absorbing interests to produce poetical writings of lasting worth? The answer seems clearly to be *no*. His poetic craftsmanship could not plumb the deep wells of human feeling, but remained on the surface—purely objective.

In the field of prose, however, Wilson came a long way both by native ability to observe, combined with his inherent love of nature, and by the long schooling he gave himself with the out-of-doors. To all his prose writing he was able to bring an originality of expression, and a real facility with words. This quality, however, is entirely lacking or very rare in his verse. Nevertheless, after the unhappy affair in Milestown, Wilson gave much attention to verse-writing and published several pieces in newspapers and magazines, but he could not earn a living at it, and soon returned to teaching.

By application to the trustees of Union School in the township of Kingsessing, Wilson was assigned to the school at Gray's Ferry, only four miles from Philadelphia.

Although in his own words he resumed "that painful profession with the same sullen resignation that a prisoner re-enters his dungeon, or a malfactor mounts the scaffold," his life took a definite turn for the better by this change. In a few weeks he was a neighbor of the famous naturalist, William Bartram, and a warm friendship grew up between them.

The Schoolmaster at Gray's Ferry

The poverty and bitterness that had distorted his outlook and that is so clearly reflected in several of his American poems were softened in the pleasant atmosphere and surroundings of the Bartram home. This was a charming stone dwelling set in eight acres of ground, that sloped down to the Schuylkill River. The elder Bartram, John, father to William, had assembled gardens of great interest from his travels in quest of rarities for British and continental horticulturists. It was as simple Quaker home, but because of its gardens, it was also a Mecca for visiting naturalists from abroad, as well as other travelers, and Wilson at last could mingle with the learned and the cultured.

There were books in the Bartram library with which he spent long hours, especially Mark Catesby's two-volume *Natural History of Carolina, Florida and the Bahama Islands* (1731), and George Edwards' four-volume *Natural History of Birds* (1751), both full of accounts and plates of American birds. Wilson already, from his long pedestrian journeys, could detect many errors in these earlier works.

He discussed his findings with William Bartram and all the daylight hours he could spare from his school work he spent in the field, gradually adding new specimens to his little collection that he had been building up since the day he shot the red-headed woodpecker.

At the Bartram home he met a fellow-countryman, Alexander Lawson, an artist and engraver, who offered to teach him how to etch. The English ornithologists Catesby and Edwards, had done their own etching, and Wilson thought he, too, could learn. Soon he had, as he expressed it, an "insatiable itch" to draw birds, and as fast as he accumulated a few drawings, he sent them to Bartram for criticism and begged that he mark them in pencil with the proper names. Bartram became his mentor and Lawson his instructor in his study of the delineation of American birds, and gradually he conceived the plan of portraying all the common American birds in a manner suitable to their great interest and beauty. Poetry was slipping to a second place in his affections and birds became his consuming passion. But the irksome task of "pedagoging" was still his only source of a livelihood.

It was 1804—ten years after his arrival in America. Wilson's school was prospering; it was even crowded with pupils. After school he studied his lessons first, then drew pictures of birds by candlelight. Poetry, too, was not yet abandoned, for to this period belong some of his better efforts: *The Solitary Tutor* and *The Rural Walk*, both published in the *Literary Magazine*, and several poems on birds, for example, *The Bluebird, The Osprey,* and *The Tyrant Flycatcher.*

But drawing was uppermost in his mind and as his finished plates increased in number, he envisaged a monumental work, *The American Ornithology.* Birds from the St. Lawrence to the mouth of the Mississippi and from the Atlantic to the interior of Louisiana were his goal. To his engraver he said, "Do not throw cold water on my notion, as Shakespeare says, quixotic as it may appear. I have been so long accustomed to the building of airy castles and brain windmills that it has become one of my earthly comforts, a sort of rough bone that amuses me when sated with the dull drudgery of life."

The Trip to Niagara Falls

Wilson furthered this ambitious plan by making a foot journey from Philadelphia to Niagara Falls in 1804—a fantastic undertaking at that time; his companions, William Duncan and a young friend, Isaac Leech. He took note of every incident and minutely described the changing scene the whole way, all of which he transposed into a long poem *The Foresters*, consisting of 2210 lines of heroic couplets. This epic of hardship has small literary value, yet Wilson entertained high hopes of literary fame accruing from it. It was published serially in the magazine *Portfolio* which at that time was taking an interest in American scenery, but Wilson, struggling for a bare living, received nothing for this, his major effort in verse.

The entire distance traversed was upwards of 1200 miles, but his companions could not match either Wilson's endurance nor his enthusiasm, and left him on the return trip. The expedition took fifty-nine days and the last day Wilson walked forty-seven miles, arriving back in mid-December, 1804.

While at Niagara he had sketched the Falls, and returning via the Mohawk River, he collected two birds unknown to him. He introduced drawings of these birds against the background of the Falls, and sent the whole picture to President Jefferson. The reply received from the President, expressing his appreciation and offering queries on other birds delighted Wilson, and encouraged him to apply for an assignment as collector on the Zebulon Pike Expedition to the sources of the Mississippi River, which was then being organized.

This letter to the President was apparently not received, for Wilson did not hear from him. He was disappointed, but by no means crushed, as some commentators have interpreted the incident. On the contrary, his letters of this period indicate a healthy sense of potential accomplishment with plans for study and travel. He was scarcely home from Niagara when he expressed hope of a southeastern journey for he felt sure that many undescribed birds were to be found there. However, he wisely deferred it.

Wilson in Philadelphia

Hard upon the failure of his letter to secure him the Pike assignment, he was offered a position as assistant editor on Rees New Cyclopedia. This tribute to Wilson's ability was almost transporting. He resigned his teaching position and took up his residence in Philadelphia in April, 1806. We may imagine the difficult change, immured as he was among books with nothing to look at but walls and chimneys and the noise of the city in his ears. His flute and violin were comforting and by getting up at dawn he could dash to the outskirts of the city after birds.

The new work was quite exacting, for not only ornithology but the whole field of zoology, with also botany and geology, were to be revised. In addition to this, Wilson served as tutor to the two young sons of Mr. Samuel E. Bradford, the publisher, yet he did not abate his efforts to accumulate a series of bird plates and a knowledge of the haunts and habits of common species.

In fact, it seems probable that Wilson welcomed his call to the staff of a publishing house, not only for the substantial stipend of $900.00 per annum, but also as a possible outlet for his own work on ornithology.

After a year at his new post, the *American Ornithology* rapidly took form. Bradford agreed to publish it, and as early as 1807 a prospectus of all the proposed ten volumes was ready for distribution. A copy went at once to William Bartram for criticism, and Wilson received a letter of approval in three days.

Launching the American Ornithology

The first volume came out in September, 1808. At the same time Wilson set out on his first soliciting trip, a sample copy of his book in one arm and his faithful fowling piece across his shoulder. "Like a beggar with his bantling," he said. Yet he preserved a friendly, dignified, and sophisticated interest in all persons who examined it. Writing from Boston to a friend October 10, he said he had heard "nothing but expressions of the highest admiration and esteem." Passing through Pennsylvania on his return trip, however, he met a certain judge who bluntly refused to examine his work, which he said was "undemocratic" and "too good for the commonality." In the face of this rebuff, Wilson stuck to his guns. To a friend he wrote: "If I have been mistaken in publishing a work too good for the country, it is a fault not likely to be soon repeated." These were prophetic words, but Wilson forged ahead in his plans, making useful contacts throughout his journey, "so that," as he put it, "scarcely a wren or tit would pass from York to Canada but I shall get intelligence of it."

By a study of the prefaces of Wilson's volumes, one can learn much about the author's hopes, plans and difficulties in connection with the publication of the *American Ornithology*.

In Volume 2, for instance, with swiftly-developing pride in things American, he tells of some beautiful pigments from the laboratory of Messrs. Peale and Son, of the Peale Museum, which he substituted in place of certain French products, with excellent soft results. Here, also, he solicits specimens and correspondence from interested persons, and gives detailed directions for the care of birds in the flesh and for making skins. He sought to cultivate the study of birds on the American side of the Atlantic, for it seemed to him humiliating to be obliged to apply to Europe for an account of the fauna of his adopted country.

The second part of his soliciting journey took him through the coastal cities and down to the deep South. After three months he had obtained his goal of two hundred and fifty subscribers and was encouraged by favorable comments on his work in the southern paper, *Republican*.

The environs of Charleston and Savannah and the dark cypress swamps of the Santee River took him back in thought to his predecessor, Mark Catesby, who had roamed that area some eighty years earlier. Though aware that Catesby's knowledge of plants and trees was far better than his, he was proud of his own better knowledge of the birds, and bent every effort to get a good collection of southern species.

The people, however, were disappointing to Wilson with his Spartan outlook on life. Said he of the persons he wished to interview: "At nine they are in bed, at ten, breakfasting, dressing at eleven—gone out at noon and not visible til ten the next morning." In Savannah a fever attacked him, but since he intended to return to New York by ship, he said with a gibe at his indisposition: "I hope the sea air and sea-sickness will carry it off."

But the privations of this southern journey and his persistent carelessness about his health, combined to undermine his general condition.

Wilson's journals of his American experience have never been found, although his biographer, George Ord, makes frequent reference to them. However, we have another source in Wilson's letters to his friends, where we can follow his travels and business contacts, and gather his impressions of many parts of the United States. On return, Wilson plunged into his double job, his writing for Rees Cyclopedia and the preparation of other volumes on American birds. As soon as two were ready, he wrapped then carefully and sent them to his father by an acquaintance returning to Paisley.

The Trip Down the Ohio River

Only a few months elapsed before Wilson was deep in plans for his long-contemplated trip down the Ohio River. The journey to Pittsburgh in Western Pennsylvania he made on foot and his expenses he limited to a dollar a day. To this rigorous excursion Wilson in all good faith invited his friend, William Bartram, a man twenty-seven years his senior, and a home-loving man who could not even be lured to the Chair of Botany by the University of Pennsylvania.

So once again Wilson set out alone. Many stops were made for collecting birds and soliciting subscriptions—Lancaster, Hanover, Chambersburg, Shippensburg, Greensburg, and Pittsburgh. Four days in Pittsburgh secured him nineteen subscribers from the city's most prominent residents. Here he purchased his small skiff, which he christened, "The Ornithologist." Then he laid in his modest stores of biscuit and cheese, tucked in a gift bottle of cordial and a tin can for bailing the boat. In high hopes of rich collecting and flouting all advice against going alone, the intrepid oarsman launched downstream for Cincinnati. With difficulty he dodged the floating masses of ice, but in a day's voyage toward the south, these quite disappeared.

Wilson was happy in his solitary journey, the hazards of which were great, but he seemed equal to every emergency. Starting on February 24th, 1810, he suffered every discomfort, but felt rewarded by the magnificent scenery and the opportunity to study the settlers and their hardworking way of life. Above all, he valued his increasing knowledge of American birdlife, and dreamed and planned about the volumes he was going to write after returning home. At Big Bone Lick he encountered his first paroquets and besides securing several for his collection, he wingtipped one, which became his little companion.

Seven hundred and twenty miles the ornithologist voyaged downstream before the lights of Louisville, Kentucky became dimly visible. He then moored his skiff securely to a large Kentucky boat in Bear Grass Creek above the rapids of the great river, and by the time he had groped his way across a swamp, carrying his satchel, his gun and pet paroquet, it was late when he arrived at the Indian Queen Tavern and asked for a room.

Wilson had four letters of introduction to prominent persons in Louisville, and lost no time in fitting in these calls during the next few days of bird-hunting. He dropped into other places, too, if they seemed to hold promise of a subscription, and by a strange coincidence, he entered the store of John James Audubon, then an obscure merchant of this frontier town. This man, who twenty years later published the famous *The Birds of America* in "Elephant Folios" was, in 1810, having but indifferent success.

Audubon had started an importing business with his partner, Ferdinant Rosier, but the Embargo Act of President Jefferson in 1807, which prohibited traffic in foreign goods, had greatly curtailed his business.

Naturally Wilson had no letter of introduction to this little-known shop or its owner, so he came quickly to the purpose of his visit, laid his books on the counter, explained the scope of the work, and asked Mr. Audubon if he would care to subscribe. The price was $120.

Audubon leafed it through without much comment and, taking the pen from the counter, was about to sign the subscription list. Just then his partner Mr. Rosier, speaking French from the adjoining room, interrupted him. His words according to Audubon's account of the incident were to the effect that since Audubon's drawings were superior and also since his knowledge of American birds must be better than this gentleman's, why should he subscribe?

Always susceptible to praise, Audubon laid down the pen.

Wilson, until that moment feeling safe in the uniqueness of his enterprise, was stunned. Not much of a French student, he had nevertheless gathered Rosier's meaning and managed to ask if Audubon had drawn many birds.

He had, and he reached for a large portfolio of his work which lay on an upper shelf in his shop, and proceeded to show his drawings to the astonished Wilson.

Many European birds which Audubon had drawn as a youth in France, before he took up his residence in America in order to engage in business, and also many American species were among the beautiful and striking portraits.

In October 1808, a year and a half previously, Wilson had said that a work such as his own was not likely to be soon repeated.

Yet here before his eyes he was outdone.

In spite of this heavy blow not a word about this meeting escaped his lips or his pen We search in vain in his letters of this period and his accounts of birds for some mention of Audubon. He seems sedulously to avoid it but writes in detail of many other events and incidents. Only in George Ord's biography of Wilson published in 1828, nearly eighteen years after the meeting of the two ornithologists, do we find two entries supposedly from Wilson's Journal which can be construed as referring to Audubon:

March 19—Rambling about town with my gun. Examined
Mr. ——'s drawings in crayons—very good.
Saw two new birds he had: both motacillae.
March 21—Went out this afternoon shooting with Mr. A.
Saw a number of sandhill cranes. Pigeons numerous.

These journal entries and a few others are put in between quoted letters and are chronologically out of place, without bearing on the letters, and they are without comment by Ord except in that they are offered as samples of Wilson's "unstudied narratives."

Ord's biography of the ornithologist is told largely by quoting his letters so that the student learns little that he does not already know if he has read the letters, and he is left with the feeling that Ord intentionally withheld enlightening information.

Be this as it may, we cannot in the space of this account go into the welter of conjecture and biased published material about the professional rivalry of these two men. So far as can be learned Wilson never broke his sardonic silence on the subject and although Audubon told him in his shop that he had no plans to publish, Wilson of course knew it was only reasonable that eventually Audubon would bring out his work.

Two days after this historic meeting Wilson left Louisville crushed with disillusionment. He sold his boat, parted with his paroquet to the innkeeper and took off southwardly into the wilderness on horseback. We can judge of the impact of Wilson's discovery of Audubon by the desperate concentration with which he went at his work from 1810 on.

The southward course of his journey to New Orleans, his ultimate destination, took him through the Chickasaw and Choctaw territory, a very difficult stretch of wilderness and swampland, where Wilson, in truth, broke his health.

He happened to stop one night, 72 miles south of Nashville, at the house of a Mrs. Grinder, where the famous explorer, Captain Meriwether Lewis had died. His grave lay neglected by the trail, and Wilson, though sick and poor, gave money for a post fence around it. But many nights he slept where darkness forced him to stop, and in a letter to his brother, David, he confessed to spending weeks in the wilderness three hundred miles from a white settlement and so reduced in strength as scarely to be able to stand, or even ride his horse. Friendly Indians told him to live on raw eggs and wild strawberries, and this diet partly restored him.

In spite of all this misfortune Wilson continued to collect and draw birds, and sent home many which were intended for his third and fourth volumes. This parcel was lost in the mail, however, and consequently his work was retarded at a very critical time.

Philadelphia Again

He returned to Philadelphia by ship from New Orleans August* 2, 1810, and faced the task of bringing out the balance of his ten volume work, only two of which had been published. While deep in southern swamps, badly nourished and infected by contaminated water, he had suffered several attacks of dysentery. But he never would, nor could he, in such isolation, take time to get well. The great body of work before him in such a weakened condition caused him to reduce the proposed ten volumes to nine. It is significant that the next four volumes came out during 1811 and 1812. This had entailed another hard journey in 1812—up the Hudson River, across rough mountain country to Lake Champlain and north to Burlington, Vermont. At Haverhill he was taken for a Canadian spy and arrested, but after explaining his travels in the interest of science, he was released.

Returning to Philadelphia, he was heartened by the favorable reception accorded the published books, but at the same time, he was thwarted and

* *Several accounts say Sept. 2.*

dismayed by the loss of all his colourists. He could not pay them. He could not even pay Lawson properly for his engraving. Wilson worked incessantly to collect the birds, write the text and make and color the drawings, himself.

He was having a race with death.

The rest of his short span was spent in several trips to the New Jersey coast after water birds with his new friend, George Ord, later his biographer, a man fifteen years his junior, highly educated, wealthy, and very prominent in Philadelphia.

The work on the water birds was difficult for Wilson. Most of the ducks breed in central and northern Canada; hence it was impossible to familiarize himself with their complete life histories and the same is true of nearly all the shore birds. However, to balance these lacks, Wilson studied the European accounts and he made many dissections which he incorporated in the eighth volume. It is impressive to see the well-organized information set forth with such care, 'ere he forever laid down his pen and brush.

So near was he to the completion of his task that his collapse in August, 1813 evokes profound sorrow.

A bird he had long wanted to possess, he chanced to see one day while talking with friends. He went after it at once and secured it, but suffered complete exhaustion, from which he did not rally, and he died on August 23rd. His friend Ord was not in Philadelphia at the time, but Mr. Jones, with whom Wilson lived, provided the burial site in the churchyard of the old Swedish Church, Gloria Dei, where Wilson had attended services.

George Ord, by previous understanding with Wilson, completed the eighth volume, for which Wilson was doing the coloring when he died. Ord likewise brought out the ninth volume on water birds in January 1814, although Wilson had completed only a few of the plates. To this Ord added a biography of the author, and as long as he lived he sought to bring Wilson recognition for his copious and authoritative studies of American birds.

Wilson's Accomplishment

Wilson drew from life or from freshly killed specimens 320 portraits of American birds, of which 39 were new to science. They were meticulously skinned, numbered, and presented to Peale's Museum in Philadelphia. A few specimens went also to Trowbridge's Museum in Albany. But both of these repositories, after a struggling existence, closed their doors, the collections were divided and sold, and some were destroyed by fire. A very few of Wilson's specimens still exist at the Academy of Natural Sciences of Philadelphia.

The deterioration of Wilson's scientific collection must go down in the pages of history, but in the hearts of American naturalists and bird lovers, six birds that bear his name will always call: the Wilson plover and the Wilson snipe from the sandy beaches and wet meadows of New Jersey; the Wilson phalarope from coastal marshes; the Wilson petrel from all oceans save the Pacific; and the Wilson warbler and Wilson thrush from the cool woods of our northern states and Canada.

Though Wilson did not live to enjoy the plaudits of fame, which he ardently yearned for, and though he was not able to lift himself out of poverty, he did attain certain honors, which must have solaced him in his final years.

He was elected to the Society of Artists of the United States in March 1812 and was chosen a member of that distinguished group of Philadelphia scientists who in 1812 were founding the Academy of Natural Sciences of Philadelphia, but he did not live to sign the register. The honor which he valued most of all was his election to the American Philosophical Society in April, 1813, four months before his death.

MEADOW

LARK

Alexander Wilson

T HOUGH this well-known species cannot boast of the powers of song which distinguish that "harbinger of day," the Sky Lark of Europe, yet in richness of plumage, as well as in sweetness of voice (as far as his few notes extend), he stands eminently its superior. He differs from the greater part of his tribe in wanting the long straight hind claw, which is probably the reason why he has been classed, by some late naturalists, with the Starlings. But in the particular form of his bill, in his manners, plumage, mode and place of building his nest, nature had clearly pointed out his proper family.

This species has a very extensive range; having myself found them in Upper Canada, and in each of the states from New Hampshire to New Orleans. Mr. Bartram also informs me that they are equally abundant in East Florida. Their favourite places of retreat are pasture fields and meadows, particularly the latter, which have conferred on them their specific name; and no doubt supplies them abundantly with the particular seeds and insects on which they feed. They are rarely or never seen in the depth of the woods; unless where, instead of underwood, the ground is covered with rich grass, as in the Choctaw and Chickasaw countries, where I met with them in considerable numbers in the months of May and June. The extensive and luxuriant prairies between Vincennes and St. Louis also abound with them.

It is probable that in the more rigorous regions of the north they may be birds of passage, as they are partially so here; though I have seen them among the meadows of New Jersey, and those that border the rivers Delaware and Schuylkill, in all seasons; even when the ground was deeply covered with snow. There is scarcely a market day in Philadelphia, from September to March, but they may be found in market. They are generally considered, for size and delicacy, little inferior to the quail, or what is here usually called the partridge, and valued accordingly. I once

From *American Ornithology; or, The Natural History of the Birds of the United States*, in 3 vols. New York and Philadelphia: Collins & Co., 1828.

met with a few of these birds in the month of February, during a deep snow, among the heights of the Alleghany between Shippensburg and Somerset, gleaning on the road, in company with the small snow-birds. In the states of South Carolina and Georgia, at the same season of the year, they swarm among the rice plantations, running about the yards and outhouses, accompanied by the Kildeers, with little appearance of fear, as if quite domesticated.

These birds, after the building season is over, collect in flocks; but seldom fly in a close compact body; their flight is something in the manner of the grous and partridge, laborious and steady; sailing, and renewing the rapid action of the wings alternately. When they alight on trees or bushes, it is generally on the tops of the highest branches, whence they send forth a long, clear, and somewhat melancholy note, that in sweetness and tenderness of expression is not surpassed by any of our numerous warblers. This is sometimes followed by a kind of low, rapid chattering, the particular call of the female; and again the clear and plaintive strain is repeated as before. They afford tolerable good amusement to the sportsman, being most easily shot while on wing; as they frequently squat among the long grass, and spring within gunshot. The nest of this species is built generally in, or below, a thick tuft or tussock of grass; it is composed of dry grass, and fine bent laid at bottom, and wound all around, leaving an arched entrance level with the ground; the inside is lined with fine stalks of the same materials, disposed with great regularity. The eggs are four, sometimes five, white, marked with specks and several large blotches of reddish brown, chiefly at the thick end. Their food consists of caterpillars, grub worms, beetles, and grass seeds; with a considerable proportion of gravel. Their general name is the *Meadow Lark;* among the Virginians they are usually called the *Old Field Lark.*

The length of this bird is ten inches and a half, extent sixteen and a half; throat, breast, belly, and line from the eye to the nostrils, rich yellow; inside lining and edge of the wing the same; an oblong crescent of deep velvety black ornaments the lower part of the throat; lesser wing-coverts black, broadly bordered with pale ash; rest of the wing feathers light brown, handsomely serrated with black; a line of yellowish white passes over each eye backwards; cheeks bluish white, back and rest of the upper parts beautifully variegated with black, bright bay, and pale ochre: tail wedged, the feathers neatly pointed, the four outer ones on each side, nearly all white; sides, thighs, and vent pale yellow ochre, streaked with black; upper mandible brown, lower bluish white; eyelids furnished with strong black hairs; legs and feet very large, and of a pale flesh colour.

The female has the black crescent more skirted with gray, and not of so deep a black. In the rest of her markings the plumage differs little from that of the male. I must here take notice of a mistake committed by Mr. Edwards in his *History of Birds,* Vol. VI, p. 123, where, on the authority of a bird dealer of London, he describes the Calandre Lark (a native of Italy and Russia) as belonging also to N. America, and having been brought from Carolina. I can say with confidence, that in all my excursions through that and the rest of the southern states, I never met such a bird, nor any person who had ever seen it. I have no hesitation in believing that the Calandre is not a native of the United States.

THE HAWK

AND

THE TERN

Henry Beston

Thoreau admired especially the makers of the woodcuts which adorned seventeenth-century books of natural history. "These men," he wrote, "had an adequate idea of a beast, of what a beast should be . . . and they will describe and will draw you a cat with four strokes more beastly and more beast-like to look at than Mr. Ruskin's favorite artist draws a tiger. They had an adequate idea of the wildness of beast and of man."

Henry Beston, whose The Outermost House is one of the recent classics of American nature writing, here pays a tribute to the even earlier artists of ancient Egypt.

O N Monday morning last, as I sat writing at my west windows, I heard a tern give a strange cry, and on looking out and up I saw a bird harrying the female marsh hawk, of whose visits to the dunes I have already told. The sea bird's battle cry was entirely new to my ear. "Ke'ke'-ke'-aow," he cried; there was warning in the harsh, horny cry, danger and anger. The greater bird, flapping her wings as if they were spreads of paper—the winging of this hawk, near earth, is sometimes curiously like the winging of a butterfly—made no answer, but sank to earth slowly, wings outspread, and rested for a long half minute on the shell-strewn floor of the sand pit forty feet back from my house. Thus perched motionless, she might have been a willing mark. Scolding without pause, the tern, who had followed the enemy down into the pit, then rose and dived on her as he might have dived on a fish. The hawk continued to sit motionless. It was an extraordinary scene. Regaining level wing just above the hawk's head, the tern instantly climbed and dived again. At his third dive, the hawk took off, flying ahead and low across the sand pit. The battle then moved into the dunes, and the last I saw of

'From *The Outermost House*. New York: Rinehart and Co., 1928, 1949.

the affair was the hawk abandoning the hills and flying south unpursued far out over the marsh.

Watching the hawk thus a-squat on the sand in a summer intensity of light, with the grey sea bird angrily assailing her, there came into my mind a thought of the ancient Egyptian representations of animals and birds. For this hawk in the pit was the Horus Hawk of the Egyptians, the same poise, the same dark blood-fierceness, the same authority. The longer I live here and the more I see of birds and animals, the greater my admiration becomes for those artists who worked in Egypt so many long thousand years ago, drawing, painting, carving in the stifling quiet of the royal tombs, putting here ducks frightened out of the Nile marshes, here cattle being herded down a village street, here the great sun vulture, the jackal, and the snake. To my mind, no representations of animals equal these Egyptian renderings. I do not write in praise of faithful delineation or pictorial usage—though the Egyptian drew from his model with care—but of the unique power to reach, understand, and portray the very psyche of animals. The power is particularly notable in Egyptian representations of birds. A hawk of stone carved in hardest granite on a temple wall will have the soul of all hawks in his eyes. Moreover, there is nothing human about these Egyptian creatures. They are self-contained and aloof as becomes folk of a first and intenser world.

THE

BIG DAY

Roger Tory Peterson

If there is any man who literally "needs no introduction" to bird watchers it is Roger Tory Peterson, bird painter and bird identifier extraordinary, who invented and introduced a new system which made it easy for the beginner to recognize and name any bird he saw. Peterson's various Field Guides *are probably more widely used both here and, recently, in Europe than any other similar works. He is also a walking encyclopedia of global ornithology and his life is the story of a consuming passion for everything connected with bird life.*

AT three o'clock in the morning a large open touring car parked just off the highway in the hills of northern New Jersey. After switching off the ignition and the headlights, the driver relaxed while the other occupants of the car leaned out and listened. Two state police saw the suspicious-looking automobile. The six silent, roughly dressed men within appeared to be a hardboiled and dangerous lot.

"What do you gents think you are doing?" inquired one of the patrolmen.

"Listening for the whip-poor-wills," replied the driver.

"Wise guys!" retorted the officer.

It took these men a full hour to convince the skeptical police that they really were listening for whip-poor-wills. Furthermore, they were trying to find as many birds as they could within a twenty-four hour day. They were starting with the night birds; that is why they had parked in this lonely place.

Some years ago, when the star of the field-glass ornithologist was rising and it was no longer necessary to check every observation over the sights of a shotgun, some fellow with good legs and sharp eyes found he could list over 100 species of birds in a day. In the north this would be in mid-May, at the time the spring migration was at flood tide.

From *Birds over America*. New York: Dodd, Mead & Company, 1948.

This all-out May-day tournament was something I had never heard of before I came into contact with the birdmen of the big cities along the East coast. New Yorkers and Bostonians call it the "Big Day"; the New Jerseyites the "Lethal Tour"; Philadelphians the "Century Run," and Washingtonians the "Grim Grind." One museum man, with a note of scorn, has dubbed it "ornithogolfing." Lately it has become tradition, planned for weeks in advance. Each hour is mapped out so that the most productive places are visited at the most opportune time. From dark to dark the field-glass forces invade the realm of the birds with military thoroughness. Crossing a field, they deploy their ranks on a wide front so that no bird slips by. Fast travel between strategic areas, with a tankful of gas and good brakes, is part of the tactics.

A dozen pairs of eyes are better than one pair, or two; and although there is dead wood in every Big Day party, the larger the group the better the list. In Massachusetts, half a dozen of us usually went together, led by our commanding general Ludlow Griscom. I remember particularly the day we piled up a grand total that broke all previous records for New England.

The evening before we held a council of war over the telephone. Griscom had studied the weather maps and the tide tables. He had outlined where we would stop and when, but each of us offered amendments. Even though the trip was planned as precisely as a train schedule, we left some room for flexibility. In migration, birds seemed to gather in "pockets." It is a waste of time to linger where not much is stirring.

I got my gear together before I went to bed, so there would be no delay. My trousers were of a sort that could not be ripped easily on barbed wire. I prefer sneakers to boots when the weather is warm for they let the water out as well as in, and they dry quickly. I dug out a hat with a good brim to shade my eyes from the sun. Although I had a pair of 12-power glasses, I decided to use my eights. They had a very wide field and were better for warblers and other small birds than the larger glass. Griscom would have his Zeis telescope, with its three rotating oculars, so if we saw any shore birds on a bar too distant to identify them with our glasses, we could magnify them as much as forty times if need be.

My alarm went off at two that morning. Although I hate alarm clocks and choose to ignore them, suffering as I do from some sort of compulsion complex, at the sound of the bell this morning I jumped from bed like a fighter from his corner. At the diner, three blocks away, I gulped my coffee and scrambled eggs while little gray mice played among the boxes of breakfast food on the shelf. I do not know what birdmen would do without diners! They are as much a part of early-morning bird trips as the robin chorus and the rising sun.

I met Griscom and the others at Harvard Square, in Cambridge. Although it was black as pitch, Griscom said there was no time to lose. We had to reach Boxford, thirty miles down the turnpike, to listen for owls before it got light. We made only one stop. Pulling to the side of the road, we turned off the engine and listened. The sound of the motor still hummed in our ears and at first we could hear nothing. Then Griscom announced. "There it is—number one!" We strained, and faintly above the chorus of the spring peepers came a nasal *beezp!* It was a woodcock, the first bird of the day. A moment later came the chirping whistle of its wings as the "timber-doodle" took off on its aerial song-flight. Higher and higher it climbed against the descending moon; until, reaching the zenith, it spilled forth its ecstatic bubble-pipe-like warblings and twisted headlong back to earth. All was silent again as we climbed back into the car. We did not wait to hear the performance again nor did we search out the singer. A bird heard is as good as a bird seen, and there were other night birds to be recorded before dawn rolled back the darkness.

We turned off the main highway onto a dirt road, went as far as we could, parked, and walked down the narrow path leading to Crooked Pond. Faint lisps and chirps dropped from the blackness above us, a good sign that meant there would be a flight. It is almost impossible to be sure of these tiny night voices beyond identifying them broadly as warblers or sparrows, but the thrush notes are quite distinctive. There was no doubt, either, about the whip-poor-will that lashed out with its nocturnal chant. It went down on our list as number two.

Griscom, leading the party single file through the dew-drenched grass, stopped abruptly as a strange call came from the second-growth woodland to our left. Dove-like yet frog-like, we could not place it. "Long-eared owl," Griscom announced finally. "It had me guessing for a minute." The rest of us had never heard that note before, so we could not dispute the verdict. Yet we had not expected the long-ear. The real reason we were walking down this trail was to try for the pair of barred owls that lived near the pond. Owls won't "talk" every morning, but that day we were favored; a few hoots from Griscom in his best strixine falsetto brought a muffled answer. The second bird gave moral support to the first, and we left Crooked Pond with both owls whooping and caterwauling at the tops of their lungs, in defiance to the strangers who had invaded their wilderness.

By the time we reached the car, the east was streaked with light. The robin chorus was in full voice and, although we had not yet seen a single bird, our list had already passed twenty. Song sparrows, field sparrows and catbirds announced themselves. A pheasant squawked. We had to hurry. Marsh birds are at their best around sunrise, and if we did not reach the Lynnfield Meadows early, we might miss the rails.

Dawn on a marsh is the most vocal time of day—even on a New England marsh, which is, at best, a pale reflection of the teeming duck marshes

[24] Trumpeter Swans

[25] Trumpeter Swans

[26] Great Northern Shrike (t
at twenty degrees below zero)

[27] Turkey Vulture

[28] Catbird

Hermit Thrush

Nuthatch

[31] Chickadees at Feeding Station

[32] Downy Woodpecker

[33] Blue Jay

[34] Evening Grosbeaks

Whiteheaded or Bald Eagle, by Alexander Wilson, 1766–1813
Catesby, Audubon, and Fuertes versions)

[36] LOWER LEFT, Great Horned Owl, by Alexander Wilson (cf. Edward Howe Forbush, "The Great Horned Owl"). Also in picture TOP, Barn Owl, UPPER RIGHT, Small-headed Flycatcher, and, LOWER RIGHT, Hawk Owl

[37] LOWER RIGHT, Water Thrush, or Water-Ouzel by Alexander Wilson (cf. John Muir, "The Water-Ouzel"). Also, CENTER, Belted Kingfisher, UPPER LEFT, Black and Yellow Warbler, UPPER RIGHT, Blackburnian Warbler, and, RIGHT, Autumnal.

1. Mottled Owl. 2. Meadow Lark. 3. Black and white Creeper. 4. Pine creeping Warbler.

[38] BELOW, Meadow Lark, by Alexander Wilson (cf. Wilson, "Meadow Lark"). Also UPPER LEFT, Mottled Owl, UPPER RIGHT, Black and White Creeper, and, MIDDLE RIGHT, Pine-creeping Warbler.

Passenger Pigeon

[40] Red-tailed Hawk. This bird could fly only in circles, as its eyesight had been damaged during a slaughter of migrating hawks.

[41] Snowy Egret

[42] Netting and banding

[43] Leg band on Canada Goose

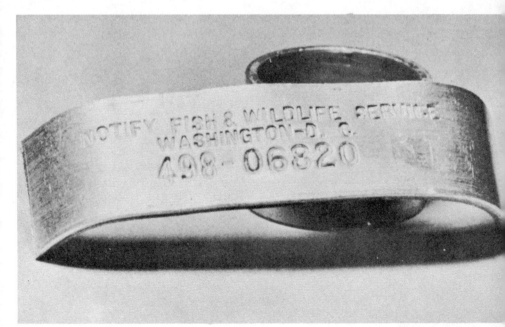

[44] Bird bands

UPPER LEFT, Bald Eagle, by Louis Agassiz Fuertes, 1874–1927 (cf. Catesby, Audubon, Wilson versions). Also, UPPER RIGHT, Golden Eagle, CENTER, immature Bald Eagle; rican Rough-legged Hawk, LOWER LEFT, Dark phase, LOWER RIGHT.

[46] California Condor, by Louis Agassiz Fuertes (cf. Peter Matthiessen, "Our Vanishing Condors")

[47] Northern Shrike, by Louis Agassiz Fuertes (cf. John Burroughs, "The Great Shrike")

[48] Chestnut-backed Chickadee, b
Louis Agassiz Fuertes

49] Roadrunner, by Louis Agassiz
'uertes (cf. George Miksch Sutton,
'Titania and Oberon")

[50] Poorwill, by Louis Agassiz Fuertes (cf. Edmund Jaeger, "Does the
Poor-will 'Hibernate'?")

[51] Catbirds, by Louis Agassiz Fuertes
(cf. Elliot Coues, "The Maligned Catbird")

[52] Eastern Meadowlark, by Louis
Agassiz Fuertes (cf. Alexander Wilson,
"Meadow Lark")

further west. Following the high dry cinder bed of the railroad, the one way in and out of the Lynnfield Meadows, we were soon in the heart of the great swamp. Patches of fog still clung to the sodden earth, or, stirred by the dawn wind, drifted off in milky wisps. Chilled, we could have done with a second cup of coffee, but this would have to wait. Our luck at Lynnfield would have much to do with the success of the day. Perhaps we might pick up a rarity—a king rail, big and rusty, or even the small elusive yellow rail. In this we were disappointed. Lynnfield was particularly poor. We heard the bittern's hollow pumping, and detected both marsh wrens: the long-bill gurgling in the cattails and the short-bill stuttering from the more grassy part of the swamp. We heard the grunting of the Virginia rail but once and missed the whinny of the sora entirely. Usually these little chicken-like birds sound off all over the swamp in the early morning. We laid their silence to the cool breeze that had sprung up, rattling the sabers of the reeds.

We had already picked up a large number of small land birds in the sparse groves at the edge of the swamp, but we placed our biggest hopes for these on Nahant, a narrow-waisted headland that juts out into the ocean. There on the spacious estates would parade the warblers and other migrants, concentrated in this natural bird trap by the barrier of the sea. We found buffy-breasted Lincoln sparrows and smart-looking white-crowns on the lawns, as we had hoped, but we had not expected the flock of ten purple sandpipers that scrambled over a dripping, tide-exposed rock. These hardy junco-colored sandpipers are uncertain enough on these barnacle-encrusted boulders, even in winter. In May, they were a genuine surprise for us. We were doing well, but it looked as though our luck would taper off; it was beginning to rain.

Mount Auburn Cemetery, in Cambridge, was our last stop before starting on the long run to the Cape for shore birds. By the time we entered the wrought-iron gates the drizzle had stopped and the gray clouds were breaking up. This famous old cemetery, where ornithologists have hunted warblers among the tombstones since the days of William Brewster, was full of birds, brought in by the southwesterly wind of the night before. Quickly we rounded out our list of warblers, adding the Tennessee, Blackburnian, Canada, Wilson's and bay-breast. Our warbler list alone was twenty-two, not bad for New England, although twenty-five or even more, is a possibility.

Our total list had reached eighty by 8:00 A.M.; a hundred by 10:00 A.M. But this furious pace slowed down to a walk by noon. New birds were harder to find; our limbs had become weary from the ten-hour grind; eyelids were heavy and heads nodded in the back seat, while the driver doggedly held to the endless ribbon of concrete unwinding toward the Cape. We went by way of Carver to take in a colony of purple martins, one of the few breeding colonies of this big glossy swallow in eastern Massachusetts. A detour at Wareham gave us the hermit thrush, singing beside a cranberry bog in the barrens, and three bald eagles, lured by the myriads of shad that swarmed into the inland ponds to spawn and die.

Nothing is duller for birds than most pine-barren country, so we spent little time on it. The outer Cape was a long haul, and it was late in the day before we reached Chatham, with its white houses and wind-swept silver poplars. There we changed into a hired beach wagon with low-pressure balloon tires for gripping the loose beach sand.

There were not more than two hours of daylight left when we started down Monomoy, the long peninsula of sand dunes and mud flats that stretches southward for ten miles or so into the Atlantic from the crooked elbow of Cape Cod. Here we hoped to wind up the day in a burst of glory. Nor were we disappointed. Shore birds swarmed the flats like sand fleas on a beach. There were a thousand ruddy turnstones all in high rufous breeding plumage with orange legs and harlequin-like head markings. We estimated 300 black-bellied plovers, 3000 sanderlings and countless numbers of the smaller "sand peeps." Our shore-bird list rose to fifteen species.

In the surf bobbed belated groups of those rugged sea ducks, the scooters. All three species were in sight and among them six American eiders, males with white backs, stragglers from the great flocks that make Monomoy their winter headquarters.

Like a magician, plucking rabbits from a hat, Griscom pulled out the two "fanciest" birds of the day. Ordering the driver to stop, he put his glasses on a lone bird swimming beyond the surf. Quickly appraising, he called out "Brunnich's murre." The telescope was brought to bear on the piebald swimmer and without a hint of chagrin, Griscom retracted the first guess. "Sorry!" he apologized, "just an old-squaw." Even Griscom makes mistakes, but he is usually the first to correct them.

We had hardly gone several hundred yards further down the beach when another lone swimmer caught our attention. Griscom squinted, hesitated and blurted "Brunnich's murre." We respectfully reserved judgment while he tensely hauled out the telescope again. In a moment he relaxed. "Don't you believe me?" he queried. "Look for yourselves!" We did. There was no doubt about it; the bird was a murre, that black-and-white sea bird that reminds one so much of a penguin. It was in changing plumage and the proportion of the bill and the light-colored mark along the gape showed it to be a Brunnich's! This curious coincidence did much to increase our ever-growing awe of Griscom. No one but he would have dared cry "Brunnich's murre" again so soon after making a blunder.

The pay-off came a short distance further down the beach when a third lone sea bird was spotted, bobbing up and down in the wave troughs. With hardly a moment's deliberation Griscom electrified us with

"Atlantic murre!" That was too much! To get both murres in one day was an extremely rare event in Massachusetts even in the dead of winter. It was next to impossible in May. Surely Griscom was getting tired— probably he had too much sun. But the telescope backed him up. The bird *was* an Atlantic murre in winter plumage. The thin pointed bill and the dark line behind the eye left no doubt about it.

At the tip of Monomoy we found the usual great congregation of gulls and terns resting on the high crown of the shell-studded beach. Facing in one direction, into the wind and the setting sun, rested five kinds of gulls and four of terns. Besides the tiny least terns with yellow bills and the familiar common tern with black-tipped vermilion bills, there were a number of roseates with blackish bills, and a few arctics, grayer than the others, with bills blood-red to the tip. This is one of the southernmost spots in America where the arctic tern can be depended upon. Indeed, I know of no better place anywhere to study the several most confusing terns side by side. An hour with these birds at the tip of Monomoy is worth months of experience with them elsewhere.

With the sun setting in a coppery haze on the horizon, we sped up the beach, satisfied with Monomoy and with ourselves. We were blissfully pleased but tired—faces windblown, eyes bloodshot and hair filled with sand. Griscom, always a martinet, said we would not stop for food until we had done one thing more—not until we had tried for the great horned owl back in the barrens.

We got not only the great horned, which was obliging enough to hoot once or twice in stentorian tones, but also a screech owl that timidly answered my bad imitations of its lonely wail. Four kinds of owls in one day was not bad. We had done about all we could, and we were hungry!

Dinner never tasted so good. When the apple pie had been followed by coffee and we had taken out our check-list cards, we counted the day's total. It came to 148! This was a new high for Massachusetts and for all New England.

Riding home, we put our trust in our driver while we dozed and fitfully dreamed of murres with blood-red bills, like those of Arctic terns. At midnight we reached Boston. We had been on the go for twenty-two hours, but we had hung up a record.

For a decade, no one bettered that score in Massachusetts. But on May 20, 1945, after three cold rainy weeks in which the May migrants had become dammed up, a platoon of bird-watchers found 160 species—all in Essex County! Three years later, on May 23, 1948, with identical freak weather conditions in our favor, we nosed out this short-lived record by one species. Late at night the cooperative barred owls of Crooked Pond responded to Griscom's whoops just as they had done on nearly every Big Day for the past fifteen years, and thus became No. 161 on our list.

Among the most famous of all Big Day trips were those which the

late Charles Urner organized in New Jersey. Starting in the swampy
Troy Meadows before daybreak, running up to the mountain ridges near
Boonton for migrating warblers and down through the pine barrens to
the southern New Jersey coast for shore birds, Urner's itinerary resembled that of the excursion I have described in Massachusetts. Urner's lists,
however, were larger, seldom fewer than 150, once as high as 173. There
were more participants, also, sometimes fifteen or twenty; as a result,
hardly anyone came within ten of seeing every bird in the day's total.
Some of the less experienced men complained it was a dog-eat-dog affair,
that once a bird was ticked off no one would wait for the slower fellows
to find it.

In the Lower Rio Grande Valley, I think it would be possible to upset
Urner's record, if a man had some knowledge of the country. Lists of
200 in one day should be possible in this strategic bird paradise where
east meets west and Mexican bird life laps across our border.

A variation of the Big Day is the "Roundup." In this there are no
restrictions on distance or number of parties, providing they start from
the same point. A number of lists are combined at the end of the day. At
St. Louis, Missouri, a "Roundup" recorded 187 species in one day, while
the Delaware Valley Ornithological Club checked off 214 between the
mountains and the New Jersey shore.

These ornithological sprees do not allow one fully to enjoy the birds or
to spend much time watching them. But there are values beyond the
excitement of the chase. If exact numbers of each species are kept, a year-
to-year comparison gives a hint of increases or declines. Redstart-*common*
does not mean much, but redstart-58 does. The conscientious field-man
keeps a diary of the outstanding behavior of the birds, his impressions of
the sweep and movement of migration and the weather.

No one would want to engage in one of these endurance tests every
week end, but once or twice a year it is great sport, a test of the skills
acquired by months and years of bird watching. We are waiting for the
inevitable day when someone will try by airplane or helicopter.

GOOD BAG

IN

CENTRAL PARK

Geoffrey Hellman

When nature gets into that most urban of magazines, The New Yorker, *it is usually to remind its readers that the entire earth is not yet covered by what some of them call "God's concrete."*

SEVEN o'clock sharp the other Tuesday morning found us at Seventy-seventh Street and Central Park West, all set for a Central Park bird walk—the last of a series of five during the fall migration that were sponsored by the Museum of Natural History and conducted by Miss Farida A. Wiley. A dozen ladies and half as many gentlemen, all equipped with field glasses, had already assembled. One of the ladies opened a paper bag and drew out a tiny dead bird. "Golden-crowned kinglet," she said, parting the feathers on its head to show a bright-orange patch. "A friend of mine got it from a cat near Trinity Church yesterday."

A minute later, hard on Miss Wiley's "My watch says it's getting about time to meander," we plunged into the Park. A bird flew over us almost immediately. "Myrtle warbler," said our leader.

"Whoopsie! Here we go!" someone said to us as eight birds, traveling fast, moved overhead. "Warblers—they're going so fast, you can't tell what kind. You'll find all the insect-eating birds, like the warblers, move very fast and very erratically."

As we headed east toward the lake, several robins and herring gulls were described. "The black bands across the tail tell you what age herring gulls are," Miss Wiley said. She pointed to some black ducks and a male and female mallard on the lake. "They're going through some courting antics," she said. "That's a funny one *this* time of year!"

From *The New Yorker*. October 31, 1953.

A bronzed grackle in an ailanthus tree came next, then a blue jay, then a hermit thrush. "You can tell by his tail he's very nervous," a lady in trousers said. "It wiggles."

"Here's a whole flock of robins," said Miss Wiley. "Oh, grackles—I beg your pardon. The robin was making a noise and the grackles were going over."

A male walker picked something up and showed it to Miss W. "Predaceous ground beetle," she said.

Suddenly, all the walkers focussed their glasses on a bush.

"Olive-backed thrush, isn't it?" said one lady.

"No, a hermit," said another. "If the tail is more russet than the back, it's a hermit."

Other hermit thrushes were sighted overhead. "Well, the hermits are really going through this morning," said Miss Wiley. She circled a bush. "That's a—you can't tell till he turns around—it's a gray-cheeked thrush."

The next few minutes yielded a flycatcher, a chewink, a phoebe, and more hermits. "It's hermit day, I guess," Miss W. said. "The hermits are *really* going through." She beckoned her followers to a clump of bushes. "The sharp chirp that you hear is a myrtle warbler," she said. "Most of the birds you see now have been nesting in the Far North and are just passing through. About the only birds that nest in the Park are robins, sparrows, grackles, mallards, and a few sparrow hawks."

A latecomer, male, caught up with us and pulled a largish dead bird out of a paper bag.

"Virginia rail," the ladies chorused.

"Fire Island," said its owner. "Probably flew into a high-tension wire."

"Cedar waxwings!" a cry went up. "See the rosy breasts."

We spotted a colleague training her glasses on a patch of foliage near a brook. "Now, why don't you turn around and show your rump?" she said. "Be accommodating. Oh, it *is* winter wren! My crush! I'm just crazy about winter wrens! His tail stands straight up and it's very, *very* short."

Several white-throated sparrows, flickers, brown creepers, thrushes, and sparrow hawks later, as we gained a point on the lake near the lower end of the Mall, a ruby-crowned kinglet hove into sight. "When he shoots his scarlet crest, it's awfully pretty," the winter-wren lady said. "It's like a little fan. He shows it when fighting. Oh, look! A goldfinch! Note the undulating flight."

Six large, majestic birds were parading along the sidewalk, and these, it appeared, were Canadian geese, on their way from Hudson Bay to the Carolinas. A lady rushed up to Miss Wiley in great excitement. "There's a wood duck out on the lake with the blacks," she said. All glasses were trained on this prize.

"A male wood duck," said the winter-wren lady. "Oh, golly-wampus!"

Miss Wiley lent us her glasses, and we made out a hell of a brilliant-colored duck. "Unusual to see one here," she said. "Unlike most ducks, which nest on the ground, it builds in natural cavities in trees, sometimes sixty feet up. We've really had a wave this morning. You never know what you're going to get in Central Park."

"I listened to the radio last night and it said northwest wind and cold, and I thought, Oh, that's the morning for me," said the lady who had brought along the Trinity Church kinglet. "It certainly has been."

NATURAL

HISTORY

IN

TIMES SQUARE

Edwin Way Teale

It is a sad fact that the animals who compete most successfully with man in his cities are those he likes least—rats, cockroaches, fleas, and bedbugs, along with the too often maligned pigeons and sparrows. Various more attractive creatures do, nevertheless, either wander into or, sometimes, manage to survive even in New York City. William Beebe wrote a whole book on the subject, Unseen Life in New York. *It had interested also Edwin Way Teale who wrote the following striking account of the birds he has seen, not only in parks and backyards, but in Times Square itself.*

I N the course of a single day, a quarter of a million people may pass through Times Square, in New York City. They pour out of the side-streets. They eddy around the bases of the skyscrapers. They funnel downward into subways. Like a great heart, Times Square endlessly draws in this stream of human corpuscles and sends it flowing away again, year in and year out, all day long and far into the night.

Here, amid the throngs, the buses, the dodging taxicabs, the changing streetcars; here, among the gaudy billboards and the glaring colors of the nighttime spectaculars; here, in this public and populous spot—fenced in by glass and brick, stone and asphalt, cement and steel—is a world so divorced from that of the open fields and woods that it seems impossible that the two should ever meet. A naturalist in Times Square seems almost as much out of place as a botanist in the stratosphere.

Yet, during the dozen years my life was spent in a New York office, when I was one of those whom Herman Melville describes in *Moby Dick* as "pent up in lath and plaster, tied to counters, nailed to benches, clinched

From *The Lost Woods*. New York: Dodd, Mead & Company, 1945.

to desks," I discovered—during odd and rare moments—surprising events in natural history taking place in the heart of the great city. . . .

In his *The Book of British Waders*, Brian Vesey-Fitzgerald speaks of the wildness of the curlew's call. "That cry," he writes, "the high, forlorn double note from which the bird receives his name, is the spirit of the wildest wildness, whether you hear it above a populous city, or on heath, or down, or lonely shore or deserted estuary." For me, a wild bird's call takes on added, immeasurably added, wildness when heard amid the concentrated civilization of a great city.

Twice, in Times Square, I caught such a sound amid the traffic. One of these occasions was on a raw, gray mid-afternoon in March. Pedestrians were hurrying along the street with coat collars turned up and the day-long twilight of the overcast sky had brought on office lights by three o'clock. Above the sound of taxi wheels rushing through the slush on the pavement, there came high overhead a faint, raucous call. It brought back a vivid remembrance of that winter day in the Lost Woods. The call was the cawing of a crow.

Another time, in the brilliant sunshine of Indian Summer, I heard above the clatter and screech of Broadway traffic a sound that came like a breath from a lonely pine woods. It was the high, wild, rolling cry of a flicker. Rising and falling in its flight, the golden-winged woodpecker was passing over the skyscrapers, and the Grand-Canyon gulches between them, on its way to Bryant Park.

Only a few steps from the spot where I heard the flicker that day, a motorist had an adventure that gave him a surprise that he never forgot. It also demonstrated that, even in Times Square, Nature can be counted on for the unexpected. The driver had pulled up for a red traffic light and was just getting under way again when a brilliant-feathered cock pheasant fluttered down and struck the fender of his car. The bird was unhurt. A wild pheasant hunt ensued in the midst of this populous Crossroads of the World. The motorist finally retrieved the bird and turned it over to the American Society for the Prevention of Cruelty to Animals. How the cock pheasant reached Times Square remains a mystery to this day.

Other odd bird visitors to the great city include a horned owl that perched in a tree near City Hall; a glossy ibis, seen for weeks near Van Cortlandt Park; a red phalarope, one of the so-called "swimming snipe"; and a thrush that lived all winter in a florist's shop on Madison Avenue and flew away again when spring came. One autumn, a duck hawk stayed for weeks on the Paramount Building, high above Times Square, and preyed on the pigeons of the neighborhood. And across the East River in Brooklyn, a visiting hawk created a first-class mystery by snatching freshly killed chickens from a line in the rear of a restaurant.

During the migration season, birds of many kinds stop off in parks, back-yard-gardens, and even on the window-ledges of skyscrapers. At the hanging gardens, high up on Radio City, an American bittern—a bird we associate with lonely marshlands or wild, boggy dells—settled down to rest one autumn as it was winging its way south over the miles of city buildings. For a quarter of an hour, this shy swampland wader perched there, high above the traffic, and then took off again. In one back-yard garden, in the heart of New York and not many blocks from Times Square, migration time brought such interesting visitors as a wood peewee, a scarlet tanager, a white-throated sparrow, a Baltimore oriole, a woodcock and a hermit thrush. A cardinal, one winter, attracted the attention of tens of thousands of people by feeding among the pigeons and sparrows in Bryant Park, one block east of Times Square.

Pigeons and sparrows are always present in Times Square. Probably the English sparrow population has decreased since the change from stables to garages. But the number of pigeons appears to remain about the same year after year. Every so often, one of these birds gets its picture in the papers. One had its leg set at Bellevue Hospital and was listed as a patient; another hatched a brood of young on a window-ledge of a hospital maternity ward; a third, in the heart of a motorized city, produced a nest made largely of paper clips and rubber bands.

To one who grew up surrounded by wild birds, by flickers and orioles, brown thrashers and bluebirds, the tame and discolored pigeons of Times Square always seem a sorry lot. The only thrill they provide for me is when they shoot from building to building on a windy day, navigating with half-closed wings the aerial rapids and whirlpools of the city canyons. . . .

SNOBBER—

SPARROW DE LUXE

Edwin Way Teale

Some students of animal behavior scorn pet owners and their observations, which they dismiss as usually anthropomorphic and overinterpreted. In actual fact, however, close association with human beings often brings out unexpected potentialities in the animal very much as they appear in a "savage" who has received a civilizing education. One recent English book, Len Howard's Birds As Individuals *so astonished professional bird students with its accounts of the varying "personalities" of tame birds of the same species that Sir Julian Huxley undertook a personal investigation of Miss Howard's pets and testified that her surprising observations deserved full credit. No story of a civilized and humanized bird is more remarkable than that of an English sparrow who regularly entered an apartment house window 160 feet above the sidewalk to spend the evening studying with his young friend.*

I N Vineland, N.J., last summer, pedestrians were astonished when an English sparrow darted down from the branches of trees, alighted on their shoulders, and peered intently into their faces. Housewives were equally amazed when the same bird flew in at their open windows. It fluttered about, examined their rooms, and flew out again. The mystery grew for several days. Then the following advertisement appeared in the *Vineland Times-Journal:*

"Lost. Tame female English sparrow. Reward. Call 1291J."

That advertisement brought about the return of a remarkable pet. It also revealed a boy-and-bird companionship which is as interesting as it is unusual. The boy is Bennett Rothenberg; the sparrow, Snobber. They were visiting the boy's uncle near Vineland when the bird became lost.

The boy and the sparrow live on the eleventh floor of a great apartment building across from the Planetarium, on Eighty-first Street in New York City. The bird is never caged. It is free to come and go. At will, it flies in and out of the apartment-house window more than 130 feet above

From *Audubon Magazine*, November–December, 1944.

the street and the Planetarium park. Each night, it sleeps on top of a closet-door left ajar near Bennett's bed.

On rainy days, the sparrow makes no effort to mount upward along the sheer cliff of brick and glass to Bennett's apartment-window. Instead, she rides up on the elevator! Flying in the front entrance of the apartment-house, Snobber alights on the shoulder of the elevator operator, Frank Olmedo. When they reach the eleventh floor, Olmedo rings the bell at the apartment and when the door opens, the sparrow flies, like a homing pigeon, to the boy's bedroom. A year ago, during a month when Bennett was away at a summer camp, Olmedo cared for the the bird and the two became fast friends.

It was in the spring of 1943 that Bennett, then fourteen years old, found a baby sparrow in Central Park. He carried it home and installed it in an empty robin's nest in his room. With the aid of a medicine dropper and a pair of tweezers, he fed it at hourly intervals. On a diet of flies, bits of worms, water and pieces of eggbiscuit, it grew rapidly. It gained weight and the whitish fuzz on its body developed into scores of strong and glossy feathers. A snobbish tilt of its beak when it had had enough food gave it its name.

The boy taught Snobber to fly by placing it in low trees, offering food, and chirping to it. The sparrow now recognizes his chirp and will fly up to the apartment window from the trees below when he calls. To the uninitiated, all sparrows seem to chirp alike. But not to Bennett. He says he can recognize Snobber's chirp in a tree full of sparrows. By the sound, he can tell whether she is angry, curious, or excited. When they go for walks together, they often seem to be carrying on a conversation, chirping back and forth, as the sparrow darts ahead from tree to tree. On reaching Eighty-first Street, Snobber flies on ahead and then waits—like a dog—at the entrance of the apartment-house for Bennett to cross the street.

A friendly bird, she often is much in evidence when the boys of the neighborhood are engaged in playing games. In the middle of a baseball game, she sometimes alights on the shoulder of the batter or settles down directly on the baseline to attract attention. At other times, when the boys are flipping playing cards in local version of "pitching pennies," Snobber will dart down, grasp one of the cards in her bill, and fly away with it. Any small, shiny object instantly arouses her interest. When she finds a dime on Bennett's dresser, she picks it up and darts this way and that, flying until she is tired. Two marbles in a small metal tray on the boy's desk keep her occupied for a quarter of an hour at a time. She pushes them about with her bill, apparently delighted by the jangling sound they make.

Her interest in bright-colored objects prevented Bennett, last fall, from keeping track of the position of Allied armies by means of colored pins on a large wall-map. No sooner did he put up the pins, placing them carefully to show the location of the lines, than they would disappear. He would find them lying on his bed, the dresser, his desk. Snobber, fluttering like a flycatcher in front of the map, would pull out the pins with her bill. Red-headed pins seemed her first choice with yellow-headed pins coming second. She became so interested in this game that she would perch on Bennett's shoulder, or even his hand, while he inserted the pins. Then she would pull them out as soon as he had finished his work. When he substituted tiny flags in place of pins, her interest rose to an even higher pitch. In the end, Bennett had to give up his efforts and the game ended for Snobber.

One August, in Central Park, one of the eminent ornithologists of The American Museum of Natural History—a scientist who had journeyed as far away as Equitorial Africa to observe bird-life—was surprised to see something entirely new to his experience. A sparrow darted down, perched on a boy's shoulder, and began to eat ice cream from a cone. The sparrow, of course, was Snobber and the boy was Bennett.

Ice cream, pieces of apple, and small bits of candy are delicacies of which the bird is passionately fond. Boys in the neighborhood share their candy and cones with her when she alights on their shoulders. As soon as she sees a piece of candy, she begins to chirp and flutter about. Bennett and a companion sometimes play a game with her for five minutes at a time by tossing a piece of cellophane-covered candy back and forth. Like a kitten pursuing a ball, Snobber will shuttle swiftly from boy to boy in pursuit of the flying candy.

Along Eighty-first Street, pedestrians are often as surprised as were the people of Vineland to have a sparrow swoop down and alight on their shoulders. The reaction is varied. One woman jerked off a fur neck-piece and swung it around in the air like a lasso to ward off the supposed attack. Several persons have made a grab for the sparrow. But, always, Snobber is too quick for them.

One day, last summer, an elderly gentleman, stout, near-sighted and wearing a derby hat, was walking down the Planetarium side of Eighty-first Street reading a newspaper held close to his face. In his left hand he clutched an ice cream cone from which he absent-mindedly took a bite from time to time. Snobber was perched on the lower limb of a tree. She cocked her head as he went by; she had spotted the ice cream. Swooping down, she alighted on the cone and began nibbling away. Just then, the man put the cone to his mouth abstractedly to take another bite. The cone bit him, instead! Or, at least, that was the impression he got when Snobber pecked him on the lower lip. Unable to believe his eyes, he peered near-sightedly at the cone and bird. Then he began to wave the cone in circles in the air. Like a pinwheel, the cone and the pursuing sparrow whirled above his head.

Seeing the commotion, Bennett ran across the street to explain and to catch Snobber. But in the process he accidentally knocked the cone from the man's hand. Thinking he was being set upon from the air and the ground simultaneously, the nearsighted gentleman clutched his newspaper in one hand and his derby hat in the other and sprinted, puffing, down the street. At the end of the block, he stopped, turned, shook his fist, and hurried around the corner.

Indoors, when Snobber gets hungry she perches on a seed-box as a signal to the boy. Two of her favorite foods, aside from seeds and bits of biscuit, are cornflakes and maple sugar. She gets greens by eating pieces of leaves from time to time. If the sash is down when she wants to fly out the window, she will dash about the room in a special manner which Bennett has learned to understand.

As might be supposed, the sparrow had difficulty at first in picking out the right window among the vast number which pierce the masonry of the great apartment-house. Once, after Bennett had chirped with his head out the window he was called back into the room and when he looked out again he was just in time to see the sparrow come flying out of a window on the floor below. As a guide, he has tied a ribbon ot the iron bar of a window-box outside his bedroom. Before dusk, Snobber always returns to the apartment. The only time she has spent the night outdoors was during the days when she was lost near Vineland.

From the beginning, Bennett determined that if she ever wanted to go free, he would not try to restrain her. The train-trip to Vineland, last summer, was one of the few times when she has been locked in a cage. The ride was bumpy and she disliked it, chirping most of the time. Bennett spent his time during the journey explaining to interested passengers about the sparrow in the cage. At his uncle's farm, Snobber was ill at ease. She had never seen a rocking chair before and the unstable perch it provided when the boy was sitting in it, disturbed her still further.

On the second day there, she dashed from an apple tree in pursuit of two wild sparrows, flew too far, became confused, then hopelessly lost. Four days later, when Bennett recovered her through his advertisement, she was several miles from his uncle's farm in the direction of New York City. She recognized the boy in an instant and flew chirping to his shoulder. A small American flag in the window of the house where she was found resembled the ribbon tied to the window-box of the apartment-house and may have influenced her in choosing that particular place. When chasing among the trees, with wild sparrows of the Planetarium park, she seems to prefer Bennett's companionship to that of any bird. She is always slightly suspicious of other sparrows. When dusting herself with others of her kind, she always stays on the edge of the group. If one of the birds becomes too familiar, she will charge it with lowered head and open beak. Bennett once brought home a young sparrow to keep her company. She refused to have anything to do with it. He then placed a canary in the bedroom as a playmate for Snobber. When he returned to the room to see how they were getting along, he found her holding the hapless bird by the bill and swinging it around in the air. The next day, she lured the canary out on the window-ledge and then chased it away down the street. After that, the boy ceased trying to find a bird companion for her and Snobber is well content to let matters rest as they are.

This spring, although she had not mated, Snobber was overcome by the impulse to build a nest. Tearing up a robin's nest and a song sparrow's nest, which Bennett had in his room, she used the material to create a nest of her own. She was busy with this task for days, sometimes flying about the room with straws fully a foot in length. In the nest, she laid two eggs. Neither hatched and one now rests on cotton batting in a small box which bears this notation on the lid: "English Sparrow Egg Laid By Snobber."

When Bennett is doing his homework, during winter months, Snobber often perches quietly on his book or on the desk beside him. And, at night, when the boy is sleeping in his bed, the sparrow is lost in slumber on the top of the closet door, its head tucked in its feathers. Often, it sleeps on one leg. At such times, it has the appearance of a ball of ruffled feathers, with one leg sticking down and a tail sticking out at right angles to the leg.

As soon as it is daylight, Snobber is awake. Bennett doesn't need any alarm clock. He has Snobber. She hops down, perches on his head, begins tugging at individual hairs. If he doesn't wake up, she often snuggles down near his neck for an additional nap herself. If he disturbs her by moving in his sleep, she gives him a peck on the chest. As a consequence, Bennett often keeps moving back toward the far side until when he wakes up he is lying on the edge and the sparrow is occupying most of the bed.

On the floor of Bennett's bedroom, there is a shiny spot six or seven inches in diameter. This is where the sparrow takes her imaginary dust-baths. Alighting at this spot, she squats down, fluffs up her feathers, turns this way and that, goes through the motions of taking a real dust-bath by the roadside.

Like Mary's famous little lamb, Snobber sometimes tries to follow Bennett to school. He rides to and from classes on the subway. Winter mornings, he always tries to leave the apartment-house without the sparrow seeing him. But the bright eyes of the little bird miss little that is going on. Several times, just as he was sprinting into the entrance of the subway a block from his home, he has heard a lively chirping behind him and Snobber has fluttered down on his shoulder. Twice he has had to explain to teachers that he was late for classes because a sparrow delayed him! At the school he attends, however, both teachers and pupils know all about Snobber. In fact, whenever Bennett gets an extra good grade, his classmates have a standing explanation: Snobber has helped him!

AN ADVENTURE

WITH A

TURKEY VULTURE

George Miksch Sutton

George Miksch Sutton is one of the most distinguished of contemporary ornithologists, teachers of ornithology, and painters of
birds. Among many other things he has been Curator of Birds at
the great Cornell department of ornithology and he is an outstanding
field observer as well. Roger Tory Peterson has written of him in
Birds over America: "I think the test of a good field observer is how
quick and accurate he is away from home. I am sure you could put
George Sutton, the bird artist, anywhere on the continent and he
would know immediately what to look for in that particular area."

I N Texas we lived in a big white house that stood on a hill southwest
of the city of Forth Worth. About us stretched the rolling prairies,
gay in Summer with red and yellow daisies and the tall spikes of blooming
yucca, and studded with clumps of prickly pear cactus and feathery mes-
quite trees.

Not far to the south of us the Trinity River slipped through a dense,
low woodland. Here I spent much of my time, eager to watch, and
capture if possible, the strange and interesting creatures which lived
thereabouts. Flying squirrels built their globular nests of twigs high in
the slender pecan trees. Chuck-will's-widows fluttered up from the leaves
like gigantic moths. Raccoons and opossums searched for food along the
banks of the slow-flowing streams, leaving their neat lacy track-patterns
in the mud.

In the pale far sky drifted wide-winged, sable-coated Turkey Vultures,
their pinions motionless for hours at a time as they ascended in slow
spirals, breasted the wind, or swung low to the level of the tree tops. I
never ceased to marvel at their clean-cut outline, and the ease with which
they handled themselves in flight. I was all unconscious, in those days, of

From *Birds in the Wilderness*. New York: The Macmillan Company, 1936.

the probability that centuries, ages perhaps, had slipped by while the Turkey Vulture was learning to conquer the air. It did not occur to me then that thousands upon thousands of the gaunt creatures had perished in the eternal struggle for survival, that those dreamily swinging spots of ebony might enchant me for an hour! Drowsily, majestically, unceasingly they drifted about, many just above the low-hung fluffy cloud masses, some gently moving amid the ribbed cirrus of the dizzy sky plains. Lying on the warm earth, I watched them. I could hardly think; I only dreamed myself a sky bird, a playmate of the clouds. I was vaguely, sadly conscious, perhaps, that while my race had for ages been developing my brain into an organ of doubtful utility, it had at the same time been reducing the length of my forelimbs, solidifying my bones—in short, condemning me to four-score years and ten as a terrestrial being without the slightest glimmer of hope that I should one day spread my black wings and, rustling like heavy silk, mount to the blue. Never, never could I be a vulture!

I was roused from my reverie by the swish of dusky, stiff quills above me, as one of the vultures, made curious by my motionless, supine form, swung low. What a different creature! The naked head and pale bill were evil in appearance. There entered my mind the thought that, had I been a corpse, that white beak would have sought with its hooked tip the innermost chambers of my heart! The plumage of the drab fowl was rusty and ragged; its wing tips spread out like slender, heavily nailed fingers! The vulture, close at hand, was a revolting creature. I shuddered because the vile body and macabre pinions had cast their shadow across my face.

Walking one day in the depths of the woodland, near a stagnant pool, I came upon a huge, partly decayed, hollowed log. Instinctively curious, I peered cautiously into the darkness, half expecting to discern the taut form of a wildcat crouched for a spring, or the lazy, pulpy coil of a water moccasin, white-mouthed and venomous. I could see nothing, though I strained my eyes. I went to the other end of the log, lay upon my side, and peered through. From this position I could see light at the other end. The dim interior became more sharply defined. What was that strange shape? Was there a movement, just the slightest movement? Did I hear a noise? My back stiffened.

Then it dawned upon me that I was gazing at the silhouette of a Turkey Vulture—a mother bird, probably, sitting upon her eggs. Eager, fairly breathless, I dragged two large stones to one end of the log, closing the opening there, and instantly sprang to the other end of the log, half expecting to be greeted by a rush of wings. Assured that the bird was still within, I sat down. For a moment I pondered. The log was almost twenty feet long; I could not make the bird come to me by punching it with a stick, and there was danger of breaking the eggs. I could not smoke it out, because I had no matches and I doubted my ability to start a fire by twirling a pointed stick against a piece of wood. My course was plain. I would have to go through the log.

I entertained certain misgivings. Could I force my way through the dark, moist tunnel? What would I encounter there? Would the mother vulture try to pick out my eyes?

Nevertheless I started, to find at once that the aperture was not so large as it had appeared to be. Arms outstretched in front, hair and face scraping the musty wood, I inched forward, my toes digging doggedly into the earth. Within a short time the entire length of my body was inside the log. My face pressed against the wet wood; my body ached with the strain of the unnatural position, but I could not bring my arms back because there was no room for such movement.

Perhaps, after all, I should not attempt this strange tunneling! In a panic I tried to back out, only to find myself powerless. It appeared that in my toes, which could push me forward, was my only propellent power. I was doomed to stay, or to go ahead! I breathed hard, spent with exertion. There did not seem to be enough air in the place. My ribs were crowded. But I must go ahead! Digging my fingers in the soft wood, shoving forward with all the force of my feet, I made slow progress. A flake of wood somehow got into my eye. I could do little more than shed tears over this unfortunate happening, for my arms were so long that I could not reach my face with my fingers. And my handkerchief was in my trousers pocket!

I realized now, without question, that I should have not come into this log, that freedom of movement and plenty of fresh air were really all I had ever desired in the world. But I could not go back. Perhaps I remembered, in that dark moment, certain lines of Joaquin Miller's poem on Columbus. At any rate I squirmed on. I heard dull sounds as the buttons of my shirt gave way. My trousers stayed on only because of the strength of the leather belt, the straps of cloth which held it, and the endurance of my pelvic bones. The slipping downward of my shirt did not improve matters any. Wads of cloth seemed to be knotted all about my body.

I found myself wondering how much more an imprisoned, half-suffocated, tortured boy, miles from home, could endure, when suddenly I realized that the mother vulture and I were not the only inhabitants of this hollow log.

Tripping ever so daintily, his fine leg-threads just brushing the surface upon which he trod, came a grand-daddy longlegs, disturbed in his noonday sleep. A grand-daddy longlegs, considered impersonally, is an interesting creature. His legs are amazingly long and thin; his airy body is a strangely plump hub for those eight filamentous spokes which mince along so questioningly. I do not mind having a grand-daddy longlegs walk across my hand, in fact.

But to have a grand-daddy longlegs, and perhaps four hundred of his companions, suddenly decide to wander all over my face, neck, and back is another story. The first tickle of the advance guard's feet upon my nose drove me nearly frantic. I plunged my face into the wood, crushing my adversary. The odor of his body was unpleasant. Already his companions were bearing down upon me. I writhed and shuddered in exquisite torture. By waiting a moment, then wiping my face deliberately across the damp wood, I could kill or disable whole squadrons at a time. The situation was not improved by the fact that I could see only imperfectly in the dim light and because of the bit of wood in my eye.

Gradually the queer spiders learned that they were safer when they moved toward the light. I could see their dancing, trembling forms slowly withdraw from me. Nervous, full of reproach for my foolhardiness, I tried to relax, to think of something besides the vise in which I was fixed.

Was this soft thing my hand felt a fluff of milkweed down? Was it a bit of silk, so oddly out of place in this nether world? It was the nest of a pair of white-footed mice—dainty, bright-eyed little creatures whose noses quivered with terror, whose bodies shook with dread, as they felt rude fingers upon their nest. Frantically they rushed forth. Instinctively they leaped for the darkest crevice they could find. Owing to the effective stoppage of my end of the log, those havens of refuge were naturally near me. Trim, sharp-clawed feet raced over my back, under my shirt, about my neck. Can mice run nimbly? Can they use their toes in holding on? Do they learn of the unknown in the darkness through touching objects with their silken whiskers? The answers to these questions, and to many more, I learned within our hollow log. I was half afraid the jewel-eyed gnomes would bite my face or that one of them would pounce into my mouth as I strove to get a deep breath of air. Could all this torture be actual? Was I having a nightmare? Would it never end? One of the mice crawled between my body and the wood. I gave my shoulder a frantic shrug; there was a tiny squeak, and the sharp nails which had been digging into my skin instantly went limp. The other mouse lodged himself somewhere in a fold of my trousers. Poor little creatures! They had sought only the safety of darkness. They could have harmed hardly a living thing. But I am sure they wrecked a thousand nerve cells in my quivering body.

Again shoving forward violently with my toes and digging my fingers into the soft structure of the tree, I pressed onward. The passageway became larger; I moved more freely. It was heavenly to be able to rest my weary body, and to breath more deeply.

But I was yet to meet my most amazing, my most uncomfortable adventure! Suddenly the mother vulture stood up, hissed, coughed a little, and began vomiting decayed flesh she had eaten earlier in the day. I had somehow forgotten the vulture. I found myself wishing with all my heart that I had not sealed up the other end of the log. Summoning courage, and wriggling forward as rapidly as I could, I struck the great bird an awkward blow. She hobbled off, hissing hoarsely and leaving a new object exposed.

I could not see very well; but I had enough strength and interest in my strange expedition to permit me to realize that I was face to face with a lovely newborn creature—a baby vulture, no more than a few hours old. It was downy white, its legs and naked head were gray, its infant eyes had no expression. Breathing evenly, quietly, it rested beside a large egg which was of soiled white splotched with blackish brown.

The mother continued to cough and hiss, but she could not produce any more food. I was thankful that the digestive process in birds is so rapid that food does not, as a rule, stay long in the crop or gullet!

Lifting the young vulture as well as I could, and rolling the big egg ahead of me, I wormed my way onward. The dusky parent retreated. At the end of the log I grasped her by the feet, pushed the obstructing stones away as well as I could, and breathed the fresh air in deep gasps. Nearly worn out, I trembled from head to foot. Most of my shirt was somewhere in the log; the underclothes which had covered my shoulders and chest were wound in tatters about my trousers. I was scratched up considerably, and bleeding in several spots. It must have taken me fifteen minutes to get out of the log, for the exit was small.

When I finally reached the outer air I sank to the leaves, awkwardly tied the vulture to a sapling, using a shred of torn underclothing, and panted and trembled as I picked grand-daddy longlegs from my hair, eyes, and neck, and a dead mouse from my clothing. The belt had dug deep into the skin and had worn raw grooves all about my waist. But I was free! I could breathe the air, the cool, fresh air of heaven!

I hobbled over to the pool. In the rustic mirror I could see that I was no lovely vision. I washed my face and hands, smoothed back my hair, and pinned my torn clothing together with a thorn or two.

Then I returned to my captives. Somehow the little white baby seemed pitiably friendless in this bright world of the open. The eyes of the mother were hard and fierce and frightened. The egg was infertile. I could hear the liquid contents slopping about inside when I shook it.

Had I been less weary or had my predatory instinct been more keen, I might have killed the mother vulture and tossed her aside; or I might have carried her home. But I couldn't bring myself to take that woods baby away, or leave it there an orphan. I put it back in the damp shadow of the hollow log. I rolled aside the stones I had brought for sealing the opening. And then I put the mother back beside the cottony infant, which by this time was peeping faintly. The mother bird did not attempt to rush away. Mouth open, she eyed me impersonally. I moved off through the woods quietly, hoping that my retreat would not frighten her, or that if she did fly away she would return to her charge.

I was famished and exhausted when I reached home. I mounted the stairs to my room with stiff and weary feet. When I took off my trousers a bright-eyed mouse whisked out of a pocket and scampered behind the bookcase.

BALD EAGLES

ON THE

HUDSON RIVER

John Kieran

John Kieran, sports writer, radio performer, and naturalist we have met before. He is one of the best illustrations of the fact that a first-rate bird watcher does not need to be a monomaniac. One of the secrets of his charm is that he manages to combine wide knowledge of natural history with a gay amateur spirit.

FULL knee-deep lay the Winter snow as the Medical Student and I started out on New Year's Day to make note of what birds we might find in the vicinity. The snow was new and clean and soft underfoot. There would be tracks in it when we reached wild territory. We knocked at the Artist's door but he said reluctantly that he couldn't go along; he had just started on a fresh canvas and he felt it incumbent upon him to stick at the easel. That was his error. Not more than half a mile from his house we found the neat footprints of a fox in the snow. Whether it was a Gray Fox or a Red Fox we had no way of knowing. We have both in our area. But a fox track in New York City—barely a mile from a subway station—is something to gloat over, and in reporting the matter later to the Artist the impulse was to repeat gleefully what Henry of Navarre said to the valiant Crillon, who somehow missed the great battle at Arques: *"Pends-toi, brave Crillon; tu n'y étais pas!"*

There is, of course, no mistaking a fox track for that of a dog, which is a gross, lumbering animal compared to a fox. Reynard leaves his delicate footprints behind him in almost a straight line, whereas a dog leaves a pattern of parallel prints that overlap sloppily and are often askew. A cat comes closer to leaving a track like a fox, but a cat takes shorter steps and would have to brush through snow of some depth over which a taller fox would trot with calm dignity. The Medical Student and I followed the fox trail for a hundred yards or so. We could see that Reynard had

From *Footnotes on Nature*. New York: Doubleday & Co., 1947.

been searching for mice, but nothing came of it up to the point where we abandoned the trail and crossed the railroad tracks to walk along the banks of the Hudson River.

We knew we would find some ducks and seagulls on the river. If there were any distinguished visitors among them, we wanted to start the New Year right by "logging" them. I keep a record of the birds I see each year and the date on which I first see them, to which I add in the case of many migrant species that date on which I last see them in the Autumn. It's remarkable how closely the migrants stick to a calendar schedule year after year. Where there are any considerable variations in such dates, the variations are probably my fault; I wasn't on the job to make note of what I should have seen.

But we weren't expecting migrants on New Year's Day. We were merely looking around for permanent residents and Winter visitors. Going down through the woods and along the open stretch of brush before reaching the railroad tracks and the riverbank, we had seen some Crows, half a dozen Black-capped Chickadees, a Downy Woodpecker, a Hairy Woodpecker, two White-breasted Nuthatches, a flock of twittering Slate-colored Juncos, about a dozen Goldfinches, a few Blue Jays, two Song Sparrows, five White-throated Sparrows and a cheerful group of Tree Sparrows calling musically as they flew from one tall dried stalk to another where they were feeding in a patch of Great Ragweed. There were, of course, many House or English Sparrows and innumerable Starlings to be seen before we left the residential area for uncultivated territory, and just as we crossed the railroad a Red-tailed Hawk sailed lazily overhead.

The river was dotted with ice floes, some in great packs and some in scattered cakes of all sizes. We swept the ice and the open water with our field glasses for gulls and ducks. When they are not flying, the ducks prefer to stay in the water, whereas the gulls prefer to sit on the ice. It always has amused me to watch ice cakes floating down the river with a dozen dignified gulls getting a free ride. Sometimes we see one gull standing solemnly on a small cake and gazing steadily ahead, looking for all the world like a ferryboat captain in command of his gallant craft.

There were several thousand Herring Gulls on the ice or in the air over the river. The Herring Gull is the common cold-weather gull in our vicinity, but we seldom fail to find a few Great Black-backed Gulls if we are patient and go over the river slowly with our glasses. These "Black-backs" are easy to pick out among the paler Herring Gulls because they wear, like Hamlet, an "inky cloak" or black mantle, the feature that gives them their common name. They bully the smaller Herring Gulls into surrendering some of the food they find by scavenging. Highway robbery is a popular pastime in the wild, and the Great Black-backed Gull makes a career of piracy over the full extent of its salt-water range. All the "Black-backs" and most of the Herring Gulls leave the river for more northerly waters in warm weather, and the Summer representative of the gull family on the river is the small, handsome and, in season, black-headed Laughing Gull.

When we had taken stock of the gull situation—we had spotted two "Black-backs" among a horde of Herring Gulls on a distant floe—we searched the water for ducks and found just about what we expected. Far out in midstream we saw lines of American Mergansers, gaudy males and sober females, swimming slowly against the tide. Here and there we spotted a Black Duck. Then we found a group of American Golden-eyes feeding by diving. They were appearing and disappearing as though they were being manipulated by a magician. The male American Mergansers and American Golden-eyes are strikingly handsome ducks in Winter plumage, and it was good to see them on the water, but the Medical Student wasn't satisfied. He wanted to see an eagle. He didn't expect to see a Golden Eagle, of course, but he knew that Bald Eagles were regular Winter visitors on our stretch of river. We had walked about a quarter of a mile up the riverbank when the Medical Student, peering through his glasses, said:

"By golly, I think I have one—away over near the far side—on the north end of that big ice floe—see it?"

As I adjusted my glasses I remarked that an eagle on a distant ice cake looks like a chunk of dark timber, an abandoned keg or a lost coal scuttle. This is particularly true of the adult Bald Eagle, whose white head and tail feathers blend with the surrounding ice and snow. When I am looking for eagles on the ice I sweep the floes with my glasses until I see something that looks like a far-off coal scuttle and then—

"You'll have to hurry to see this coal scuttle," interrupted the Medical Student. "It has just taken off and is flying low up the river."

Sure enough, it was a mature Bald Eagle, and the Medical Student, lowering his glasses, said that we had started the New Year in proper fashion by seeing such a great bird. Later in the season the Artist and I saw six Bald Eagles at once along the same stretch of river, four of them sitting on one cake of ice. We soon discovered the reason for this aquiline conference. One of them had a chunk of food and the others were envious. There was a bit of sparring with talons and wings now and then, but the owner clung to the food and finally flew off with what was left of it.

HOW TO

GET ALONG

WITH BIRDS

Robert C. Miller

Most of the vast literature of ornithology is deadly serious. Your bird lover may jest about trivial things like politics, love, and religion, but his feathered friends are sacred. Say one word against them and he will put you down as a heretic and a blasphemer, unfit for the society of either man or bird.

The Director of the California Academy of Sciences is one of the last men from whom one would expect blasphemy but here is the evidence in an essay which is deceptively entitled "How To Get Along with Birds" but of which the conclusion is that it can't be done. The problem is not how to attract them but how to protect your garden and how to get a reasonable quota of early-morning sleep. "The poetry of earth is never dead," wrote Keats, who then went on to praise the grasshopper for taking up when the birds leave off at midday. Dr. Miller says in effect that the poetry of earth may also be described as an unceasing, infernal racket. Since he has devoted his life to the study of nature he probably feels differently most of the time but it was doubtless a relief to get this charming if rebellious protest out of his system.

Hundreds of books and magazine articles have been written on how to identify birds, how to study birds, how to attract birds, how to encourage them to take up residence about the house and garden. There are reams of literature on how to build bird houses, bird baths, and feeding trays, and how to plant your back yard so that birds for miles around will gather to admire it. But hardly anybody has dealt with the problem of how to get along with birds after you have them.

The first and worst thing to be noted about birds is that they get up too early in the morning. This in itself would not be so bad if they didn't make so much noise about it; but like other early risers they act as if

From *National League for Women's Service* Magazine, March 1950.

nobody else had a right to sleep. They start greeting the dawn before the night is much more than half over, and one is tempted to think they don't know the difference between Aurora and aurora borealis.

If you live in the country you awaken to the crowing of roosters, the cackling of hens, and the quacking of ducks. If you dwell in a suburban retreat, the robins gather round and join their voices in a rousing matutinal chorus. If you live in the city, the sparrows and house finches take over. These categories, moreover, are not mutually exclusive. If you select your habitat with sufficient care, you can have every one of these avian voices, plus a lot of others, greeting your ears in the pale, chill dawn.

There is a common rural expression about "getting up with the chickens," and you might as well do just that if you live within two hundred yards of a flock of poultry, for they are not going to let you sleep if they can help it. One of Aesop's fables tells of a maid who wrung a cock's neck because he was instrumental in waking her up at a given time every morning. Thereafter her mistress, with no rooster to act as an alarm clock, took to rousing the maid at all hours of the night, so she was worse off than before. Anybody who has ever raised poultry will agree that this is a fable, because roosters, far from being accurate in their timing, crow *ad lib* anywhere between midnight and morning. For this they deserve to have their necks wrung, which is not the moral, if any, that Aesop intended to draw.

Happily, most birds are more regular in their habits. Chaucer, it is true, remarks:

> *And smale foules maken melodye*
> *And slepen all the night with open ye.*

But doubtless he referred to nightingales. With a few noteworthy exceptions, birds restrain their paeans until at least the first faint streaks of dawn are visible on the eastern horizon. This at all events brings the problem within bounds, and makes it slightly easier to cope with.

Let us digress at this point to consider the question of why birds sing at all. Maybe you think it's because they are happy, but that is not to be taken for granted. Bear in mind that morning song commences before it is light enough for the birds to see to begin feeding. Some of the finest bird music is produced on an empty stomach, and it is hard to see how even a bird can be that happy at breakfast.

Scientists have come up in recent years with a new explanation, one that is not at all romantic, not on first thought very convincing, and possibly not even true. Anyway this is the theory: birds sing to enforce their property rights—to announce that possession has been taken of a certain area, and to warn other birds of the same species to keep out.

As a rough analogy, let us suppose that your neighbor has been taking a shortcut through your yard, trampling down your peonies and wearing a path across the lawn. Instead of arguing or quarreling with him, or putting up "No trespass" signs, or building a fence, you climb a tree, sit on a branch and sing "O Sole Mio" at the top of your lungs, starting at dawn and continuing at intervals till after sundown. This is guaranteed to produce results of some kind. It will probably be effective in keeping your neighbor off the property, at least until you are committed to an institution.

Well, whether birds sing because they are happy, or hungry, or real estate minded—sing they do; and they are going to keep right on singing in the early hours of the morning when even their best friends and sincerest admirers prefer to sleep. It's no use to turn and toss and raise your blood-pressure, much less go out and throw rocks at them when it is still too dark to see. There are only two courses to pursue. One is, again to quote Chaucer, "To maken vertue of necessite"—to get up and dress and pretend you like it, thinking meanwhile of all the old maxims on the advantages of early rising. The other, and better, is a technique I learned from a friend in college, who used to set his alarm clock an hour early just for the fun of turning it off and going back to sleep.

I have a robin who takes up a stance outside my bedroom window and warbles stridently in the pale gray dawn: "Get up, get up—you better get up, you better get up—see?" He varies this at intervals with a stacatto "Beep, beep, beep, beep, beep" in a descending scale. He does everything except honk like an automobile or whistle like a train. Do I allow myself to be annoyed? No. I just say, "Pfui! my fine feathered friend, go chase a worm." Then, with a deep sense of comfort and well being, I turn over for another snooze, thankful I *don't* have to get up with the birds.

Now about this matter of attracting birds, so you can properly enjoy your beauty sleep, the books all say to plant pyracantha, cotoneaster, toyon, and sun-flowers. These may be all right for certain places; but everyone who has ever tried it knows that the real way to attract birds is to plant a vegetable garden. The moment you walk out in the yard with a spade they begin to gather round, and they follow the progress of events with increasing interest and enthusiasm. Robins work the place over looking for worms, and flickers go over it again looking for ants. As tender shoots begin to appear above the soil, the white-crowned sparrows feel a sudden urge to get their vitamins. Finally the quail come out and snuggle down and dust themselves in what remains of the lettuce patch.

There are again two ways to look at this. You can practice psychology and try to feel glad that you have been able to assist our little feathered friends. Or, if you want to raise a garden, you can take some practical steps. Most damage by birds is done to the tender shoots, before the vegetables are one inch high. If you can get them two inches high they are practically immune. This can be accomplished by covering your vegetables with paper caps, either the commercial variety known as "hotcaps" or just plain waxed paper propped up in the middle and staked out along the rows. Such procedures not only give protection from birds, but offer the advantage of a little temporary hotbed.

Probably the best of all possible ways of protecting a vegetable garden from birds is that developed by Italian fisher folk. Get old fishing nets and spread them around over your garden, with suitable supports two or three feet high. The vegetables will grow and thrive. The birds may feel frustrated, but that is *their* problem. You can enjoy both ornithology and gardening, once you learn to get along with birds.

SPRING

IN THE

KINGDOM

Ada Clapham Govan

Birds that come and go are—such is human perversity—usually more welcome than those which stay with us. Here is an account of one woman's experience with hordes of visitors.

ASIDE from the visits of the field sparrow and the finches, our visitors up to that time consisted of a regular assortment of juncos, downy woodpeckers, brown creepers, tree sparrows, red-breasted nuthatches, white-breasted nuthatches, five darling chickadees, and, as a finishing touch, two golden-crowned kinglets. With these I was content and the days slipped by, pleasantly enough, till just two days before Easter. On Good Friday morning, I looked out of my window and discovered one lone fox sparrow feeding in the yard; eleven more were keeping him company by afternoon. The flock numbered fifty-three by Saturday noon, and more were arriving constantly. Apparently a migration of fox sparrows was keeping pace with spring. To have as guests fifty-three of these superb singers was something long to be remembered.

Meanwhile, five robins, a flicker, a gorgeous cock pheasant, and one unwelcome grackle had arrived in time for dinner; but it wasn't until Easter Monday that things really began to happen.

Easter Sunday was a mellow, sunny day, but a blizzard broke that night, catching the migrating hosts in their northward flight and slaying them by thousands and tens of thousands. The noise of that wild storm and a mixed chorus of bird calls outside awakened me at daybreak. Every feeding box was inches deep in snow; yet birds were everywhere, and in spite of the storm, they were singing lustily, joyously, as I had never heard birds sing before. By six o'clock I had scattered two large pans of food all over the yard. The manner in which it disappeared left no doubt of its being sadly needed.

From *Wings at My Window*. New York: The Macmillan Company, 1940.

Some gay little song sparrows joined the fast-growing assembly, and fox sparrows arrived in an ever-increasing stream. A few purple finches joined the throng, and strangers whom I could not identify, for their coloring was changed and dulled, so sodden were they all from the gale's buffeting. Why did so many come to us? What had told them that here they would find sanctuary?

There they stood within a few feet of the house, body-deep in slush and snow, blown and battered by the gale—between three and four hundred birds (nearly three hundred of them fox sparrows), and all singing gloriously. Any migration under such conditions would be unusual, but a gathering of almost three hundred fox sparrows, plus many other birds, in one back yard, is an event of a lifetime. To see a flock of even one hundred Foxies in our locality is something to boast about. No wonder people came from all over town, and farther, to hear them sing. Their song carried for blocks! The promise of springtime had betrayed them, yet it seemed that no sleet or snow or fiercely beating hail could quench the joy of homecoming in those valiant hearts.

Then I heard the squeaking of a wheelbarrow chorus far in the distance, and saw a cloud of midnight blackness coming towards me. Settling in the woods across the road, it quickly disintegrated into hundreds of rusty blackbirds still groaning their crazy song.

The peak of the invasion reached us on Tuesday morning. In one group there were more than eighty fox sparrows; two other groups were nearly as large, and there were several smaller bands. For several days we fed about four hundred birds, who consumed twenty pounds of wild bird seed and many pounds of sunflower seed, suet, and scraps, in less than three days.

Soon warm weather and a few sunny hours thinned the ranks of those who had come to us in their time of stress; but across the years I can still hear the wonderful singing that was wafted on high from dawn to dark in a never-creasing chorus of thanksgiving.

THE

PASSENGER

PIGEON

John James Audubon

Perhaps no story about birds has been more often told than that of the passenger pigeon which once migrated in flocks of incredible size over eastern North America though it is now "as dead as the dodo." Perhaps its disappearance was inevitable, not only because it was slaughtered recklessly by both hunters for food and "sportsmen" killers, but also because the clearing of the forest deprived it of the immense food supply necessary to such prodigious numbers. The fact remains that the extinction of the species, like the loss of some great work of art, is absolutely irretrievable. And it is startling to realize in how short a time the irretrievable loss can occur. In 1813 Audubon saw passenger pigeons passing hour after hour sometimes at the rate of 163 flocks in 23 minutes. Just 101 years later the last living specimen died in the Cincinnati Zoological Garden.

THE Passenger Pigeon, or, as it is usually named in America, the Wild Pigeon, moves with extreme rapidity, propelling itself by quickly repeated flaps of the wings, which it brings more or less near to the body, according to the degree of velocity which is required. Like the Domestic Pigeon it often flies, during the love season, in a circling manner, supporting itself with both wings angularly elevated, in which position it keeps them until it is about to alight. Now and then, during these circular flights, the tips of the primary quills of each wing are made to strike against each other, producing a smart rap, which may be heard at a distance of thirty or forty yards. Before alighting, the Wild Pigeon, like the Carolina Parrot and a few other species of birds, breaks the force of its flight by repeated flappings, as if apprehensive of receiving injury from coming too suddenly into contact with the branch or the spot of ground on which it intends to settle.

I have commenced my description of this species with the above

From *Birds of America*, Vol. 5. Published by George R. Lockwood and Son, 1870.

account of its flight, because the most important facts connected with its habits relate to its migrations. These are entirely owing to the necessity of procuring food, and are not performed with the view of escaping the severity of a northern latitude, or of seeking a southern one for the purpose of breeding. They consequently do not take place at any fixed period or season of the year. Indeed, it sometimes happens that a continuance of a sufficient supply of food in one district will keep these birds absent from another for years. I know, at least, to a certainty, that in Kentucky they remained for several years constantly, and were nowhere else to be found. They all suddenly disappeared in one season when the mast was exhausted, and did not return for a long period. Similar facts have been observed in other States.

Their great power of flight enables them to survey and pass over an astonishing extent of country in a very short time. This is proved by facts well known. Thus, Pigeons have been killed in the neighbourhood of New York, with their crops full of rice, which they must have collected in the fields of Georgia and Carolina, these districts being the nearest in which they could possibly have procured a supply of that kind of food. As their power of digestion is so great that they will decompose food entirely in twelve hours; they must in this case have travelled between three and four hundred miles in six hours, which shows their speed to be at an average of about one mile in a minute. A velocity such as this would enable one of these birds, were it so inclined, to visit the European continent in less than three days.

This great power of flight is seconded by as great a power of vision, which enables them, as they travel at that swift rate, to inspect the country below, discover their food with facility, and thus attain the object for which their journey has been undertaken. This I have also proved to be the case, by having observed them, when passing over a sterile part of the country, or one scantily furnished with food suited to them, keep high in the air, flying with an extended front, so as to enable them to survey hundreds of acres at once. On the contrary, when the land is richly covered with food, or the trees abundantly hung with mast, they fly low, in order to discover the part most plentifully supplied.

Their body is of an elongated oval form, steered by a long well-plumed tail, and propelled by well-set wings, the muscles of which are very large and powerful for the size of the bird. When an individual is seen gliding through the woods and close to the observer, it passes like a thought, and on trying to see it again, the eye searches in vain; the bird is gone.

The multitudes of Wild Pigeons in our woods are astonishing. Indeed, after having viewed them so often, and under so many circumstances, I even now feel inclined to pause, and assure myself that what I am going to relate is fact. Yet I have seen it all, and that too in the company of persons who, like myself, were struck with amazement.

In the autumn of 1813, I left my house at Henderson, on the banks of the Ohio, on my way to Louisville. In passing over the Barrens a few miles beyond Hardensburgh, I observed the Pigeons flying from north-east to south-west in greater numbers than I thought I had ever seen them before, and feeling an inclination to count the flocks that might pass within reach of my eye in one hour, I dismounted, seated myself on an eminence, and began to mark with my pencil, making a dot for every flock that passed. In a short time finding the task which I had undertaken impracticable, as the birds poured on in countless multitudes, I rose, and counting the dots then put down, found that 163 had been made in twenty-one minutes. I traveled on, and still met more the farther I proceeded. The air was literally filled with pigeons; the light of noon-day was obscured as by an eclipse; the dung fell in spots, not unlike melting flakes of snow; and the continued buzz of wings had a tendency to lull my senses to repose.

While waiting for dinner at Young's inn at the confluence of Salt River with the Ohio, I saw, at my leisure, immense legions still going by, with a front reaching far beyond the Ohio on the west, and the beech-wood forests directly on the east of me. Not a single bird alighted; for not a nut or acorn was that year to be seen in the neighbourhood. They consequently flew so high, that different trials to reach them with a capital rifle proved ineffectual; nor did the reports disturb them in the least. I cannot describe to you the extreme beauty of their aerial evolutions, when a Hawk chanced to press upon the rear of a flock. At once, like a torrent, and with a noise like thunder, they rushed into a compact mass, pressing upon each other towards the center. In these almost solid masses, they darted forward in undulating and angular lines, descended and swept close over the earth with inconceivable velocity, mounted perpendicularly so as to resemble a vast column, and, when high, were seen wheeling and twisting within their continued lines, which then resembled the coils of a gigantic serpent.

Before sunset I reached Louisville, distant from Hardensburgh fifty-five miles. The pigeons were still passing in undiminished numbers, and continued to do so for three days in succession. The people were all in arms. The banks of the Ohio were crowded with men and boys, in-cessantly shooting at the pilgrims, which flew lower as they passed the river. Mulitudes were thus destroyed. For a week or more, the population fed on no other flesh than that of Pigeons, and talked of nothing but Pigeons.

It is extremely interesting to see flock after flock performing exactly the same evolutions which had been traced as it were in the air by a preceding flock. Thus should a Hawk have charged on a group at a certain spot, the angles, curves, and undulations, that have been described by the birds, in their efforts to escape from the dreaded talons of the plunderer, are undeviatingly followed by the next group that comes up. Should the bystander happen to witness one of these affrays, and, struck with the rapidity and elegance of the motions exhibited, feel desirous of seeing them repeated, his wishes will be gratified if he only remain in the place until the next group comes up.

As soon as the Pigeons discover a sufficiency of food to entice them to alight, they fly around in circles, reviewing the country below. During their evolutions, on such occasions, the dense mass which they form exhibits a beautiful appearance, as it changes its direction, now displaying a glistening sheet of azure, when the backs of the birds come simultaneously into view, and anon, suddenly presenting a mass of rich deep purple. They then pass lower, over the woods, and for a moment are lost among the foliage, but again emerge, and are seen gliding aloft. They now alight, but the next moment, as if suddenly alarmed, they take to wing, producing by the flapping of their wings a noise like the roar of distant thunder, and sweep through the forest to see if danger is near. Hunger, however, soon brings them to the ground. When alighted, they are seen industriously throwing up the withered leaves in quest of the fallen mast. The rear ranks are continually rising, passing over the main-body, and alighting in front, in such rapid succession, that the whole flock seems still on wing. The quantity of ground thus swept is astonishing, and so completely has it been cleared, that the gleaner who might follow in their rear would find his labour completely lost. Whilst feeding, their avidity is at times so great that in attempting to swallow a large acorn or nut, they are seen gasping for a long while, as if in the agonies of suffocation.

On such occasions, when the woods are filled with these Pigeons, they are killed in immense numbers, although no apparent diminution ensues. About the middle of the day, after their repast is finished, they settle on the trees, to enjoy rest, and digest their food. On the ground they walk with ease, as well as on the branches, frequently jerking their beautiful tail, and moving the neck backwards and forwards in the most graceful manner. As the sun begins to sink beneath the horizon, they depart *en masse* for the roosting-place, which not unfrequently is hundreds of miles distant, as has been ascertained by persons who have kept an account of their arrivals and departures.

Let us now, kind reader, inspect their place of nightly rendezvous. One of these curious roosting-places, on the banks of the Green river in Kentucky, I repeatedly visited. It was, as is always the case, in a portion of the forest where the trees were of great magnitude, and where there was little under-wood. I rode through it upwards of forty miles, and, crossing it in different parts, found its average breadth to be rather more than three miles. My first view of it was about a fortnight subsequent to the period when they had made choice of it, and I arrived there nearly two hours before sunset. Few pigeons were then to be seen, but a great number of persons, with horses and wagons, guns and ammunition, had already established encampments on the borders. Two farmers from the vicinity of Russelsville, distant more than a hundred miles, had driven upwards of three hundred hogs to be fattened on the Pigeons which were to be slaughtered. Here and there, the people employed in plucking and salting what had already been procured, were seen sitting in the midst of large piles of these birds. The dung lay several inches deep, covering the whole extent of the roosting-place. Many trees two feet in diameter, I observed, were broken off at no great distance from the ground; and the branches of many of the largest and tallest had given way, as if the forest had been swept by a tornado. Everything proved to me that the number of birds resorting to this part of the forest must be immense beyond conception. As the period of their arrival approached, their foes anxiously prepared to receive them. Some were furnished with iron-pots containing sulphur, others with torches of pine-knots, many with poles, and the rest with guns. The sun was lost to our view, yet not a Pigeon had arrived. Everything was ready, and all eyes were gazing on the clear sky, which appeared in glimpses amidst the tall trees. Suddenly there burst forth a general cry of "Here they come!" The noise which they made, though yet distant, reminded me of a hard gale at sea, passing through the rigging of a close-reefed vessel. As the birds arrived and passed over me, I felt a current of air that surprised me. Thousands were soon knocked down by the pole-men. The birds continued to pour in. The fires were lighted, and a magnificent, as well as wonderful and almost terrifying, sight presented itself. The Pigeons, arriving by thousands, alighted everywhere, one above another, until solid masses were formed on the branches all round. Here and there the perches gave way under the weight with a crash, and, falling to the ground, destroyed hundreds of birds beneath, forcing down the dense groups with which every stick was loaded. It was a scene of uproar and confusion. I found it quite useless to speak, or even to shout to those persons who were nearest to me. Even the reports of the guns were seldom heard, and I was made aware of the firing only by seeing the shooters reloading.

No one dared venture within the line of devastation. The hogs had been penned up in due time, the picking up of the dead and wounded being left for the next morning's employment. The Pigeons were constantly coming and it was past midnight before I perceived a decrease in the number of those that arrived. The uproar continued the whole night; and as I was anxious to know to what distance the sound reached, I sent off a man, accustomed to perambulate the forest, who, returning two hours afterward, informed me he had heard it distinctly when three miles distant from the spot. Towards the approach of day, the noise in some measure subsided long before objects were distinguishable, the

Pigeons began to move off in a direction quite different from that in which they had arrived the evening before, and at sunrise all that were able to fly had disappeared. The howlings of the wolves now reached our ears, and the foxes, lynxes, cougars, bears, racoons, opossums, and pole-cats were seen sneaking off whilst eagles and hawks of different species, accompanied by a crowd of vultures, came to supplant them, and enjoy their share of the spoil.

It was then that the authors of this devastation began their entry amongst the dead, the dying, and the mangled. The Pigeons were picked up and piled in heaps until each had as many as he could possibly dispose of, when the hogs were let loose to feed on the remainder.

Persons unacquainted with these birds might naturally conclude that such dreadful havoc would soon put an end to the species. But I have satisfied myself, by long observation, that nothing but the gradual diminution of our forests can accomplish their decrease, as they not unfrequently quadruple their numbers yearly, and always at least double it. In 1805 I saw schooners loaded in bulk with Pigeons caught up the Hudson River, coming in to the wharf at New York, when the birds sold for a cent apiece. I knew a man in Pennsylvania, who caught and killed upwards of 500 dozens in a clap-net in one day, sweeping sometimes twenty dozens or more at a single haul. In the month of March, 1830, they were so abundant in the markets of New York, that piles of them met the eye in every direction. I have seen the Negroes at the United States Salines or Saltworks of Shawanee Town, wearied with killing Pigeons, as they alighted to drink the water issuing from the leading pipes, for weeks at a time; and yet in 1826, in Louisiana, I saw congregated flocks of these birds as numerous as ever I had seen them before, during a residence of nearly thirty years in the United States.

The breeding of the Wild Pigeons, and the places chosen for that purpose, are points of great interest. The time is not much influenced by season, and the place selected is where food is most plentiful and most attainable, and always at a convenient distance from water. Forest-trees of great height are those in which the Pigeons form their nests. Thither the countless myriads resort, and prepare to fulfill one of the great laws of nature. At this period the note of the Pigeon is a soft *coo-coo-coo-coo*, much shorter than that of the domestic species. The common notes resemble the monosyllables *kee-kee-kee-kee*, the first being the loudest, the others gradually diminishing in power. The male assumes a pompous demeanour, and follows the female, whether on the ground or on the branches, with spread tail and drooping wings, which it rubs against the part over which it is moving. The body is elevated, the throat swells, the eyes sparkle. He continues his notes, and now and then rises on the wing, and flies a few yards to approach the fugitive and timorous female. Like the domestic Pigeon and other species, they caress each other by billing, in which action, the bill of the one is introduced transversely into that of the other, and both parties alternately disgorge the contents of their crop by repeated efforts. These preliminary affairs are soon settled, and the pigeons commence their nests in general peace and harmony. They are composed of a few dry twigs, crossing each other, and are supported by forks of the branches. On the same tree from fifty to a hundred nests may frequently be seen:—I might say a much greater number, were I not anxious, kind reader, that however wonderful my account of the Wild Pigeon is, you may not feel disposed to refer it to the marvellous. The eggs are two in number, of a broadly elliptical form, and pure white. During incubation, the male supplies the female with food. Indeed, the tenderness and affection displayed by these birds towards their mates, are in the highest degree striking. It is a remarkable fact, that each brood generally consists of a male and a female.

Here again, the tyrant of creation, man, interferes, disturbing the harmony of this peaceful scene. As the young birds grow up, their enemies, armed with axes, reach the spot, to seize and destroy all they can. The trees are felled, and made to fall in such a way that the cutting of one causes the overthrow of another, or shakes the neighbouring trees so much, that the young Pigeons, or *squabs*, as they are named, are violently hurled to the ground. In this manner also, immense quantities are destroyed.

The young are fed by the parents in the manner described above; in other words, the old bird introduces its bill into the mouth of the young one in a transverse manner, or with the back of each mandible opposite the separations of the mandibles of the young bird, and disgorges the contents of its crop. As soon as the young birds are able to shift for themselves, they leave their parents, and continue separate until they attain maturity. By the end of six months they are capable of reproducing their species.

The flesh of the Wild Pigeon is of a dark colour, but affords tolerable eating. That of young birds from the nest is much esteemed. The skin is covered with small white filmy scales. The feathers fall off at the least touch, as had been remarked to be the case in the Carolina Turtle-dove. I have only to add, that this species, like others of the same genus, immerses its head up to the eyes while drinking.

In March, 1830, I bought about 350 of these birds in the market of New York, at four cents apiece. Most of these I carried alive to England, and distributed them amongst several noblemen, presenting some at the same time to the Zoological Society.

This celebrated bird is mentioned by Dr. Richardson as "annually reaching the 62nd degree of latitude, in the warm central districts of the Fur Countries, and attaining the 58th parallel on the coast of Hudson's Bay in very fine summers only. Mr. Hutchins mentions a flock which visited York Factory and remained there two days, in 1775, as a very remarkable occurrence. A few hordes of Indians that frequent the low flooded tracts at the south end of Lake Winnipeg, subsist principally on the Pigeons, during a part of the summer, when the sturgeon-fishery is unproductive, and the *Zizania aquatica* has not yet ripened; but farther north, these birds are too few in number to furnish a material article of diet." Mr. Townsend states that this species is found on the Rocky Mountains, but not on the Columbia River, where the Band-tailed Pigeon, *Columba fasciata* of Say, is abundant. Whilst in Texas, I was assured that the Passenger Pigeon was plentiful there, although at irregular intervals. In the neighbourhood of Boston it arrives, as Dr. T. M. Brewer informs me, in small scattered flocks, much less numerous than in the interior of that State.

My friend, Dr. Bachman says, in a note sent to me, "In the more cultivated parts of the United States, these birds now no longer breed in communities. I have secured many nests scattered throughout the woods, seldom near each other. Four years ago, I saw several on the mountains east of Lansinburgh, in the State of New York. They were built close to the stems of thin but tall pine trees (*Pinus strobus*), and were composed of a few sticks; the eggs invariably two, and white. There is frequently but one young bird in the nest, probably from the loose manner in which it has been constructed, so that either a young bird or an egg drops out. Indeed, I have found both at the foot of the tree. This is no doubt accidental, and not to be attributed to a habit which the bird may be supposed to have of throwing out an egg or one of its young. I have frequently taken two of the latter from the same nest and reared them. The Wild Pigeons appear in Carolina during the winter at irregular periods, sometimes in cold, but often in warm weather, driven here no doubt, as you have mentioned, not by the cold, but by a failure of mast in the western forests."

A curious change of habits has taken place in England in those Pigeons which I presented to the Earl of Derby in 1830, that nobleman having assured me that ever since they began breeding in his aviaries, they laid only one egg. My noble friend has raised a great number of these birds, and has distributed them freely. It is not, therefore, very surprising that some which have escaped from confinement have been shot; but that this species should naturally have a claim to be admitted into the British Fauna appears to me very doubtful. The eggs measure one inch five-eighths in length, one inch one-eighth and a half in breadth, and are nearly equally rounded at both ends.

CARE

AND FEEDING

OF

WILD BIRDS

John K. Terres

Birds have been cruelly persecuted but on the other hand no other group of animals has been the object of more solicitude. Unfortunately, this solicitude is often bungling and a few suggestions from an authoritative source are very much worth having.

RULES for becoming a successful foster-parent:
Every year, bird's nests are blown out of trees by violent storms and newly-hatched, or half-grown young birds, scattered on the ground. If the nest and fledglings can be replaced in the tree or bush, it is far better to do so and let the bird-parents go on with an exacting job for which they alone are best suited. But if you enjoy being a foster parent, the experience of establishing a nursery for young birds can be rewarding. When the nest has been destroyed, and the youngsters seemed doomed to perish without your care, take them in if you are prepared to devote yourself to the task of feeding them at 15-minute intervals for at least 12 hours during the day. Here's how one of our correspondents, an expert at caring for baby wild birds, does it.

If the nest has been destroyed, she puts the helpless young birds in a box in a substitute nest, perhaps of grass, lined with soft cloth or cotton so that the birds' feet have something pliable to push against. She keeps them warm by covering them with a cloth and protecting them from drafts. If the fledglings are old enough to perch, she puts them in a large cage, or better, gives them the freedom of a room in which they can learn to fly.

Young birds should be handled as little as possible and not fed too much at a time. Feed them only during daylight hours, but feedings should be frequent, at least every 15 minutes or, at most, half an hour apart. Young birds are like our own children; they demand all the attention they can get, but regularity of feeding gives the best results.

Foods and Feeding

Feeding is common sense, with a dash of ingenuity. Many people try to feed foundling wild birds simply on bread, even offering it to owls and griebes.

Our correspondent's basic food for very young songbird nestlings, other than hummingbirds, is equal parts of finely-mashed yolk of hard-boiled eggs and finely-sifted bread crumbs, *slightly* moistened with milk or cod-liver oil. This mixture will agree with starlings, blue jays, cardinals, towhees, robins, catbirds, orioles, sparrows and other small birds. Good supplementary foods are canned dog-food, bits of grapes, cherries, bananas, or soft apple pulp, pieces of earthworms that have been "squeezed out," and bits of scraped or finely chopped meat. One woman with an orphaned yellow-billed cuckoo got a supply of insects for it each night by attracting insects to a light in her window.

At first, older fledglings may not eat. To forcefeed them, hold the bird by enclosing its body and closed wings in your left hand, and with your forefinger and thumb, gently pry open the bill at its base. In your right hand hold a medicine dropper, or an improvised narrow wooden spoon, or better, a small paint brush to pick up food on the tips of its bristles. Poke the food down the bird's throat, but not too much at once or it will choke. In a short time the youngsters will learn to open their bills for food. Continue the feeding until the bird's crop is full, and it should be especially full at nightfall, just before the bird goes to sleep.

To supplement her basic diet, our correspondent includes chopped nasturtium and watercress, rich in calcium and vitamins, and cottage cheese for added protein.

Most seed-eaters—cardinals, grosbeaks, and finches—also need fine gravel and charcoal, crushed seeds, chopped greens, fruits, mealworms and insects.

Young woodpeckers eat a mixture of dog-food and the basic finely-mashed egg yolks.

For baby hummingbirds supply a syrup in equal parts of sugar and water fed with a medicine dropper. After about 10 days, our correspondent feeds the hummers their first protein—dried dog-food very finely-sifted and thoroughly mixed with the syrup.

Young hawks and owls require meat, preferably meat with the fur or feathers on it which aids the digestion of raptorial birds. Feed them on freshly-caught rats and mice, or poultry and raw beef sprinkled with cod-liver oil, with which chicken feathers may be mixed.

Water and Sunshine

Small birds are quickly killed by forcibly giving them water. Before
they learn to drink, they receive sufficient water for their needs from
their food. When they are old enough to sit on a perch, water may be
offered in a shallow dish. You may also dip their bills into a water-cup
until they learn to drink by themselves. Young birds must have some
sunshine too, but they should be shaded from the heat of the mid-day
sun. Birds, like humans, welcome a cool retreat in hot weather.

When the Bird Grows Up

No matter how attached we may become to the birds we have raised,
we must remember that we have been their protectors, not their captors;
that wild birds belong to the State. As soon as a bird is strong enough,
it should be allowed to forage for itself and should be turned loose as
soon as it is able to fly. If the foundlings are not encouraged to return
to a wild, free life, they will learn to depend upon human assistance which
may bring them disaster when they are suddenly thrown upon their
own.

THE

BIRD DOCTOR

Paul H. Fluck

Feeding birds is one of the commonest and on the whole the safest ways of trying to be kind to them, though even that has its dangers—as for instance when a food supply is suddenly cut off after dependence upon it has led to overpopulation and perhaps to a delay in moving to more suitable winter quarters. Tending sick or wounded specimens is a ticklish business and should not be undertaken by those who do not know what they are doing and are not willing to go to endless trouble.

I HAVE two Doctor's Degrees. The first was presented to me twenty years ago at a graduation ceremony at the Academy of Music in Philadelphia. That diploma hangs on the wall of my office. It is printed on sheepskin and awes my medical patients into paying my fees. My other Doctor's Degree was presented to me by a blue-eyed freckled child. That diploma was written in pencil on a scrap of notebook paper. It came wrapped around a box that contained a battered robin. It read:

Dear Bird Doctor:
My robin is dying. Mother said you could save it if I brought it to you. Please do.

Carol.

I did save it. Carol's letter made me an *amateur* Bird Doctor. I waited almost ten years for another scrap of paper to make me a *professional*. It was a check for ten dollars, drawn on a bank in Hatboro, Pennsylvania. Written in the lower left corner were the words: "For the Care of One Sparrow Hawk."

It makes no difference that I never received another fee for such services. That check, duly cashed and listed on my income tax return, made me a *professional* Bird Doctor.

There are thousands of doctors, and all kinds of them, but I suspect there are fewer "paid" Bird Doctors than any other physicians.

From *Nature Magazine*, June 1956.

Looking back now over ten years of aiding birds, I see that I always intended to be a Bird Doctor. I knew it that first day, when I held a crippled blue jay, her bill completely snipped off by the washing-machine motor. Holding the bird in my hand, I dashed to my medical kit for a piece of oxidized cellulose to stop the bleeding. I held the cellulose over her bloody face for almost half an hour, while the phone jangled in vain with calls from human patients. When the bleeding stopped, I snipped off most of the cottony stuff and looked hopelessly at my patient. The bird's eyes sparkled behind the bloody clot, and her tiny tongue flicked in and out, in pain. I considered putting the jay in a box with some chloroform on cotton. But my wife said "No."

I said, "How will she eat?"

My wife said, "We'll see about that when the time comes."

When the time came, my wife chewed up food, and the bird picked it from between my wife's lips. For three weeks the bird ate everything in that way. Then she began to eat mashed potatoes and milk by herself, and finally her bill grew back far enough to cover her tongue.

While the jay was getting well her recovery was making news, and the door-bell was ringing. Children were bringing in crippled grackles, robins and sparrows. A policeman brought in a heron and a duck, and I was finding injured birds along the highway and in the park. The bird doctor business was booming. Birds were in boxes, in cages, in the bathroom, and in closets. If I had stopped to look ahead, I would have seen the impossibility of keeping up with the crippled bird business. For Humans a ration of one doctor for every seven hundred patients is about average. But there are said to be seven billion birds in these United States, and I was the only practicing Bird Doctor in the Delaware River Valley.

Besides being the lowest-paid profession in the world, bird-doctoring is the most demanding, physically. I have carried a flicker around from ant hill to ant hill for hours on a hot August day when the thermometer stood at 100. I have chased grasshoppers and leaf-hoppers during July, August and September to feed a kingbird and a scarlet tanager. For fifteen months I drove eight miles every day to stuff a pound of perfectly good beef liver down the throat of a blind barn owl, which never hunted a mouthful for himself all the time he was in my care. After the owl passed on, a rowdy red-shouldered hawk took his place, and for a year I drove the same eight miles to stuff more fifty-cent-a-pound beef liver down his throat. Every day I came home with blood oozing from my hands, and many evenings in my office I could not give a hypodermic injection with my bandaged fingers.

But bird-doctoring pays off in a big way. If you have the stamina to take it, and enough closets, and bird cages, and bathrooms, and back porches to house them, birds make the best patients on earth. They never complain. They never hire lawyers to sue you. They never sign hospital releases and go home. And while it is true that get-well rate of 50 percent is hardly ever obtainable, you can be sure that you will spend some of the most interesting hours of your life when bird-doctoring.

I feel sorry for people who have unintelligent parakeets and canaries for pets. These have been reared in captivity and deprived of the urge to be free. Wild birds are part of Nature. Many flow north with the spring and south with the fall as unhinderable as water pouring over a waterfall. They roost, eat, fight, drink, sing, bathe, and scheme escapes. Some of the most unforgettable hours of my life I have spent with a red-tailed hawk on my arm. The most affectionate friend I ever had was a blue jay. The most beautiful thing I ever had in my hand was a bluebird dying of footpox. If I sound like I am a bit soft in my head, mull this over in your own. Barney, the blind barn owl who lived in the old house in Washington Crossing Park, drew crowds of hundreds of people every Saturday and Sunday afternoon. Many drove more than a hundred miles to just stroke the feathers on his ugly head for a few seconds. In those fifteen months Barney did a job for conservation. His fans came in sleet, snow, fair weather, and during the terrible Delaware Valley Flood of August, 1955. Barney appeared on TV, and he got fan mail. Some real tears are shed when I tell visitors that the owl died on Halloween.

Actually, here and now, *and with emphasis*, let me make it clear that bird-doctoring is a ninety per cent unnecessary profession. Most small birds with broken wings make out far better if they are left to fend for themselves in a thicket of honeysuckle or blackberry briars near a spring or a brook. I have cold-heartedly released as many as a dozen birds that could not fly from wing injuries, in snow and sleet, in such locations. And in six instances I have recaptured those birds again. The bands on their legs proved that they were the cripples—completely recovered!

One song sparrow flew weakly from my hand and collapsed under a spice bush. I worried about it all night. At dawn I got up and spread enough bird seed around that bush to feed a hundred canaries. I did not see that bird again, for two years, and blamed myself for letting him go in the snow. Then one day I picked him out of a bird trap, and read his band. I thought I was seeing things. I read the number over again, and had two friends read the number. That little scamp came back every day for a month or so. He had so much zip that I could not handle him. I still think that on that first afternoon he was playing "possum," and that if I had kept him overnight he would have died!

Again I say, the best thing for an untrained bird doctor, and that probably means you, to do with a bird that cannot fly is to let it go at once, in the safest place you can find.

Most of the bird patients I have treated have been special patients, large birds like hawks and owls; blind birds; birds with hemorrhages, birds with diseases that might have infected wild birds. It made no difference how hopeless the case looked, I treated every bird exactly as I would have treated a human patient. Then I put the bird in a dark closet, except for owls, which I place in a lighted closet, and I wait twelve hours, or as much as twenty-four. Then I can predict the outcome. Dead birds are buried, or given to a taxidermist to mount. Live birds are treated exactly the same as well birds. Just as it is with chronic patients among people, birds that can never get well, or never care for themselves again, are the most difficult problems. But there is a place even for them.

At the bird programs at Washington Crossing Park my crippled birds pinch-hit for me on days when birds refuse to go into banding traps, or when rain or sub-zero weather makes banding too uncomfortable. From the reaction of the 35,000 people who have come to the bird programs in the Park in the last four years, I am sure that many like the crippled birds best.

Peanut, the scarlet tanager, will never fly again, but he can drink Coca Cola from a straw! Rosie, my helpless rose-breasted grosbeak, has posed for more Kodachromes than any grosbeak on earth. Saucy, my eleven-year-old blue jay with the deformed bill can dance like a strutter at the Mardi Gras. Unlike too many chronic human patients, birds do not give up. They keep on trying to get well. They keep on learning new tricks because new tricks mean more attention.

I have seen a red-shouldered hawk knock itself out two weeks in a row, becoming violently impatient as he waited his turn to be carried outside for the crowd to see. Barney, the blind barn owl, would limp over to the attic door, and wait to be carried outside at exactly 4 o'clock every Saturday and Sunday. On weekdays he always remained in his box in the corner.

Birds under my care are rarely given medicine. Although I can calculate a dose of almost any drug for a newborn baby, I am completely licked by the mathematics involved in figuring a dose for a two-ounce bird. Even whiskey I have found to be too strong as a stimulant for most songbirds. Vitamin drops are essential to almost all wild birds in captivity. I put the vitamin drops in the water dish daily.

Splints for broken wings are useless in most instances. Wing injuries, if they are not hopeless from the start, usually heal themselves in seven to ten days. Occasionally when the wing is dragging on the ground, a doll's sock, or a child's sock with the toe cut off can be slipped over the bird, and two holes can be cut out for the legs. But, after ten years of bird-doctoring, I am inclined to do less splinting.

Small cages cause birds more suffering than almost any ailment. A storeroom, a bathroom, a screened-in porch, or a packing carton, make far better quarters for crippled birds than canary and parrot cages. A few birds do well in cages, but only a few. If you must put a wild bird in a cage, be sure to cover the top of the cage, and the sides if necessary. Pine needles in the bottom of the cages make cleaning an easy task. And the pine needles are almost ideal for bird's feet.

My most ungrateful bird patients have been herons. Great blue herons and night herons have long, dangerous bills, which you have to get a grip on first, before you can feed them or give them a diagnostic looking-over. Feeding a heron calls for patience and a nose clamp. I usually use smelts, and work them all the way down the heron's neck. It is like squeezing mud out of a garden hose. But finally the smelt slips inside, and you turn your back to pick up another. Then you suddenly discover your first smelt lying there, ready for another try.

The best place for herons is in a safe, secluded pond or brook where there are plenty of fish and tadpoles, and no dogs, or children. Taking care of crippled herons is a dangerous and smelly business. The next time I treat one, I am going to have a galvanized bucket on my head with holes cut for my eyes.

Many visitors to Washington Crossing Park will recall the old crow that suffered with asthma. He was one of the few birds who had his own medicine bottle. A few drops would relieve his gasping, but the crow despised the medicine so much he hopped out of an open window one day, and even though he was almost completely blind with cataracts, and had one wing completely shot off, he managed to disappear in the woods and we never found him again.

Few birds have to be destroyed to end their suffering. Usually all that is necessary is to put the dying bird in a tightly covered box, in a completely dark closet. The suffering bird reacts exactly as any bird (except an owl) reacts to night. He will remain absolutely quiet. If men could die as easily as birds, narcotics would be almost unnecessary.

In spite of the low fees, and the dubious future of bird-doctoring, I will be a bird doctor forever. Or until I become hard-hearted enough to send a child on her way with a box containing a dying robin.

HAWKS

Brother Hubert Lewis

This is a brief account of one man's observation on the habits of hawks with special reference to food habits and the balance of "good" and "bad" from the standpoint of man's prejudices.

BECAUSE of the large number of used hawks' nests noticed on our hikes a year ago, we decided to make a study of our local hawks. The results were a revelation to me.

How there can be any balance in animal life is now harder for me to understand than ever. The same persons who are complaining of rodents, crows and other destructive small animals wantonly kill the hawks who would easily take care of these and save shells and plenty of money and land if let live.

In all we located five redtail, one broadwing and a cooper's hawk's nest. The latter pair was persuaded to abandon their nest in the "chicken house valley." The redtails being early nesters, we numbered the nests in the order in which they were found. We decided at first to go up to the nests not more than once a week but after we saw the food they were eating we went up more often.

We concentrated on nests 1 and 3 because they were nearest the school and because they were comparatively easy to climb to.

The food which we found in nest 1 was over 90% rodents: mice, gophers, moles and a squirrel. This nest was located near 200 acres of abandoned farm land covered with a ten-year's growth.

The food found in nest 3 was 90% reptiles: blacksnakes, a copperhead, lizards and a crushed turtle. The only other food found at this nest was mice, young crows, a woodpecker, and an immature great horned owl. This nest is located on property partly owned by a man connected with the St. Louis Zoo and who brought the surplus of harmless snakes to the Glencoe area and released them.

Mice seem to be the standard baby food for hawks; we found that to be true for Minnesota redtails also. Snakes seem to be standard for fledglings about to leave the nest. I found five garter snakes on one nest in Minnesota also.

From *The Bluebird*, May 1948.

Getting back to the young crows, on one of my trips to nest 3 I met one of our neighbors through whose lespedeza I was crossing. We both noted the excited calls of some crows. We thought they were after an owl. It was decided to investigate because I knew that there were young crows in this nest, which seemed to be the center of disturbance. As we pushed through the brush the male redtail took to the air from the hawk's nest farther up the valley. While we watched him, bedlam broke loose at the crow's nest. Instead of an owl we saw the unmistakable red tail as the female redtail squirmed to avoid a dive from a crow. She had in a talon what we later found to be a young crow. The speed of the crows as they dived made the hawk appear to be stationary in the air. When the pursued and pursuers approached the hawk's nest the male angled his wings and dove. At least one black wing feather fell. Examination of the crow's nest revealed three where there were five fledglings ten days before. We found the young crow in the hawk's nest.

The boys and I had located seven crows' nests within a mile of the school. These all had clutches of four or five eggs each. As the crows grew we noticed that they were being taken from the nests. We decided that it was the work of owls or other animals. After the above incident we noticed the redtails and broadwings were the causes of some of the crows' frustrations. We then found two nests cleaned out before the crows were able to fly. One of these two was within a block of a broadwing's nest. Of seven crows' nests with 33 eggs only 7 young crows survived.

The same people who are using shells on both hawks and crows could save money and their breath, or is it ink, if nature were allowed to take its course.

The only bird's feathers found about these six nests were a sora rail, a woodpecker, a great horned owl and young crows mentioned before. There was a decided odor of tainted meat from the partly eaten owl. This was the only odor detected about any of the hawks' nests. From a former nest here and two in Minnesota there was a fish odor from nests in which there were large young. I find that all hawks are very clean about the nest. Bones, hair or feathers are removed from the nest as soon as the young are finished with them.

On one trip to nest 3 we could hear a two-weeks old hawk continually calling. I was amused to find that a young hawk is a poor judge of what his stomach will hold. I found a 14 inch blacksnake in a graceful curve; half of it remained unswallowed. He was unable to get it up or down; nor could I help him get it up. His greed retarded his growth for more than a week and nearly ended his life. He was very weak when I went up a few days later.

We did not find a trace of domestic birds being fed to the young on the nest, nor did we find any chicken feathers near any of the nesting sites.

During the summer and early fall when the immature hawks are apparently on their own at least one came near our chicken inclosure and repeated the redtail call by the hour from some dead branch while watching 1000 white young chicks and their elders. Everybody seemed much concerned about the future of the chickens. One of the boys told me he had "hawk trouble." He reported that he found a large hawk walking among the young chickens and that the chickens did not pay any attention to the hawk nor did the hawk harm them. I put his story down as a wild statement. I determined to get first hand information. I concealed myself within shooting distance of the place. I found that the chickens were disturbed even by the calls of a crow, but not by the call of the hawk. The hawk would not come in that day. A few days later word was sent that a hawk was among the chickens. I arrived in time to see the dog chase the hawk into the large trees near the inclosure. It had no chicken with it. The dog was chained and I concealed myself. I did not have to wait long. The immature redtail came down from branch to branch and made the last five or six feet by a short glide into the inclosure and proceeded to walk among the chicks, who, busy pecking at the vegetation, gave the intruder no more than a glance and walked away from what must have appeared to be a giant to them. He made no attempt to strike. On the contrary he seemed to want to find what the chickens were so busily eating. I was able to walk in the open within a hundred feet of the hawk. It took off to its perch near the tops of the trees.

I have since noticed this habit of immature hawks perching near farm yards and repeating their call. I fear that many times it is their undoing. My guess is that the white chickens bring back their associations with the downy companions of the nest.

These reactions will be given further observation this year and I hope others will take a chance also.

Just this week, March 1, a pigeon hawk flew within ten feet of these same chickens which are laying hens now. The hens gave the small hawk one look without showing any signs of fear.

We have a well-trained German shepherd which keeps hawks and crows on the move. He is very solicitous for his chickens.

We had a chance to see how the balance in "nature" works in reverse on hawks. From reports, a broadwing hawk has been nesting near our orchard for several years. The past year the nest was about one quarter of a mile from the school near a road, as is their custom.

The pair was making a good job of clearing our orchard of mice and excess rabbits. On May 14th the first egg was laid. On May 30th, the day on which the squirrel season opened, our illegal hunter "sportsman" shot the male hawk near the nest, though the nest is in the center of a Wild Life Refuge with signs about 100 ft. around the property.

On June 14th only two of the young remained. An egg or a young hawk had disappeared. Crows and blue jays were fighting the mother hawk nearby, as we were to the nest. We were hardly down to the ground when the mother hawk returned to the nest pursued by crows and blue jays. The next day there was but one downy youngster and he was calling; I think for food because his mother could not leave him unprotected. The next day there was no sign of life about the nest. Was it that while the mother was trying to appease the hunger of the youngsters the crows and blue jays put the law of reprisal into action?

Our most unusual hawk episode happened on December 28th, just as we were to start on our winter census hike. I had put out an extra large supply of feed on my window feeder, left the window open 3 or 4 inches and was cleaning the binoculars when a chickadee and a tufted titmouse dashed into the room amid a shower of sunflower seeds and other feed. The chickadee flew against the closed west window crying continuously. The titmouse fastened itself to an open clothes closet door emitting a noise not unlike a large snake. Looking out the window for the cause, I saw a small hawk clinging to the edge of the feeder. I tried to open the window so as to capture him for identification. He watched my hand in an unafraid manner until I made a lunge for him. He flew about 20 feet into a white oak tree and paid no more attention to me. I then went out and found him watching three or four boys. We added a sharpshinned hawk to our list.

With his usual deliberate or assured manner the hawk darted at a spirea bush from which he took an English sparrow with him for a morning snack. He then flew off over the tops of the large trees with his characteristic few flaps and a glide.

BIRD VOICES

OF THE

AUTUMN

Robert Cunningham Miller

Robert Cunningham Miller, Director of the California Academy of Sciences, will be remembered by readers of this volume as the author of a humorous complaint against birds as nuisances. Here he has recovered his composure and looks upon them with favor.

IN the Pacific states Indian summer brings us some of our finest weather, and in coastal regions where there is considerable summer fog it constitutes quite a definite, well-marked season—the long, warm, golden interlude between summer fog and winter rain. It is almost a second springtime, only more subdued and mellow, with more subtle nuances of light and color and sound.

Nature has to be learned by ear as well as by eye. Every experience of the out-of-doors has a sound accompaniment—the crash of a waterfall, the roll of thunder, the sighing of wind in the trees, the crackling of twigs or the swish of grasses as little animals move about their business, the voices of insects and birds. Indian summer has it own complement of musicians, and its own musical score which, lacking the wild rapture of spring, requires more careful listening. If spring provides the crescendo of the symphony, autumn gives us nature's chamber music.

There is the industrious hum of bees, the rhythmic stridulation of grasshoppers, and the cheerful chirp of crickets which—as the weather grows cooler—will find their way indoors to sing their autumn song around the fireplace. And there are the voices of the birds, almost unnoticed till we try to contemplate what an Indian-summer day would be without them.

On a sunny morning in September the juncos pursue one another with cheerful trills and twitters, their song more playful and varied than the somewhat monotonous "territorial" chant of spring—a serious

From *Pacific Discovery*, September–October, 1951.

business then, when the males take up their posts and by persistent song announce their possession of the nesting area and their intention to defend it against all comers. Now the responsibilities of the nesting season are over, food in the form of ripened seeds of weeds and grasses is abundant, the sun is warm, and life is good. Flashing the white inverted V of their outer tail feathers, the juncos dart about with all the happy abandon of children on a picnic.

One hears the nasal *yank, yank, yank* of a wandering nuthatch, the shrill cry of a sparrow hawk, the loud shouts of jays—hardly musical sounds, yet each contributing in its own manner to the character of an Indian-summer day. From the distance comes the lilting trill of a white-crowned sparrow, while close at hand a Bewick wren tries a few exploratory notes, like someone practicing scales and runs on the piano. A pair of wren-tits, mated throughout the year, slip unobtrusively about among the shrubbery, conversing with one another in lovely, liquid syllables, occasionally interspersing gently scolding notes that provide just the right accent to this otherwise too perfect example of conjugal felicity.

The robins begin to gather into flocks. One notices half-a-dozen robins in the yard, and thinks perhaps it is a robin family. Then he sees a score or more of robins on a neighboring lawn, and presently they are going about in flocks of two or three hundred. Robins at this season are comparatively silent, especially considering the size of their flocks; however, they frequently give familiar robin calls, and occasionally, on any sunny day, a short phrase of song.

Many of the bird voices of autumn seem vaguely plaintive and at least one, the *tiu, tiu, tiu* of the rufous-crowned sparrow, sounds downright querulous. Happily it is unlikely that the little feathered complainants feel as dejected as they sound.

Most familiar of the plaintive voices of the autumn is that of the goldfinch, which in its several local races is found throughout most of North America. As goldfinches move about in little flocks in September and October, feeding on weed seeds or flicking out thistledown, their purling calls, marvelously sweet yet tinged with melancholy, bring to Indian summer the gentle sadness of remembered yesterdays.

There is another autumn voice that is still more poignant. As the days grow shorter and the noonday shadows lengthen to the northward, there comes one day a call so indescribably sad and sweet that it might almost be the voice of a disembodied avian spirit. Three notes there are in a descending cadence, not in the diatonic but in a chromatic scale. They have been compared to the opening bars of "Three Blind Mice," but this is only a loose approximation. "Oh, dear me," says the bird, recounting its woes, and then in a different key and with altered emphasis, it repeats, "*Oh, dear* me," as if its heart were bursting with all the sorrows of the avian world. This is the song of the golden-crowned sparrow, newly arrived on its winter feeding grounds; and when one hears it, he inevitably thinks of the lines of William Cullen Bryant:

"The melancholy days are come, the saddest of the year,
Of wailing winds and naked woods and meadows brown and sear."

But nature never leaves us to despair. Even the melancholy days hold promise of happier ones to come. Just as the tide of out-door life seems at its lowest ebb, in the late, dark mornings of December, the Anna hummingbird begins its courtship, and in coastal California the song sparrow bursts forth with its nuptial song. Nature seems ever to be looking forward. Even as the dying year approaches its end, there are bird voices to remind us that we have passed the winter solstice, and that already the days are lengthening toward spring.

THE POPULAR
NAMES OF BIRDS

Ernest Thompson Seton

In most branches of natural history the instructed amateur is likely to call animals or plants by their official Latin names. For some reason or other, bird students as well as mere bird lovers seldom do. They say "house wren" instead of "Troglodytes aedon" and "yellow-bellied sapsucker" instead of "Sphyrapicus varius." This does very well for common birds but it leads in the end to precisely the sort of confusion which the Linnaean system was invented to avoid. The same species gets different names in different regions and the same name is given to different species in different parts of the country.

Hence the attempt on the part of official bodies to standardize popular names and, in effect, to make them "scientific" rather than popular. The attempt is still being made without notable success and it may well be doomed to perpetual failure. In a letter to the editors of The Auk *in 1885, one of the most popular of American naturalists examines the problem and comes to some very sensible conclusions.*

To the Editors of *The Auk:*
The "powers that be," I understand, are preparing a "Check List" and revising the scientific and popular names of our birds.

There is no doubt that scientific names are entirely in the hands of scientists, but it seems to be overlooked that popular names are just as completely in the hands of the people. Scientists may advise, but not dictate on this point. A short analysis of the principle of common names may place the matter in a new light.

A bird's name, to be popular, must be distinctive, and in accordance with the genius of our language. Examples of such are Thrush, Rail, Heron, Hawk, Crane, Nightjar, and many others. These are truly popular names, evolved originally out of description, handed down and condensed and changed until they have assumed their present terse, abrupt,

From *Ernest Thompson Seton's America,* edited by Farida Wiley. New York: Devin-Adair, 1954.

and to a foreign ear uncouth forms, but, nevertheless, forms in accordance with the pervading spirit of the Saxon tongue; or, in other words, they are *really* popular.

On the other hand, look at the so-called popular, but really translated, scientific, spurious English names given to our birds, taking as examples the following: Baird's Bunting, Leconte's Sparrow, Wilson's Green Black-capped Flycatching Warbler, Bartram's Sandpiper, Sprague's Lark, Wilson's Thrush, Black Ptilogonys, Semiplamated Tattler, Fascinated Tit, Florida Gallinule.

Surely, the gentlemen whose names are applied to these birds have not so slight a hold on fame as to require such aids as these to attain it, if indeed aids they be, which I question; for such nomenclature *cannot* stand the test of time.

If you show an "out-wester" the two birds mentioned above as Baird's Bunting and Leconte's Sparrow, and tell him that these are their names, he will probably correct you, and say one is a "Scrub Sparrow," and the other a "Yellow Sparrow." Convince him he is wrong, and in a month he will have forgotten all but the names he formerly gave them; they are so thoroughly appropriate and natural that they cannot be forgotten. The next name in the list above is clumsy enough to strangle itself with its own tail. A lad on the Plains once brought me a *Neocorys spraguei*, and asked its name. I replied it was Sprague's Lark. Soon afterward he came again; he could not remember that name; so I told him it was a "Skylark," and he never forgot that. On the Big Plain that seed was sown, and not all the scientists in America can make, or ever could make, the settlers there call that bird anything but "Skylark." And I consider that lad precisely represented the English-speaking race; he rejected the false name, and readily remembered the true one, and was aided by that which was apt and natural. No better illustration could be given of the fact that phraseology may be the life or death of a cause, according as it is happy or unfortunate.

A similar instance is the case of the "Bartram's Sandpiper." Ever since Wilson's time this name has been continually thrust into the face of the public, only to be continually rejected; "Upland Plover" it continues to be in the East, and "Quaily" on the Assiniboine, in spite of Bartram and Wilson, and will continue so until some name, answering all conditions, is brought forward; for here, as elsewhere, the law of the survival of the fittest rigidly prevails. As an example of the fit ousting the false, note how, in spite of the scientists, "Veery" is supplanting "Wilson's Thrush" throughout the length and breadth of the land.

The spurious English names scarcely need comment, they so evidently contain in themselves the elements of their own destruction. Imagine a western farmer being told that a certain songster was a "Ptilogonys."

In spite of the books, the three examples cannot hold ground against "Willet," "Ground Wren," and "Waterhen," respectively.

The purpose of a check list that includes English names is, I take it, not to attempt the impossible feat of dictating to our woodmen what names they should give their feathered friends, but rather to preserve and publish such names as are evolved in the natural way—names which are the outcome of circumstances. Only in cases of egregious error is a common name to be superseded; and in doing this it must be remembered that no name can be popular unless true to the principles of the English tongue. It must be short, distinctive, and, if possible, descriptive. Of this class are Veery, Junco, and Verio. These are the only successful artificial names that I can at present recollect. Among natural English names for American birds are Bobolink, Chewink, Kingbird, and many others. Such as these not only more than hold their own, but are as great aids to the spread of knowledge as the Ptilogonys kind are hindrances; while such as Wilson's Thrush can only be accepted as provisional, until better knowledge of the bird and its surroundings shall result in the evolution of an English name founded on true principles.

ERNEST E. T. SETON
of Manitoba

Glen Cottage, Howard Street,
Toronto, March 21, 1885

HOW LONG

DOES IT TAKE

TO PAINT

A BIRD PICTURE?

Athos and Sara Menaboni

Athos and Sara Menaboni appeared earlier in this book as bird lovers as well as bird painters. Here is some account of how they work as artists.

THE vultures were cheated of a meal when, on the way back from Florida, we picked up a little pig that some automobile had killed. We brought it to Valle Ombrosa[1] as a gift. . . .

I think I had better go back to the beginning of this story. It will answer in still another way the question that is invariably asked by everyone we meet for the first time: "How long does it take to paint a bird picture?" This story, then, will give some idea of how long it took a certain picture to come into being. It is infinitely more important, however, as an instance of how people enter into the picture of our lives.

One day we received a letter from an unknown sergeant stationed at Fort MacPherson, just outside Atlanta, who was working as an entymologist, although in civilian life he had studied ornithology. He had seen Mr. Menaboni's bird pictures and would like to meet the artist. But perhaps he should get a formal introduction from one of the ornithological professors at Cornell University?

We do not like formality. Cornell was "way up yonder" in New York State. I wrote to the sergeant that all that was necessary for him to do was to telephone us and set a time when he could come to Valle Ombrosa. The following Sunday afternoon he came. We dismissed formality, and right away started swapping bird lore.

In the course of the conversation, the sergeant said that he had written

From *Menaboni's Birds,* New York: Rinehart & Company, 1950.
[1] Valle Ombrosa, the Menabonis' home and bird refuge in Atlanta, Georgia.

an article about a golden eagle he had once had, and he asked if Athos had ever had a living eagle? When Athos answered in the negative, he told us how sorry he had been to have to refuse an offer from the San Diego Zoo of a young golden eagle, because he was just at that time entering the service. Did Athos want the eagle, if it was still available? Imagine asking Athos if he *wanted* a golden eagle!

Our new friend wrote to the director of the San Diego Zoo about the matter, who answered that the golden eagle would be given to Athos if he would pay the transportation costs. Imagine asking Athos *if* he would pay the express charges!

When the express company notified me over the telephone that the crated eagle had arrived in Atlanta, I drove blithely into town to fetch our new bird. But after I saw the size of the roomy crate, my heart sank; there was no possible way to put it into the automobile or tie it on. I should have to get a delivery truck.

The sympathetic expressman started calling transfer companies for me. The reply he got was: "The OPA[2] will not let us deliver that far into the country. It is out of our zone." Company after company he telephoned, in vain. The expressman was beginning to feel very sorry for me, and I was becoming frantic. Here was a bird, the like of which we had never expected to own, but which Providence had sent our way. He had crossed the entire continent and now there was no way of getting him transported a measly fourteen miles to Valle Ombrosa. Something was vitally wrong in the setup.

The expressman called the number of the last transfer company in the telephone book, then quickly handed the receiver to me, saying, "You see if you have any luck!" I am a long-winded talker, and I gave my spiel so fast and pleadingly that the man at the other end of the line had no chance to insert a hasty "No." Finally he interrupted me: "Listen, lady, let me say a word, will you? Just where is Cook Road?"

I told him, and he said that he lived not far from me. We began chatting about the neighbors we both knew, how much we liked the section in which we lived, and at long last he said, "This evening I am taking a load of pipes to my home on my truck. I'll put the eagle box on top of the pipes and route my way home via your house and drop off the eagle for you."

I wanted to shout in sheer gratitude but I only thanked him for getting me out of a fix.

When the man arrived at Valle Ombrosa with the eagle, he was so interested in our birds and enjoyed himself so much that he did not want a fee for the delivery, and we had to force it upon him.

Through the wire we could see the huge bird, with fierce eyes and

[2] This was during World War II.

menacing-looking talons. Frankly, I was afraid. Athos admitted that two persons would be necessary to handle the strong bird, so I telephoned to the sergeant to come help take the eagle from the crate, since he had had experience in handling eagles.

My fear had been unjustified, for all John and Athos had to do was wrap the eagle in a leather jacket while they put jesses on the legs, attached a chain to these specially fashioned leather straps, and fastened the chain, which had a swivel, to a post. It might be a simple matter for people with experience, but I noticed that they worked with hands encased in heavy leather gloves. What kept the procedure from being difficult or really dangerous was that the eagle was already tame.

After the eagle was settled and beginning to get his bearings, we discussed how we were going to feed him. In a separate little box the San Diego Zoo had put two live guinea pigs, with instructions for the trainmen to kill them on certain days in transit. But after they had killed one and it had not been eaten, they used good sense in not offering the other. The sergeant suggested that he bring a mate for the guinea pig, then guinea pigs could be raised for eagle-food. The following Sunday he brought the guinea pig from the Medical Laboratory, and thus began a new experience for us, for we'd never had guinea pigs at Valle Ombrosa. Also, he brought three dead rabbits that had been used for experimental purposes. He said that he would continue to bring rabbits until the guinea pigs multiplied in sufficient numbers, for he felt a joint ownership-responsibility for the eagle.

That day a girl was here who asked, "What will you name the eagle?" I told her that she could name him for us.

She thought for a few minutes, looked at the sergeant's uniform insignia, and said: "Since he got the eagle for you, let's name him 'The Sergeant'—Sarge for short." (Later, when our friend was promoted to a lieutenant, the Sarge retained his former rank.)

The Sergeant was not happy. He refused to eat the rabbits or anything else offered to him. We worried considerably during the two weeks he fasted until finally he decided to eat. He did not learn to go inside his house during rain or the hot midday, but stayed on his outside post, or flew the length of the chain. It was not pleasant for us to watch him from our windows in this unhappy state, angrily chewing at the leather jesses that he knew fettered him. The Sergeant did not like dogs, and Yama[3] kept a respectful distance from this king of birds. However, when we approached him, he was not afraid of us, ate from our hands, and would let us scratch the back of his neck.

One day Athos was painting and happened to look out the window

[3] Yama, the Menabonis' dog, who helped pamper and care for their birds.

toward the eagle outside. In a mad scramble, he ran to the door, yelling to me, "The eagle has got loose!"

I dashed to the door, then stopped still in my tracks as I saw Athos make a football player's lunge at the eagle on the terrace wall as the bird was about to spring into the air. My thought was: Athos's hands will be torn to shreds—what is the doctor's telephone number?

In a split second, Athos had grabbed both the legs at the same time, and was holding them tight, with the talons away from his body. As calmly as you please, Athos held the Sarge in his arms and I let out a sigh of relief.

As per instructions, I carried the leather jacket to Athos and helped wrap the eagle in it. Then we stood for ten minutes discussing what to do next. The Sergeant did not struggle; patiently he waited for us to make the decision not to put jesses on him again, and to abandon the special eagle-house that had been built for him by the wall of the front terrace and which he had disliked from the first.

I chased some silver Sebright bantams from one of the "rooms" of the aviary, and the Sergeant was put there. He liked it! No more jesses on his legs, a nice roof to get under during rain and hot sun, a suitable perch, lots of room in which to fly. He made himself at home.

Never again could we scratch the back of his neck, but we could go into his cage whenever we wished. He allowed photographers to enter, but he did not enjoy the procedure of being photographed by strangers. After many such experiences, one day the Sarge got tired of everybody crowding into his cage chasing him around to get him in good photographic positions. It was as though he said aloud, "I'm going to put a stop to this," for he raised his head feathers in anger—the danger signal, which Athos recognized—and made a motion that indicated he was about to attack. Athos said, "We must scram!" and we cleared out of the cage in record time!

The Sergeant realized his triumph, for the next day he did the same trick to clear photographers out of his private domain. No more strangers in his lair! They could look at him through the wire, and he would show off his seven-foot wingspread, but they had to respect his rank by not being too familiar. Athos and I could enter his cage, yes, for we were home folk, but no one else.

Of course by now you have guessed that the dead pig we brought home from our trip to Florida was for the Sarge. Food for him was a real problem during wartime rationing of meat; besides, meat from the butcher was not a proper diet all the time. Our friends entered into the spirit of the hunt, and it was amazing what a quantity of rabbits, squirrels, and opossums could be found dead on roads. However, the last-named were not relished, and I informed the fortune-hunting friends not to get possum any more. Mind you, all this was during gasoline rationing also, and our friends used their precious gas to drive to Valle Ombrosa, or I used ours to go miles for the prizes. Everyone had problems and we managed somehow; every morning the Sergeant wanted his breakfast.

Shortly after we got the eagle, some friends who knew we had open house every Sunday afternoon, brought their out-of-town visitors to Valle Ombrosa. Right then a Long Island couple fell in love with the Sergeant and asked Athos to paint a portrait of the bird.

They had to wait a year and a half for the picture. Athos studied the bird in a thousand poses, sketched him in the cage, and while painting the actual picture, returned time after time to look at the coloration. When the picture was finished, our friends came to Atlanta again. After they had seen it, they insisted that we must have a dinner party downtown, and hurriedly assembled our mutual friends to celebrate that night. With champagne, we drank a toast: "To the Sergeant!"

It is hard to answer the question, "How long does it take to paint a bird picture?" It is not a matter of how many days Athos works at his easel. I believe it would be more pertinent to ask: "What goes into a Menaboni bird picture?"

And this is not the kind of a story that ends abruptly, for today I am paying a price in loneliness for the Sergeant's sake. Athos has gone off for the day hunting with a friend to try to get some rabbits for the Sergeant. The food problem is always with us.

EAGLE

MAN

Ted Shane

If we may believe the many articles in the better magazines the problem of the retired businessman who doesn't know what to do with his so-called "golden years" is second in seriousness only to juvenile delinquency. Unfortunately, the solution is not usually as easy or as satisfactory as it proved to be in the case of Charles Lavelle Broley, who had had the good sense to develop a hobby during the course of his career as a banker. Most men of sixty would not take kindly to the suggestion that they should become eagle watchers and learn to climb into nests high in swaying treetops. But Mr. Broley was already a confirmed bird watcher and he promptly specialized in eagles with the results detailed below. Perhaps it is worth mentioning that "bald eagle" is so called because "white" is the older meaning of "bald" and as every patriotic American knows, it is the white-headed and not the golden eagle which is our national symbol.

EN route from Winnipeg, Canada, to Florida in January 1939, Charles Lavelle Broley stopped at the headquarters of the National Audubon Society in New York. Crowding 60, he had just retired as a bank manager; as a confirmed bird watcher, he wondered if he could put his new leisure to use for the society.

Wildlife custodians were worried about the bald eagle, our national symbol, which was in danger of extinction. Little was known about its migratory and personal habits, and it was being shot on sight as a common chicken thief.

Richard Pough, now chief of conservation for the American Museum of Natural History, gave Broley a few aluminum identification tags, and suggested he try banding eagles. Only 166 of the birds had been banded; their eyries were perched dizzily in tall trees or other inaccessible places. "Naturally you won't be able to do any climbing," Pough said. "Get a boy for that, and you can do the easy part—the banding."

From *Lifetime Living*. January 1953.

In the Tampa Bay area of Florida, it was then common to see the big white-headed birds soaring regally over the shorelands. Broley found himself a brash 16-year old and went eyrie-hunting. They sighted Nest One in the deep-tangled flatlands back of Gibsonton. From a distance it looked like a clump of Spanish moss. Up close it was as big as a small car, cup-shaped, near the top of a sturdy pine whose lowest branch was 40 feet from the ground.

The ex-banker was slightly nervous. There were no handbooks on banding eagles, and Broley's equipment was homemade. Would Mama and Papa Eagle interfere? How do you catch a falling boy?

Broley, an old lacrosse player, took aim and threw a lead weight tied to a fishline over the 40-foot limb. As he hauled up a rope ladder via the line, two eagles zoomed up from the nest. The lad mounted the swaying ladder and pulled himself up into the huge stickpile. Broley heard a yell, saw him seize a stick from the nest and begin fencing with an unseen adversary. Then a young bird backflipped from the nest into the underbrush 500 feet away.

Broley found the eaglet cowering under a saw palmetto. It was a magnificent dark-brown youngster, about 11 weeks old but still unable to fly. When he grabbed the bird's legs, it slashed out with its scimitar beak and its big talons hooked deeply into his hand. Painfully he pried them out with his banding pliers and lugged the bird like a chicken back to the tree. There he found his assistant, white-faced and bleeding. Wrestling the eaglet, they got it banded and into a canvas bag for the return trip to the nest.

Broley hadn't shinned up a tree in 45 years, but since the shaking boy was in no condition to go, he began the giddy climb up the rope ladder. In the nest he found another eaglet. He approached with caution, but this baby did not protest when he banded it.

As he runged down the quivering ladder he was sweating, and he was bloody. "But," he says, "I had banded my first eagle. And I knew I was going to like it."

After that, Broley did his own climbing. He ran out of bands and telegraphed for more. Pough sent them with the reminder, "Don't let your boy take unnecessary risks."

When the nesting season slacked off in March, the ex-banker had banded a total of 44 young eagles. He had lost 15 pounds, had thrown away his outdoor glasses, and had never felt better in his life. He was also learning that the eagle is a much-libeled bird. Not one adult had attacked him, and he has yet to see an eagle toting anything but the food it normally eats—large fish. [Of 800 nests he has examined, he has found chicken bones in only two.]

While Broley spent that summer at his home in Ontario, one of his bands was "recovered" near Poughkeepsie, N.Y., 1100 miles from Florida; its wearer had died for alleged chicken theft. Another band was found in New Brunswick, Canada; a third on Prince Edward Island. Like any tourist, the Florida bald eagle appeared to summer in the North. The following winter, provided with a gross of bands and a U. S. Fish and Wildlife badge, Broley returned to Florida and found so many eyries he had to number and map them. Citizens began phoning the police to report a crank who was climbing trees. Three times Broley was clapped in jail for "molesting birds." Back-country folk, suspecting he was a "revenooer," lit brush fires while he was aloft, to burn his car and maroon him.

His 1940 Florida score was 76 bandings. That summer he tackled 20 eyries in the elms of Ontario—some of them 110 feet up. He tied two ladders together to reach lower branches 60 feet high, then steeplejacked himself into the penthouses to find them tenanted by northern cousins of his Florida babies—slightly larger, and equally sharp-clawed and spirited.

What had begun as a casual hobby was now a new life. Broley began tackling the 115-foot Florida cypresses, wading waist-deep through the swamps with his 65 pounds of ladders, ropes, tools, cameras and snakebite juice poised atop his bald head, marking his way in and out with the skill of an Indian.

In 1946 Broley became the Babe Ruth of banding—tagging 150 eaglets, 14 in one day. That report alarmed Richard Pough. His protege was 67 now, an age when elderly gentlemen climb into rocking chairs, not eagle roosts. He tried to get him to quit. "What would I do, play shuffleboard?" inquired Broley. "I don't know how."

His banding trips are mostly lone affairs, but recently some have become public events, with as many as 1000 spectators. Fan mail has found him which was addressed simply: "Eagle Man, Tampa, Fla."

As Broley accumulated eagle lore, he set out to correct public misunderstanding. At schools and club meetings, on radio and TV, he has plugged for preservation of our national bird. Watching his splendid slides and movies of eagle life, his audiences have done more falling than he. "I fell out of every tree you climbed!" one woman gasped at him.

He has had some close calls. When one nest gave away beneath him, he saved himself by grabbing an overhanging branch. Next day he came back and jacked up the nest with two-by-fours. Another time, a limb he was standing on snapped under him. His sickening plunge was stopped short when his pants caught on a branch stub. "I felt foolish," he admits, "just hanging there. It took me an hour to squirm around and rip my pants open, then slide down the trunk. I was lucky to get home even in a barrel."

"What brings my heart to my mouth," Mrs. Broley says, "is seeing him stand on a branch 80 feet up, nonchalantly toss a rope over a higher branch, and climb that. I don't like it when he has to pull the ladder up after him to get into very high nests. That means he has to come down with the ladder not fastened at the bottom at all, and he swings and sways dizzily, especially if there's a high wind."

Broley never knows what he'll find when he steps into an eagle's nest. The great horned owl, a militant character with a six-foot wing-spread and murderous claws, often takes over an eyrie. Last year Broley was nearly knocked out of an eyrie when a mother owl swooped in noiselessly on her down-lined wings. He has been besieged by hornets and by irate flying squirrels.

Ornithologists agree that Broley hasn't climbed in vain. He has proved that the Florida eagle practices "reverse migration"—it nests *before* it goes north—and travels as far northwest as Lake Winnipeg, 2400 miles away. It flies at great speeds: one bandee left Tampa on May 21, and was "recovered" on May 24 near the Arctic Circle. The $500 fine for shooting the bald eagle or taking its eggs and young from the nest for commercial zoos stems from the publicity Broley has given the monarch of the air.

Nevertheless the number of birds shows a steady, tragic decline. Since the 1946 peak, Broley's score for bandings has dwindled alarmingly each year. Ten percent of the 1200 birds he has banded have been shot. The way things are going, ornithologists gloomily predict, the bald eagle may be extinct by the year 2000. Here and there eagle lovers have chipped in and brought eyrie trees, and recently W. K. Vanderbilt set aside 12,000 acres near Venice, Fla., as a sanctuary.

Today, at 73, Broley is a lithe and sinewy 150-pounder of medium height. He opens his day with a dozen hoists on a chinning bar, eats only breakfast and dinner, doesn't smoke or drink. Radiating physical and mental health, the Eagle Man has proved that retirement can be just the beginning of life. "When you sit in a treetop and look out over the world," he explains, "it does something to your point of view."

TWENTIETH-CENTURY AUDUBON

Cedric Larson

We have met Roger Tory Peterson before. Perhaps no one else in all history has done more to popularize "bird watching" both as a hobby and as a serious study. He is also a fascinating personality of whom the following gives some interesting glimpses.

A GENERATION ago the study of birds was chiefly for museum men and a sprinkling of university professors. Today it is estimated that there are close to five million adult Americans and hundreds of thousands of school children who have an interest of some kind in birds.

This phenomenon is not confined to this country, for here and abroad the study of birds has gained a widespread popularity in the past fifteen years which is nothing less than astonishing.

Roger Tory Peterson—one of the world's foremost authorities on birds and a man whose bird books in 7 languages are currently selling 100,000 copies a year—has an explanation all his own for this prevalent interest:

"Birds can fly where they want to when they want to," he observes. "At least so it seems to us, who are earthbound. They symbolize a degree of freedom that we would nearly give our souls to have. Perhaps this is why bird watching has almost become a national hobby in Britain and is rapidly becoming one here.

"It is an antidote for the disillusionment of today's world, a world beset by pressures it has never before known. Many men in business and the professions find in birds a much-needed balance, a release from their highly complex affairs and the artificiality of the city.

"Housewives find in birds a pleasant relief from the routine of the home, and children enjoy their pursuit for the outlet it gives their abundant energies. Boys in their teens make the keenest bird recorders, for once they fall under the spell of the 'lure of the list,' they play the game for all it is worth."

Dr. Peterson points out that in the eastern half of the United States,

From *Natural History*, May 1956.

from the Atlantic Ocean to the 100th meridian, which runs from central North Dakota through central Texas, there are approximately 440 different kinds of birds. In 35 years of watching, Peterson has seen all but 4 of them.

This modern-day Audubon is what a sports writer might call a triple-·threat man. Besides being an ornithologist of the first caliber, he is a skilled artist, a lecturer, a writer, and an expert photographer. He is the author of scores of articles and booklets on birds, and his *Field Guide to the Birds* has sold 350,000 copies in its eastern editions alone.

Dr. Peterson has traveled on four continents studying and photographing birds. In a typical year, he will be away from his home half or perhaps two-thirds of the time, either in the field or lecturing.

When Dr. Peterson is not on a bird safari or another errand having to do with birds, he may be located for brief periods with his wife and two boys in their Connecticut home. The Peterson home is situated on a 55-acre estate at Old Lyme, Connecticut, near Long Island Sound, on an eminence overlooking the Connecticut River estuary.

They purchased this home in the fall of 1954, and already their address is known to thousands of bird lovers on five continents. Their house, fittingly enough, is surrounded by a dense and bushy forest, where scores of species of birds nest and fly about in gay pageantry.

For the first eight years after World War II, the Petersons rented a place overlooking the Potomac River in the Washington suburb of Glen Echo, their home being remodeled slave quarters high on a river bluff. After years of searching, they finally decided on their present location—midway between Boston and New York.

This proved an ideal place, for here Peterson is only a short way from the headquarters of his publishers—Houghton-Mifflin in Boston—and not too far from the headquarters of the National Audubon Society in Manhattan, of which he is now a member of the Board of Directors.

The Peterson story starts in Jamestown, New York, where Roger was born on August 28, 1908. His father was Charles Gustav Peterson from Värmland, Sweden, who came to this country at the age of four. When the family settled in Jamestown, it was virtually a Swedish community. The town lies in the hills of western New York near famed Lake Chautauqua, a district rich in wildlife. Roger's grandfather died when his father was only eleven, making it necessary for the boy to go to work in the factories and mills at an early age.

When Roger was born, his father was a craftsman in the Art Metal Construction Company, one of the city's furniture factories. Few of Roger's grade-school teachers would have regarded him as a budding genius or a model child. He was, in fact, something of a problem, and he still holds the dubious distinction of having been spanked oftener in the sixth grade than any other boy in the history of the school. Seven times in one term he marched the dreary path to the principal's office.

But the seventh grade proved a turning point in his life. His science teacher, Miss Blanche Hornbeck, organized an Audubon Junior Club and obtained leaflets that turned Roger's attention to birds. So, at the age of eleven he embarked, in a sense, on his life's work. He still feels that his great interest in birds at that age stemmed from the fact that these winged creatures were symbols of freedom in his maladjusted youth. And he can still recall the exact date of every bird trip he made during the first five or six years of his new-found enthusiasm.

Dr. Peterson recalls with a smile that Miss Hornbeck knew little about birds but learned with the class. They studied the Audubon Junior leaflets together—leaflets that he was to rewrite and reillustrate 20 years later. Miss Hornbeck had the children copy the pictures, and Roger was launched on a career that was to win him world-wide recognition as a bird artist. He used to decorate the margins of his arithmetic and history books with pictures of eagles, hawks, and owls.

As a boy of eleven, he searched the environs of Jamestown and Lake Chautauqua for birds. He would even range along the southern shores of near-by Lake Erie—about 25 miles north—to find waterfowl. Later he wrote: "The mere glimpse of a bird would change my listlessness to fierce intensity. I lived for birds."

His preoccupation with birds did not evoke wholehearted support in the minds of his parents. His father was a practical man and was plainly worried about his son's obsession. Roger seemed not to care how long he was away from home or how muddy or torn he got his clothes, as long as he could watch birds. Once his father stopped the boy's English teacher on the street in Jamestown and said: "Roger likes you a lot. I wish you'd tell him there are other things in the world besides birds. He'll never make a living out of them."

At other times, his father seemed to take pride in his son's knowledge of birdlore. "He can name any kind of bird he sees," he would boast to his intimates. "And he can draw them all." As the years have proved, he missed by a mile in thinking that Roger could not make a living from birds.

Training in art

After leaving high school, Roger came to New York to attend the Art Students League and also the National Academy of Design. He studied under such well-known artists of the day as John Sloan and Nikolaides. His skill as an artist is so considerable that he can draw or paint almost anything with great success, but he limits himself mostly to birds.

When the depression of the 1930s terminated his five years of art training, he obtained a teaching position with a boys' school in Boston, where he taught natural history, art, and astronomy. He admits today with a twinkle in his eye that his knowledge of astronomy at the time was nil and that he kept just one lesson ahead of the boys all through the year. He taught in this Brookline, Massachusetts, school for four years. It was during this time that fate, in the form of a friend who was an ornithologist, intervened in Peterson's life to set him on the road to fame and fortune.

Up until this time, most books on bird identification were formidable scientific treatises, bristling with technical jargon and phraseology confusing to the layman. Peterson, who had taught himself bird identification without help, was an expert in his hobby. During his trips to New York, he took frequent bird walks with a friend he had met at the American Museum of Natural History—conservationist William Vogt (of *Road to Survival* fame). Vogt was astounded at the speed with which Peterson could identify birds and persuaded him to write some magazine articles on this subject.

It was apparent to Vogt that Peterson had a revolutionary system, a magical short cut, as it were, to bird identification. After the magazine articles, Vogt advised Peterson to put his system in book form and illustrate it with his own patternistic drawings.

A few months later, the book manuscript was finished, but this was during the height of the depression, and first books by new authors were not easy to place. None of the first five publishers to whom he submitted it were interested. One or two of them were scornful, telling him he was a nobody in the bird field and that his book would not sell.

But the Houghton-Mifflin Company in Boston had two bird enthusiasts on its editorial staff. After much deliberation, they decided to take a flyer on the book, albeit with qualms and misgivings. They cautiously printed 2000 copies, after first stating that the author would get no royalties on the first 1000.

The book proved to be the kind that publishers dream about. It had a runaway sale, and the first edition sold out in five days. Five thousand more copies of Peterson's *Field Guide to the Birds* were rushed off the presses. A month later they were all gone. The book had made a great hit among bird lovers, and Peterson found himself something of a celebrity overnight.

This all happened in 1934. Since then a third of a million copies have been sold, and the book has been revised twice. The last revision was in 1947, when Dr. Peterson rewrote the whole book and reworked the entire system. Now Houghton-Mifflin never prints fewer than 50,000 at a time. A companion volume, *A Field Guide to Western Birds*, published in 1941, has sold 115,000 copies. And a similar volume, *A Field Guide to the Birds of Britain and Europe,* has recently been issued in Britain. Editions of this are being published in Dutch, French, German, Spanish, Italian, and the three Scandinavian tongues. The text in these various editions may vary somewhat, but the Peterson system is the same. Since 1934, more than 900,000 copies of Peterson's books have been sold throughout the world.

His *Guide* has been so widely accepted that bird watchers simply call it "Peterson," giving rise to the quip that "Peterson has gone out with more women on Sunday afternoon than any man in history." Recently an ardent bird lover in Philadelphia wrote: "The *Field Guide* is now being called around Philadelphia 'The Gospel of Saint Peterson.'"

Interestingly enough, the Army and Navy were influenced by the Peterson system in teaching plane-spotting in World War II. In that field, as in bird identification, it served better than any other method. The system is based on shape, pattern, and the simple but clever idea of using "pointers" on recognition pictures of birds, designed to bring out the crucial points of difference.

His book showed how to spot a bird quickly and accurately from its silhouette and pattern and stressed the one or two characteristics that set it apart from other or similar birds. Gone into the discard was the need for floundering through tedious technical descriptions. With Peterson's book, the most amateurish bird watcher could not only identify a bird in an instant but could do it at a distance. It has been called the most practical bird guide ever to appear.

This book won for Peterson a job with the National Audubon Society in New York as Educational Director. While serving in this capacity, he spent his evenings and vacations preparing his *Field Guide to Western Birds,* which covers the birds west of the 100th meridian.

Varied war work

Then came the draft in World War II. The Army gave him a job doing technical manuals at Fort Belvoir, Virginia, where he spent two years on such topics as defusing land mines and building bridges. He was assigned to the Engineer Corps to utilize his artistry for camouflage, but he was trained as a combat engineer. Toward the end of the war he was shifted to the Air Corps, where he was put to work studying the effects of D.D.T.

Before entering the Army, Roger met, in the film and photography department of the National Audubon Society, a young lady named Barbara Coulter, who was from Seattle. They were married in 1943 and now have two boys: Tory, age ten, and Lee, six.

After the war and out of the Army, Roger and his wife made a big decision. Instead of going back to a regular job, he would try freelancing.

He rewrote the *Eastern Field Guide* and redid its pictures. He painted many birds for national magazines and illustrated a series of a dozen articles in full color, for *Life* Magazine. He prepared a "primer" edition of his *Field Guide* in a 35¢ edition, which sold 250,000 copies. He was deluged by requests for paintings and lectures.

· He launched a series of bird prints, rivaling Audubon's and selling in lithographed copies for $5 to $15 each. He painted about 30 of them, and collectors snapped them up. An enterprising New York City department store copywriter once advertised them as "Genuine Audubon prints by Peterson."

Dr. Peterson published his *Birds Over America* in 1948 (Dodd-Mead), a 342-page book illustrated with 105 photographs by the author. This book was a great success and won thousands of new converts to the ranks of the bird watchers. It won for its author the coveted John Burroughs Medal, bestowed by the John Burroughs Memorial Association, for meritorious nature writing.

Since 1945, Dr. Peterson has made repeated trips to Europe and has ranged all over North America, visiting many other out-of-the-way places. He has become an expert photographer, both in still and motion pictures, and he worries his budget-minded wife by his frequent investments in costly photographic equipment. One of his movie cameras is equipped with a special 12-inch Kilfitt lens. He lectures for the National Audubon Society one month each year and tries to reach a different region of the U.S.A. each time. He regards his lecture tours as a good antidote to his hermit's life in his Connecticut studio.

Sometimes people ask Dr. Peterson if scientists haven't just about discovered all there is to know about birds. He smiles patiently at such naïve questions and points out that there are about 8600 species of birds in the world, not counting subspecies. North America alone has more than 650 resident species north of the Mexican border.

"We have today only scratched the surface in our study of birds—particularly in the field of bird behavior," he declares. He places the present bird population of the U.S.A. at five to six billion breeding land birds and an unknown number of water birds. He says that the notion that man has displaced birds on this continent is open to considerable doubt. There may be fewer hawks, owls, and large game birds than in Columbus' time, but many ornithologists are sure that there are more songbirds.

Birds, he points out, are hardy creatures. They have to be to survive. And—perhaps more important—they are highly adaptable. Songbirds seem to thrive better in the broken, semiopen country that follows civilization than in virgin forests or tropical jungles.

Since World War II, Roger Peterson has distinguished himself in other aspects of natural history, although ornithology is his primary love. He has edited field guides on butterflies, mammals, flowers, trees, minerals, reptiles, and other subjects.

Recognition

In 1952 he received the honorary degree of Doctor of Science from Franklin and Marshall College. He is a fellow of the American Ornithologists Union and was awarded this scientific society's Brewster Medal for the second edition of his *Field Guide*. From 1951 to 1953, he served as president of the American Nature Study Society, a group composed of teachers and others who are concerned with nature study.

Around Jamestown, New York, Dr. Peterson is the shining example of the "local-boy-makes-good" tradition. They have forgotten his one-time childish pranks, such as going down the fire escape when the dismissal bell rang in school. A year or two ago, the Jamestown Chamber of Commerce had a Roger Tory Peterson Day and presented him with a special Certificate of Recognition.

We asked Dr. Peterson about his rather unusual middle name, Tory. He explained with a smile that it did not identify him as an ultraconservative in politics. Rather, it was a sort of special variant of the Swedish name "Thure," by which his uncle was called. When he had to tell his first-grade teacher his middle name, he could pronounce it but not spell it, and she wrote it down just as it sounded to her—"T-O-R-Y." That rendering of a good old Swedish name has stuck to him through life.

One of his close associates, Carl W. Buchheister, senior vice-president of the National Audubon Society and director of the Audubon Camp of Maine, thinks that Peterson has probably done more to promote popular interest in birds than any man since Audubon, which is quite a tribute, coming from a professional colleague.

No story of Peterson's career would be complete without an account of his record-breaking grand tour of North America. For 100 days he traveled in company with the distinguished British birdman James Fisher (described as Peterson's "opposite number" in Britain and Europe). The idea arose because James Fisher had left no stone unturned in assisting Peterson in his European travels and in his writing on Europe's birds. They had collaborated on some work, and a firm friendship had sprung up between them. So in the early 1950s, Peterson planned a tour for his friend. He felt it highly desirable for some opinion-making European to see the full grandeur of North America, and especially our conservation work and wildlife management. The trip was a sort of "ambassadorial gesture," as Dr. Peterson puts it, to enable James Fisher to interpret a different phase of America to Europe than the average European gets on a trip to America.

The outcome was the now-famous 100-day tour. It commenced on April 10, 1953, when they met in Newfoundland. It ended in mid-July, when James Fisher left his friend in the Alaskan area and returned to Britain. It has been said that not even John James Audubon in all his lifetime covered as much of the North American wilderness as did Roger Tory Peterson and his distinguished English colleague in those 100 adventurous days.

A little over a century after Audubon, and partly tracing his trail, they started in Newfoundland and went south along the Appalachian highlands to Cape Sable and the Dry Tortugas, America's coral islands. They then struck west and south into the cloud forests of Mexico. Passing over the continental divide and deserts to the Coronado Islands, they traveled up the entire length of the Pacific coast to Alaska, where their journey reached its climax in the Pribilofs. There they saw the 1,500,000 fur seals of the fabulous seal islands.

Fisher covered in all some 30,000 miles. The two naturalists made the trip by car and plane, driving in Dr. Peterson's station wagon in most of continental United States and Mexico. They probably covered more wild country of North America in a single trip than anyone has ever done before.

The voluminous notes that both men took on this trip finally metamorphosed into a fascinating, profusely illustrated book entitled *Wild America*, written by them jointly. It received prominent notice in the book and scientific world. Both the *Chicago Tribune* and the *New York Herald-Tribune* featured it with page-one reviews, and it has been a bestseller in its field around the country since. This 434-page book is illustrated by scores of drawings by Roger Tory Peterson—wild animals, reptiles, forests, mountains, trees, Eskimos, and plant life, with, of course, more birds than any other category. It is the kind of book that could scarcely have been written prior to our era of airliners and superhighways.

Anyone who gets to know Dr. Peterson cannot help but be struck by his almost boyish enthusiasm for his work. He embarks on every field trip with all the ardor of a sort of super boy scout, and every trip is a new adventure, every day brimming with fascination. Yet this enthusiasm for birds and birdlore has nothing sentimental or immature about it. It is rather the manifestation of a deep-seated love of occupation, too often missing in adults, the passion of a man whose vocation in life is also his avocation.

He loves nature in a philosophical way, yet he sees natural phenomena in a lucid, objective, and realistic manner. He has a gift for expressing his feelings about nature in a simple, forthright style. His writings for children have been especially successful. Most of his books are illustrated with his own photographs or drawings. Dr. Peterson likes to be with children and will let formal appointments wait while he talks to a teenager about the wonders of the outdoor world. Seven million children have read his pamphlets in the Audubon Junior Clubs.

Dr. Peterson is a man of genuine humility and his honors have never changed him a bit. What better testimony could there be of the influence that the world of nature can have on the personality of one who has become absorbed with its beauties and mysteries?

BIRD BANDING—

THE HOWS

AND WHYS

Department of the Interior

Bird banding is a relatively modern technique but it has added more than perhaps any other to our knowledge of bird life. Millions of metal or plastic tags have been attached to millions of legs and an astonishing proportion of them have been recovered, often in distant lands. A band makes a bird an individual—you know who he is, where he has been, how long he has lived since he was first captured. The momentary discomfort of the captured bird is trivial and there is perhaps no other experimental interference with his life which so completely avoids even a suspicion of cruelty.

THREE Pintail ducks from North America were shot in widely separated places in far distant parts of the world. One duck was taken near Cali, Colombia, South America; one on an island in the Pacific, and the third along the Dart River in England. The South American hunter learned that his duck had come from North Dakota. The weatherman in the Pacific discovered that his bird had been in northern California, more than 4600 miles away, just 3 months before. The English sportsman found that his Pintail duck just 21 days before had been in Labrador, some 2200 miles across the Atlantic. How did these men know that their ducks had come from North America?

It really isn't such a mystery as it might seem. On the leg of each duck the hunter had found a small aluminum band. The band carried a number and a request that the finder of the band report to the Fish and Wildlife Service in Washington, D.C., U.S.A. Each hunter did exactly that. When their letters reached the Service in Washington they were sent to the Bird Banding Office. Records of the wild birds banded in North America are kept in this office. Here it is that the band number, species, date of banding, place of banding, and name of the bander are recorded. When some one sends in a band he has found, the record can be located quickly.

From *Conservation Notes*. Washington, D.C.: U. S. Department of the Interior.

Coming back to the letters of the three hunters—workers soon found the three numbers among the 11 million banding records registered in the office. Then they sent each hunter a letter telling him the kind of bird he had taken, when and where it had been banded, and who banded it. Since banders are interested in knowing what happens to the birds they band, a letter was sent to the bander of each Pintail duck to tell him who had recovered the banded bird and when and where it was found.

As far as we know the first bird band ever to be recovered was found on a Gray Heron in Germany in 1710. The heron had been banded in Turkey several years before. Modern bird banding really had its beginning with Hans Christian Mortensen, a schoolteacher of Viborg, Denmark. In 1899 he began putting metal bands on the legs of teals, pintails, storks, starlings, and 2 or 3 kinds of hawks. The bands had his name and address inscribed on them. As his banded birds began to appear in many places in Europe other bird students became interested in bird "ringing," as they say in Europe. In a short time bird banding was "catching on" in America. As more and more bird students began to band birds in the United States they decided they could accomplish more if they worked as a group. Thus, in 1909, the American Bird Banding Association was formed. During World War I, however, banding lagged. Biologists in the Bureau of Biological Survey (now the Bureau of Sport Fisheries and Wildlife) were convinced that banding birds was most worthwhile. They felt it had much to tell us about the habits of birds, especially their migrations. So to further the banding of birds in America the Bureau and its Canadian counterpart, the Canadian Wildlife Service, offered to take over the work of the American Bird Banding Association. The offer was soon accepted and since 1920 banding of migratory birds in the United States and Canada has been under the joint direction of the Federal Governments of the two countries.

Banding birds has shown us many things about the individual bird as well as the species or group to which it belongs. We know that many birds live as long as 10 years. Some live even longer; for example, the Red-winged Blackbird that was banded in New York and shot 14 years later in North Carolina; or the Black Duck banded on Cape Cod and taken by a hunter 17 years later in Newfoundland. The longest a North American bird has been known to live in the wild is 26 years. The holder of this record was a Caspian Tern. It was banded in Michigan in 1925 while still in the nest, and shot in Ohio in 1951.

When banded birds are recaptured at various places and released unhurt the banding information tells us the routes they were following. Thus, when large numbers of birds of a migratory species such as the Bobolink, Scarlet Tanager, or Redstart, and various ducks and geese are banded, we can map the general route the species takes between its wintering and nesting grounds. From banding information we have learned that some birds, as the Atlantic Golden Plover, do not return south in the fall over the same route they took north in the spring.

How did we learn that the Arctic Tern makes the longest known migration flight of any living species? It was from bands returned from such faraway places as Nigeria, West Africa, and Natal and Cape Province, South Africa. It is now known that this bird makes an annual round-trip flight of about 25,000 miles. It nests near the Arctic Circle and winters in the Antarctic.

Many ducklings and goslings are banded each summer on their nesting grounds. When hunters return bands they find on these birds during the hunting season they may be helping to improve their own future hunting. From the bands turned in from hunting areas, wildlife workers can figure pretty closely just how numerous certain ducks will be along the various migration routes during the following hunting seasons. Knowing approximately how many Redheads or Canvasbacks or Mallards could possibly be in an area during the hunting season gives a pretty good basis for saying how large a bag limit should be established for the hunter. The game managers want to be sure that enough pairs of these birds escape the guns to provide the next season's breeding stock. Otherwise excessive shooting could seriously reduce the number of ducks.

Specially designed traps are used to catch the birds for banding. The bird bander must take extreme care in trapping and handling the birds to avoid injuring them. The bander regularly visits his banding trap each day. If he has trapped a bird he removes it from the trap, and if he can identify it he carefully fits the aluminum band to its leg and releases it. Birds should not stay in the trap very long, so the bander visits the trap about every 2 or 3 hours on the days he operates the trap. The last trip is made at dusk—birds are never left in a trap overnight.

Authorized banders receive bands without charge from the Service's Bird Banding Office. That office also keeps a record of the numbers on the bands it sends each bird bander. When a band is put on a bird's leg, the bander records the number on a form he receives from the Bird Banding Office. He also records the species, age, and sex of the bird and the place and date of banding. Later the bander returns the completed form to the Bird Banding Office.

Fifteen different sizes of aluminum bands are used in banding birds. Very small bands are needed for tiny birds such as the warblers, vireos, kinglets, and hummingbirds. Large bands are used on swans, geese, or eagles. Besides the serial number, each band bears the name and address of the Fish and Wildlife Service in Washington. Thus the finder of a band knows where to send it and the Bird Banding Office has a number to use in locating all the banding information on a particular bird.

Anyone who is at least 18 years old and knows how to identify all the common birds in their different seasonal plumages may apply for a banding permit from the Fish and Wildlife Service. The applicant must furnish the names of three well-known bird banders, bird students, or naturalists who can vouch for his fitness as a bird bander. Only those persons who are well qualified will be issued banding permits.

Not everyone can or wants to band birds. But we can all help the work of bird banding by sending in bands we find. In fact, this important study of American birds would fail were it not for the many people who send in bands they find. Banding is only one phase of the work—the bands must be found and returned.

Where are we most likely to find bands? Hunters should always look at the legs of ducks, geese, woodcock, and other game birds they shoot. Many of these birds carry bands. Dead birds along our highways and birds washed up at the seashore may have bands on them. Fishermen sometimes catch banded birds in their nets and on their lines. Sometimes banded ducks are found in beaver and muskrat traps.

When you find a band, straighten it out and attach it securely to a piece of heavy writing paper. With the band send in the following information:

1. Your name and address (plainly printed)
2. All letters and numbers on the band
3. The date you found the band
4. The place where you found the band (nearest town, with County and State)
5. Tell how you found the band (on a bird found dead, shot, trapped, or some other way)
6. Place in an envelope and send to the following address:
   Bird Banding Office
   Patuxent Wildlife Research Center
   U. S. Fish and Wildlife Service
   Laurel, Maryland

What do you do if you find a live banded bird? *Do not* remove the band but read the number on the band, write it down, and release the bird carefully. We may learn more about where it goes or how long it lives. Send in all the information you can about finding the banded bird to the Bird Banding Office. If it is a tiny bird you will not see the name and address of the Service on the band; it will be on the inside of the band. There isn't room for it on the outside. And remember, *don't take the band off, you might injure the bird*. Later you will receive a letter from the Bird Banding Office telling you where the bird was banded, what kind it was, and who banded it. The person who banded it will also learn that you found the band. Each year more than 40,000 band recovery reports are processed and acknowledged in the Bird Banding Office.

Birds pay no attention to State or National boundaries. From our banding work we have learned that many species of birds have long migration routes that carry them through or into a number of countries. A species may nest in Canada, migrate through the United States, and winter in Mexico or Central America. Some go on down into South America, others cross the Atlantic Ocean to Africa. For this reason, if bird banding is to be worthwhile, many groups must work together. The bird-banding work and study of bird migration and distribution are the particular responsibility of the Bureau of Sport Fisheries and Wildlife. But the Bureau must have the help of State conservation departments and of private groups and persons interested in conservation. People in Canada and Mexico as well as people in some South American Republics help us trace the movements of many far ranging birds.

As we have seen, some birds (very important to us, too) spend parts of each year in different countries. These birds need places to feed and rest safely wherever they go. Protecting and feeding them in one country is not enough. All the countries through which they pass must be interested in saving them. Bird conservation is not one country's problem; it is an international problem.

THE

REMARKABLE HISTORY

OF BIRD ANTING

Maurice Burton

Birds of many different species all have the curious habit of picking up ants and then rubbing them into their feathers. More than a hundred years ago John James Audubon commented casually upon the fact that he had seen turkeys "roll themselves in deserted ants' nests." But no other ornithologist seems to have had his curiosity aroused until much later. At the present moment, however, "anting" has become one of the most discussed of the many mysteries of bird behavior. Precisely what is it that they do and why do they do it? Observations are many and theories almost as numerous. Here is a clear, careful presentation of the fact and the problem—though the latter is still unsolved.

THERE is probably no finer example of misplaced skepticism than is to be found in the story of anting.

In 1876, Abbott M. Frazar, wrote an account, in the Bulletin of the *Nuttall Ornithological Club* of the remarkable things he had seen a crow do with some ants. During the next sixty years, from time to time, a similar story would appear in the press or in the lesser scientific journals. What these stories amount to was that several people had seen a bird on the ground or near an ants' nest with its wings half spread forming shields over the flanks and breast and the tail half drawn up under the body. In this quite unusual attitude the bird could be seen picking up ants with its beak and placing them among its feathers. As often as not the ants were placed on the underside of the wings and into the base of the tail. During the course of this strange procedure the bird might topple to one side or perform a half somersault. There was, however, no limit to the variety of contortions to which this anting, as it was later to be called, might lead, but always they were bizarre and outside the range of postures or attitudes normally assumed by birds. It was, indeed, the very fantastic nature of these alleged postures, together with the lack of any

From *Animal Legends*. New York: Coward-McCann, Inc., 1957.

obvious purpose in the whole procedure, that caused these accounts to be treated with skepticism.

We speak of them as alleged postures, for the general opinion was that "it was not possible." Several leading zoologists, and naturalists more especially, expressed either intense skepticism or complete disbelief and the now-familiar story of bird anting would still be in the category of the impossible but for the persistence of a boy of twelve years of age.

In 1934, Peter Bradley, then a schoolboy living in one of the suburbs of Melbourne, Australia, was at play when he noticed some starlings picking up ants and stowing them away among their feathers. He wrote to the *Melbourne Argus* about this. There seem to have been one or two letters in reply from people more knowledgeable than Peter Bradley pointing out that this was just another of those stories. The boy was persistent, however, and he seems to have adopted the attitude that if they did not believe him he would show them. At all events he was persistent, and one of the people he ultimately wrote to was the Australian orni-thologist, A. H. Chisholm, who wrote in the *Victorian Naturalist* in 1940: "Frankly, I doubted the evidence of the boy's eyesight." It so happened, however, that Chisholm was looking through some of his earlier notes, and among them he came across one which he had forgotten all about. It was from a man living in Sydney who had written describing how he had seen certain soft-billed birds placing ants under their wings.

Chisholm then goes on to describe how he searched the books and journals devoted to the study of birds, in Australia, in Britain and Amer-ica, and could find in them no reference to bird anting. He began to wonder, therefore, whether this was a habit confined to Australia. At all events, in the same year that young Bradley put the ants among the starlings, Chisholm published his *Bird Wonders of Australia*, and included therein a mention of this new idea. As he himself recorded later: "Then events began to happen—and they have been happening ever since, in four continents. There have been, so to speak, international complications; and all because of that boy who spied on starlings!" If this was true for 1940, it is even more true for today. Ornithologists the world over are seeing all kinds of bird anting; and those that have not yet witnessed the phenomenon nurse, as likely as not, the secret ambition to do so. Not for the first time in the history of mankind the bursting of the dam of dis-belief has heralded a flood of enthusiastic belief amounting almost to a religious fervor.

Soon after Chisholm's book was published, his note on bird anting was seen by Professor Erwin Stresemann, of the University of Berlin who published a note in a German ornithological journal *Ornithologisches Monatsberichte*, calling attention to this strange phenomenon and asking anyone who had seen anything like it to let him know. From all over

Germany letters poured in giving first-hand observations or—even more remarkable in view of what has already been said—supplying references to notes previously published in German journals that had been overlooked or forgotten.

It was Stresemann who, in publishing the results of his inquiry, gave this behavior the German name of "einemsen," which was later rendered in English as "anting." It is as good a name as any, but as we shall see, it represents only half the story. Stresemann published this new name in 1935, and between then and the present time there has been published a mass of evidence on the same subject, leaving no doubt that this trick of behavior does occur, notwithstanding the skepticism prior to 1934. In that period of time, the impossible has become the commonplace and, what is more important, its full ramifications have been shown to be more fantastic than the earliest accounts, which were flatly rejected by the skeptics.

Although in this chapter the credit for the first recorded observation of anting has been given to Abbott M. Frazar, there are in fact two earlier claimants to it, although neither of these gave such a precise expression to it as did Frazar. The first is contained in words written by the eminent American ornithologist, John James Audubon (1780-1851). In his *Birds of America*, published in 1844, he describes how turkeys "roll themselves in deserted ants' nests to clear their growing feathers of the loose scales and prevent ticks and other vermin from attacking them, these insects being unable to bear the odour of the earth in which ants have been." Although Audubon refers to *deserted* ants' nests, he clearly implies some cleansing or therapeutic quality in the formic acid left behind in the earth by ants. Moreover, as we shall see, anting does not always require the presence of ants.

The second claimant combines with Frazar and Audubon to keep the blue ribbon on the American side of the Atlantic Ocean. His account published in 1947 tells of West Indian grackles, crowlike birds of America, rubbing their feathers with limes that had fallen to the ground. If we choose 1844, the year Audubon's book was published, then we have ninety years of skepticism followed by twenty years—out of which we must take five years of global war when little of this kind of literature was published—during which the literature on the subject became so extensive that one can do no more than summarize it briefly. To a large extent this has been done in Frank W. Lane's *Animal Wonderland*, published in 1948, a book more worthy of close study than its title might suggest. The notes that follow are drawn partly from that book and partly from my own researches.

Before going further, let us be clear what the anting posture is like. I have often found that people mistake sun bathing for anting.

Certainly, in sun bathing, birds strike some curious attitudes, but once you have seen a bird "ant" there is no possibility of your ever confusing it with anything else, or of confusing anything else with it. When anting the wings are brought well forward of the body, at the same time being arched outward, and the tail is twisted to one side and under the body. The whole action is rapid and vigorous.

About half the species of songbirds have been included in the list of those actually observed anting, but the habit is not necessarily restricted to the smaller birds. At least one species of parrot has been seen to indulge in the habit, and, as we have seen, so did Audubon's turkeys. Anting may be carried out by the bird picking up the ants and placing them on its feathers or by sitting on an ant hill and allowing the ants to crawl over it. The ants may be taken up in the beak one at a time, or they may be picked up several at a time. In the last case they may be crushed and their juices rubbed on to the feathers. Sometimes the ants are subsequently eaten. Jays have been seen to wallow in ants' nests laid bare in the course of farm work. Starlings have buried themselves in an ants' nest, throwing the ants over their shoulders. Water birds, such as dippers, will ant, and a young dipper when first presented with ants was seen to pass one after the other through its feathers. Birds like grosbeaks that are normally quarrelsome when in too close contact with one another will remain on the most amicable terms when anting although so crowded that they are continually jostling each other. Finally, bouts of anting may last up to half an hour, the birds, so far as it appears to the human eye, enjoying every minute of it.

The harmony and unusual friendliness noted in the grosbeaks seems to be a not uncommon feature of anting. Charles K. Nichols, of the American Museum of Natural History, has given us a most graphic description of the anting of the American robin. One of the robins was going through the customary evolutions associated with anting and, in addition, was seen sometimes to press its breast to the grass and, using it as a pivot, partly rotate the body. In the middle of this seeming ecstasy another of its kind came on the scene and appeared to drive it away. Then the second robin settled on the same spot and behaved almost exactly as the first had done. Soon a third robin appeared and took its place. After a few minutes the three were taking it in turns to revel in the attractions of this particular spot on the lawn.

Chisholm, returning in 1944 to the problem of anting, gives the story of a tame magpie that would fill its beak with ants in the garden, go into the house, seek out someone smoking a pipe, fly up on to that person's shoulder, dip the ants into the tobacco ash and put the whole mixture under its wings. Clearly anting is not just anting but something more, and this is borne out by the account in the *Victorian Naturalist* for 1945 by 'T. E. Givens. He watched in Northern Queensland a flock of red-browed finches visiting daily a smoldering log and disporting themselves in the smoke. One after another the dozen or so finches would fly on to the log. "Upon reaching the smoke, each bird stood as upright as possible, using its tail as a support. The wings were opened slightly and drooped a little forward and down. Then the head was swept forward, down and under the wing in a circular motion, the bird meanwhile vigorously shuffling its wings and body feathers, often toppling backwards from the violence of its efforts. These actions were rhythmically repeated as many as eight or ten times, when the bird usually rested before repeating the whole process."

Givens watched all this from a distance of six feet, where he was more inconvenienced by the smoke than the birds that were actually flying into it appeared to be. He also made another very important observation, from which it would appear that anting has something in common with ritual dancing. On several occasions, when there was not enough smoke to go round, those left out would go through the motions of anting even when a few feet away. This suggests that the mood associated with anting can be infectious, thereby justifying the use of the words "ecstasy" and "enjoyment" or others suggesting emotional qualities.

I have from time to time received letters from people, with no claim to being naturalists or ornithologists, telling of having watched jackdaws or starlings behaving in a curious way in the smoke coming out of the chimneys of houses. The descriptions have often been imperfect, but they have been sufficiently detailed to leave little doubt that these various correspondents had in fact been watching a behavior closely similar to that of the red-browed finches over the smoldering log in Queensland.

Jackdaws are by no means uncommon in Britain. Anything like their exact numbers would be difficult to compute. Starlings are even more numerous and can only be described as abundant. The number of house chimneys throughout the length and breadth of Great Britain must be little short of fifty million. There are 365 days in each year, with one extra every fourth year, and for about one half of each year some 25 per cent of these chimneys will be emitting smoke for the greater part of the daylight hours. I have asked a number of ornithologists of greater or lesser experience whether they had seen a jackdaw or starling "anting" in the smoke of a chimney. So far I have failed to find one that has seen it. Therefore, in my experience, this particular natural phenomenon alleged to have been observed by a dozen or so laymen has not been by a scientist. According to the usual scientific standards for the acceptance of evidence, therefore, it would be necessary for me to suppose that jackdaws and starlings do not "ant" in the smoke of chimneys—had I not since seen it for myself.

It must be confessed that before having my attention drawn to it I had not noticed this particular facet of the behavior of birds. The words "this particular facet" are used advisedly, for we have not yet exhausted the subject by any means. For example, one American writer reports how when moth balls had been thrown out on to the flower beds a bronze grackle came down and used these precisely as it might have used ants. Other grackles have been observed using the juice from husks óf walnuts. A pet parrot made a practice of taking a piece of apple or a string of apple peel and inserting it beneath its wings or in the feathers between its shoulders, a thing it did with no other article of food. A cockatoo had the habit of rubbing its feathers with apple peel.

Helmut Hampe, writing in the *Ornithologisches Monatsberichte* in 1935, tells of tame starlings that would put ants among their feathers at every opportunity. They would also use the juice or pulp of a lemon in the same way, even vinegar and beer. One of their delights, apparently, was to find the bowl in which had been a salad dressed with vinegar and to bathe in it. He also had a tame jay that showed a similar fondness for orange juice. Every time an orange was being peeled it would draw near to intercept the spurting juice and go through the motions of bathing.

From the many observations now set on record it would seem that birds ant in good health or ill. Some do so systematically, some casually; some perform the rite with seeming ecstasy, others do so with an air of indifference. In some species the performance is carried out simultaneously by a group; in others it is done in solitary state. In some cases the ants were also eaten, in other cases not; when eaten some may be crushed and others not; or none may be eaten. Some birds ant regularly, returning to the same spot each day, and carrying out the process in the same way; others do it spasmodically.

The catalogue of substances used includes ants, both those with and those without formic acid, pungent beetles, strong-smelling bugs, wood lice, meal worms, various berries, juice, pulp or rind of lemon, juice and rind of limes, orange juice, vinegar, beer, apple pulp, apple peel, walnut juice, moth balls, hot ashes, smoke, cigar butts and cigarette ends. Starlings in Australia have been seen fluttering among the foliage of the bush *Diosura alba*, the aromatic leaves of which were afterward found to have been crushed, presumably by the birds with their beaks. Then we have recorded instances of birds that will pick up a lighted cigarette from an ashtray and hold the smoldering end to the undersides of the wings.

So far, so good: Following the preliminary stages of disbelief, and when the mood of skepticism has been broken down, anting is seen not only to be widespread but to take all manner of forms. If, however, we are to accept the testimony of the one man who, more than anyone else, has made a close study of anting in birds, the phase of disbelief has been succeeded by a phase of wild belief, in which a most surprising variety of behavior is accepted under this one heading. That man is H. Roy Ivor, of

Canada. His evidence is sober, and tends to contradict much that is contained in this summary.

H. Roy Ivor tried scattering a shovelful of earth containing several hundred ants over the floor of his aviary. He then lay down on the ground, often with his face within sixteen inches of the birds, and watched them closely. After sixteen experiments, in the course of which twenty out of the thirty-one species in the aviary anted, some of them actually on his hand, he found no obvious or fundamental difference in the actions of families, species or individuals, the only variation being in the position adopted.

Ivor carried out his work in a thoroughgoing fashion. He used over a hundred birds representing some forty species of song birds, made thousands of observations, took two hundred feet of normal-speed and a hundred feet of slow-motion film, mainly in color, scrutinized many of the frames through a viewer and had several of them printed and enlarged. This was up to 1946. Not only was he unable by any of his methods to discern any variation in the pattern, his motion pictures did not show the bird placing the ant on any part of the plumage other than the undersides of the primaries and the tail. He did add, however, that the crow and magpie were exceptions to this, and he did not exclude the possibility of individual idiosyncrasy. He also agreed that this did not mean that his experiments had proved conclusively that there is only one way in which a bird ants. What he had proved, however, was that the many birds which he had under observation for several years had a definite pattern which never altered. He took the view that too many of the records of anting were based upon observation of the event from a distance. In addition, he pointed out that the action is extremely rapid, that there is the surprise element in viewing a behavior hitherto unseen, and that one has to reckon with the human failing of not seeing accurately what really happens.

During the past three years, I have had especially good opportunities of watching "anting" carried out by several species of birds using different substances to set it going. More will be said about this in the next chapter. Meanwhile, I would confirm all that Roy Ivor has said about the definite pattern, and I agree with him that the birds do not place the ants or any of the substitute materials on any other part of the plumage than the undersides of the primaries and the tail.

It might not be unreasonable to add another clause to Ivor's summing up: that when, following a period of intense skepticism, the dam bursts and the flood of belief pour over a particular field of study the resulting credulity becomes as facile as the incredulity it displaces was stubborn. There seems no doubt, however, especially from the careful and persistent researches of Ivor, that this habit which has been named anting does exist, that it is widespread especially among the song birds, that it does conform more or less to a pattern which may vary conceivably on occasion following the idiosyncrasies of the individual. The question then arises: What is the function of anting?

We have seen that the first possible reference to it, somewhat indirect, perhaps, was that of Audubon in 1844, which implied that it might be for cleansing the feathers or for getting rid of parasites. The next, more direct, reference to the habit is that of Frazar, in 1847, and Frazar said he had seen the ants seize the parasites and bear them away. There have been other similar observations since. In this connection it is of interest to note that Frank W. Lane draws our attention to the known practice among human beings in various parts of the world of laying verminous clothing on large ant hills for the purpose of cleaning it, the clothing being left until it was judged that the vermin would have been removed, after which the garments are shaken free of ants and replaced on the body.

Other suggestions must readily spring to mind, and these have been summarized by Chisholm who sees four positive functions. They are: Formic acid given off by the ants acts as a stimulant to the skin; the formic acid cleanses the skin of parasites; the odors of the formic acid and other pungent substances are attractive to the birds; and it frees the ants of their formic acid before they are eaten. These represent the consensus of views advanced at some time or other by various writers on the subject. Some writers have suggested, following up the idea that the acids or other pungent substances might act as a skin stimulant, that the effect may be similar to the well-known ruffling of the feathers with the fingers, which tame birds seem to enjoy. A more outlandish suggestion was that the ants were stowed away among the feathers to act as a kind of emergency rations during migration.

Ivor states categorically that in none of his extensive observations did he see anything to suggest that the habit was related to the need for getting rid of vermin. I heartily concur with this. He emphasizes also that only two parts of the plumage are anointed, the undersides of the primaries in the wings and the underside of the tail, and these he suggests are the two parts with the exceptions of the head and neck most inaccessible to the bird's bill. He concludes: "This accounts for the contortions of the body and, in my opinion, precludes the possibility of accepting any of the suggestions previously made as to the biological significance of anting, with the possible exception of the pleasure derived. Even this, however, does not seem logical, for, were it done for pleasure, there are many parts of the body more readily accessible."

This conclusion seems to be supported by several telling arguments. Thus, the bluebird and the American robin, closely related and anatomically very similar, have different nesting habits. The former nests in cavities and might be supposed to be more prone to skin parasites, yet it does not ant, while the robin nesting in more open sites does. A pet crow observed by Ivor did not ant in the normal way. It would, however, sit among ants and allow them to crawl over its body, and he noticed that if an ant seized the tip of a feather and bit it or tried to pull it, the crow closed its eyes and remained quiet for minutes at a time, apparently enjoying the action. Thirdly, aviary-kept birds, when given an opportunity to ant, would do so at first with great enthusiasm, later growing tired of it.

It is natural now to ask whether anting is peculiar to birds. There is only one record of a mammal anting. Aaron M. Bagg, of Massachusetts, writing in the *Journal of Mammalogy* for 1952, described seeing a gray squirrel performing in a remarkable manner at the foot of a Colorado blue spruce. It crawled on its belly across this spot, rolled on its shoulder and on its back, rolled on its side like a kitten playing with a ball, and performed a forward somersault. During this performance the squirrel was seen to scratch itself several times. Examining the spot afterward, Bagg found a trail of ants crossing it and several ant holes opening on to it. The variety of movements described here, including the forward somersaults, are used in pure play by the gray squirrel, even when ants are not present. And squirrels often stop whatever they are doing to scratch—ants or no ants.

Play in animals has been shown beyond reasonable doubt to be pleasurable and indulged in for the enjoyment of it. There is no ground for supposing that Mr. Bagg's squirrel was not stimulated to play by the presence of the ants and was anting in the sense, and for the same reasons, as Ivor's birds, for the pleasure so derived. Indeed, the whole performance bears a strong resemblance to the manner in which dogs and cats will luxuriate in a growth of aromatic herbs.

It would be wrong to conclude this discussion without reference to a legend from the East about pangolins. These animals have long low bodies supported on short legs and ending behind in long tails, the whole covered with large overlapping scales, sharp-edged and somewhat pointed, with a few hairs growing between the scales. The animal's under surface is soft and protected by a few sparse hairs only. To obtain a meal a pangolin rips open an ants' nest with its foreclaws, the third toe of each forefoot being armed with an extra long claw. It flicks its long extensile tongue into the tunnels with lightning speed to pick up the ants. While this is going on it may happen that some ants climb over the pangolin's body. These are shaken off with a quick quivering movement, and, as if to demonstrate its complete mastery of the situation, a pangolin, having cleaned out a nest, will sweep the fragments from it together with its tail and search these with its tongue for any remaining ants. So it makes a clean sweep of the ants, including any that wandered over its body.

Everything in the pangolin's anatomy and behavior seems to be directed toward giving the maximum protection from ants, even from the dreaded hard-biting soldier ants. There is the stout armor covering the body, the ability to shake off any ants straying over it, the clean sweep made of a nest. In addition, the nostrils are narrow and easily closed, the eyelids thick and swollen looking, giving maximum protection to the small eyes; the mouth even when open is slitlike with room for no more than the passage of the slender tongue with any ants that may be adhering to it. In the face of this, the behavior with which the pangolin is credited in the folklore of China, Malaya and Japan would seem to be impossible. This is that after tearing open an ants' nest a pangolin may erect its scales, wait until as many ants as possible have crawled under them, then it will suddenly depress its scales, crushing the ants beneath. After this, it goes into water, once again erects its scales, allows the ant carcasses to float off, and then proceeds to enjoy a meal of the dead ants floating on the surface of the water.

There may be nothing in this story. It certainly would seem contradictory that an animal so heavily protected against ants, and able so thoroughly to dispose of them in another way, should choose this method either for the purpose of killing the ants or of obtaining a meal. On the other hand, an armor of overlapping scales must be an ideal cover for harboring small skin parasites. Moreover, the build of the pangolin must make for difficulty in cleaning the body by any of the more familiar methods used by mammals. It should not be surprising then to learn that the pangolin has adopted some unfamilar ways of keeping itself clean, or of ridding itself of parasites, stimulating the soft skin at the bases of the scales or just enjoying itself. Certainly, remembering the history of our knowledge of bird anting, the eastern legend cannot be rejected out-of-hand. What methods do armadillos use to these ends? And the porcupines? Both these animals might be worth watching to see what light they may shed on these and allied problems.

It is no function of this chapter to assess the significance of anting nor to offer a complete account of the evidence so far available, less still to give a final verdict on the subject as a whole. Its aim is strictly limited to establishing the following points:

1. That skepticism even in informed quarters is no proof that a particular event or phenomenon is impossible;

2. That incredulity can be as misleading as credulity;

3. That there can be fashions in scientific belief as in anything else, and that such fashions follow the known course of all fashions, vogues and crazes, namely, they are slow, even stubborn in starting, and that once started they rise to a peak in a relatively short space of time to go beyond reasonable bounds, only to return to normal when the first flush of enthusiasm has expended itself;

4. That scientists are sometimes as prone as anyone else to accept ideas for which there is little or no foundation while stubbornly refusing to see the truth before their very eyes;

5. That animals have idiosyncrasies as well as human beings, and that there are traits outside the more familiar and normal behavior which are capable of no simple explanation;

6. That because no reasonable explanation can be advanced for a particular event or line of conduct it does not thereby follow that it does not exist.

Part

Five

EXTINCTION AND CONSERVATION

AND I

OUGHT TO KNOW

Will Cuppy

The late Will Cuppy, otherwise known as the Hermit of Fire Island, could never seem to make up his mind whether he was a nature lover or, like Samuel Johnson, Sydney Smith, and Charles Lamb, a nature hater. His various books dealing with natural (and unnatural) history are pretty sure to delight any reader but none so much as those who know enough about both to appreciate fully the curious facts, deliberate fallacies, and puckish comments which he blended in a version which was his alone. One of his best pieces is this one from a section in a book appropriately called How to Become Extinct. *It contains among much other curious matter some comments on the ambivalence of ornithologists who, when they know that a species is threatened with extinction, are torn between the desire to keep it going and the urge to get as many stuffed specimens and skins as possible into the museums.*

THE last two Great Auks in the world were killed June 4, 1844, on the island of Eldey, off the coast of Iceland. The last Passenger Pigeon, an old female named Martha, died September 1, 1914, peacefully, at the Cincinnati Zoo. I became extinct on August 23, 1934. I forget where I was at the time, but I shall always remember the date.

The two Great Auks were hit on the head by Jon Brandsson and Sigurdr Islefsson, a couple of Icelandic fishermen who had come from Cape Reykjanes for the purpose. A companion, Ketil Ketilsson, looked around for another Great Auk but failed to find one, naturally, since the species had just become extinct. Vilhjalmur Hakonarsson, leader of the expedition, stayed in the boat.

The main reason why these particular fishermen went birding that day is part of history. It seems that bird lovers and bird experts everywhere were upset over the disappearance of the Great Auk from its accustomed haunts and its extreme rarity even in its last refuge, the little island of Eldey. Since there was grave danger that it would soon

From *The Great Bustard and Other People*. New York: Rinehart & Company, 1941.

become entirely and irrevocably extinct—as dead as the Dodo, in fact—
it looked as though something would have to be done and done quickly.

Well, something was done. As always, one man rose to the occasion.
Mr. Carl Siemsen, a resident of Reykjavik and quite an ornithologist on
his own, hired Jon and Sigurdr and the rest of the boys to row over
to Eldey and kill all the Great Auks they could find, in order that
they might be properly stuffed and placed in various museums for which
he acted as agent and talent scout. And of course that was one way of
handling the situation. It was pretty tough on the Auks, though, wasn't
it?

I don't say the museum people themselves would have hit the Great
Auks on the head, or even that they would have approved such an act.
I do say that ornithologists as a class, so far as I have been able to observe
them, generally from a safe distance, do seem to suffer from a touch of
split personality when faced with a dwindling species of bird. They appear to be torn between a sincere desire to bring that bird back to par,
at any cost to themselves and to certain well-to-do persons whose names
they keep in a little black book, and an uncontrollable urge or compulsion to skin a few more specimens and put them in a showcase at the
earliest possible moment. I don't pretend to follow their line of reasoning,
if such it may be called. To do that you have to be a Ph.D. in birdology.
It takes years of hard study, and I guess you have to be that way in the
first place.

Right here I might offer a word of advice to the Ivory-billed Woodpecker, now the rarest bird on the North American continent and one
that is going to come in for more and more attention. Keep away from
bird lovers, fellows, or you'll be standing on a little wooden pedestal with
a label containing your full name in Latin: *Campephilus principalis*. People will be filing past admiring your glossy blue-black feathers, your
white stripes and patches, your nasal plumes in front of lores, your
bright red crest and your beady yellow eyes. You'll be in the limelight,
but you won't know it. I don't want to alarm you fellow, but there are
only about twenty of you alive as I write these lines, and there are more
than two hundred of you in American museums and in collections owned
by Ivory-billed Woodpecker enthusiasts. Get it?

Yes, I know that many ornithologists are gentle, harmless souls without a murderous thought in their whole field equipment. I should like
to remind them, though, that even a bird has a nervous system, and I am
thinking especially of the Roseate Spoonbill, one of our few native birds
with a bill shaped like a soup ladle. It can't help the Roseate Spoonbill
much to go chasing over hill and dale practically twenty-four hours a
day, aiming binoculars at it from behind every bush—as if it didn't
know you were there!—clicking your cameras, watching every move
and that sort of thing. There must be Roseate Spoonbills who haven't

had a decent night's rest in years. No sleep, no nothing. And you wonder why they're neurotic.

I should like to add that the habit of climbing up into trees and rubber-stamping the eggs of birds threatened with extinction in order to warn wandering collectors away from the nests might well be abandoned in the interests of whatever remnants of sanity may still be left among our feathered friends.

Coming back to the Great Auk, if I may, I am rather surprised that I brought up the subject at all, for it is not one of my favorite birds of song or story. I lost interest some years ago when I learned that it was only as large as a tame Goose, and some say smaller—the Great Auk, mind you! When I think of the precious hours I once wasted thinking how wonderful it would be to see a Great Auk, I could sue.

Besides, it was one of those birds that lost the power of flight through long disuse of their wings, and surely that is no fault of mine, to put it no closer home. I am always a bit impatient with such birds. Under conditions prevailing in the civilized world, any bird that can't make a quick get-away is doomed, and more so if it is good to eat, if its feathers are fine for cushions, and if it makes excellent bait for Codfish when chipped into gobbets. Such a bird, to remain in the picture, must drop everything else and develop its wing muscles to the very limit. It does seem as though that should be clear even to an Auk.

Flightlessness alone, however, does not explain the fate of this species to my satisfaction, since it is a well-known fact that fish do not fly, either—that is, most fish. By the way, there are grounds for believing that the Great Auk regarded itself as more of a fish than a bird, for it made its annual migrations to Florida by water, and largely beneath the surface at that. Still and all, it didn't work out in the long run. I cannot avoid the feeling that birds migrating under water is something Mother Nature will stand just so long and no longer.

I'm afraid the Great Auks were pretty foolish in other ways, too. Like Dodos, they had a tendency to pal with just anybody. Whenever they noticed some one creeping up on them with a blunt instrument, they would rush to meet him with glad little squawks of welcome and stick out their necks. Both species did this once too often. Maybe you never heard that duodo, the earliest version of Dodo, is Portuguese for simpleton. You didn't know the Portuguese had a word for that, eh?

We should now be in a position, if we're ever going to be, to form some opinion on why the Great Auk became extinct. It would be too easy, and not very scientific, to say that it happened merely because Jon Brandsson and Sigurdr Islefsson were running amuck on the morning of June 4, 1844. But why were there only two Great Auks left on Eldey? What had been going on in this species? Just how far had *Alca impennis* evolved, whether rightly or wrongly? As Richard Swann Lull states in

Organic Evolution, "Extinction in phylogeny has two aspects, each of which has its equivalent in ontogeny." And two aspects is putting it mildly.

Let's not be too quick to blame the human race for everything. We must remember that a great many species of animals became extinct before man ever appeared on earth. At the same time it is probably true that when two husky representatives of *Homo sapiens*, with clubs, corner the last two birds of a species, no matter how far they have or have not evolved, both the phylogeny and the ontogeny of those birds are, to all intents and purposes, over. For the present I shall have to leave it at that.

Since I mentioned two other extinct individuals in the first paragraph of this article, my readers may expect me to bring them into the story. To the best of my knowledge and belief, Martha, last of the Passenger Pigeons, is now one of the treasures of the Smithsonian Institution. After life's fitful fever she can do with a good rest. No more of those incredible, sky-darkening flights amid general uproar and pandemonium. No more dodging bullets. No more roup. Martha was far from a Squab when she left us in 1914, having reached the age of twenty-nine. Her name, by the way, is no whimsical invention of mine. She was really Martha, as anybody will tell you who knew his Cincinnati around the turn of the century.

We are not quite sure why the Passenger Pigeon became extinct as a species. Some say that all the Passenger Pigeons in the world—except Martha, presumably—were caught in a storm and perished during their last migration southward over the Gulf of Mexico. The weakness of this theory is that Passenger Pigeons never went near the Gulf of Mexico on any pretext, let alone made a habit of flying over it in a body. I grant you there have been some bad storms over the Gulf, but that also holds true of other bodies of water.

My own view is the economic one. The food supply of those birds probably gave out, and there they were. Only the other day I came across the statement that the chief food of the Passenger Pigeon was beech-mast, a commodity which could never have been abundant enough in this country to last them forever. I never even heard of it myself except in this connection. I do think our scientists, instead of spinning pictur-esque yarns about the disappearance of the Passenger Pigeon, mere guess-work for the most part, might well devote themselves to the question: Whatever became of the beech-mast? Then we might get somewhere.

So much for *Ectopistes migratorius*. Nevermore, alas, will they alight in our forests by the billion, breaking down and killing the trees for miles around by the weight of their untold numbers, destroying the crops for thousands of acres in every direction, wrecking havoc and devastation upon whole counties and leaving the human population a complete wreck from shock, multiple contusions, and indigestion. People miss that sort of thing, but you needn't look for any more Passenger Pigeons. They have gone to join the Great Auk, the Labrador Duck, the Eskimo Curlew, the Carolina Parakeet, the Heath Hen, and the Guadalupe Flicker. You won't find any of them. They're through.

What is more, sooner than we think we may see the last of the California Condor, the Everglade Kite, the Trumpeter Swan, the Whooping Crane and the Limpkin, not to mention some of the Godwits, which haven't been doing any too well here lately. It's enough to made Donald Culross Peattie go and hang himself.

But look, Mr. Peattie, only last June a thing called a Cahow, supposed to be extinct, turned up in Bermuda as chipper as ever. It wasn't extinct at all. Does that help any? And I honestly don't think we need worry about the Whooping Crane. There will always be people who will see to it, if it's the last thing they do, that there are plenty of Whooping Cranes around. Life has taught me that much at least.

If I may close on a personal note, I'm sorry but there seems to be some doubt whether I became extinct on August 23, 1934, or whether the date will have to be moved ahead a few years. That day was one of my birthdays and it was not my twenty-first or my thirtieth—or even, I am afraid, my fortieth. And it got me to thinking. Since then I have had more birthdays, so things haven't improved much in that respect. I find, however, that it is technically incorrect to call anybody extinct while he is still at large. I must have made a mistake in one of the minor details. Some day that can be fixed in a jiffy by changing a numeral or two, and then everything will be right as rain.

Anyway, you can see how the thoughts of a person who fully believed himself to be extinct, even if he had talked himself into it, could be a bit on the somber side. Yet I had my moments, for I assure you that becoming extinct has its compensations. It's a good deal like beating the game. I would go so far as to say that becoming extinct is the perfect answer to everything and I defy anybody to think of a better. Other solutions are mere palliatives, just a bunch of loose ends, leaving the central problem untouched. But now I must snap out of all that. According to our leading scientists, I am not yet extinct, and they ought to know. Well, there's no use crying about it.

As I look back over the period since 1934, I guess I didn't go into the thing quite thoroughly enough. I never really classed myself with the Dodo, a bird we always think of as the ultimate in extinction, though I suppose the Dodo is no more extinct than anything else that is extinct, unless it's the Trilobite. Maybe I'm more like the Buffalo, which seems to be coming back now in response to no great popular demand that I can see. Did I ever tell you what happened to the Buffaloes that time? The moths got into them.

THE LAST

OF A

SPECIES

William Bridges

The reader will remember that John James Audubon saw passenger pigeons in incredible numbers. Probably no bird ever seemed to him less likely to disappear. But disappear it did and we know exactly when.

THE whole world was beginning to take fire on the first day of September, 1914, so it is understandable why the death of a pigeon in the Cincinnati Zoological Garden passed, if not quite unnoticed, at any rate with a minimum of general interest. The Cincinnati *Enquirer* gave it a third of a column; no doubt the wire associations sent a paragraph to other American newspapers. I cannot find that the New York *Times*, usually receptive to significant news, bothered about the little obituary, for the Battle of the Marne was in the making that September day and the extinction taking place in western Europe transcended, in news value, the extinction of any bird.

Nevertheless, all of us interested in animal life must wish that some editor with a sharpened sense of history—natural history—had assigned a reporter to record every minute detail of the drama that was taking place in Cincinnati, because the dying pigeon was Martha, the last Passenger Pigeon in the world. The very last of a race, sole relic of flocks comprising uncounted billions of individuals.

It was an opportunity for someone to record an event that may never occur again—the final exit of a species before human eyes. Other forms of wild life will go out of existence; many large and spectacular creatures are almost surely doomed today. But in all probability they will drift from existence into nonexistence while no man watches or is aware, just as the Great Auk and the Carolina Parrakeet and the Heath Hen disappeared, and we will realize they are gone irretrievably only when the

From *Animal Kingdom*. Bulletin of the NYZS, October 18, 1946.

last known individual fails to appear in its accustomed haunts. The stars, whispering leaves, the bright eyes of some small startled animal may be the only witness of their passing.

Our chance to see a species expire came only with the Passenger Pigeon, for its circumstances were unique. In 1914 it had already vanished as a wild bird, a stealthy and obscure disappearance, but the race had lingered a long time in captivity and the approach of its doom could be seen and measured and recorded. For once, we could know to the hour and minute when a great phase of American life came to an end.

But much as we regret it now, no reporter kept a deathwatch beside Martha's cage and sought out all the ascertainable facts of her life, and as things stand, the published and scattered accounts are confused and conflicting. After the lapse of only thirty-one years and while the guardians of her last hours are still alive, it has been difficult to reconstruct accurately and in detail the story of her end and her apotheosis.

In running down as much of the story as is still recoverable, I have had the cordial assistance of Director Joseph A. Stephan of the Cincinnati Zoological Garden, of his father, General Manager Emeritus Sol A. Stephan, and of Dr. Herbert Friedman, Curator of Birds of the U. S. National Museum.

To set the stage for the exit of Martha, it is necessary to recall what the Passenger Pigeon was, and something about its natural history. A whole generation has grown up since the last captive bird died and the wild birds had disappeared more than a generation before 1914, so that there are many grown men and women today who never heard of the Passenger Pigeon. Mention it, and they think of the Carrier Pigeon or the Homing Pigeon.

The Passenger Pigeon, despite its name, did not carry messages nor did it have a highly developed homing instinct. It was something entirely different from the specialized breeds of the common domestic pigeon; it was a true wild pigeon, native only to North America. Slender-tailed, bluish, with a slaty-blue head and breast of purplish-brownish-red, it was big and handsome. It had a wingspread of almost two feet and it weighed about 12 ounces.

The "Passenger Pigeon," it was called, presumably because it was constantly wandering over areas of several hundred square miles in search of food, or making sun-darkening flocks to its roosting or nesting grounds. In the early years of the last century the wild pigeon flocks roamed almost the whole of the United States where the hardwood forests existed, and they consumed unbelievable quantities of acorns, beechnuts, chestnuts and other tree seeds, of blueberries, huckleberries, raspberries, wild cherries, pokeberries and even caterpillars and other insects.

In 1832 the conservative ornithologist Alexander Wilson estimated that a single flock he encountered near Frankfort, Kentucky, contained *at least* 2,230,270,000 birds. Audubon cited equally prodigious flocks. Wilson's birds, if they ate only one pint of beech mast each in the course of a day, would consume 34,847,968 bushels a day.

Their nesting sites in Kentucky, Indiana, Michigan and elsewhere in the Middle West have been described by competent naturalists in the early and middle years of the last century. Millions of pigeons nested in the same forest. Over an area of a hundred square miles every tree would be loaded with nests, often as many as a hundred in a single tree. Great branches would break from the weight of the nesting birds.

Concentrated as they were in flocks, roosts and nests, their extermination was easy. Netters could take 3000 birds at the spring of a single trap. The methods of slaughter, for market or for sport, were many and varied and often cruel and wanton. By the "seventies" the vast flocks were gone from many parts of the country and by the "Eighties" the end was in sight everywhere.

In 1879 dead Passenger Pigeons were selling for 35 to 40 cents a dozen on the Chicago market. Live birds that could be fattened and fed up for increased tenderness were worth $1 to $2 a dozen.

Already voices were crying in the wilderness, warning that the Passenger Pigeon was not an inexhaustible resource. In 1878 or 1879 (the record is confused), the Cincinnati Zoological Society bought four pairs of live Passenger Pigeons near Petoskey, Michigan, and paid the (comparatively) exhorbitant price of $2.50 a pair. These were put on exhibition in the Zoo and were, it appears, the progenitors of the last, ultimate survivor of their race.

As I said before, I wish some trained reporter had nominated himself Historian to the Last Passenger Pigeon, for the printed records are sadly in conflict. Edward Howe Forbush, the notable ornithologist of "The Birds of Massachusetts," thought the sole survivor in the Cincinnati Zoo had come (as I read his rather ambiguous remarks), from the Whittaker flock in Milwaukee.

Ruthven Deane attributed the last bird to the Whitman flock in Chicago (*The Auk*, 1911, page 262)—and, incidentally, stated that she was "about fourteen years old" then (1911). All the Cincinnati Zoo sources I have seen indicate that Martha was 29 years old at the time of her death.

(On second thought, maybe it would have been better to have *two* trained reporters keeping the history of Martha—each one checking on the other!)

The moot point of Martha's age (29 years is a remarkably advanced age for a pigeon), probably depends on whether one believes she came from some late generation of the Whittaker-Whitman flocks, or whether one accepts the Stephan family version of her origin—for both Director Joseph Stephan and his father have repeatedly and positively asserted that Martha was a direct descendant of the Cincinnati Zoo's own birds, that she was hatched in the collection, and passed her whole life within the confines of the Zoo.

The conflicting evidence extends even to the time of her death—some accounts saying 1 o'clock in the morning, some 1 o'clock in the afternoon. It has even been said that Martha died on September 2 instead of September 1.

Unable to reconcile all these contradictory statements, I wrote to Director Stephan and by return post came a sheaf of longhand and typewritten notes that his father had compiled around the time of Martha's demise. They, I thought, would settle matters once and for all. Instead, they offered some new contradictions!

Once more I queried the amiable Director of the Cincinnati Zoo, and his reply (airmail special delivery), was as specific as anyone could wish. He had even, I noticed, put a new and boldly black ribbon on his typewriter. There could be no question of illegibility.

"Martha died," he wrote, "at 5:00 P.M. September 1, 1914. My father, Sol A. Stephan, Director of Animals, now 96 years old, and myself were with her at death, as she was very feeble and had to be assisted to eat.

"Martha was hatched at the Cincinnati Zoo with many others, but outlived her sisters and brothers. She was named after Martha Washington. We still have the aviary covered with the same wire, that caged all the Passenger Pigeons and also have a sign erected to indicate that. Of course these birds were outdoors 12 months a year, with protection from the strong winds.

"I as a boy would take the eggs that dropped out of nests and put them under tame pigeons to hatch in my pigeon loft. Sometimes when they were about to hatch I put them in a Passenger Pigeon nest to let them finish the incubation, and when hatched, they mothered them O.K.

"On Sundays we would rope off the cage to keep the public from throwing sand at her to make her walk around; during her last five or six months she was not able to fly up to her perch."

So much for the time and date of Martha's death. I know of no one better qualified than Director Stephan and his father to say exactly when it occurred.

The United States Weather Bureau tells me that September 1, 1914, was a partly cloudy day in Cincinnati, with no rain but a fairly high humidity of 74 per cent, and a temperature range of 72 to 89 degrees. A warm, rather muggy day, it would appear, typical of so many midwestern summer days. The problem of what to do with Martha's body —long since promised to the Smithsonian Institution—must have required an immediate answer. I had seen a statement somewhere (which

Dr. Friedman of the Smithsonian had been unable to confirm), that she was frozen in a block of ice for shipment to Washington.

Director Stephan was positive about that:

"I took her to the Cincinnati Ice Co. plant personally and supervised the placing of her body in a tank of water, suspended by her two legs, and froze her body into a 300-lb block of ice," he wrote me.

Martha reached the United States National Museum on the morning of September 4, and the experts—taxidermists and anatomists—immediately went to work on it. A full account of the anatomical work was subsequently published (with a ghastly plate of the skinned carcass), in *The Auk* (1915, page 29), by Dr. Robert Wilson Shufeldt, sometime Honorary Curator of the Smithsonian Institution and in 1914 an associate in zoology.

"I found," he wrote, "the bird to be an adult female in the moult, with a few pin feathers in sight, and some of the middle tail feathers, including the long, central ones, missing . . . It had the appearance of a specimen in good health, with healthy eyes, eye-lids, nostrils, and mouth-parts. The feet were of a deep, flesh-colored pink, clean and healthy, while the claws presented no evidences indicative of unusual age, though not a few of wear."

Eventually the anatomists and the taxidermists did their work and Martha was ready to be presented to posterity that would never see her kind again in flesh.

"This specimen is still on exhibition in the U. S. National Museum," Dr. Friedman wrote. "The bird is mounted perched on a branch of a tree which, in turn, is inserted in an old-fashioned mahogany stand. The specimen is shown in our synoptic series of North American birds with no special trimmings. There is no background and the bird is not in a case by itself. The case is one of those which has glass on both sides and consequently there are two labels, one on either side of the bird. These labels read as follows:

"Ectopistes migratorius (Linnaeus)
Passenger Pigeon.
Exterminated. Formerly very abundant throughout a large part of North America. This is the last known individual. It died in captivity in September, 1914.

"Ectopistes migratorius (Linnaeus)
Passenger Pigeon.
Last of its race. Died at Cincinnati Zoological Garden, September 1st, 1914.
Age 29 years.
Presented by the Cincinnati Zoological Garden to the National Museum.
Adult female, 236650."

Such are the few stray bits of information that may now be gleaned about Martha's life and death. Thirty years ago a historian could have garnered other, and more pertinent, facts. I wish he had—but I wish even more that the grandparents of the present generation had not thought the Passenger Pigeon was indestructable.

FIFTY YEARS OF PROGRESS—

THE NATIONAL AUDUBON SOCIETY

John H. Baker

The National Audubon Society, with its affiliated local clubs, is probably the largest and also the most influential association in the world for the protection, appreciation, and study of birds. Here is something of its history.

WHEN the National Association of Audubon Societies for the Protection of Wild Birds and Animals, Inc. was launched in January 1905, market gunning and sport shooting, practically without restriction, were widespread in the United States. Quite a few states, as a consequence of local Audubon movements, had adopted the Audubon model law protecting songbirds, so that the practice, commonly prevailing before the 1890s, of using robins, meadowlarks, and other songbirds for food, had been largely stopped. But there was almost no protection of non-game species of wildlife, other than songbirds, and very little protection of game.

Commercial dealers in game were doing a thriving business. I remember very well watching gunners shooting small sandpipers for the pot on the beaches in the early 1900s. The eggs of coastal nesting birds such as gulls, terns, and skimmers were being widely used locally for food. The commercial traffic in wild bird plumage, mainly for millinery purposes, was bringing millions of dollars annually into the coffers of the importers and wholesalers.

There was at that time no soil conservation concept or recognition of the need for governmental action. There certainly was no water conservation concept; everyone seemed to think there always would be plenty of water for all purposes. The forest conservation concept was just developing. There was little concept of wildlife conservation outside of the small groups constituting the then-organized Audubon So-

From *Audubon Magazine*. January–February, 1955.

cieties. There was little, if any, awareness of the interdependence of wildlife, plants, soil, and water, or their relation to human progress. The beneficial role of predatory animals was not at all appreciated and even today, may I say, it is little appreciated. Our children's children may look back on the present destructive attitude toward predatory animals with the same feeling we have today about those who shot small sandpipers for the pot, used robins and meadowlarks for food, or wore the plumage of wild birds as hat trimmings.

The wildlife protective organizations in existence toward the end of the last century, and early in this one, tended to be highly specialized in objectives. As a consequence, there were apt to be conflicts that tended to weaken the whole movement. I have, in the past, likened this situation to one in which the theoretical Society for the Preservation of the Chickadee was constantly warring with the theoretical Society for the Preservation of Sunflower Seeds.

Appreciative uses of the out-of-doors—other than to view the scenery, hike, hunt or fish were, generally, not indulged in. Certainly there was no training of teachers in effective presentation of nature and conservation subjects from the outdoor approach. True, there was teaching of nature study, but almost wholly from the indoor laboratory approach and not outdoors in nature's laboratory.

While the original stated purposes of the National Association included the protection of other animals than birds, the great bulk of the Society's activities, and of the interest of its members and affiliated societies, concerned bird protection. There was need to develop public opinion to support the passage of basic laws restricting or ending the slaughter of wild birds and other animals. Insofar as the commercial traffic in wild bird plumage was concerned, it was a long battle. The key actions were: (1) the passage in New York State in 1910—New York City being the place of business of more than 90 per cent of the importers and dealers in such plumage—of a law banning possession for sale, offering for sale, and sale of the plumage of wild birds; (2) the Federal Tariff Act of 1913 banning the importation into the United States of wild bird plumage with, however, certain provisions that provided loop-holes; (3) the Federal Migratory Bird Treaty Act of 1918, giving power to the federal government to prescribe allowable take, if any, of those families and species of birds defined in that Act as migratory; (4) the 1941 New York State law eliminating legal loop-holes of which advantage had been taken; and (5) the 1952 amendment of the Federal Tariff Act for the same purpose. In obtaining the passage of these basic bird protective laws the National Association of Audubon Societies played a leading part.

It might well be said that during nearly the first half of the Society's existence we were in the era of protection, and that in the second half we have been in the era of conservation.

With the growth of public awareness of the recreational pleasures to be derived from appreciative use of the out-of-doors, new industries have developed, providing ever better cameras and projectors, binoculars, nature books, bird nesting boxes, feeding stations, and field guides for identification, not only of birds and flowers, but of trees, mammals, insects, reptiles, and all other forms of plant and animal life. There is no question that the National Audubon Society has played a substantial part in the development of such public interest. At the turn of the century anyone who was interested in observing birds was apt to be regarded as odd; now almost everyone is apologetic if he does not know one bird from another.

During the second half of your Society's existence the scope of objectives and program has been greatly widened in recognition of the fact, learned from experience, that with increasing population pressure, neither birds nor plants can, in the long run, be saved from extinction through protection alone; recognition that it is essential to preserve the carrying capacity of their habitats in terms of food, cover and water; recognition of the complex interrelationships of soil, water, plants, and wildlife, and their direct impact upon human progress.

As recently as 25 years ago, there were no summer camps for the training of teachers and other youth leaders to present nature and conservation subjects from the outdoor approach, and none that stressed the interrelationships of the resources. There were no wildlife tours by station wagon and boat under guidance of trained naturalists and conservationists, taking people into the field to observe first-hand the existing soil, water, plant, and wildlife conditions in an area, in order to learn of the history and results of man's alteration of that environment; to see what a national park, monument, federal, state, or private refuge or sanctuary is like; and to learn something of the management problems in connection with them.

There were no nature educational centers in the vicinity of great metropolitan populations where groups of school children and scouts might be taken by busloads with their teachers and leaders. Here they go out on the trails under the guidance of well-qualified nature and conservation teachers, receive instruction while visiting trailside museums, and so better their chances of living healthy and happy lives, and of helping, as voting citizens, to preserve those resources and environments on which their health and happiness depend. It is not merely to increase recreational pleasures that your Society strives to develop public conservation opinion. It is, in the last analysis, to prevent human impoverishment through promoting human progress.

Although bird lectures, and some on other animals, were given in the early part of this century, the volume was small. Usually they were not presented by organizations, but by individual lecturers seeking personal profit or acclaim. The big jump in public attendance at wildlife and conservation lectures came with the development of Audubon Screen Tours in the past ten years, now reaching an estimated 700,000 persons annually in North America.

The organization of children in schools and other groups into clubs receiving informative leaflets about birds began as far back as 1910, and surely has been an outstanding factor in our generation in the development of public opinion favoring conservation. It was only during the past 20 years, however, and to some extent very recently, that the scope of the informative material furnished both the children and their teachers and leaders was broadened to include the protection of habitats and the interrelationships of all renewable resources.

It might be said that a primary objective of all of the new programs of the second half of your Society's existence has been to provide opportunity to members and other friends to participate in doing, as distinct from being urged, told, or aroused.

While the value of intangibles has surely been recognized to some degree ever since man was released from cave-man status, it is only in this century that an appreciation of those intangible values has received volume expression; for example, the value of a sunset, a snow-capped range of mountain peaks, human health and happiness. Every year more and more people realize that it is not only impossible but unreasonable to attempt to evaluate intangibles in dollars or other monetary terms.

We are still far from our goal. No doubt there will be new developments in regard to policy and objectives with succeeding generations, but it would seem that, insofar as the scope of your Society's objectives is concerned, it now "covers the waterfront." Governments may come and go and policies change, but the need for conservation, like the law of supply and demand, goes on forever. Conservation affects profoundly the physical, spiritual, and economic welfare of every man, woman, and child, bar none, everywhere and always.

To me it seems that the greatest progress in conservation in our generation has been the growing recognition of its basic relation to human progress. With this has come the broadening of horizons and the scope of the operations and goals of the organizations working in the conservation vineyard.

It is easy to be pessimistic, in the face of human population pressures and the obstacles of human fear and greed, but it is truly remarkable how much progress has been made in so little time. It takes stamina, persistence, determination, and faith to keep forging ahead toward our objectives. It is gratifying to realize that every day the Society enjoys the encouragement of more and more people. We have hitched our wagon to a star, and we intend to keep on "going places" in the attainment of our goals.

SNOWY EGRETS

AT EAST RIVER

ROOKERY

Helen G. Cruickshank

Conservation sometimes seems like a perpetually losing battle, but it has won great victories, one of the greatest being its victory over commerce and fashion, both of which seemed bent upon the destruction of several especially beautiful birds—including the egret. In the one year 1914, 21,528 ounces of this bird's plumes are said to have been sold on the London market alone and this meant the death of nearly 130,000 adult birds plus the death of their orphaned nestlings, since the birds are in full plumage only at the time when they are raising their families. Many of the plumes came from Venezuela but in the United States a chief source was Florida. In England the Royal Society for the Preservation of Wild Birds conducted a campaign which shamed fashion into abandoning the vogue responsible for so much cruel slaughter and in the United States County Life *also mounted a protest.*

In Florida one of the Audubon Society's wardens in a sanctuary was murdered by a poacher who was promptly acquitted by a jury. Nevertheless, here also fashion changed; strict laws protecting the egret were passed; and today women seem to get along very happily without the borrowed plumes bought at the cost of so much inhumanity.

THE snowy egret is one of those unusual birds that fully lives up to its name. Its plumage glistens with the white usually associated only with new-fallen snow in bright sunlight. Dense masses of fragile, recurved plumes, as delicate in appearance as snowflakes, develop during the breeding season. These plumes may be held close against the body or lifted and spread until the entire bird is clothed in a frail, misty veil of white. Then it seems to me the most beautiful of all birds. Its legs are black and shine as if lacquered, and the feet are golden. The bill is black, the lores are clear yellow. The eyes are yellow, too, making a sharp contrast with the black pupils.

From *Flight into Sunshine*. New York: The Macmillan Company, 1948.

Late in the nineteenth century the beauty of these birds aroused the cupidity of man, and fashion fanned the flame of greed. For some time after the turn of the century, it was feared that snowy egrets would be exterminated in our country. The rarer they became, the higher soared the prices of the plumes until they were literally worth their weight in gold. Finally the plumes brought as much as $32.00 an ounce. As the value of the plumes skyrocketed, it became profitable to track down even the smallest colony.

So one of the most horrid periods of bloody destruction that has overtaken our wild life was ushered in. The killing served neither the need for food nor warmth. Only silly vanity was gratified by the annihilation of these beautiful birds. Men fought and sometimes killed each other to maintain control over colonies of snowy egrets. When the eggs hatched and the instinct to care for the hungry young was strongest, the killers descended on the colonies. They shot each bird as it attempted to return to its helpless young. Soon the desecration of the nests would be complete for the instinct of the adults to shelter and feed their young was powerful enough to pull them back in the face of gunfire.

The valuable, recurved plumes grow in definite patches known as scalps, and after the adults were killed, they were "scalped." Then the bloody, mangled bodies were thrown aside, and the killers withdrew to find a market for their ill-gotten booty.

Meanwhile the young birds were left to certain death. Some met a merciful death at the claws or teeth of some hungry wild creature, but others died slowly of heat, cold or starvation.

For many years the destruction continued until the snowy egrets, once common as far north as New York City, were seen no more. Even in the remote southern marshes where once clouds of them had filled the sky, there remained but a tiny remnant.

Just in time, the National Audubon Society was organized and hastened to combat the ruthless killing of this beautiful creature. The society fought a glorious and winning battle. It fought for humaneness and with a desire to conserve precious beauty for future generations. It fought against gangs organized to exploit, for personal gain, wealth which belonged to the nation.

It was a long and bitter fight. Bands of killers that had fought one another for possession of the birds turned upon the law-enforcement officers. More than one of those officers who gallantly gave his life to save the birds, gave it for an ideal and a vision of the future. On wild and lonely Cape Sable not far from one of the great snowy egret rookeries of today, lies Guy Bradley, an Audubon warden who gave his life for the cause of conservation. His unflinching courage in the face of danger gives him a permanent place in the story of American bird conservation.

Those who made sacrifices for bird protection made no futile gesture. Slowly, under that protection, the snowy egrets increased in numbers and spread farther and farther northward. Today they are once more nesting as far north as New Jersey. During their postnuptial wanderings they are again seen in New York and even as far north as Massachusetts.

THE
GUY BRADLEY
STORY

Charles M. Brookfield

The Audubon Society wardens stationed at its various sanctuaries are its shock troopers and its troubleshooters as well. As guardians they are by no means always popular with those who would hunt for "sport" or for commercial exploiters and they have more than once been victims of violence.
The story of Guy Bradley is given here.

ACROSS the calm waters of Florida Bay a series of distant shots cracked faintly in the still summer air. It was the eighth of July; the year 1905. Young Guy Bradley, Audubon Warden of Monroe County, reached for his .32 caliber revolver, gave his wife, Fronie, a hasty kiss, the two small sons a pat on the head, jumped into his boat, and took off toward the sound of shooting. Near Oyster Keys he could see a schooner anchored. Bradley recognized the boat—Walter Smith's. This was to be a dangerous business—the arrest of a tricky violator who had already threatened to kill him.

As Bradley drew closer, a man aboard the schooner fired a shot in the air. The warning was heeded by the rookery raiders ashore—two men came off in a skiff, one carrying dead birds. But they were too late. Before the schooner could get underway, Bradley's boat was alongside.

"I want that boy—the one with the birds," called Bradley. "He's under arrest."

"You ain't got no warrant. I'll be damned if you'll get him," answered the man with the rifle who stood on the schooner's deck above Bradley.

Two shots rang out. The little .32 ball lodged in the schooner's mast but the heavy Winchester rifle bullet entered the left side of Bradley's neck, ranging downward through his body. The little boat bearing a crumpled body slowly drifted with the gentle southeast breeze. A thin red stream trickled through the floor-boards and mixed with the bilge-water below. The schooner sailed away.

The chain of events leading up to this tragedy began years before, shortly after the Chicago fire, when Edwin Ruthven Bradley brought his wife, Lydia, and two sons to Florida.

Arriving in the state about 1870, the Bradleys were Florida pioneers. The eldest boy, Louis, was four, and little Guy still a baby. The Bradleys settled in the pine woods near Orlando, cleared the land and started a citrus grove, but Edwin who had been a post office employee in Chicago, had a hankering to be near salt water. They moved to Melbourne, Florida, then to Lantana. Old grandfather E. C. F. Bradley, a civil engineer who had laid out many of Chicago's streets, came south to avoid cold winters and to visit the family in Lantana.

Although Edwin's two boys, Louis and Guy, spent most of their time hunting and fishing and had little formal education, their father became for a time Dade County Superintendent of Schools. This position, in that day, could not have been too arduous, for though the county stretched along the coast from the St. Lucie River to Florida Bay, the population in 1880 was but 257 persons. No doubt Guy Bradley picked up some knowledge of surveying from his grandfather. Their mother taught both boys to play and read music. Louis played the "big fiddle" and Guy the "little fiddle." With others, they formed a string band that played for dances and parties at the big hotel in Palm Beach. Each young man received five dollars to play all night. Guy Bradley became quite a musician.

Development of Florida's east coast was well under way in the early 1890s when Edwin Bradley became assistant superintendent of the Florida Coast Line Canal and Transportation Company, then engaged in dredging the East Coast Canal. He met J. E. Ingraham and became agent for the Florida East Coast Land Company, later the Model Land Company. The Bradleys, lured by free land, moved again from church and school to the remote Cape Sable country. Edwin and the boys each "took up" one quarter mile of waterfront, as all the settlers had agreed, extending as far back from the shore as they cared to go. Settlers grew potatoes, tomatoes, and eggplants without fertilizer in the rich hammock land, and raised numbers of chickens. Produce was carried by sailboat to Key West and sold. Those who were less industrious lived by fishing and hunting egrets for their plumes.

By 1900 the settlement at Flamingo could boast a post office and a schoolhouse with one teacher. Edwin Bradley was postmaster and his son Louis sailed the mailboat to Key West. W. R. Burton opened a general store, the only one in Flamingo, and married Edwin Bradley's daughter, Margaret. Their descendents live in Miami today. One day a strange west coast schooner put in at Flamingo with two brothers named Vickers and their sister, Fronie, aboard. Guy Bradley fell in love with Fronie. They married and within a few years two sons, Ellis and Morrel, arrived to add to their happiness.

Commercialization and "living off the country" always takes toll of wildlife. It was not surprising that by 1900 our beautiful plume birds —American and snowy egrets—were almost extinct in Florida. The rate of slaughter was tremendous. In the nesting season of 1892 just one of the many "feather merchants" in Jacksonville shipped 130,000 bird "scalps" (skins with the feathers on) to New York for the millinery trade! The big profits from the sale of egret scalps went to the milliners. Plume hunters got only $1.25 per scalp at Brickell's store on the Miami River. Even so, if a thousand parent birds were shot at a rookery, the heartless effort was well repaid. Several thousand young birds starving to death in the nests meant little where such pay was involved. Whites and Indians raided and killed with no thought of the future. Since the parent birds have plumes only in the nesting season, killing for plumes brought death to the season's young. Florida had no effective law to prevent the slaughter.

A small group of earnest conservationists began fighting this destruction. In May of 1901, William Dutcher, first president of the National Committee of Audubon Societies and Chairman of the Committee on Bird Protection of the American Ornithologists' Union, came to Tallahassee, secured the introduction of a model non-game bird bill and advocated its passage before the Florida State Legislature. The bill was enacted into law and is still the basis for bird protection in Florida.

In those days there was no Florida Game and Fresh Water Fish Commission. The Governor appointed one "game warden" for each county on recommendation of the county commissioners. But Monroe County included vast stretches of wilderness—mangrove and everglades—on the mainland. Key West, the only town and the county seat, was an island. One warden could not be very effective.

The National Association of Audubon Societies, as the National Audubon Society was then called, at its own expense, employed four men to guard the remaining egret rookeries in Florida. One of these first Audubon wardens was Guy M. Bradley, and he was faithful and courageous at his job. When the ornithologist, Frank M. Chapman, returned from a trip to a rookery with Guy Bradley in 1904, the New York *Sun* quoted Chapman as follows: "That man Bradley is going to be killed sometime. He has been shot at more than once, and some day they are going to get him."

Sanford L. Cluett, vice president of Cluett, Peabody and Company, had known Guy Bradley since 1888 in Palm Beach. In 1905 Mr. Cluett visited Flamingo and talked with his friend. Years later he wrote: "I spent several days there, and Guy told me of his connection with the

Audubon Society—and further told me that he was going to arrest a poacher who was a dangerous character. This matter worried him much, and he showed me his nickel-plated, I believe, .32 caliber pistol which he carried. I told him I thought it was altogether inadequate. We said good-bye on my leaving there—in fact, he came out in his rowboat with his little boy to say farewell."

Exactly what happened on that July day in 1905 will never be known. After the shooting, Walter Smith and his sons sailed to Key West. Guy's boat drifted into Sawfish Hole, near East Cape Sable. Here his body was found by the Roberts boys who were attracted to the spot by a flock of vultures wheeling in the air overhead.

Smith, in default of $5000 bond, was held in jail in Key West pending action of the grand jury. The National Association of Audubon Societies retained State Senator W. Hunt Harris of Key West and Col. J. T. Saunders of Miami to assist the prosecution. Two weeks later the newspapers carried headlines: *Indignant Neighbors Burn Smith's House—Flamingo People Incensed Over Killing of Guy Bradley*. With Key West dateline, the story went on: "The Negro and his wife, who were occupying Smith's house since he came to give himself up, were ordered to move out, and as soon as they were out the torch was applied and everything that would burn was destroyed. This act shows that the residents of Flamingo are indignant over the killing of Guy Bradley and that it would be unwise for Smith to return there, if he is released."

And Smith was released—five months later. The prosecution failed, despite the additional legal talent, and the testimony of S. L. (Uncle Steve) Roberts. "Uncle Steve" quoted Smith as admitting that in April Bradley had arrested Smith for shooting in the rookery, that Smith had a Winchester rifle, and had told him that if Bradley ever attempted to arrest him again, he would certainly kill the warden. The grand jury at Key West "deemed the evidence of the State insufficient to bring the accused to trial and failed to present a true bill." For Smith, this was the same as an acquittal.

But Guy Bradley did not give his life in vain. His death focused national attention on bird protection. Florida conservationists were outraged. President William Dutcher spoke for the National Association of Audubon Societies: "Every movement must have martyrs, and Guy Bradley is the first martyr to bird protection. A home is broken up, children left fatherless, their mother widowed, a faithful and devoted warden cut off in the movement. Heretofore the price had been the life of birds. Now human blood has been added." The National Association of Audubon Societies raised funds and bought a house in Key West for Guy's widow, Fronie, and the children.

The killing of Bradley, followed by the brutal murder of Audubon Warden McLeod by bird plume hunters near Charlotte Harbor, South

Carolina, in 1908, caused a shift in the conservation battlefront. The Audubon Society struck at the very heart of the traffic in bird "scalps" —the millinery trade in New York. The "Audubon Plumage Bill" was introduced in the Legislature at Albany. T. Gilbert Pearson, President of the Society, successfully spearheaded the fight for passage of this bill to outlaw the commercial use of wild bird feathers in New York State. Signed by Governor Charles Evans Hughes in 1910, the bill was enacted into law.

It is a great source of satisfaction that the Cape Sable country, scene of Guy Bradley's efforts and death and home of the wild birds he died to save, is preserved forever within the boundaries of the Everglades National Park. Ill-considered drainage canals ruined the land for farming by letting spring tides flood it with salt water. Hurricanes destroyed most of the original buildings, but the village lingered on for a time as a group of fishermen's shanties on stilts.

Out on the lonely sand beach of East Cape Sable stands a gravestone inscribed:

GUY M. BRADLEY

1870–1905

Faithful Unto Death

As Game Warden of Monroe County
He Gave His Life for the Cause
to Which He Was Pledged.

THE STORY OF

HAWK MOUNTAIN

Maurice Broun

The three greatest threats against the survival of wildlife in America are probably these (in decreasing order of importance): (1) the spread of cities and the exploitation of natural resources which involve the inevitable destruction of habitats and food supplies; (2) the reckless killers who sometimes call themselves "sportsmen"; (3) well-meaning but uninformed "nature lovers" who want to protect the "nice" and the "cute" animals by destroying their natural enemies— without whom the balance of nature upon which the welfare of all depends cannot preserve itself.

The "sportsmen" and "nature lovers" are the modern successors of the old-fashioned gamekeeper who classified all living creatures as either "game" or "vermin" and did his best or worst to exterminate the latter. Neither realized what modern research has demonstrated again and again: namely that the natural enemy of the species is also an indispensable friend without whom the balance of nature upon which the welfare of all depends cannot maintain itself.

In the past hawks were—and to a lesser extent still are—conspicuous victims. For years large companies of gunners used to station themselves at a certain season under the flyways along which these birds migrated in order to shoot them down—some gunners frankly indulging the lust to kill, others offering the more or less sincere excuse that they were "protecting" other birds from the villains who preyed upon them. Here is the story of one highly successful effort to put an end to this stupid and cruel practice.

I GREW up in the heart of Boston—a poor environment, perhaps, for anyone to cultivate a love for wild birds. But I was fortunate. I met many expert and amateur bird students in the city park, and all were helpful and encouraging to the small boy consumed with the bird passion. Within five years, with borrowed binoculars and books, I had learned and identified more than two hundred kinds of birds within

From *Hawks Aloft*. New York: Dodd, Mead & Company, 1948.

five miles of the State House. And then my career with birds really began with a research job in the State House, in the Department of Agriculture, under two master bird men: Edward Howe Forbush, dean of American ornithologists, who for forty years until his death in 1929, had been State Ornithologist of Massachusetts; and his assistant, Dr. John B. May. It was a privilege to be associated with these men, both of whom were a tremendous stimulus and an inspiration to me. I helped Mr. Forbush for three years in the compilation of his monumental *Birds of Massachusetts and Other New England States*.

Mr. May was an authority on hawks. He understood hawks better than anyone else I knew. Perhaps it was my daily contact with Dr. May that crystallized my interest in hawks. In any event, the occasional hawks that I was fortunate to see in and around the outskirts of the city quickened my blood "like fiercely ringing bells or far-off bugles."

I learned with pain that not everyone felt about hawks as I did. My sentiments were akin to Thoreau's, who wrote "I would rather never taste chicken's meat or hen's eggs than never to see a hawk sailing through the upper air again. This sight is worth incomparably more than chicken soup or a boiled egg." But mankind in general seemed bent on the extinction of the birds of prey, whose depredations on game birds could never be compared with the depredations of man himself.

Then, late in 1932, I learned about the graveyard of hawks at Drehersville, in east-central Pennsylvania. At that time I was a research associate at the Austin Ornithological Research Station, on Cape Cod. A fresh copy of *Bird Lore* on my desk carried the shocking intelligence in a few words, signed by Richard H. Pough: "On top of Blue Mountain above Drehersville, Schuylkill County, an appalling slaughter is going on . . . Blue Mountain is a long, continuous ridge along which thousands of hawks pass in migration. First the broad-wings in September, and out of this flight I would say 60 were shot. Then came the sharp-shinned and Cooper's hawks—thousands of these were killed. The enclosed photographs show 218 birds picked up in about an hour last Sunday morning at one stand. Among others I have found 5 ospreys, a protected bird, of course, but one that will be shot every time, along with eagles, sparrow hawks, flickers, blue jays, so long as hawk-shooting of this sort is permitted. When 100 or 150 men, armed with pump guns, automatics, and double-barreled shotguns are sitting on top of a mountain looking for a target, no bird is safe. The birds are seldom retrieved, and I have found many wounded birds, some alive after several days."

To a young conservationist, deeply sensitive to the value and beauty of our native hawks, *Bird Lore's* fragmentary picture of carnage was profoundly shocking. And the worst of it was, I thought, that little if anything could be done to stop that slaughter, since Pennsylvania laws at that time provided merely nominal protection to but three kinds of hawks: the osprey, the bald eagle, and the sparrow hawk.

Until recent years the extensive fall migrations of hawks and eagles along the Kittatinny Ridge were almost unknown to ornithologists. This is remarkable, for the flyway begins but a few miles above New York City. The Kittatinny Ridge, with a maximum elevation of two thousand feet, extends in unbroken relief from southeastern New York southwest across five states, and elsewhere along the ridge groups of men sought out favorable spots to kill the migrating hawks. By far the most popular, and most infamous, shooting grounds were located on a spur of the ridge, above Drehersville.

The topography of this ridge (designated as Blue Mountain on U.S. topographic maps) must be understood if we are to appreciate this concentration point of hawks and eagles. The long ridge, along which the hawks fly southward with a minimum of effort, riding the ascending air currents, here narrows to a slender bottleneck: a focal point for all migrating hawks. The razor-back ridge ends abruptly; its wooded slopes merge into a broad cross-ridge which zigzags southward. Jutting conspicuously from the trees of the cross-ridge are a series of promontories, in the line of flight of the migrating birds, affording a wide sweep of view down the valleys and across the ridges. A road winds up from Drehersville, crossing the broad cross-ridge. Every fall, for more years than most local residents could remember, hunters gravitated to this place in the mountains to enjoy a week's holiday. As many as one hundred and fifty to four hundred hunters swarmed over the mountain "lookouts" on Sunday, and perhaps half as many were on hand during week days. Some of the hunters came from points sixty to a hundred miles distant, so attractive was this "sport" to the hunting fraternity.

The hawk-shoots had long been known to the Pennsylvania Game Commission. The Game Commission apparently favored the killing. In the early '20s the hawks had one articulate friend, the Honorable Henry W. Shoemaker. He tried to induce the Game Commission to put an end to the shooting but his efforts were fruitless. The Game Commission was responsible, in 1929, for legislation placing a five-dollar bounty on goshawks, a hawk that is rare in Pennsylvania. Not one hunter in a hundred would know a goshawk if he should ever see one. A goshawk bounty is really an incentive to kill all hawks, with the agreeable feature that the state has to pay the bounty only on goshawks.

Meanwhile the "hawk-shoots" were being well advertised in local newspapers. A typical example follows, quoted from the Pottsville Journal of October, 1929: "SPORTSMEN SHOOT MIGRATING HAWKS. Pottsville Hunters Knock Down Pests from Point of Vantage in Blue Mountains. Kill 300 in single day.

"Thousands of huge hawks, redtails, marsh and goshawks, borne by a stiff northwest wind over a steep pinnacle in the Blue Mountains . . . are daily challenging hunters and sportsmen of Pottsville and vicinity.

"Chilled by the early October winds, many thousands of hawks are sweeping past the mountain pinnacle, inviting extermination, a challenge that has been accepted by local sportsmen and hunters who are shooting hundreds every favorable day.

"Impressed by the unusual opportunity to wipe out thousands of enemies to bird and game life in the State, a Pottsville sportsman today urged local hunters to cooperate in killing hawks.

"The migrating birds pass within a few feet of the ground at the mountain pinnacle, generally between the hours of 10 A.M. and 3 P.M., only when a stiff northwest wind is blowing. With ordinary shotguns, 300 hawks were killed last Friday . . .

"For years, hunters have been seeking the spot in the Blue Mountains over which the hawks pass in their migration to the south. Finally discovering the place, a number have almost daily congregated and poured many boxes of shells into the blackened skies, killing as many as eight with a single bullet. . . ."

The "sportsman" was reputed also to be a sporting goods merchant, doing a lucrative business selling shells to the local sportsmen who accepted the challenge of the hawks which were brashly "inviting extermination." It is interesting to note the familiarity with basic details of hawk flights, such as requisite wind conditions and the best time of day to be on hand. The slaughter is condoned with the usual falsehood concerning "enemies to bird and game life."

A news item similar to this, reprinted in a Philadelphia newspaper, attracted two young conservationists of that city, Henry H. Collins, Jr., and Richard H. Pough. During the fall of 1932 they made five trips to the Blue Mountain, above Drehersville. These were no pleasure jaunts such as people make nowadays. Collins and Pough were amazed and shocked. They were mad enough too to give prompt, vigorous expression to their investigations. Collins, in the *Bulletin of the Hawk and Owl Society* for 1933, called the attention of conservationists to the wanton slaughter.

"The season extends from early September to December," Collins wrote. "The height appears to be during the first weeks of October. On one occasion, sixty-four automobiles, the means of transportation of over two hundred gunners, were parked along the mountain road. On another occasion there were forty cars, with about one hundred and fifty hunters, including twelve women.

"The hunting has been going on for many years. It appears to have grown in popularity since the World War, but one hunter spoke of his father shooting there as far back as sixty years ago.

"One case of extreme cruelty witnessed was that of a wounded hawk tied to a log. When another hawk appeared in the sky, a man would jab the wounded bird with a stick to make it scream and thus attract its fellow migrant to a similar fate. Such cruelty is illegal under the humane laws of the State and all engaged in it are liable as accomplices. Wardens on duty, however, have never made any attempt to stop it. Another decoy consisted of a hawk thrown into a tree by the means of a stone on a string and left dangling there in the northwest breeze.

"Wardens, if on duty, will call out, 'It's an osprey. Don't shoot!' but usually a gun goes off anyway. The bird is killed, and in the confusion among so many hunters the guilty one usually escapes."

Blinded pigeons were also commonly used to decoy the hawks at the various shooting-stands. The pigeons were tied to a long pole, and when an approaching hawk was sighted the hunter waved the pole, causing the pigeon to flutter wildly. Almost any bird of prey could readily be lured into the gun sights by such means. Such practices are still commonly employed elsewhere in the mountains of Pennsylvania where hawk shooting persists.

While Pough and Collins were making their investigations, the S.P.C.A. was urged to stop the hawk-shooting. This organization arranged with the State Police to have two members of the police force on duty atop the mountain. If the policemen expected to halt the horror, they might as well have tried to stop the flow of black waters of the little river winding along the foot of the mountain. Years later I was to meet one of these gentlemen, Ernest Barr of Philadelphia. He told me, "We spent three nightmarish weeks on this mountain. There were as many as four hundred hunters one day, and so many birds were slaughtered that a bad odor hung over the place. We couldn't do a thing about it." So the holocaust continued.

Each fall a local resident would drive a truckload of cartridges up the mountain and ply a brisk trade. Other men, equally anxious to profit, gathered up the used shells to salvage the old brass.

Blind men! Unfolding before their eyes was the mystery, the eternal wonder of migration. But they could not see. What meant it to them, the bold, impetuous speed of the peregrine? Of what account the grace and fluency of osprey moving down the sky? Or the wings of an eagle slanting into the west like the sails of a galleon? Leonardo da Vinci perceived aerodynamics in the vibrant vans of the *Buteo;* but to these men— nonsense, *kill it!* The sky-borne freedom of the falcon was to be stopped and shattered by a shower of lead. The fierce purity of the wilderness reduced to mangled feathers on blood-stained rocks. . . .

This was sport. This was an opportunity to exhibit skill in marksmanship, to train the eye of the hunter for the coming game-killing season. Besides, so-called "sportsmen" and certain farmers considered it their divine right to kill every hawk. Were not all hawks "vermin," a plague to small game which God created especially for the hunters?

The hawks were not destroying property and were not even residents in Pennsylvania. The hunters were killing birds that belonged to the nation, and more specifically to the inhabitants of regions to the north and south, where the hawks summer and winter. But these hunters had no scruples; they merely expressed an atavistic urge to destroy. Untold thousands of birds had been massacred on this mountain peak during the sixty to seventy years of its desecration—and only three voices had been raised to save them.

Here was a dramatic opportunity to put an end to the horror. Who would make conservation history? A full year passed. In October, 1933, at a joint meeting of the Hawk and Owl Society, the National Association of Audubon Societies and the Linnaean Society of New York, Richard Pough, anxious to save the birds, reported that he had made contact with real estate agents of the owners of the mountain. The property could be bought at a low figure and on easy terms. Conservationists present at this meeting were confident that the problem was solved. But nothing happened to quiet the roar of guns above Drehersville.

The spring and early summer of 1934 passed, and still nothing was done. But one woman's sleep had been tormented with visions of the birds gasping in agony or blown to bits in the skies.

Mrs. Charles Edge, of New York City, now moved in on the field of battle. Mrs. Edge was, and still is, chairman of the militant Emergency Conservation Committee which had performed prodigies for wildlife protection. In a span of only five years the Committee had campaigned to save our vanishing waterfowl; had fought for the preservation of elk in our national parks; the saving of Yosemite sugar pines; had worked to save the bald eagle; had sent the antelope's S.O.S. across the country; and had made a plea for effective guardianship and preservation of certain of our national parks. Mrs. Edge, as the Committee's chairman, was indefatigable.

In August of that year, Mrs. Edge obtained, without difficulty, a lease of the mountain for one year, with an option to buy from the owners. The property acquired, the next problem was the pressing one of getting someone before mid-September to protect it.

Mrs. Broun and I had been spending a pleasant summer in Vermont. Our holiday was electrified in mid-August by an urgent letter from Mrs. Edge, asking me if I would assume wardenship that autumn. "We must have a warden on the property: first to post it and then to guard it and get police protection. It is a job that needs some courage," she wrote to me.

An exciting prospect, but a hazardous one. We decided on hopping from the Green Mountains to the Blue Mountains. I replied that we would "take over" without salary; the Emergency Conservation Committee could pay our expenses, I suggested. Mrs. Edge, on the eve of her departure on a trip to Panama, wrote to us enthusiastically of her satisfaction that we would tackle the situation at "Hawk Mountain," but she warned, "I anticipate you will have real trouble with lawless hunters and and I recommend that you get promptly in touch with the Pennsylvania State Police and ask for protection on Saturdays and Sundays." On her way to the steamer, Mrs. Edge stopped at her lawyer's and signed a power of attorney giving me authority and a free hand at Hawk Mountain during her absence.

Thus "Hawk Mountain" Sanctuary came into being—the world's first sanctuary of the birds of prey. It marks an epoch in conservation.

Drehersville [we found] was a cluster of tidy houses surrounding a tiny church. Hardly a soul was in sight. Hushed tranquility, deep repose, the feeling that all was well with the world pervaded the little village. This was not at all what we had anticipated; this was alien to what we had read about: blood and thunder, and swarms of gun-toting men.

I decided that we had better run into Schuylkill Haven, some twelve miles toward Pottsville, to call on the real estate agent. We had hoped to learn from him about the mountain. We also needed quantities of "no trespassing" posters.

My first act in Schuylkill Haven was to phone four local newspapers, requesting each to carry a notice, for three successive days, announcing the new status of the mountain property, that it was henceforth an inviolate wildlife sanctuary, and that the trespassing laws would be enforced. Then we called on Gordon Reed, the agent for the property. Oh, yes, he knew all about the mountain and all about the hawk-shoots; and he succeeded in filling us with gloom. I told him that I was about to put up "no trespassing" posters along the road, especially at the beginning of the trail that led through the woods to the shooting stands. When we parted, Mr. Reed suggested, "After you get your posters up, take my advice and *scram!*"

Early morning found me putting up posters along the rocky road. Where did the bounds of the property run through the woods? Not even the neighboring owners could tell exactly. Five years later a costly survey revealed to us the extent of the 1398 acres. For the time being, it was necessary to post both sides of a stretch of road one and a half miles; for the road, a public thoroughfare, bisected the Sanctuary. It was dreadfully hot. I was surprised that no hunters had come. I did not know that it was too early in the season, nor did I realize that the hawk-hunters knew just when to flock the mountain.

By mid-afternoon the lonely road flaunted posters every few yards. A local game warden, apparently startled by my newspaper notices which had just been printed, came to find out what it was all about. The warden tried to impress me with the utter futility of my job. "Wait till the coal-miners from Tamaqua come along; then you'll see," he warned me. While we argued, two carloads of hunters drove up—the vanguard. There was much guttural, explosive language from the visitors. But they left the mountain, bewildered, to say the least. In the days to follow I was to meet many such men, many of whom I tried to reason with as to why hawks should not be killed indiscriminately. Generally, these men were irritated, unwilling to listen. The game warden, a man named Jones, concluded his visit with the statement that I had the hardest job on my hands that I'd ever have in my life. "You can't stop those guys from shooting hawks up here," he said, despite the fact that I had already done so, before his eyes!

It suddenly came to me that, after all, in spite of our right, our duty to stop the hawk-shooting, we were, from the standpoint of the hunters, meddlesome outsiders, and as such we were bound to arouse indignation. Of course, it did not matter to the hunters that most of the hawks also came down from New England and New York. Did they ever give a thought to the rights of others?

Before the close of the day I prepared a thousand word statement— "A New Deal for Hawks"—defending the action of the Emergency Con-servation Committee in leasing the mountaintop to prevent the killing of hawks. It hammered out the theme of unjust persecution and the eco-nomic importance of the hawks. Every trip up and down the mountain was agony to tires, but I sent the article off the same evening to three local newspapers, whose combined circulation exceeded 200,000. The ar-ticle promptly appeared in print, and was copied in other newspapers, as far away as Scranton.

Daybreak of our third day on the mountain found me patrolling the road. I was anxious to see some hawks, but was utterly ignorant of the hawk-flights and their *modus operandi*. And, naïvely, I expected to see hunters at that ridiculous hour. During the night someone had ripped off most of the "no trespassing" posters.

As I patrolled the road that day, replacing posters, I was impressed with the countless numbers of old cartridge shells scattered along a quarter-mile stretch of road above the present entrance to the sanctuary. In the early afternoon I was thrilled to see my first flight of hawks, some fifty birds, including three bald eagles, three peregrine falcons, a few broad-wings and sharp-shins, all passing fairly low over the road.

During the day three more cars came up, with seven inquiring faces, and shotguns ready for business. But they departed promptly. One of the men made a slurring remark about the "New York chiselers going to hog all the shooting."

The following morning I found that every single one of my sixty-odd

posters along the road had been removed. It began to rain, for which I
rejoiced, since no one was likely to venture up the mountain to make
trouble. I drove into Hamburg, the nearest large town, to obtain more
posters, and to make contact with game wardens and the State Police. I
thought, naïvely, that I could obtain official protection on weekends. I
went over to the police barracks and learned that the police had their
hands full with strikes in the local industries.

The weekend was upon us. I drove up the mountain after breakfast
and in a drizzling rain I managed to nail up an entirely new set of posters.
The weather cleared in the early afternoon. A few hawks passed low
over the road. Only two cars appeared, each emptying gunners—five in
one car. These men asked if they could walk to the pinnacle, and I allowed them to do so, without their guns. Returning, an old man in the
group had this to offer: "A fellow doesn't want a gun up there; he should
bring a pair of field glasses and a camera." These were the first heartening
words I had heard on the mountain since our arrival.

Sunday brought raw, nasty weather, which suited me immensely. At
5 A.M. I was at my post of duty on the mountain road, expecting hunters
and the promised trouble. Nothing happened, expect the weather, and
obligingly it poured all through the day.

Looking back on those early, disquieting experiences, I marvel at our
great good luck with the weather. Providentially, torrents of rain fell on
three successive weekends, and the anticipated hordes of hawk-killers did
not materialize. The game wardens had warned me, however, that early
October would bring plenty of hawks and plenty of trouble in the form
of toughs from the coal region.

Mrs. Edge and her son Peter came out to the mountain in the middle
of the second week to see how everything had been going. The situation
was well in hand, and we had had no trouble—not yet—but it behooved
us to engage a deputy sheriff, I advised Mrs. Edge. Obviously we must
secure the services of someone who was authorized to make arrests, if
necessary. I had already begun to cast around for the right man and,
through the help of a sympathetic notary in a nearby town, I hoped to
engage Bob Kramer, if Mrs. Edge approved. She did. The cost of maintaining Kramer for ten weeks was another worry for Mrs. Edge, but she
did not hesitate. Bob Kramer, of nearby Auburn, a sturdy man of forty-
two, good-humored and dependable, possessed an important weapon
which I lacked: the Pennsylvania Dutch tongue. He had been engaged in
police work for years. Kramer would have agreed to work for us on
weekends only, but we took him on daily, beginning the end of September. I also engaged a surveyor, who successfully determined our important west boundary, the one nearest the hunters of Drehersville.

Meanwhile I continued my vigil, day after day, at the entrance to the
sanctuary, where few hawks are seen unless the wind is in a southerly

quarter. All sorts of men with high-powered rifles and shotguns came to indulge in the old "sport," only to learn that on *this* mountain it was a thing of the past. A few hunters came from New Jersey, and two from Delaware. My tongue wagged incessantly those first few weeks. It was no fun trying to convince those men of the folly of shooting hawks. Many were surly, and some went off with pent-up truculence. My only weapons that entire season was a ready tongue and a bold front—under which I sometimes quailed! But Kramer had a gun which was respected.

The evening of the seventeenth two young men said they had been gunning a few miles up the ridge, during the afternoon. They asked me whether or not I had seen the big hawk flight. No, I had not. Then I learned that they had counted almost two thousand hawks passing high over the ridge that afternoon; a broad-wing flight, I gathered. I was chagrined that I had missed the spectacle. Not until October 7th did I make daily visits to the mountain summit to observe the wonderful hawk-flights, while Kramer patrolled the road.

The possibility of an "invasion" of hunters now became very real. Kramer's daily presence had deterred the local hotheads from forcing their way, but I was advised that it might be necessary for me to stand guard at the old shooting-stands on the crest of the mountain. From there it was possible to observe the various approaches to the summit, through the woods from the north or from the west.

One day I learned almost with disbelief that a certain obstreperous character in Drehersville, who worked cheek by jowl with the officials of the numerous hunting clubs, had been obtaining sworn affidavits from many of the local farmers that the hawks often came down and carried off young pigs! This same man killed a red-tailed hawk and, to taunt us, he hung the bird, with wings spread, from the girder of the little bridge over which we passed twice daily. There the bird hung for about ten days. I took a picture of it which helped us in our money-raising campaign.

Now a great hullabaloo was raised in gunning circles throughout two counties against the out-of-state "chiselers." The farmers in the vicinity made the loudest squawk. They not only resented us and our assumed arrogance in taking over "their" mountain, they resented the name "Hawk Mountain" and claimed that there never had been such a place. Local newspapers belabored us and carried the usual stale message that the hawks were killing off game. A great to-do was made by the Pottsville merchant "sportsman" who used to come up the mountain on weekends, his truck loaded with cartridges to sell. We learned that the local sportsmen's clubs, representing 15,000 hunters, had engaged a lawyer to search all land titles and find loopholes which might break Mrs. Edge's lease, and to buy the mountain, if possible. The hunters were holding frequent meetings to decide what to do.

A few days later, the agitated hawk-shooters, though still contemplating the purchase of "Hawk Mountain," leased a considerable tract of land near Port Clinton. I saw their advertisement in a newspaper, urging gunners to kill hawks in this new place, about four miles down the ridge, and offering gunners "a new line of shells, at $.60 a case." Kramer investigated the Port Clinton hawk-shoots. These could be serious on days when the wind was easterly, but at no time was the slaughter comparable to that which had occurred formerly on our mountain. The place was also much more difficult of access.

Most of the hunters that I encountered had been killing hawks on this mountain for many years. Most of them were obdurate in their opinion of hawks in general and, they insisted, all hawks should be exterminated. It was useless to argue that the hawks do not feed while migrating, and that the good habits of the birds of prey involved mainly rodents. One farmer, in spite of his carping, allowed his large flock of white leghorns to roam the fields at the foot of the mountain. Why, I asked the gunners, were there so many grouse drumming in these upland woods? Here, at the greatest concentration point for hawks in the entire country, the ruffed grouse abounded; one day I had counted thirty-three of the birds in different parts of the Sanctuary. Rabbits, quail and pheasants were plentiful in the excellent cover of the old fields in the vicinity of Drehersville. But perhaps I was "seeing things," for the hawks kill off the game!

In early October much of the opposition had quieted, but it looked like the calm before the storm, and throughout the month Kramer and I anticipated trouble daily. With the fourth week approaching, a group of local hunters was planning to mob Kramer and me and force their way to the summit.

Late Friday afternoon two husky young men, built like fullbacks, appeared without guns at the Sanctuary. I was pleasantly surprised to learn that they had been recruited by Richard Pough to help us protect the place for a week or so. Pough, one of the "discoverers" of the hawk-shoots, had been in constant touch with Mrs. Edge. Knowing only too well what we might be up against with the lawless elements among the hawk-shooters, Pough generously arranged to have Charlie French and Dudley Wagar, both of Philadelphia, help us.

The following day it poured again—the fourth soggy Saturday! The four of us, Kramer, the newcomers and I spent a few hours on the mountain road, nevertheless, hunched in our cars. We even turned away a few hunters who had come from Reading.

Sunday, October 7th brought beautiful weather and ideal hawking conditions. Kramer and Wagar took the road, while French and I posted ourselves at the summit rocks. It was a day of many surprises, and some drama—but not the drama we had expected. We had plenty of company, some of it very talented. Ten members of the Delaware Valley Ornithological Club, of Philadelphia, including Richard Pough, Samuel Scoville, Jr., the writer, Julian K. Potter, the ornithologist, and Jacob B. Abbott, the artist, were among the observers at the Lookout that day. The hawk flight was disappointing—only a hundred birds of thirteen species. But to me it was tremendously exciting to see so many kinds of hawks. A special feature was an adult golden eagle. The great bird came obligingly close, an eye-opener to the ornithological gathering—and the first of many golden eagles that were to lure bird watchers from all over the country.

Early in the afternoon we heard some shooting on the ridgetop, about a half mile directly behind us. Charlie French and I and one of the D.V.O.C. men took off through the woods and presently reached the west boundary of the Sanctuary. There, on the edge of our line, marked by "no trespassing" posters, were ten men, two of them perched high in a tree, blazing away at occasional hawks passing just out of shotgun range. The men were just off the Sanctuary property. There was nothing I could do, except perhaps to wait until they killed a protected species (ten ospreys and a bald eagle were the only "protected" birds that passed), and then I would prosecute the killer. So we leaned against a tree and waited, silently. The shooting stopped, the men were maddened that we just stood there and stared at them. Each passing minute increased the tension till one of the men snapped, "Well, whatcha goin' to do about it?" I replied, "Just stay here and see what you fellows might do." The fellow lowered his gun, came up to me menacingly and said, "I'll knock your——block off." For a moment it looked like a fight—and it might have been bad business, three unarmed men against ten with guns and hot tempers—but the fellow suddenly stopped and spluttered, "You damn hawk-lovers; you're just a bunch of barbarians."

Returning to the Lookout, I found more visitors. A "mob" had indeed come! That day seventy-four men, women and children climbed to the Lookout to enjoy the beautiful scenery and the birds. It was an inspiring sight, and it augured well for the successful outcome of our "new deal for the hawks." At the entrance, Kramer had turned away thirty-two gunners, including a few women. Ten times that number of gunners might have been on hand that day had we not spent the previous weeks impressing the hunting elements that we meant business on the mountain. Pleasant weekends thereafter brought increasing numbers of bird-students and protectionists to enjoy the hawking.

Hawk-hunters, some of them hard-bitten fellows who looked as though they would as soon shoot a mother-in-law as a hawk, continued to come late into November—a month *after* the opening of the small game season—so deep-rooted was the urge to follow this perverse and cruel "sport." But in spite of all the threats and warnings and the hubbub of the shotgun squads, we had a singularly peaceful time of it along the old mountain road. At the summit, in the few weeks that it was possible to observe the hawk-flights, we had the satisfaction of seeing more than ten thousand hawks pass safely; not a single bird was killed. Not a single untoward incident occurred in that birth-year of the Sanctuary.

BIRD INVASION

Edwin Way Teale

A rare or disappearing species naturally attracts our sympathy. On the other hand any bird which is too numerous and too successful is likely to be looked upon with disfavor. The English sparrow used to bear the brunt. Samuel Johnson said he could love anybody except an American and I have known bird lovers who felt the same way about this immigrant whom we blame on England though it is actually European. Nowadays the starling, which has spread rapidly from the east coast to the Pacific and bred in such numbers that flocks sometimes almost "darken the skies," is with some almost equally unpopular.

During the nineteenth century attempts were made to introduce many exotic birds. Nearly all of them failed and the only two which succeeded too well were the English (more properly "house") sparrow and the starling. Oddly enough the latter looked at first like another failure. But in 1891 a leader of the American Acclimatism Society liberated a certain number—no one is sure just how many—in Central Park. This time the "innoculation" took. Many people are anxious to know how to attract birds. Possibly even more would now like to know how to discourage starlings. Incidentally it is another significant fact that nearly all successful introductions are of birds which had already learned how to live either in cities or in the neighborhood of cultivation.

D URING the early days of a recent winter, the deepest snow in more than half a century lay on the fields around my home. In that time of crisis for many birds, a flock of starlings demonstrated the versatile resourcefulness that has enabled them to invade America and spread from coast to coast in less than sixty years.

Starlings are primarily ground feeders. Yet during these days we saw them probing in bark crevices like nuthatches. We saw them hovering on fluttering wings like humming birds to obtain suet from a feeding stick. We saw them bracing themselves with stiffened tails on tree trunks, like woodpeckers. We even saw them pulling apart a squirrel's nest, high in a maple tree, hunting for spiders and other edible creatures hibernating in the mass.

From *Days without Time*, New York: Dodd, Mead and Company, 1948.

Sometimes starlings catch insects on the wing like flycatchers. They have been observed scooping beetles out of the air while in full flight in the manner of swallows. And, like cowbirds, they often follow cattle and sheep across a pasture to feed on the small creatures that the grazing animals stir out of the grass.

In a tree near my study window, a starling once darted upward from a branch and snatched a piece of bread from the mouth of a surprised blue jay on the limb above. On another occasion, a starling on the ground walked up to a crust of bread where an English sparrow was feeding. Grasping one edge in its bill, and with the dogged sparrow hanging on, it swung the crust and sparrow in a crack-of-the-whip half-circle through the air. Aggressive, omnivorous, resourceful, the starling is well fitted to survive under many conditions of life. In spite of man's antagonism, it has increased and spread in America. Its conquest of this country probably is the greatest, the most dramatic bird invasion recorded in natural history.

The story of the invasion begins in the spring of 1890 when a liner from Europe steamed into New York Harbor to discharge its passengers at a pier on lower Manhattan. Sixty of those passengers rode ashore in cages. They were dark, chunky birds with yellow bills. The vessel was the *Mayflower* of the starlings.

Every one of America's untold millions of these birds, according to Dr. Frank M. Chapman, has descended from one hundred immigrants—the sixty that arrived in 1890 to be set free in Central Park and forty more that reached New York the following year. Their coming was the result of one man's fancy. That man was Eugene Schieffelin, a wealthy New York drug manufacturer. His curious hobby was the introduction into America of all the birds mentioned in the works of William Shakespeare.

Skylarks, chaffinches, nightingales, as well as English sparrows and starlings, rode across the Atlantic in cages consigned to Schieffelin. He even organized a society for the importation of foreign birds and incorporated it in Albany. Today, partly in consequence of lessons learned from his activity, no foreign bird or animal can be imported without special permission from the United States Department of Agriculture. Schieffelin was only one of several to introduce the English sparrow; but he, alone, is responsible for the starling. His skylarks and nightingale soon died out but his starlings flourished like weeds of the air.

The somewhat dubious honor of being the site of the first starling nest in America belongs to the American Museum of Natural History. Soon after the original birds were released in Central Park, a pair nested in an opening under the eaves of one of the wings of the museum. That, however, was only the beginning. The starling is one of the first birds to nest in spring. It has two brood in a season—and sometimes even three

—each producing four or five new birds. The first brood is often out of the nest before many birds have laid their eggs. Moreover, starlings set up housekeeping close together, as many as five pairs of birds nesting in the knotholes of a single tree.

In the matter of nesting material, the starling has an advantage over many other birds. It uses common and easily obtained lining for its nest. And it displays an instinctive thrift in employing such material. Unlike numerous birds, if it drops the dry grass it is carrying in its bill, it stops to pick it up again. Malcolm Davis, of the National Zoological Park, in Washington, D.C., tells of a remarkable instance of the kind in a note published in *The Auk* for October, 1946. "While walking along one of the busy streets of Washington, D.C.," he writes, "I observed several starlings carrying nesting material. One with a mouthful of dry grasses flew across the street. In mid-street, it accidentally dropped the nesting material. The grass floated down upon a passing truck. Immediately, the bird dived down upon it, falcon style, recovered the grasses from the speeding truck, and flew in the direction of the nesting site. Any factor," Davis adds, "small as it may be, that contributes to the firm establishment of a species in a certain area may be well worth considering. This small display of persistent economy may be a contributing factor to the establishment of this species."

Another and paramount factor is the fertility of the starling, its early nesting and its double broods. Each year, the multiplication of these birds is something to make the ears of the fecund rabbit droop in frustration. It was not long after they were introduced before the compound interest of this fertility began to show results.

Starlings overflowed into the suburbs of New York, onto Long Island, across the Hudson into New Jersey. In the following years, Bridgeport, New Haven, Boston, Philadelphia, Washington reported the appearance of a few starlings, then many starlings, then far too many starlings. The newcomers were driving native birds—swallows, martins, flycatchers, flickers, blue-birds—from their nesting sites. They were pushing their way into feeding grounds. They were upsetting the whole balance of nature. A bird invasion was on in full force. By that time, nothing could stop the advance of the starlings.

Not that a good many people didn't try. They are still trying. People fired shotguns into trees where the birds roosted at night and were showered with falling starlings. They doused the birds with fire hoses; they set off Roman candles; they clanged bells; they stood around beneath the trees and slapped long boards together to produce artificial thunderclaps. They set out stuffed owls, electrically-charged dummy owls, aluminum owls with eyes that would shine at night, imitation owls re-enforced with explosive charges. One man painted a live starling pure white in the belief that such an abnormal bird would frighten the others away.

In Milwaukee, Wisconsin, an ingenious janitor smeared axle-grease over the grillwork at the courthouse windows so the alighting birds skidded, bumped their noses, did flipflops and generally discouraged themselves from choosing the building as a roosting place. Molasses paste was used in some places for catching the birds. In Decatur, Illinois, an estimated twenty thousand starlings were killed in the course of a two-months' campaign. And in Washington, D.C., Government men spent their evenings jiggling strings to which were attached rubber baloons containing dried peas. The peas in the baloons produced a hissing rattle that scared the starlings out of their wits—for a time.

But all these were relatively unimportant skirmishes on a long battle line. The starlings continued to advance. They followed the Great Lakes west. They spread down the Mississippi Valley. They penetrated beyond the Rockies. They crossed the line into Canada. They flew over the Rio Grande. Today, after only slightly more than half a century of rapid multiplication, the starling occupies the country from Maine to Oregon and from Mexico to Churchill, on the Hudson Bay. It is a permanent part of our bird family. Schieffelin has given America the starling—for better or for worse.

The bad side of this bird is easy to see, particularly in fall and winter. At those seasons, old and young gather together in immense flocks. They settle in the later afternoon in treetops or on the ledges of city buildings for a social hour before going to bed. The din is tremendous. I remember walking past the White House, in Washington, one October dusk and hearing a continuous, almost deafening clamor from the starlings in the treetops. In New York City, one bridge, not far from Grant's Tomb, is the roosting place of as many as forty thousand starlings. In troops and straggling bands, they come flying across the Hudson from New Jersey, across the East River from Long Island, down from Westchester feeding grounds, as sunset nears.

Another favorite starling roost in New York City is on the Metropolitan Museum of Art on Fifth Avenue. As short winter days near an end, starling flocks stream toward this structure, sometimes flying down the streets lower than the rooftops, turning corners like soldiers on parade. In Lancaster, Pennsylvania, and Paterson, New Jersey, so many starlings perched on the hands of the town clocks that the timepieces were put out of order. During one cold February, starlings were found to be keeping their feet warm by roosting on the small electric bulbs of a theater sign in the heart of Boston. In my neighborhood, the birds sometimes fly down to perch on the tops of warm brick chimneys during the coldest weeks of winter.

Along the seacoast, wherever there are stands of the high, plumed

Phragmites, the starlings find a safe roosting place. A solid mass of these cane-like plants extends for a hundred yards along one edge of the swamp at the foot of my Insect Garden. Here, from miles around, the starlings congregate as winter evenings approach. Once, as I was walking down the hillside, a Cooper's hawk shot from between the apple trees and streaked low along the slope, a starling leading it by a rapidly diminishing distance. The dark little bird gained the haven of the Phragmites clump and the hawk rose in a swift wing-over and returned to the orchard. As it curved upward, a sound as of a great wind sweeping through the Phragmites reached me. The clump was alive with roosting starlings; they all had moved on their dry supports at the sudden approach of the hawk.

In Europe, some starling roosts have been used by the birds continuously for more than a century and a half. The fact that these birds stick pretty close to man and often flock in the downtown districts of a city make their garrulousness and gregariousness the more annoying. During fall and winter months, "starling awnings" sometimes have to be put over the entrances to public buildings as a protection against the droppings of the assembled birds. Eleven tons of droppings were cleared off the Capitol roof in Springfield, Illinois, after starlings had been roosting their for years. To some people, the odor of starlings, in the mass, is objectionable. Add to these facts a few other considerations and the causes of the starling's unpopularity are obvious. In many localities the aggressive newcomer has displaced such old favorites as the bluebird and the martin. Moreover, its appetite for ripe cherries is so great that when a starling flock alights in a tree the pits seem to rain down and the branches are stripped in a single afternoon. The starling, in many ways, comes close to being the bird that nobody wants.

But whether we want it or not, we have got it. It is here to stay. And, fortunately for us, the starling, for all its faults, has a good side.

Even the mockingbird of the South hardly excels the starling as an accomplished mimic. When I started to write this, I knew of twenty-seven different birds that the starling imitates. Now I know twenty-eight. I have just heard one of these birds, perched on a lamppost, imitate the high, trilling call of the cedar waxwing. In the yard of a friend at Stamford, Connecticut, starlings gather each autumn to feed on the ripe berries of various bushes. One old male, after dining plentifully, is in the habit of expressing the pleasures of a full stomach by going through his whole repertoire. With hardly a pause, but with many a jerk of tail and twitch of wings, it will imitate the songs of the bluebird, the wood peewee, the red-winged blackbird, the meadow lark, the bobwhite, the Carolina wren, the blue jay, the whippoorwill and the flicker.

A small boy in my neighborhood was in the habit of giving a peculiar whistle when calling his chum. Soon the chum was coming out of his house, called by the whistle, when his friend was nowhere to be seen.

He discovered that a starling, balancing itself on a telephone wire, was imitating the sound. In some instances, these birds have mimicked the barking of dogs and the peeping of baby chicks. W. H. Hudson, the English naturalist, tells of a starling he encountered in a Hampshire village that cackled like a hen whenever it brought food to the nest.

In its own right, the starling has little that can be termed truly a song. It squeaks and chatters and gives rasping cries of alarm. During breeding season, the males sometimes indulge in faint little "whisper songs," produced with the bills apparently closed. The nearest a starling comes to singing is a pleasing, long-drawn whistle that sounds like "Fee-you!"

In 1826, when John James Audubon visited England, he noted in his journal that the starlings he saw reminded him of the American meadow lark. And well they might. For although an ocean separated the two, they have many traits in common. Both walk instead of hop when on the ground. Both fly in the same manner, alternately flapping and sailing. Only the starlings, however, gather together in immense flocks to perform the aerial evolutions that are a regular feature of their autumns. In great clouds, like swarming bees, thousands of birds rise and fall, turn and circle, wings moving together, individuals lost in the coordinated mass movement of the whole. From a distance, they look like wind-blown smoke. "These aerial evolutions," Dr. Frank M. Chapman, the noted bird authority of the American Museum of Natural History, once wrote, "constitute the chief claim of the starling to a place in the Bird's Hall of Fame."

From a practical point of view, however, another side of the starling's activity is even more important. This is its consumption of insects. All during its unusually long nesting season, it is searching for insects to feed the four to six ravenous baby birds that hatch from the pale bluish or whitish eggs. Cutworms, weevils, grasshoppers, crickets, beetles, caterpillars, millipedes and spiders are thrust hastily into the wide-open mouths and immediately the parent birds are off again, hunting for another course in the day-long, continuous dinner.

Government scientists who examined the stomachs of hundreds of starlings report that this unwelcome immigrant must be classed, on the basis of its food habits, as a beneficial species. Its destruction of immense numbers of injurious insects far outbalances the loss from the cherries it eats. An increase in the number of starlings in certain parts of England is given as the explanation for the disappearance of the great "cockshafer years" of former times. During such years, the beetles appeared in immense numbers, stripping the oaks of their leaves in midsummer.

In the eastern part of the United States, where the Japanese beetle has been spreading rapidly, the starlings have developed an appetite for these ,insects. They take them both young and old, as grubs and as adult beetles. I have watched starlings going over the leaves of roadside plants, picking off the Japanese beetles. I have also seen them probing lawns with their long pointed bills, seeking out the buried larvae.

One striking instance of the value of these labors occurred in Connecticut. For several years, the birds came regularly to the yard of a friend of mine to search for beetle grubs. Marching in a straggling line across the grass, they would probe the ground. Then, one spring, a cat was added to the household and the starlings were frightened away. Before the second summer was over, the consequences became dramatically apparent. Working unseen and unhindered in the ground, the grubs of the Japanese beetle sliced their way through the grassroots, killing whole sections of the lawn. This snipped-off turf could be rolled up almost like a carpet. No other bird I know is as effective in combating such injurious grubs as the starling.

In all the world, there are about seventy species of starlings. In the United States, there is only one—the one that Eugene Schieffelin's fancy turned loose the last years of the past century. That one, to many people's way of thinking, has been enough. But in the course of time, Nature's balance will be restored. The starling will finds its level. And, in the end, this noisy bird invader that has conquered a continent may be regarded as an immigrant that has developed into a beneficial and valued citizen of the country.

REFUGEE PELICANS
OF THE DESERT

Lewis W. Walker

The story of wildlife in the modern world is largely a story of de-creasing populations, narrowing ranges, and, sometimes, of complete extinction. Most of the exceptions are the result of the benevolent interference of the relatively few men who actively engaged in conservation. Occasionally however some change in an environment resulting from a slow natural process proves favorable to one species or another. Occasionally also man himself, in pursuit of his own ends, unintentionally favors the interest of a bird or beast.

Because such situations are relatively rare they are always in-teresting and especially so when, as in the case presented in the fol-lowing account, both man and nature co-operated even though the former did not consciously do so.

The great white pelican—the only inland species of pelican found in the United States—formerly populated California's famous dead Salton Sea. When it gradually shrank and shrank, they disappeared. Now that it is spreading again—no one is quite sure why—they have returned. And pelicans are, of course, among the most impressive of our birds in size, beauty, and comic charm.

COYOTES, roadrunners, and rattlers are to be expected in the desert that lies between the southern California coastal range and the muddy Colorado. They are an integral part of this torrid belt of shifting sand. However, this land has not always been reserved for them alone. Water birds such as pelicans, geese, and cranes formerly frequented the area, as is shown by bits of charred bone excavated from the refuse heaps of the Indians that once camped on the shore line of ancient Le Conte Sea.

This sea nestled in the bottom of a tremendous sink or depression that is thought to have had no outlet and to have been fed intermittently by the mighty Colorado. Whenever the big river changed its course and dumped directly into the Gulf, evaporation caused Le Conte Sea to shrink. But even to the present day the ancient shoreline levels remain plainly

From *Natural History*, December, 1949.

visible, although the waters that etched them vanished many centuries ago.

Prior to 1900, some early California subdividers visualized parts of this ancient lake bed as ideal for the growing of all-year crops, so the waters of the Colorado were diverted to supply irrigation needs. For a few years all was serene. Then unprecedented floods from Arizona's normally peaceful Gila River overtaxed the crude dams, and the full force of the Colorado spilled once more into what is now known as the Salton Sink. Two years later, when the raging torrent was finally controlled, a lake about 80 miles long by 35 miles wide was left in the heart of the arrid Colorado Desert.

During the two years of uninterrupted flow, several species of fishes as well as beaver and muskrat were carried to this below-sea-level spot, and they thrived on the spreading rushes and willows. Within a few seasons, birds commenced to settle on the body of water, and now it is the winter home for several species of geese, countless ducks, and 500 or 600 little Brown or Sand-hill Cranes.

Birds on migration that usually nested in more temperate zones looked over the shores and the tiny islands of silt at the southern end, and a few tarried to raise their young. These pioneers were queer types to be seen in the heart of a desert. Cormorants, which are more at home on wave-swept coasts, moved in and utilized the dying tops of the flooded desert trees. Grebes or hell-divers settled in the clumps of fast-growing tules, along with bitterns, coots, and rails. Even Gull-billed Terns, normal residents of the Atlantic Coast and the Gulf of Mexico, crossed to the Pacific and founded their only known western colony on these tiny islands of silt—islands that they now share with the white pelican, one of the largest water birds found in the United States.

These giants, with a wingspread that sometimes reaches almost ten feet, do not lead the same life in this burning desert that they do in their cool northern lake country. There they are comfortable when sitting on their eggs to keep them warm. Here they waddle onto the near-by shallows every 20 or 30 minutes throughout the hottest part of the day. It is tempting to conclude that they bring water on their feathers to cool the eggs. After a few rapid dips, I have seen them go back to the exposed eggs and appear to rub their dripping breast feathers over them. Then they seem to crouch over the nest to provide shade while normal evaporation cools off the eggs. But that the bird is actually aware of providing a sort of "desert refrigerator" for the eggs will doubtless be questioned. Some will say that they simply go for a dip to cool themselves and that the rest of the performance is happenstance. In any case, one can easily feel the difference in temperature between eggs that have absorbed the sun's rays for a few minutes and those that the parent has just vacated.

During the months of June, July, and early August, birds not actively engaged in family duties escape the heat by making long flights to cool mountain lakes. About mid-morning the idle ones take off in a follow-the-leader formation, and the view of these fifteen or twenty must be alluring to others of their own kind. As they swing over the islands, single recruits constantly join the air-borne procession, which soon starts to use the rising currents of warm air over the desert to gain altitude. Within a very few moments the hundreds of birds, stretching for about a mile through the sky, become mere glistening specks against the blue. A "now you see it, now you don't" effect is achieved at every banking turn. If the sun hits the white feathers at just the right angle, the birds are visible; but as they bank away they become lost.

High in the air they straighten the line and set off on a general westerly course. Perhaps from their vantage point they can see their destinations— the lakes and reservoirs that dot the higher elevations of San Diego's mountainous country.

Late afternoon brings their return. With black-tipped wings flexed and sometimes almost closed, they plummet to within a few hundred feet of the nesting islands and then, spreading their feathers, slow down and land in a conventional manner.

Newly-hatched pelicans are among the strangest of bird infants, both in texture and color. If a gob of wax with a decided salmon tint were set under the desert sun and allowed to collapse, the resulting pile would be a good facsimile of these babies. Their skin has a translucent quality and is completely naked of both feathers and down. For the first few hours of their lives they are practically helpless, and they sprawl on the ground as though dead.

Within a week, however, a gray fuzz obliterates the sickly salmon tint and provides a shield from the sun's rays. About two weeks after hatching, the young gain the power of motion. From then until flight they wander all over the colonies and sometimes form into immense wriggling heaps in which each seeks the shade cast by his shade-seeking neighbor.

At mealtime, the onlooker is treated to the high-light show of the pelican colony. The parents, wandering aimlessly, are tackled by every famished fledgling, but these hungry young are usually shoved unceremoniously to one side. Finally, by some means, the correct offspring is identified and permitted to dine. After many awkward jabs, the fledgling hits the crack between its mother's mandibles and thrusts its bill far down into her throat. During this maneuver she is in the midst of a paroxysm called regurgitation and is pumping predigested fish into her crop. The head of the fledgling remains submerged for many seconds. Then the mother, as though tired of the constant probing of her now empty gullet, shakes the infant loose. For a minute or more the gorged young one staggers about the colony as though drunk, either through fullness or possibly lack of oxygen. The reeling intoxication is always followed by a sudden stupor, and soon the young one, falling flat on its face, temporarily passes out of the picture.

If you were to walk toward a just fed fledgling, it would awake with a start and try to run. Generally, however, the food would act as ballast and keep its breast to the ground. But within a few seconds its stomach pump would go into action, and the slimy fish just devoured would be left in a pile by the fleeing youngster.

The range of these giant white pelicans has been sadly reduced in the last century. At one time small colonies existed on many lakes, but such large birds of glossy white are tempting targets to a certain class of sportsman. During the duck season in the region of Salton Sea, I have seen them shot down and left to rot where they fell. If such unwarranted wasting of life is questioned by a conservationist, he is given the old worn-out retort, "They kill sport fish." In eight weeks that I spent in the heart of these pelican colonies, I checked their foods at every opportunity. Carp, humpbacked suckers, and small mullet made up the bulk of their fare. Occasionally blue-gilled sunfish were brought in by the adults, but this was rare. The remains of bass were only detected three times in the hundreds of regurgitated fish that I examined.

Luckily, however, there are a few spots in the West where white pelicans are practically unmolested. But only a few of these breeding colonies are really sanctuaries where the birds are protected for their beauty and because their inoffensive nature is realized and appreciated. The advance of civilization has forced the birds ever backward, until now most of the dwindling colonies are in remote locations far from the haunts of man.

THE

MOST DANGEROUS

PREDATOR

Joseph Wood Krutch

Man is the most dangerous of predatory animals—to himself as well as to all other living creatures—because he alone is capable of rapidly and permanently upsetting the balance of nature. It is true that this balance commonly depends upon the relation of predator and prey but Nature, however red she may be in tooth and claw, is subject to limitations which man has escaped. What the difference is may be clearly illustrated by two stories, both of which are laid in Baja California, Mexico. Both involve a ruthless predator and the slaughter of innocence. But Nature's far from simple plan depends upon continuing co-existence while man is the only animal who habitually exhausts or exterminates what he has learned to exploit.

THERE is a tiny island, Rasa—Island—less than a mile square in area and barely one hundred feet above sea level at its highest point—which lies in the Gulf fifteen or twenty miles away from the settlement at Los Angeles Bay. It is rarely visited because even in fair weather the waters 'round about it are treacherous. Currents up to eight knots create whirlpools between it and other small islands and there is a tide drop of twelve to thirty feet, depending upon the season. It is almost bare of vegetation except for a little of the salt weed or Salicornia which is found in so many of the saline sands in almost every climate. But it is the nesting place of thousands of Heermann gulls who, after the young are able to fend for themselves, migrate elsewhere—a few southward as far as Central America but most of them north to various points on the Pacific coast. A few of the latter take the shortest route across the Baja peninsula but most take what seems an absurd detour by going first some 450 miles south to the tip of Baja and then the eight hundred or a thousand miles up its west coast to the United States—perhaps, as seems to be the case

From *The Forgotten Peninsula*, New York: William Sloane Associates, 1961.

in various other paradoxes of migration—because they are following some ancestral habit acquired when the climate or the lay of the land was quite different.

My travels in Baja are, I hope, not finished, and I intend someday to set foot on Rasa to see what goes on there for myself. So far, however, I have observed the huge concentration of birds only from a low-flying plane and what I have to describe is what Walker has told me and what he wrote some ten years ago in an illustrated account for the "National Geographic Magazine."

In late April, when the breeding season is at its height the ground is crowded with innumerable nests—in some places no more than a yard apart, nowhere with more than twenty feet between them. Because man has so seldom disturbed the gulls here they show little fear of him though once they have reached the northern shore they rise and fly out to sea at the first sight of a human being.

If this were all there was to tell, Rasa might seem to realize that idyllic state of nature of which man, far from idyllic though he has made his own society, often loves to dream. Though on occasion gulls are predators as well as scavengers they respect one another's eggs and offspring on Rasa and live together in peace. But like most animals (and like most men) they are ruthless in their attitude towards other species though too utterly nature's children to rationalize as man does that ruthlessness. They know in their nerves and muscles without even thinking about it that the world was made for the exclusive use and convenience of gulls.

In the present case the victims of that egomania of the species are the two kinds of tern which share the island with them and have chosen to lay their eggs in a depression surrounded by gulls.

Here Walker had best tell his own story: "In the early morning of the second day a few eggs were seen under the terns but even as we watched, several were stolen by gulls. By late afternoon not an egg remained. Nightfall brought on an influx of layers, and morning found twice as many eggs dotting the ground. By dusk only a fraction of the number in the exact center of the plot had escaped the inroads of the egg-eating enemy.

"The new colony had now gained a permanent foothold. Accordion-like it expanded during the night, contracted by evening. Each twenty-four hour period showed a gain for the terns and a corresponding retreat in the waiting ranks of the killing gulls.

"By the end of a week the colony had expanded from nothing to approximately four hundred square feet of egg-spotted ground and it continued to spread. The gulls seemed to be losing their appetites. Like children sated with ice cream, they had found that a single diet can be overdone."

What an absurd—some would say what a horrid—story that is. How decisively it gives the lie to what the earliest idealizers of nature called her "social union." How difficult it makes it to believe that some all-good, omnipotent, conscious and transcendental power consciously chose to set up a general plan of which this is a typical detail. How much more probable it makes it seem that any purpose that may exist in the universe is one emerging from a chaos rather than one which had deliberately created that chaos.

But a fact remains: one must recognize that the scheme works—for the terns as well as for the gulls. If it is no more than the mechanism which so many call it, then it is at least (to use the newly current terminology) a cybernetic or self-regulating mechanism. If the gulls destroyed so many eggs that the tern population began to decline then the gulls, deprived of their usual food supply, would also decline in numbers and the terns would again increase until the balance had been reached. "How careful of the type she seems; how careless of the single life"—as Tennyson observed some years before Darwin made the same humanly disturbing fact a cornerstone of his theories.

Absurd as the situation on Rasa may seem it has probably existed for thousands of years and may well continue for thousands more—if left to itself, undisturbed by the only predator who almost invariably renders the "cybernetic" system inoperable.

78   7133   12